A Special Edition for Friends of

PLANT CONSTRUCTION COMPANY, L. P.

There was a time, a century ago, when almost every family photo album in California contained at least one photograph by Isaiah West Taber. His work appeared regularly in books, magazines, and newspapers throughout America. During Taber's lifetime he achieved world recognition as perhaps San Francisco's most famous photographer. His dynamic persona combined with the elegance of his studios in San Francisco, London and Paris, and the richness of his scenic views and portraits made the name "Taber" unrivaled as a commercial success. Today his widely collected photographs still are featured in illustrated works of California history. The photography of Isaiah West Taber has withstood the test of time and is a significant contribution to the history of California and the West. Until now, however, Isaiah Taber's work has never been the subject of a book. *Taber, A Photographic Legacy*, corrects this oversight. The book pays tribute, long overdue, to a master of California photography who showed the Golden State to the world.

Have a healthy, happy and prosperous New Year!
January 2004

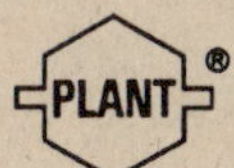

TABER: A PHOTOGRAPHIC LEGACY

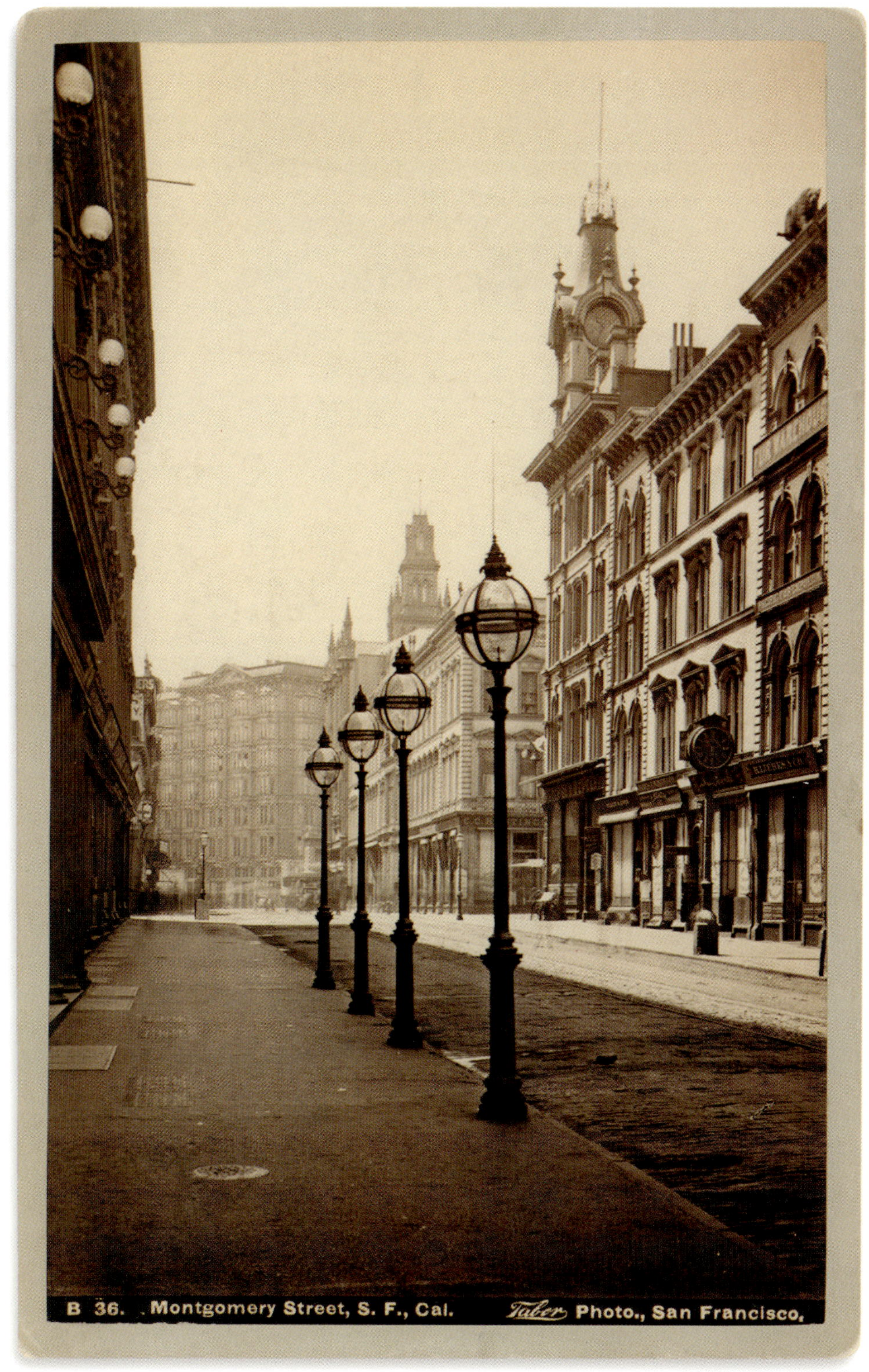

c.1879

CALIFORNIA STATE LIBRARY

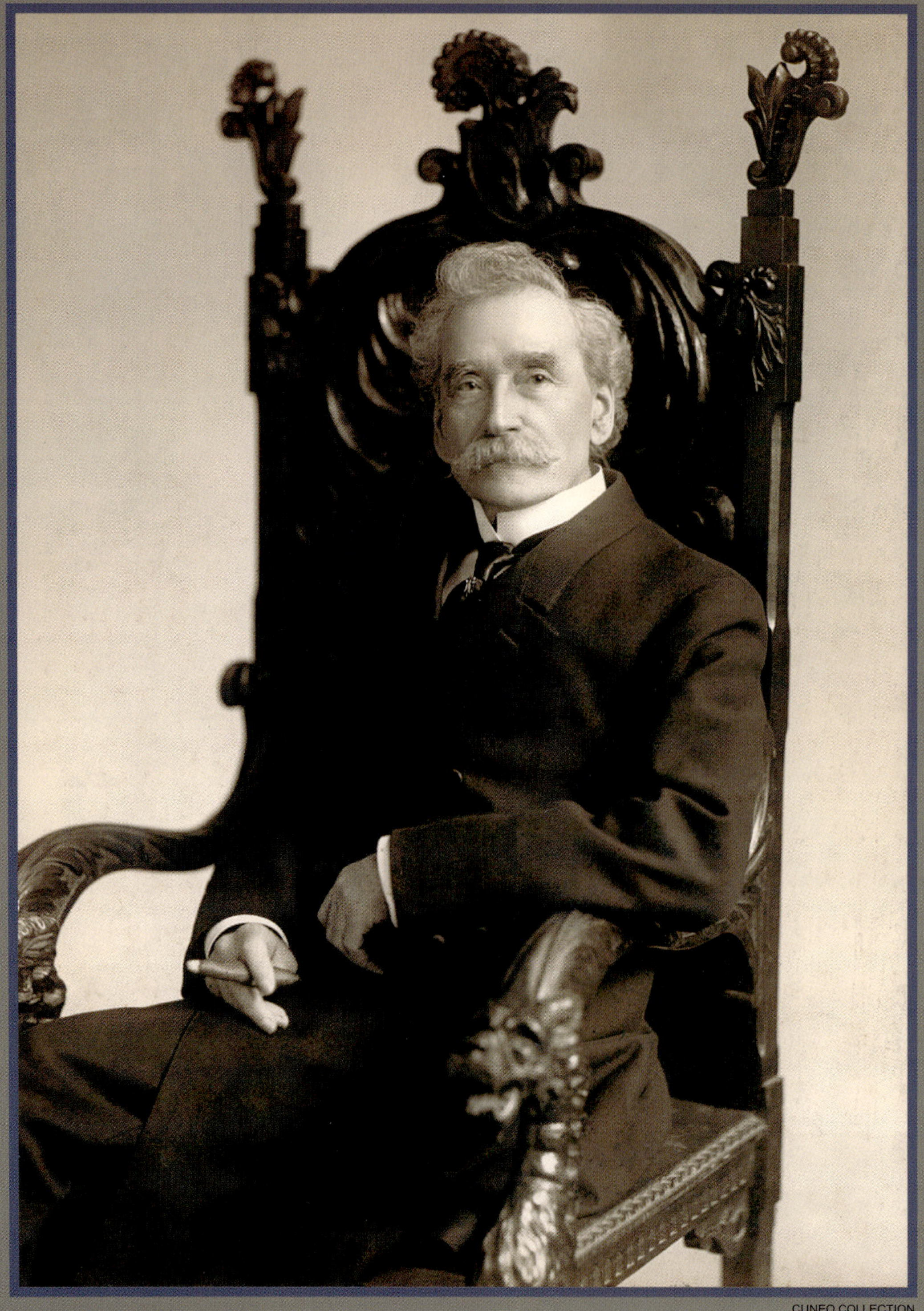

CUNEO COLLECTION

Isaiah West Taber, c.1900

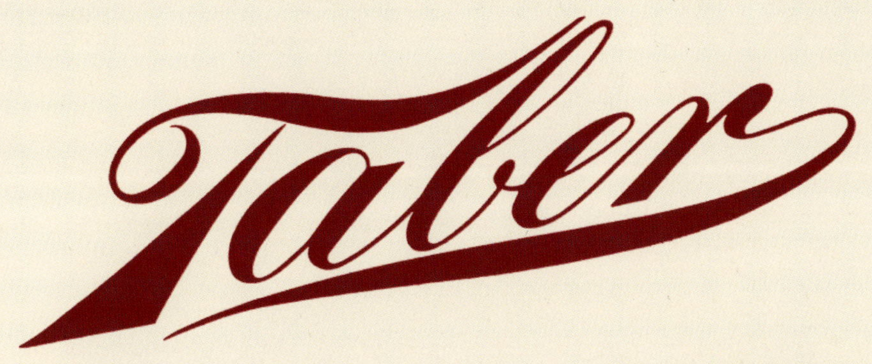

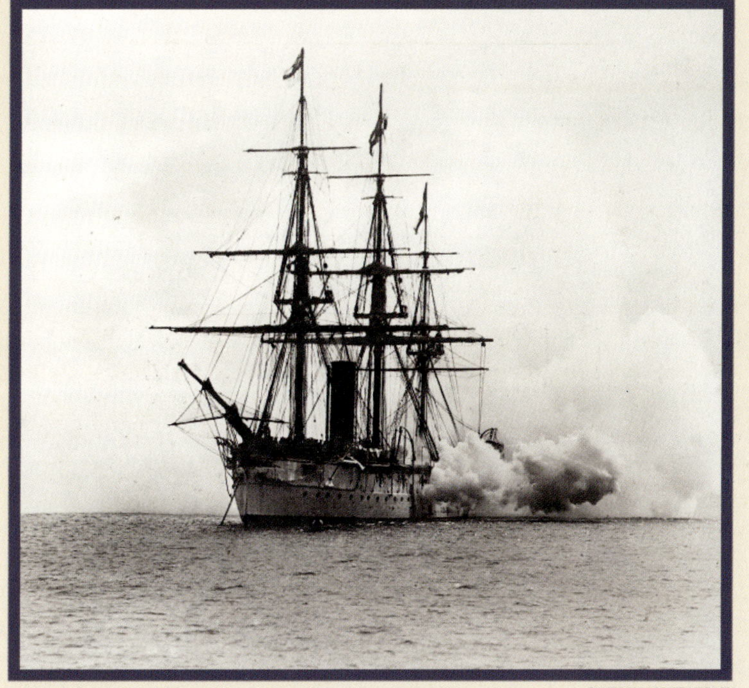

CALIFORNIA STATE LIBRARY

A PHOTOGRAPHIC LEGACY
1870 - 1900

Linda Bonnett & Wayne Bonnett

Introduction by Gary F. Kurutz

WINDGATE PRESS :: SAUSALITO, CALIFORNIA

ACKNOWLEDGMENTS

The authors wish to thank Gary F. Kurutz, Curator of Special Collections, California State Library; Marilyn Blaisdell; Glenn Koch; Susan Snyder, The Bancroft Library; Sarah Kozma, Onandaga Historical Association; and Paul Cyr, Curator Special Collections, New Bedford Free Public Library. A special debt of gratitude to Doris Cuneo Maslach, Barbara Cuneo Stone, and Gordon C. Cuneo who shared with us the Taber materials preserved by their parents, Ruth McLean Cuneo and Egisto Cuneo, close friends of Louise Taber.

PHOTOGRAPHY SOURCES
The photographs, credited on page, were provided through the courtesy of: The Bancroft Library, Berkeley, California; Marilyn Blaisdell Collection, San Francisco, California; the California State Library, Sacramento, California; the Egisto Cuneo & Ruth McLean Cuneo Collection; and the Onandaga Historical Association Museum & Research Center, Syracuse, New York. Preceeding page, HMS *Comus*, 1882, California State Library.

Copyright © 2004 by Linda Bonnett and Wayne Bonnett. All rights reserved. No part of this book may be reproduced in any form or by any electronic or mechanical means without written permission from the publisher.

First Edition

Printed in Korea by Sung In Printing America

ISBN 0915269-21-X

Windgate Press, P.O. Box 1715, Sausalito, California 94966

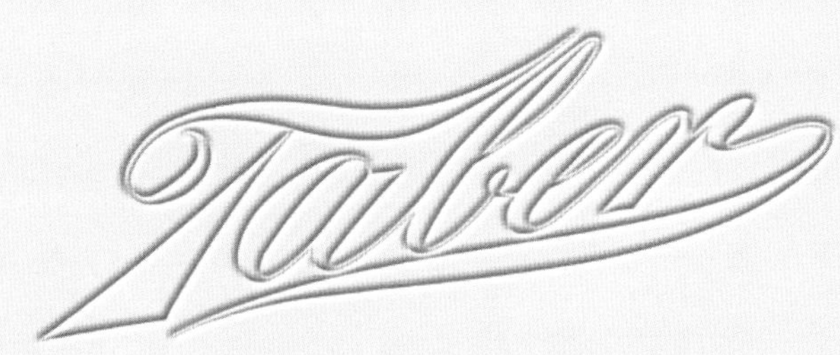

CONTENTS

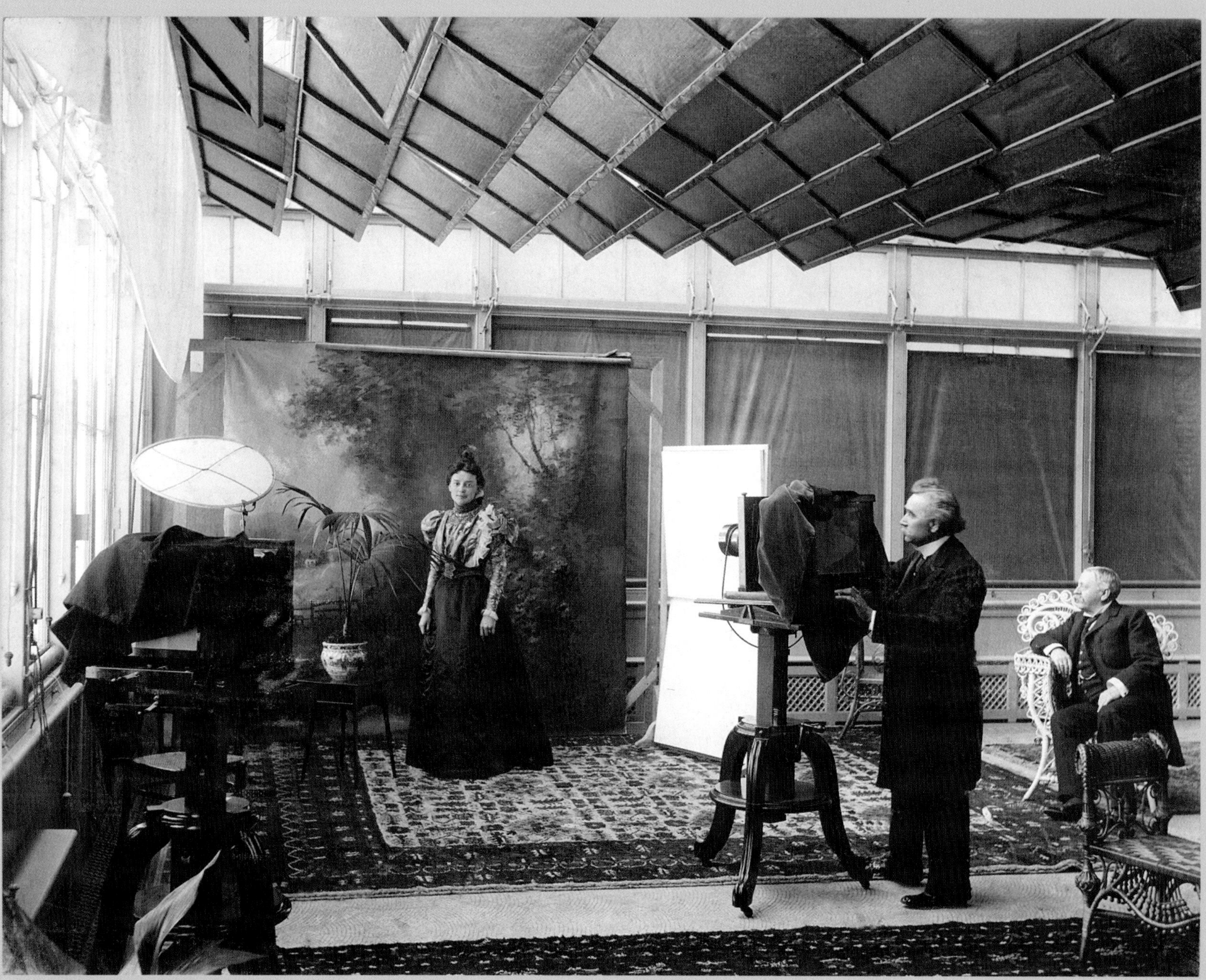

CALIFORNIA STATE LIBRARY

Isaiah Taber in his London studio, 1897. L. Birmingham, left, and Mr. Page of New York, seated at right.

INTRODUCTION

Isaiah West Taber ranks as one of California and the West's premier pioneer photographers and perhaps no other early California photographer achieved such fame during his lifetime. Over a period of forty years, this one-time gold seeker built an extraordinary collection of portraits and scenic views. The classic image of the pioneer Western photographer is one of a solitary man dressed in rugged garb leading a team of mules loaded down with glass plates and cameras into the wilderness. In contrast to that stereotype is I. W. Taber who, from an elegantly appointed salon in Gilded Age San Francisco, presided over one of the most successful photographic businesses in America. While others may have achieved fame for their artistic mammoth landscape views, this splendidly dressed man with a genteel air became famous because of his abilities as a portrait photographer, inventor of photographic styles and techniques, and collector and publisher of fine scenic views. Through skillful and dynamic marketing, he reached thousands, from monarchs to average Californians.

When Taber died in 1912, after a long and distinguished career, the editor of *Camera Craft* recognized the impact of this sophisticated entrepreneur by writing: "The late Isaiah West Taber had made his name a household word in thousands of homes throughout the country. Today, there are hundreds of thousands of photographic portraits, bearing the 'Taber' imprint, treasured by their owners."

In 1850 the twenty-year old native of New Bedford, Massachusetts, came to California during the height of the gold fever after an early youth at sea. While in northern California, he tried his hand at trading, farming, and appears to have experienced some success mining along the American River and its tributaries. Typical of most fellow gold seekers, he did not make a pile. In 1854 Taber returned home to New Bedford. There, he engaged in the profession of dentistry. However, extracting teeth and staring into the mouths of customers did not suit his adventurous interests. Instead, he turned to photography. No doubt working with chemicals and a variety of instruments assisted him as he embarked on a new livelihood. He learned the complex art of making daguerreotypes and ambrotypes, and as the technology changed, mastered making paper prints from glass plate negatives. The young cameraman moved to Syracuse, New York, in 1856 and established a successful portrait business.

In 1864 Taber left New York and joined Henry Bradley and William Herman Rulofson, the well-known pioneer San Francisco photographers. From these two pictorial pioneers, Taber undoubtedly enhanced his photographic skills and learned a great deal about the economics of operating a successful gallery in the rambunctious environment of California. After working for Bradley and Rulofson for seven years as one of their principal operators, Taber decided to go it alone. The next several years illustrate how Taber, like many photographers, went in a multitude of directions before achieving economic stability. He purchased the photography department of the Nahl Brother's Art and Photographic Gallery owned by Charles and Hugo Nahl. Charles Nahl achieved considerable fame for his historical paintings of California. Taber did retain the services of Hugo to color his photographic portraits. Following that, he worked for a short time for George D. Morse, another well-known pioneer photographer.

Taber then left Morse to start his own gallery taking with him the able technician Thomas Boyd. As traced in city directories he operated out of several downtown locations until 1878 when he established a spacious gallery at Number 8 Montgomery Street in the city's bustling commercial center. As his business unfolded during the 1880s, he found that making photographs of people posing in his gallery was particularly rewarding. In 1893 he moved his gallery and its tons of glass plate negatives to 121 Post Street. Portraiture established his reputation and created an outlet for taking and acquiring landscape views and experimenting with different forms of photography.

Portraiture in mid to late-nineteenth century California represented the "bread of butter" of a photographer's income. Artistic

Taber

Photographer AND Portrait + Artist

No. 8 Montgomery Street,

Opposite Palace & Grand Hotels, *San Francisco.*

Like M. Adam Solomon, of Paris, France; Fredericks, of New York; and Notman, of Montreal; I. W. Taber, of San Francisco, is acknowledged to be one of the most celebrated photographers in the world. He has made his profession a life-long study to bring the photographic art to its greatest perfection. The Taber photographs of San Francisco are now celebrated all over the world. Here in London they are regarded by experts as almost perfection itself. Her Majesty, the Queen, is a great admirer of the Taber photographs. She has a large collection of them in her library which represents her friends and those of her family who have visited California. The Taber photograph is one of the regular souvenirs. No one ever thinks of leaving San Francisco without a Taber photograph of themselves and their friends. His studio is within one square of the great Palace Hotel. Our London people, as well as Europeans generally, who propose visiting the United States, should make a note of this.—*Pall Mall Gazette, London, Eng., 1881.*

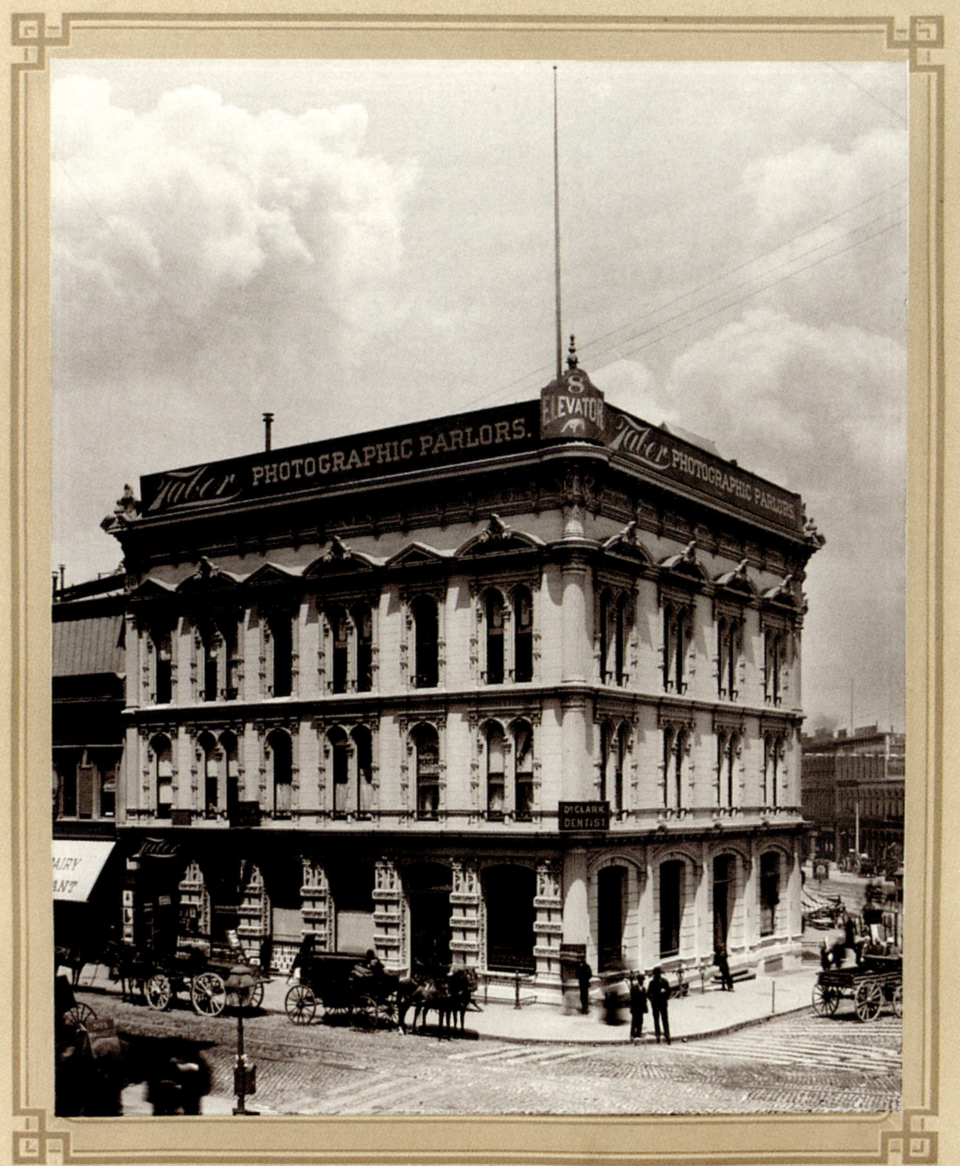

Portraits in all the NEW STYLES, and with the Most Artistic Accessories.

All Portraits and Views taken by the Instantaneous Process.

OUR EXTENSIVE VIEW DEPARTMENT

CONTAINS THE BEST COLLECTION OF VIEWS OF THE

Yosemite, Big Trees, Geysers, Columbia River, Yellowstone Park, Colorado, Mexico, Railroads, Mining, Indians, City, Japan, Sandwich Islands, etc.

CATALOGUES sent on application. *Unmounted Photographs can be safely transmitted through the Mails to all parts of the World.*

Strangers will find it interesting to visit our View and Portrait Collections, and are always welcome

Page from Taber's photographic album, California Scenery and Industries, *1884, showing Taber's gallery on the top two floors above the Hibernia Bank at 8 Montgomery Street, at the intersection of Market, Geary, and Montgomery Streets.*

CALIFORNIA STATE LIBRARY

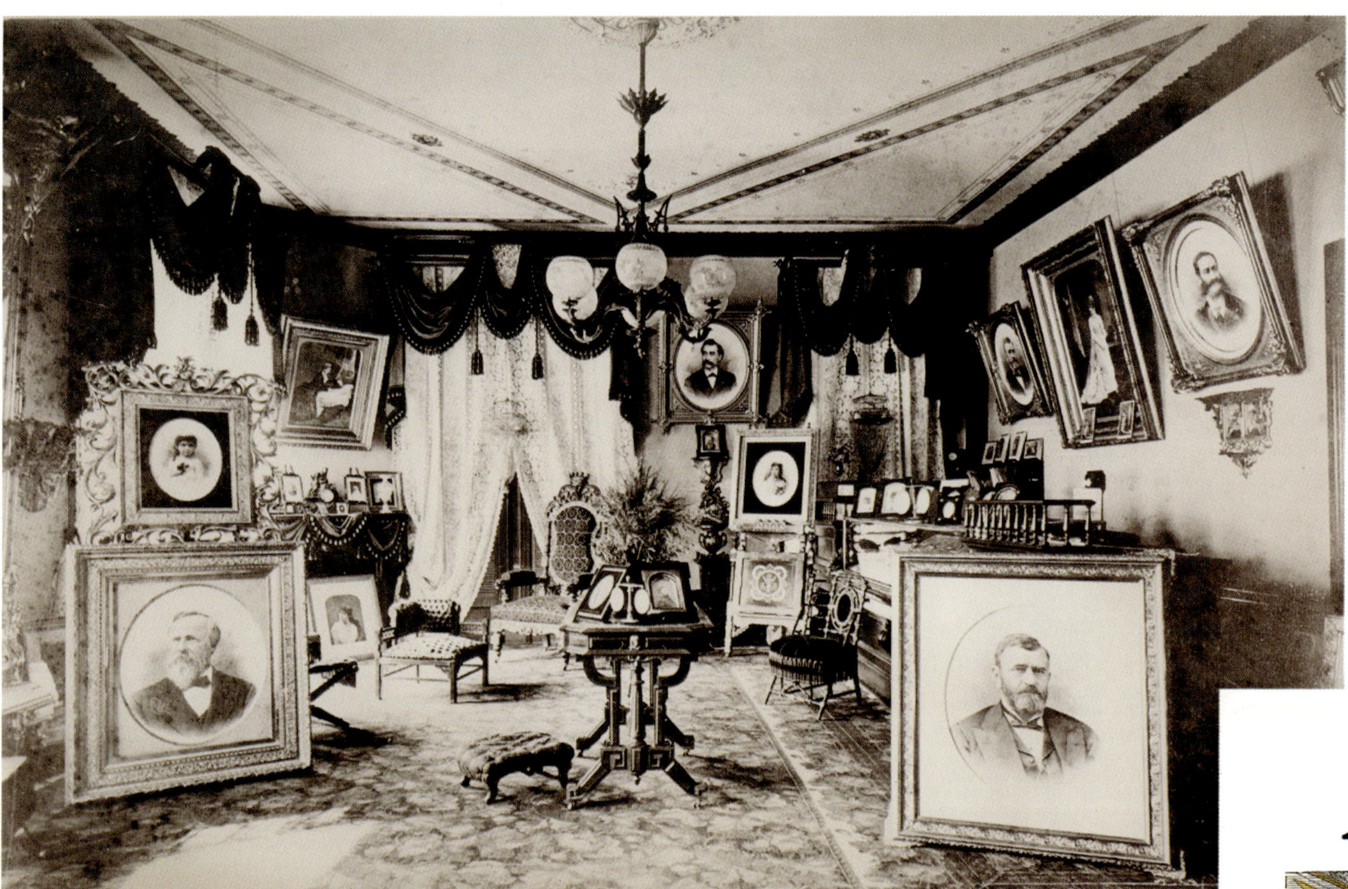
MARILYN BLAISDELL COLLECTION

Taber used this photo to advertise his Montgomery Street studio and gallery in the early 1880s. It was taken, however, in his home in Oakland, using furniture from his entry hall and parlor (See page 67). The portraits include ex-President Ulysses S. Grant, lower right, and President Rutherford B. Hayes, lower left. Taber's likeness hangs at the rear center. In the wood engraving of the same view, below, Taber has placed himself behind the counter as if waiting on customers.

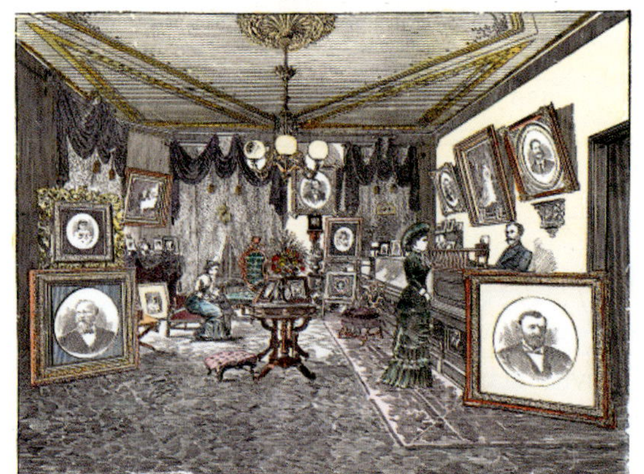

MARILYN BLAISDELL COLLECTION

land and city scapes, unless commissioned or subscribed, did not offer a stable form of income. Many photographers, with Taber as a leading example, started in the portrait business and later branched out to include scenic views. Portraiture, however, was an acutely competitive business with just about every town of any reasonable size supporting one or more portrait studios. When it came to a city as large and cosmopolitan as San Francisco, the competition was white hot. San Francisco directories during Taber's active years listed an impressive number of photographic salons, at least forty in 1880, all in the business of making portraits. One obvious method to compete and establish credibility was to make likenesses of celebrities. Endorsement by a visiting musician, actor, statesman or person of royal lineage was something to covet and promote.

Taber, with his business acumen, did not miss a trick. He created a celebrity collection and his advertisements and photographs of his galleries highlighted portraits.

To entice visitors to his establishment, he incorporated a multi-pronged strategy of a high visibility location, heavy advertising, and the latest technology. His third-floor gallery in the Hibernia Bank Building, located where Montgomery Street intersected

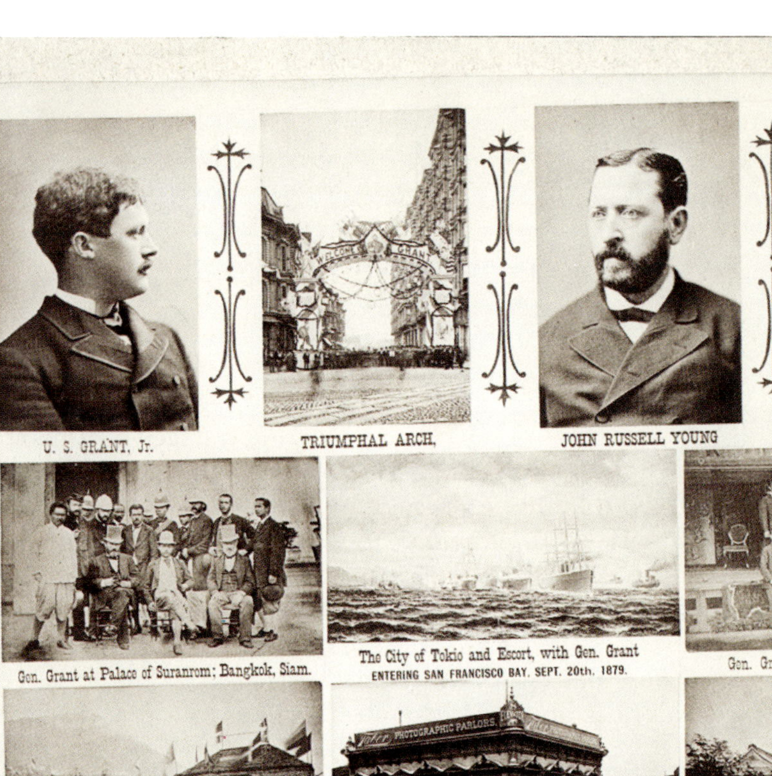

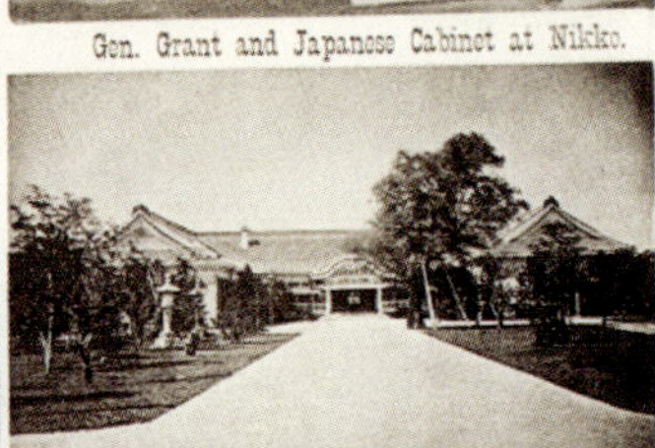

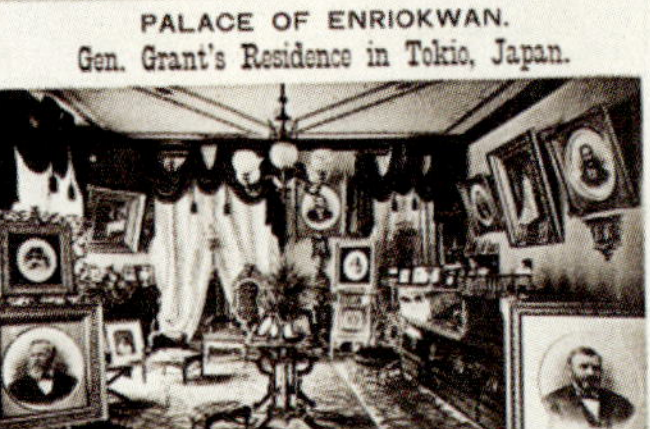

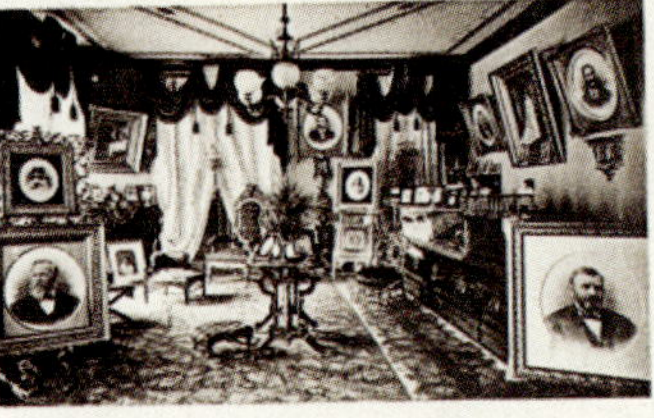

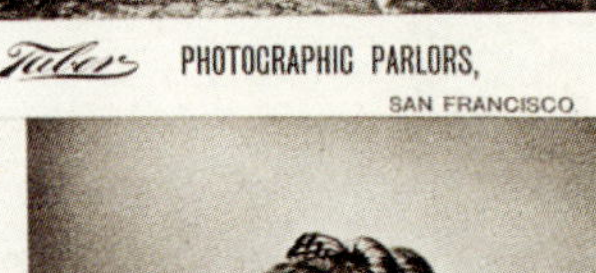

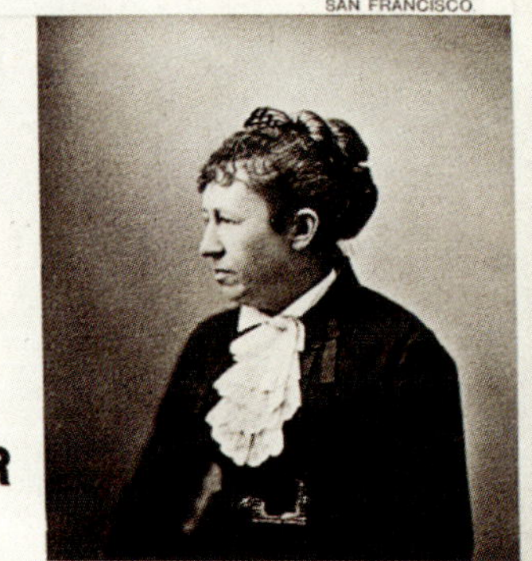

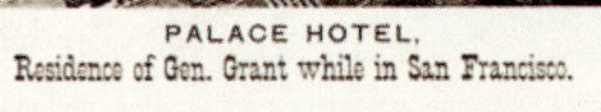

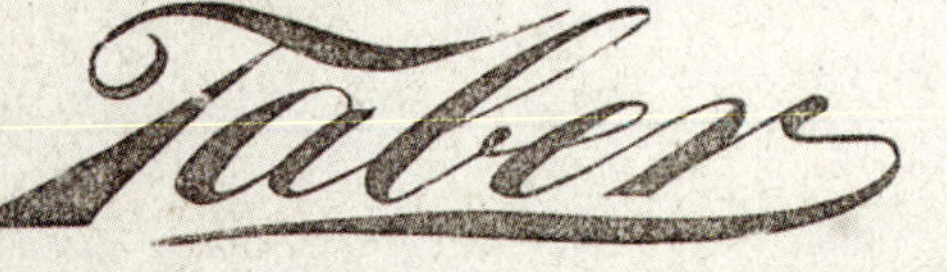

CALIFORNIA STATE LIBRARY

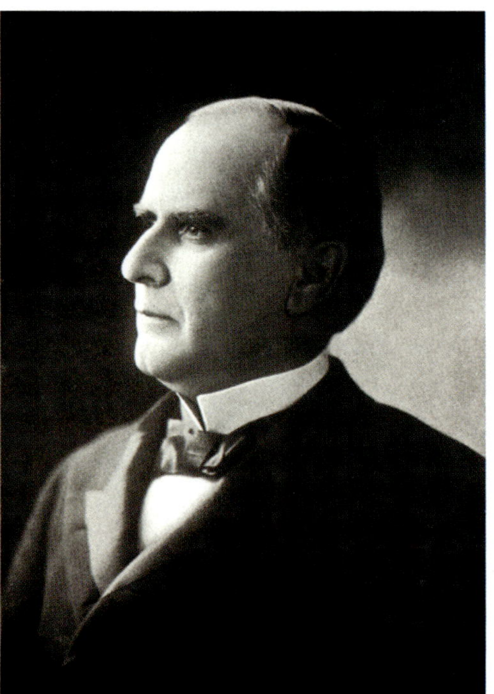

WINDGATE PRESS

WINDGATE PRESS

When former President Grant visited San Francisco in 1879 on his round-the-world tour, Taber produced a souvenir card, left, as well as several portraits of Grant and his wife. President William McKinley, top, sent a thankyou note to Taber after having his portrait taken during his San Francisco visit in 1901. Above is world-reknown horticulturist and Santa Rosa, California resident Luther Burbank, c. 1895.

Market Street, was crowned with a large sign "I. W. Taber Photographic Parlors" and could be seen by anyone strolling along this thoroughfare. Thus, guests of the nearby Palace or Grand hotels or those riding a buggy could easily spot where to have a portrait made. Once inside after a short elevator ride (a relatively new innovation), an array of smartly appointed parlors, dressing and sitting rooms awaited prospective customers. Thick carpets, ferns, fashionable wicker furniture, and elegantly framed portraits resting on easels added to the allure. He installed telephone communication to the nearest hotels; sported a new electrically operated camera that required short exposures (perfect for children and pets), and offered his mounted portraits in the latest styles.

The photographer apparently mixed well with the *beau monde* and joined a number of social clubs. He managed to put his name in front of the public whenever possible through directories, periodicals, and newspapers. Through skillful public relations, he projected himself as a "world famous" celebrity. The *Illustrated Fraternal Directory* for 1889 and John S. Hittell's *The Commerce and Industries of the Pacific Coast*, for example, both praised him for his skill and artistic achievement. The *Fraternal Directory* noted his memberships in social organizations and described him as "genial, unostentatious and generous. A man of few words, sound judgment, sensitive nature and keen intellect; and there is that happy expression or cordiality in his nature that has a tendency to charm and please all with whom he associates." Similarly, he received numerous endorsements from the local press applauding not only his work as a photographer but also his general contributions to San Francisco's prosperity. With such praise, the social and economic elite more than likely enjoyed calling upon his this "genial, unostentatious and generous" man.

When he traveled, he managed to take photographs of the most prominent people. On his 1880 Hawaiian trip, for example, he arranged a session with the island kingdom's royal family. So great was his fame that he was invited to England in 1897 to photograph Queen Victoria's diamond jubilee. Taber's success led him to establish a salon in London and Paris. In the overseas establishments, the shrewd businessman naturally marketed his views of California and Western scenery. With endorsements from the Queen Victoria and later, King Edward VII, Taber certainly brought glitter to San Francisco. Seven U.S. presidents posed for his camera. According to one newspaper account, Taber's company photographed over 100,000 individuals.

Another way to get your name out in front of the buying public was through the many fairs and expositions held in America and Europe. Taber won medals locally and internationally and, not surprisingly, incorporated references to them into his advertising.

Typical of a late nineteenth-century photography business, Taber's gallery offered reproductions in a variety of packages and styles. A cabinet card in the 1880s stated on the reverse: "Duplicate Copies at Reduced Rates. Viz: 1 dozen for $5.00—2 dozen for $9.00—3 dozen for $12.00—100 for $30.00—Glazed Finish $3.00 per dozen extra. Life size enlargements from this Negative $15.00 each, —or, finished with Crayon, India Ink, Oil, or Water Colors, for $35.00 and upwards, other sizes at proportionate rates. All enlarged pictures are printed by a new process that absolutely insures their never fading."

In this cutthroat business of portraiture, he marketed such novelties as "ivorytypes," hand-tinted images, silhouettes, porcelain miniatures, and bas-relief photographs with "iridium, platinum and roman sepia finish." Another Taber innovation was the "promenade photograph" which measured 4 x 7 inches and featured three-quarter and full-length portraits. Some of these marketing stunts elicited critical howls from purist photographers but they did generate customers and profits.

By the nature of his business, Taber had an interest in the state's young history and its colorful individuals. After all, he participated in the Gold Rush and could readily identify with the pioneers who built the state. To this end, Taber embarked on a project to create a collection of portraits and biographical data on "representative Californians." But alas, Taber's historical portraits fell victim to the earthquake and fire of April 1906 (see page 162).

His catalogs, notices in city directories, and the backs of the mounts of his photographs advertised a multitude of subjects and sizes. With his wonderfully situated Market and Montgomery Streets location, this clever entrepreneur also touted his gallery as a tourist destination. Taber's work emerged as a visual chamber of commerce for his city, state, and region. A catalog issued by his studio entitled *Pacific Coast Tourist Guide and Catalogue of Views* (c. 1882) spelled out the commercial value of his work: "This industry of Mr. Taber's induces travelers to visit our State to behold its grand and beautiful scenery, which brings a large revenue to this City. It helps to fill our hotels, brings customers to our tradesmen and encourages emigration to our shores."

A big boost in the scenic view business for Taber occurred around 1876 when he acquired Carleton E. Watkins' negatives, including those of Yosemite. At the time, Watkins ranked as California's most accomplished and famous photographer based on his vast array of spectacular scenic views, especially his world-famous mammoth plates of Yosemite Valley. The celebrated photographer lost control of his collection because of poor business practice combined with a general economic recession. His financial backer, James Jay Cook, apparently foreclosed on loans to Watkins and seized Watkins' negatives, equipment and his Montgomery Street Yosemite Art Gallery. Cook then made an arrangement with Taber to publish prints from Watkins' negatives under Taber's name. Much has been made of Watkins' lack of business skill and the possible chicanery of his financial backer, James Jay Cook. As Watkins' first biographer, Charles B. Turrill explained, "Prior to that time Mr. Taber had been known as a portrait photographer, though in those days the lines were not so closely drawn between portrait and view men." Peter Palmquist, Watkins' more recent biographer, also stated that Taber had ties to Cook. Nonetheless, Taber seized the opportunity and began marketing Watkins' views with his own distinctive logotype. To maker matters even more bitter for Watkins, Taber later hired his best photographic printer, Policarpo Bagnasco.

For publishing Watkins' views under his own name, Taber was roundly criticized. In his defense, Taber was not alone in publishing the unattributed works of others, but because of his immense business success and unparalleled inventory, his example has gained the most attention. Even the great Watkins obtained the negative collection of railroad photographer Alfred A. Hart and published them as his own views. Recognition of individual achievement did not carry the same importance in the 1870s and 1880s as it does today.

The acquisition of Carleton E. Watkins' negative collection, of course, provided additional stimulus for marketing scenic views. Taber operated in a highly competitive milieu, and like the even more aggressive portrait business, adding quality inventory became as important as obtaining the most aesthetically pleasing photograph. Photographic establishments up and down California in the 1870s and 1880s marketed scenic views and several big name itinerant photographers like William Henry Jackson of Denver and Charles R. Savage of Utah visited the region to create their own collections of Pacific Coast images. In addition to the Watkins acquisition, Taber and assistants fanned out into the California and Western countryside to obtain views. His own city of San Francisco offered spectacular subject matter and in the 1870s and 1880s, Taber made beautifully composed photographs of Nob Hill mansions, business blocks, street scenes, squares, and ships in the bay. Mindful of the state's young but colorful history, he made an effort to collect historical images even daguerreotypes and ambrotypes. These he would re-photograph or print. By the turn of the twentieth century, the photographer offered over 30,000 scenic views, an incomparable record of the West. In an era before the advent of the picture postcard, galleries like Taber's offered the best possible venue for the souvenir-conscious traveler. *Builders of a Great City*, a thick volume filled with congratulatory biographies of "representative" San Franciscans, called his landscape and city views "unrivaled."

Taber employed a team of technicians to print and mount his photographs. While offering a variety of sizes from stereoscopic view to 18 x 22 inch mammoth plates, the most common Taber single images that survive today are a 7 ½ x 9 ½ inch view and a 7 ½ by 5 inch cabinet card with a black or gray border. These sizes remained his stock and trade. Below the photograph would be a title or caption, inventory number and his distinctive script logotype. Unlike others in the city such as Lawrence and Houseworth, Bradley and Rulofson, Eadweard Muybridge, and C. E. Watkins, he did not rely on the ever-popular stereograph. Although he made mammoth-plate views (16 x 20 inches and larger), precious few are found in institutional and private collections.

Similar to his approach to portraiture, Taber enjoyed experimentation offering the latest techniques. For example, in 1889, he went to Cloverdale in Sonoma County to photograph a solar eclipse and had a special camera manufactured for the event. One image in particular Taber seemed to relish was an 1882 mammoth plate view of the H.M.S. *Comus* firing a salute in San Francisco Bay (title page). This "instantaneous" picture represented a then marvelous technological achievement in fast exposure speed capable of freezing the very moment the guns fired. To make it even more impressive, Taber took this photograph from another vessel while in motion. He modestly stated, "This photograph has been pronounced by the highest authorities in the photographic profession to be the most wonderful achievement in instantaneous photography yet accomplished."

Ever cognizant of what appealed to tourists, Taber recorded in depth San Francisco's most exotic location, Chinatown. Although overshadowed by the work of future photographic artists like Arnold Genthe, Taber created the first important body of work on this "Cathay in El Dorado." His images as well as the words of such famous writers like Frank Norris, Mrs. Frank Leslie, and Charles Nordhoff helped to create the stereotype of the Chinese in the occidental mind. Visitors to San Francisco made a point of visiting Clay Street hill with its tantalizing shops, restaurants, and fascinating population. Obtaining photographs of Chinatown would become a must.

Taber was one of the first to combine portraiture and landscape photography in one image as demonstrated by a number of his Chinatown views. Additionally, Taber directed his camera to record another stereotype of the district—the dark, dangerous, squalid, and crowded maze of Chinatown's streets and narrow alleys.

Taber, as a man of remarkable marketing skill, saw the potential of the album format. He also realized its advertising potential and the compatibility of mixing photographs with text. In addition, he received commissions to photograph places like Sutro Heights and events like the 1893-94 California Midwinter International Exposition, and for these jobs, he created specialized albums. In many respects, these impressive albums remain his most enduring legacy.

San Francisco in the 1870s and 1880s stood as the economic and cultural center of the Pacific Rim. With its commanding location, San Francisco emerged as a world emporium. To capture that enterprise and economic muscle, Taber embarked on an incredibly ambitious publishing project, the creation of an advertising volume illustrated with original photographs. Unlike city directories designed for mass distribution, Taber planned a limited-edition work probably sold by subscription to the advertisers represented in the volume. He designed it to attract a specific audience, the well-to-do and cultural elite who patronized plush hotels and booked passage on the finest steamships. It would be distributed not only in San Francisco but also in the eastern United States and several foreign countries. The result was one of the most sumptuous volumes ever produced about an American city and perhaps the most ambitious photographically illustrated work produced on the West Coast. Published in 1880, it carried the following title gold-stamped on its front cover: *The Taber Photographic Album of Principal Business Houses, Residences and Persons.* To a certain degree, it served as a forerunner of the advertising books placed in today's luxury hotels and resorts.

Gracing the folio-size pages of this morocco bound album are advertisements and approximately 130 photographs depicting an astonishing mixture of businesses and attractions. Rodger C. Birt in his doctoral dissertation on San Francisco photography wrote: "It is a visual catalog of the amenities San Francisco had to offer the tourist, the visiting businessman, or recently arrived permanent resident." In other words, a visitor to San Francisco could find just about anything and everything just as he would in New York or London. Such long-lived companies as Levi Strauss, Tubbs Cordage, W. J. Sloane, and Gladding, McBean and Company each occupied an entire page. It superbly captured San Francisco's Gilded Age when palatial mansions dominated Nob Hill and all kinds of factories and shops produced everything from boilers to blankets.

Never one to be self-effacing, I. W. Taber reserved the most prominent space in the album for himself. The very first leaf greets the reader with a smiling portrait of the mustachioed, curly-haired photographer framed by handsome typographic ornaments. The next leaf consisted of a view of his luxurious "Photographic Parlors and Art Studios" strategically located opposite the Grand and Palace Hotels. Flanking the photograph, Taber added important information about his equipment and services. He asserted: "We have the latest improved instruments for taking the most elaborate and perfect pictures known to the art of photography." This imposing advertising leaf shows that he saw his businesses as more than portraiture and making landscape views. He wrote in the polite florid language of the day, "We beg leave to inform you that we have just received the very latest improved instruments from Europe especially adapted for photographing Maps, Drawings of Machinery, Shafts, Buildings, etc., which we furnish at the lowest rates. Residence and Business Property, in any part of the city, Oakland or Alameda photographed at short notices." This was certainly more than a one-man operation. He also noted that while enjoying more than twenty-five years of experience in photography, that he employed "only the best and most experienced help."

Such a lavish publication required considerable capitalization and Taber solicited support from "the business community." A notice in the San Francisco *Daily Evening Bulletin* for January 3, 1880, provides data on the actual cost of production. The volume would cost $1,700 for the binding and printing, $1,500 for the photographs and another $1,800 for miscellaneous expenses. Major subscribers received one full page. If however, a business' sign appeared in the same photograph as one of the paying customers, Taber's technicians carefully blotted out their name.

Taber's work also represents an important example of how original photographs, in an era before photomechanical processes, were incorporated into publications. It is not known exactly how many copies Taber published but its must have been a small number. A similar volume published in 1884 by Taber consisted of only 150 copies. Production of a photographically illustrated book, however, was no easy task in the days before the mechanically produced halftone. A book with 130 photographs (copies varied in number) like the *Taber Photographic Album* would require the production of close to 20,000 original photographs! Then each print had to be carefully mounted on the page. Following this tedious procedure, Taber's bookbinder, D. Hicks and Company, bound the stiff leaves into the volume by means of linen hinges. Despite the tremendous labor required, the *Taber Photographic Album* nonetheless represents an important advance in the development of book illustration. Previously, publishers had to rely

THE BALDWIN ★

★ ★ ★ *The Leading Hotel of San Francisco, California.*

This Hotel was Completed and Opened in May, 1877, and is Conducted on the American Plan.

Over $3,500,000 having been expended by Mr. Baldwin in its construction and furnishing. The Baldwin is the Most Elegantly Appointed Hotel in the World.

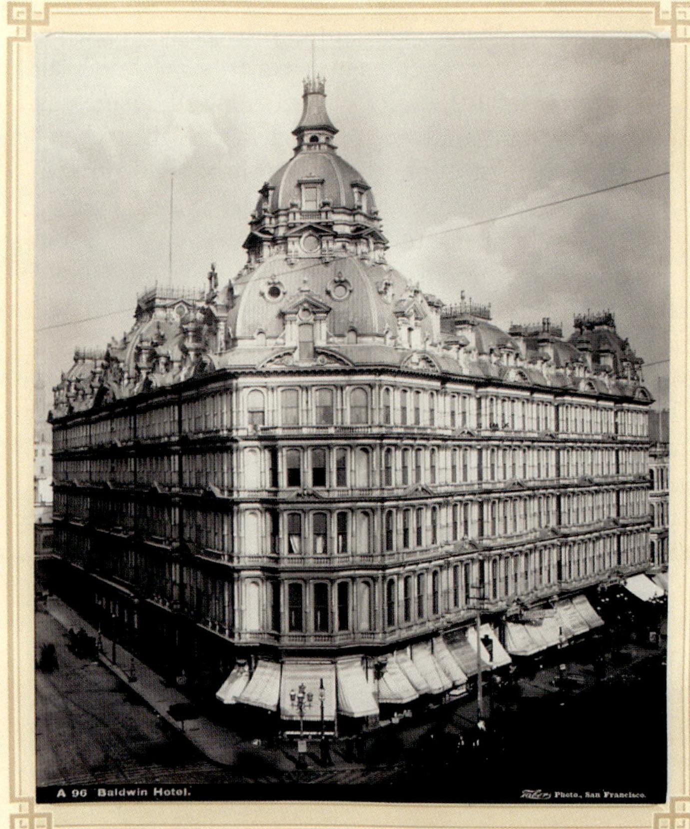

Situated on Market Street, at the intersection of Powell and Eddy Streets, and fronting on four principal streets in the business centre, it is convenient of access to and from all quarters of the City. Eight lines of Street Cars pass its doors.

HOTEL COACHES AND CARRIAGES IN WAITING AT ALL STEAMER AND RAILWAY DEPOTS.

TOURISTS' HEADQUARTERS.

Special Accommodations for Families & Large Parties.

H. H. PEARSON, PROPRIETOR.

Formerly Proprietor of the COSMOPOLITAN, San Francisco.

CALIFORNIA STATE LIBRARY

From California Scenery and Industries, *1884.*

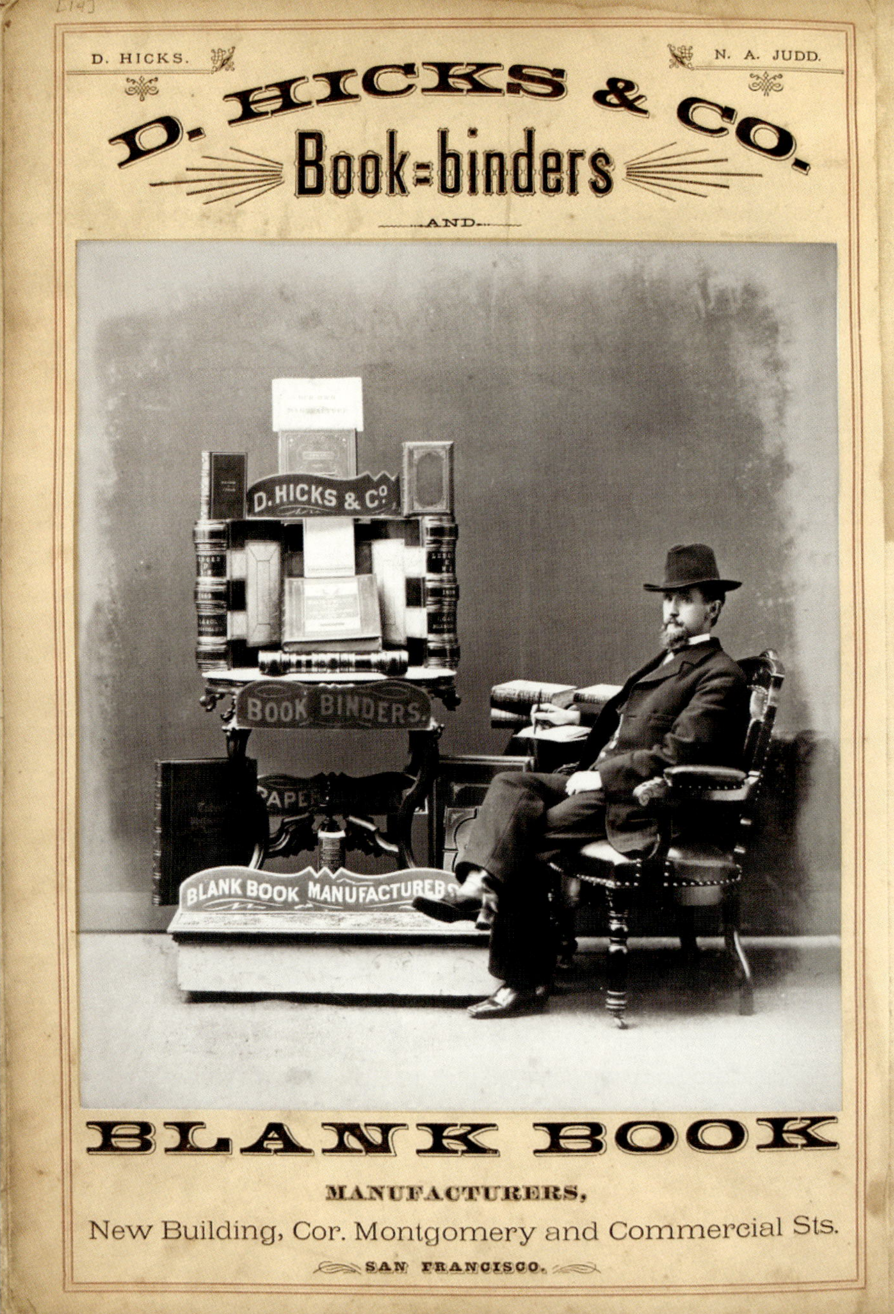

CALIFORNIA STATE LIBRARY

From The Taber Photographic Album, *1880.*

on lithographs, etchings, and engravings created by the interpretative hand of an artist. Now the bustling San Francisco business scene could be accurately portrayed by the "truthful lens."

Taber followed this album of business photographs with a smaller but equally impressive work in 1884 called *California Scenery and Industries*. The folio volume consisted of fifty-five leaves embellished with original photographs According to an advertisement in the *San Francisco Newsletter*, Taber published 150 copies requiring 8,350 original photographs all mounted by hand. While similar in format to the 1880 publication and designed to demonstrate California's commercial importance, this folio included the added feature of tourist attractions such as Yosemite, Calaveras Big Tree Grove, and regional resorts and hot springs. Business and pleasure were artfully mixed. It was a visual equivalent to the promotional books by the likes of Charles Nordhoff, Benjamin C. Truman, and John S. Hittell. Taber solicited subscriptions from a variety of businesses including wineries, newspapers, and San Francisco hotels. Naturally Taber liberally sprinkled the volume with celebrity endorsements of his photography. The last leaf is a spectacular view of his Montgomery Street gallery.

Historian Peter Bacon Hales in his seminal work, *Silver Cities: The Photography of American Urbanization, 1839-1915*, praised the two folio advertising albums:

> Taber is justly considered one of San Francisco's three greatest nineteenth-century photographers, his most significant contribution to urban photography, however, is not to be found in his spectacular views of that city's picturesque cityscape, nor in his catalogue of portraits which included virtually everyone of note who lived in San Francisco, visited it, or was a subject of interest to its residents. Rather, it is in a pair of large albums, one called *California Scenery*, the other *California Scenery and Industries*.

In addition to these costly advertising volumes, Taber's business establishment also sold individual albums. Customers could come into his studio and from his "View Department" select particular scenes from the many thousands available and have them made into albums. A number of Taber albums with scenic views of California and the west survive in institutional collections. They serve as a reminder of how this clever businessman marketed his products.

In 1886, Taber took his equipment out to Adolph Sutro's magnificent estate, appropriately known as Sutro Heights, overlooking Seal Rocks, the Cliff House, and Pacific Ocean. His growing reputation as a portrait photographer and view artist combined with his mingling with San Francisco's more famous personalities may have led to this undertaking. It is not clear if Sutro commissioned Taber or if the photographer saw this as an opportunity to expand his image stock with negatives of one of San Francisco's latest attractions. Taber made dozens of views and mounted them in albums presented to Sutro.

Taking advantage of the newly emerging halftone technology, Taber, in 1895, published a number of these Sutro-related pictures in an oblong booklet entitled *Sutro Baths, Heights and Cliff House*. The San Francisco Photo Engraving Company turned his originals into photomechanical images for mass distribution. Designed for the tourist trade, Taber's booklet borrowed an idea from his lavish 1880 and 1884 folio directories by carrying advertisements of local businesses.

A major personal triumph occurred when for Taber when he won the concession as the official photographer of the California Midwinter International Exposition. The fair, modeled after the enormously successful 1893 Columbian International Exposition in Chicago, gave San Francisco businessmen an opportunity to tout the charms of their city to the world. California and the city at the time were mired in economic doldrums. Led by *San Francisco Chronicle* publisher Michael de Young, the business community hoped the fair would rejuvenate the local economy. Held in what became Golden Gate Park, the fair represented to Taber an unparalleled advertising bonanza with exposure to a worldwide audience. As the official photographer, Taber opened up an eye-catching multistory photography pavilion on the fair grounds selling images from his considerable inventory. He advertised them as "crystal views of California." From opening day on January 27, 1894, to the fair's closing on July 6, more than 2,500,000 people enjoyed the extravaganza, and presumably, many came away with a Taber photograph as a memento.

To commemorate the fair, Taber created a number of large folio morocco-bound albums entitled *Souvenir of the California Midwinter International Exposition*. Each came embellished with approximately 130 original photographs with the majority measuring 8 x 10 inches. He did include several 10 ½ x 14 and 10 ½ x 16 ½ in size. This represented a tour-de-force of the exposition and featured a number of night views, a relatively new development in photography. Taber apparently made one album for presentation to each fair commissioner. It is not known exactly how many of these souvenir albums were produced but fewer than ten are known to exist today.

In conjunction with the fair, H. S. Crocker and Company published a much less expensive trade edition illustrated with halftone reproductions of Taber's photographs not only of the exposition but also tourist scenes of California. The Crocker Company entitled the work *The "Monarch" Souvenir of Sunset City and Sunset Scenes: Being Views of California Midwinter Fair and Famous Scenes in the Golden State.* The introductory matter described Taber as "the world-famous photographer" but also indicated that "all the photographic galleries of the State" contributed images for this project. None of the other photographers, however, were recognized. This fifteen-part oblong publication, along with the previously mentioned Sutro Baths booklet, demonstrated how photographers in the 1890s collaborated with publishers in utilizing the halftone to mass-produce their photographs. Virtually every large city by the 1890s produced souvenir publications loaded with halftones of prominent landmarks and natural wonders. Albums with actual photographs mounted on the pages, however beautiful, were just too expensive and could not be enjoyed by a wide audience.

Taber took on other commissions that centered on promoting business and tourism. A fine example is a little oblong volume with a tied-together binding with the name *Hotel Bella Vista, San Francisco, Cal.* gold-stamped on the front cover. Published in 1894, the souvenir book presents excellent documentation on how San Franciscans lived. Located at the corner of Pine and Taylor Streets on Nob Hill, the Bella Vista was classed as a "private family hotel" and more than likely catered to permanent residents rather than to tourists and traveling businessmen. For this publication, Taber contributed a mixture of thirty-four interior and exterior hotel views with his standardized tourist images of the city, Yosemite, and Stanford University. The publisher, Pacific Press Publishing Company of Oakland, then converted his original photographs to photo engravings.

When San Francisco was rocked by earthquake and scorched by fire in April 1906, the history of photography suffered an incalculable disaster. Isaiah West Taber's Post Street gallery, with its eighty tons of portrait and twelve tons of view negatives, was destroyed along with the glass plate negatives of many other important pioneer photographers including Carleton E. Watkins. Untold numbers of daguerreotypes, ambrotypes, albums, and positive prints likewise suffered a fiery end. During those horrifying four days, much of the visual history of California and the West literally went up in smoke. As stated in *Camera Craft*, "The loss [of Taber's negatives] was an irreparable one, not only to him but to the world." Symbolic of the city's resilience, however, the seventy-five-year-old Taber remained optimistic and attempted to rebuild his portrait business. Advanced age and lack of resources, however, impeded his progress. He died quietly at home on February 22, 1912, sixty-two years to the day after he first arrived in the golden city of San Francisco. Obituaries in the local press praised his long career and many contributions. Perhaps no higher praise could be elicited than from one obituary which remarked that his "name was in practically every San Francisco family portrait album before the [1906] fire."

Fortunately, Taber left a rich legacy with the spectacular albums and thousands of prints that survive. During his later years, he achieved world recognition as perhaps the most famous photographer in San Francisco and the West. His own persona and inventiveness, combined with the elegance of his studios, and the richness of his portrait and view collection made the name "Taber" as well known as any. While his celebrity portraits attracted acclaim, his well-composed scenic views and sumptuous advertising volumes did much to call attention to the delights and economic opportunities of the Golden State. Taber gave visual credence to the florid language of the booster. Carleton E. Watkins and Eadweard Muybridge may have achieved more fame as photographic artists but few could rival Taber as a commercial and public relations success. Today, Taber views are universally recognized and collected for their documentary value and for creating a lasting record, in particular, of San Francisco and California in the late nineteenth century. Twenty years before his death, the *San Francisco Call* for August 14, 1892, beautifully and proudly summed up the place of this transplanted New Englander:

> There is no branch of business of which San Francisco is more justly proud than that of photography. The work of our local galleries stands unrivaled in the world. If there is one establishment more widely known than any other it is that of the Taber Photographic Company, the excellence of whose pictures has won the favor not alone of Californians, but of every prominent foreigner who has passed through this fair city. Everyone who is anyone goes to Taber's to inspect, admire and order.

— Gary F. Kurutz
Curator of Special Collections
California State Library

Taber Photographs
1870 - 1900

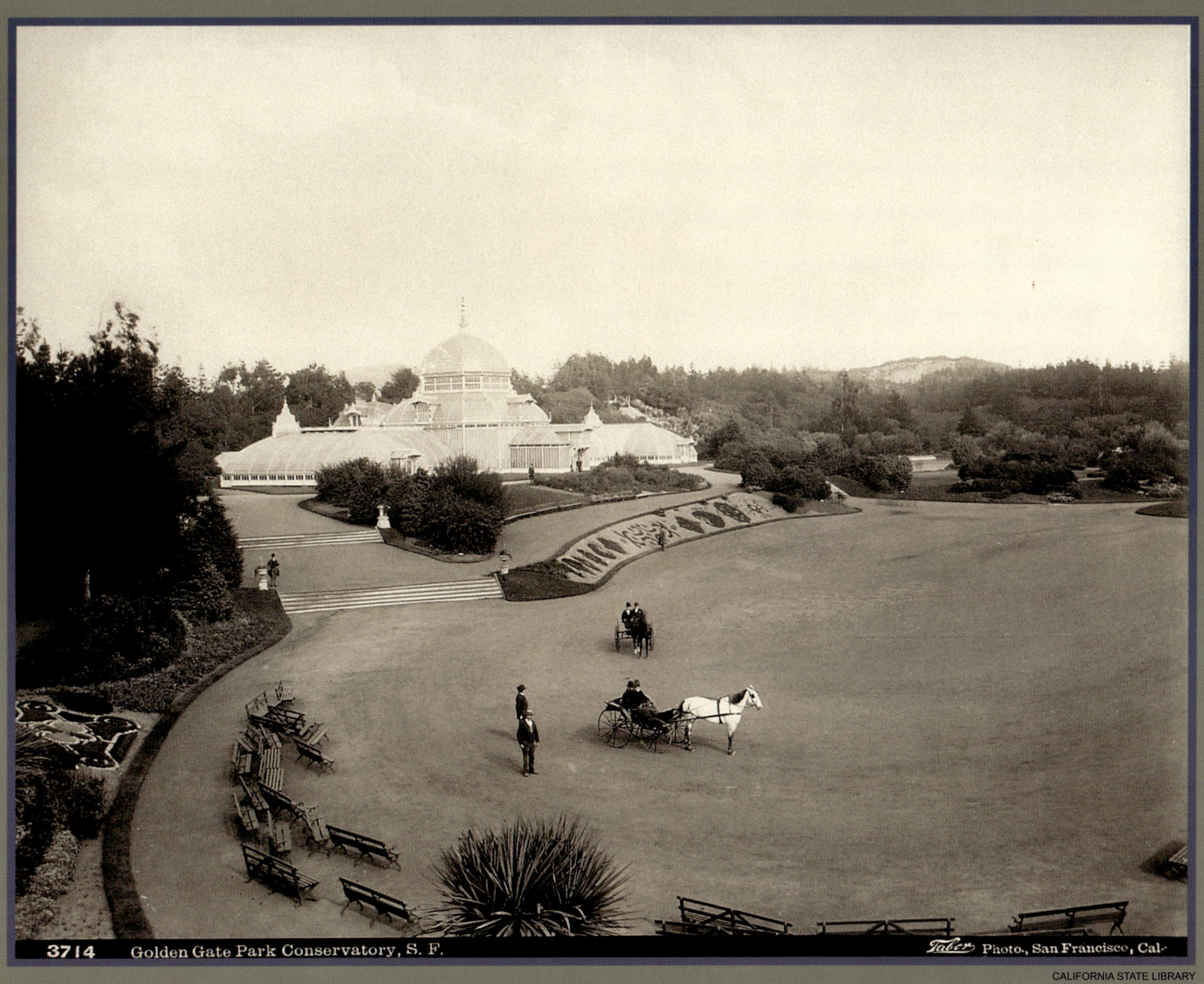

CALIFORNIA STATE LIBRARY

SAN FRANCISCO

Scenic view photographs published by Isaiah Taber between 1880 until 1906 were sold mounted or unmounted and usually printed with Taber's reverse caption and logotype along the bottom edge. Most prints were made from 8 by 10 inch dry plate glass negatives and sold in four popular sizes, 8 x 5 inches, 8 x 10 inches, 8 x 12 inches, and 11 x 14 inches. Unmounted prints were sold flat or shipped rolled around cardboard tubes. Surviving prints mounted by Taber are on high-quality board, prints mounted by others may be on board of lesser quality. The numbers printed on the lower left of the caption line primarily assisted Taber's technicians in locating the correct glass negative from among the thousands stored in the gallery. Scenic negatives and prints generally were not dated.

When Isaiah Taber shot this scene in 1882, a block west of his studio, cables had just been installed under the two center tracks on Market Street. The full-size photo on the opposite page was made from the uncropped 8 x 10 inch negative, typical of Taber's city views. The same scene, below, shows the print cropped to fit an 8 ½ x 5 ½ inch cardboard mount.

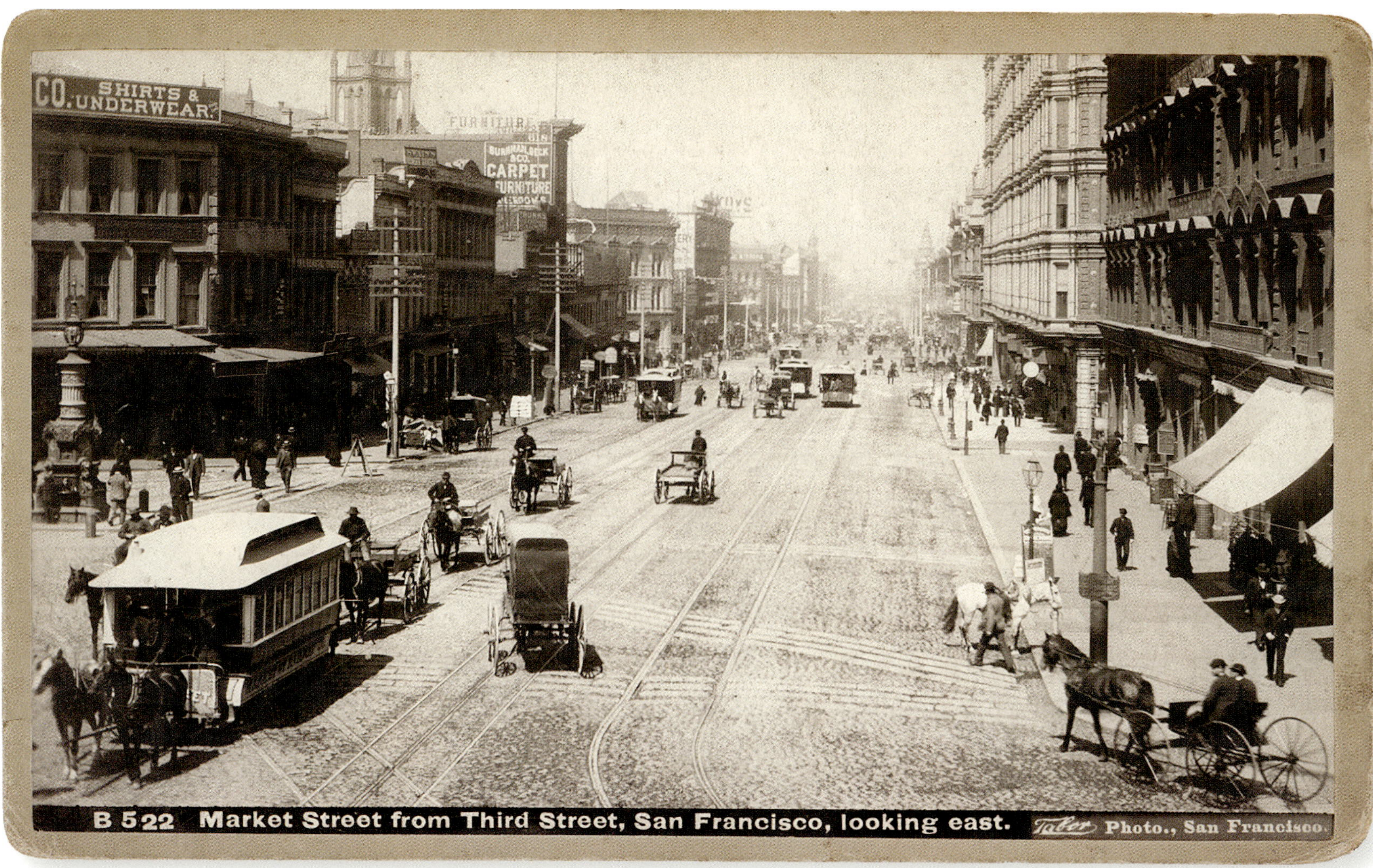

CUNEO COLLECTION

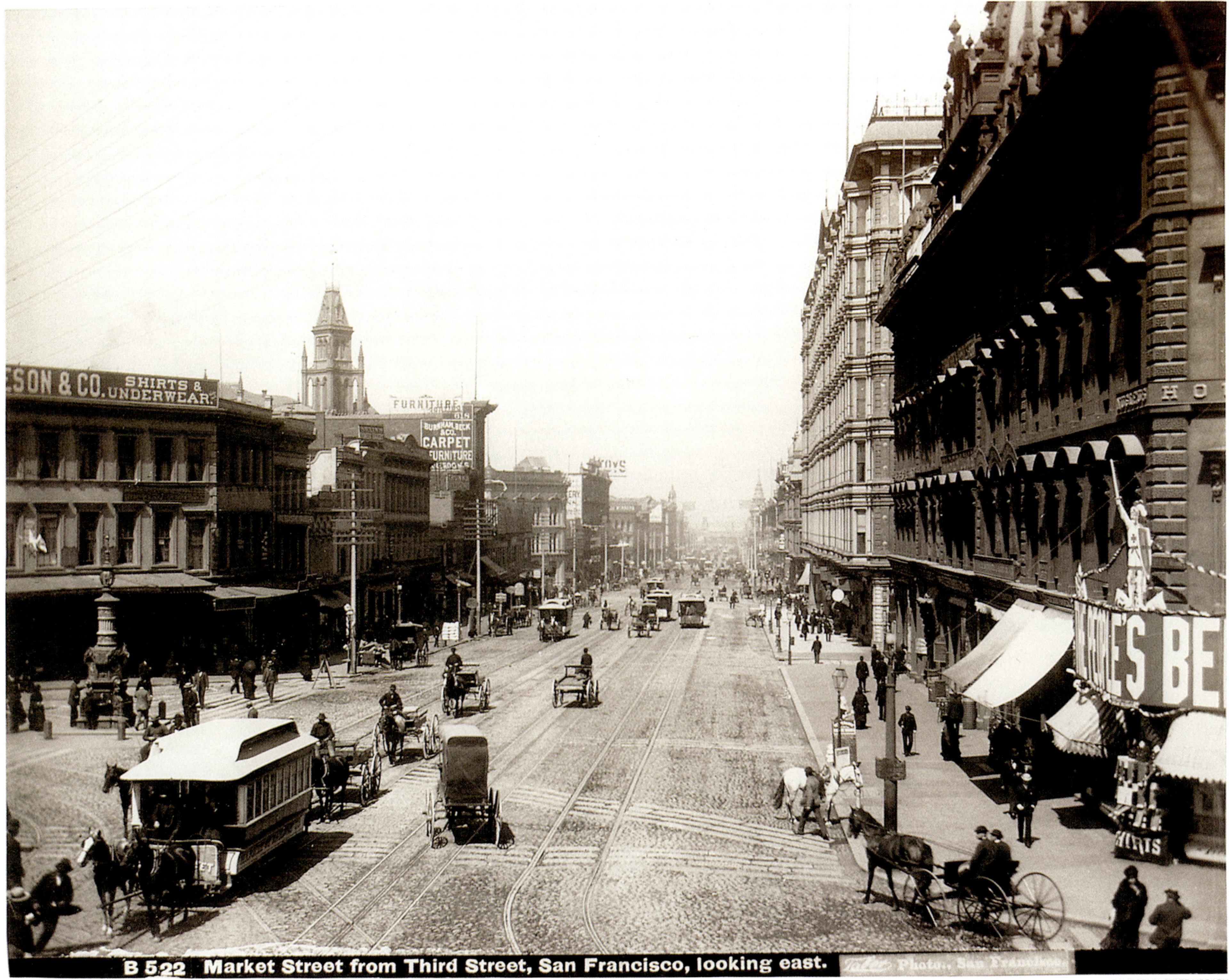

B 5:22 Market Street from Third Street, San Francisco, looking east.

CALIFORNIA STATE LIBRARY

Taber experimented with shorter exposure times and various developing chemicals to produce "instantaneous" photos, a process first made popular by Eadweard Muybridge. The short exposure times stopped action without blurring, resulting in "snapshots" like these.

Right: When snow began falling on Sunday, December 31, 1882, Taber rushed out with his camera to capture the rare event. Giddy San Franciscans gathered on Market Street in front of the Palace Hotel.
Below: A blustery day on Market Street, taken from Sixth Street looking east, with wind-blown pedestrians dodging rain puddles.

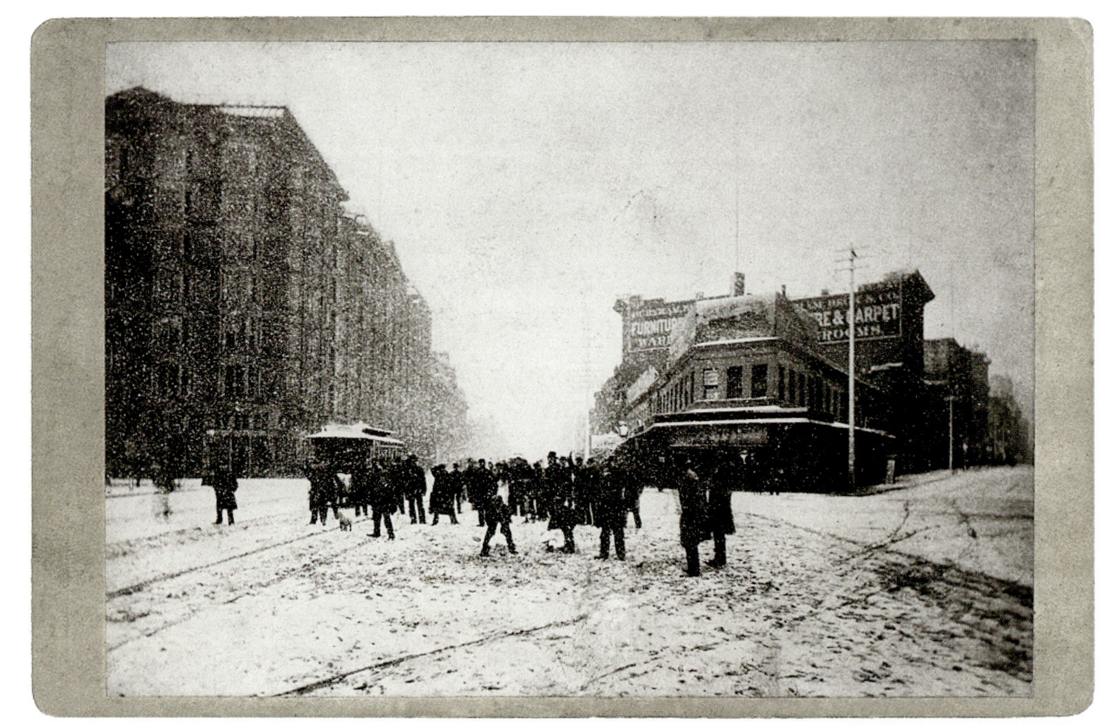

MARILYN BLAISDELL COLLECTION

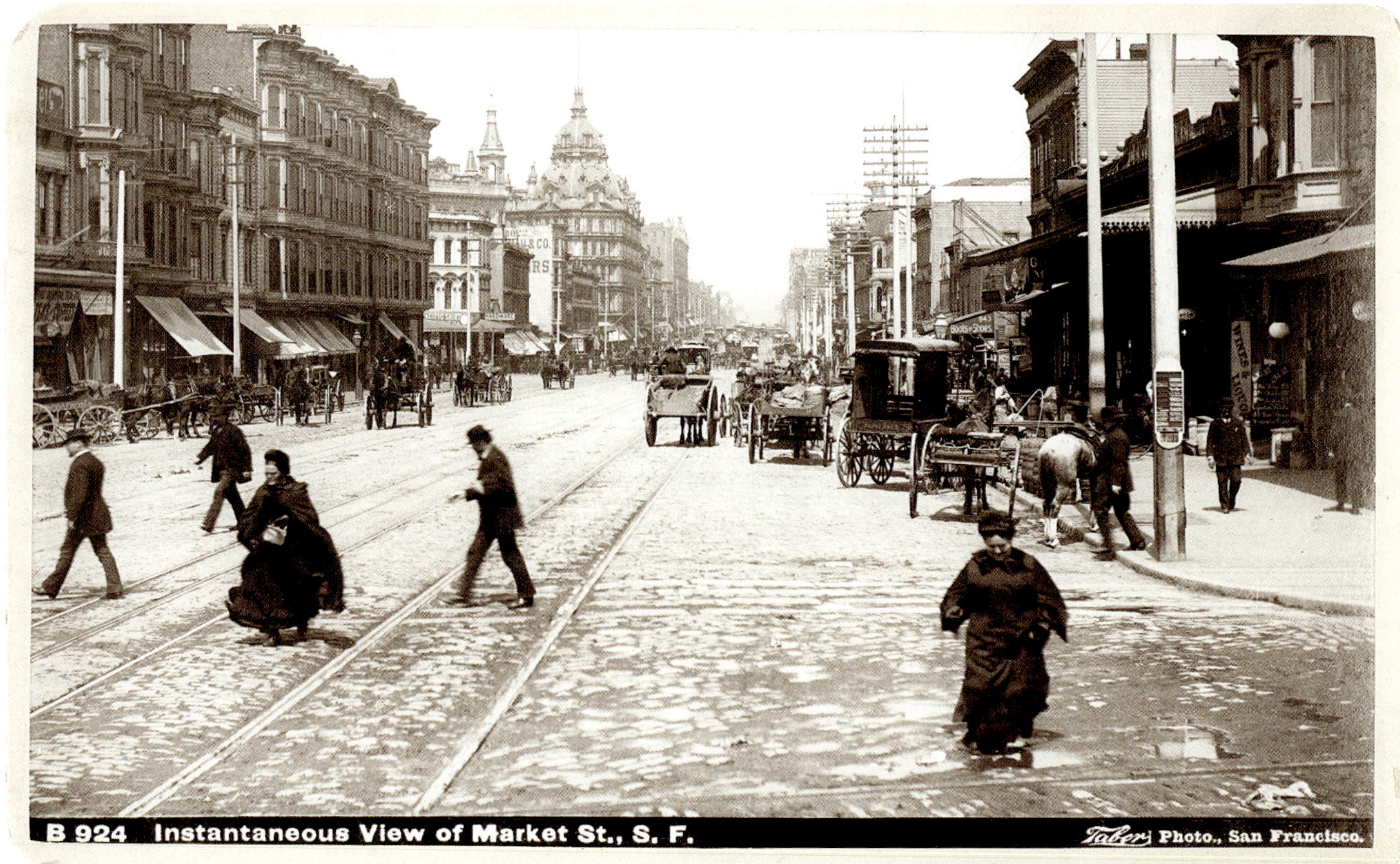

MARILYN BLAISDELL COLLECTION

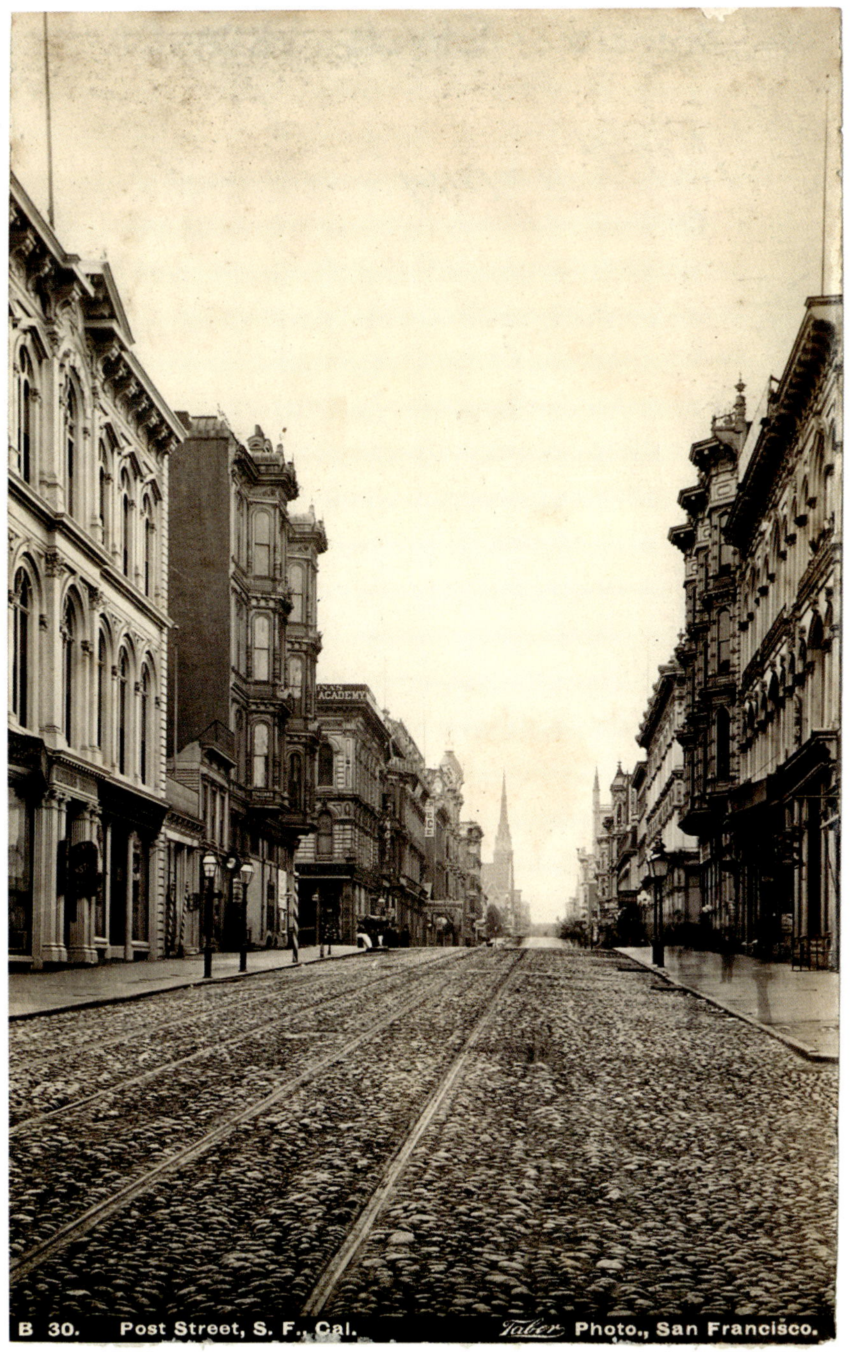

CALIFORNIA STATE LIBRARY

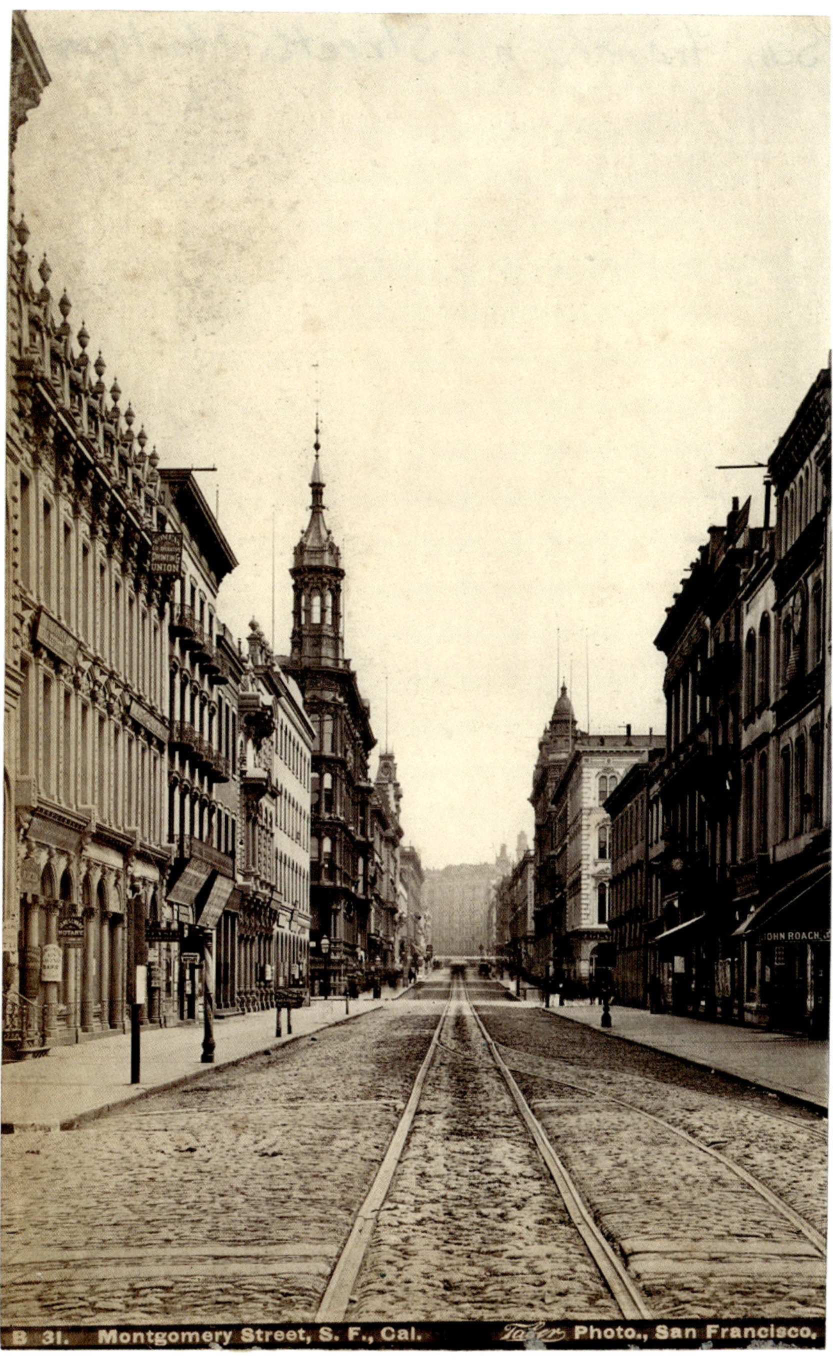

CALIFORNIA STATE LIBRARY

Early morning street scenes without traffic proved popular. These two examples, around 1884, capture the architectural feel of pre-earthquake downtown San Francisco. At left above is the Post Street neighborhood where Taber relocated his studio in 1893. Above right, looks down Montgomery Street to the Palace Hotel in the distance.

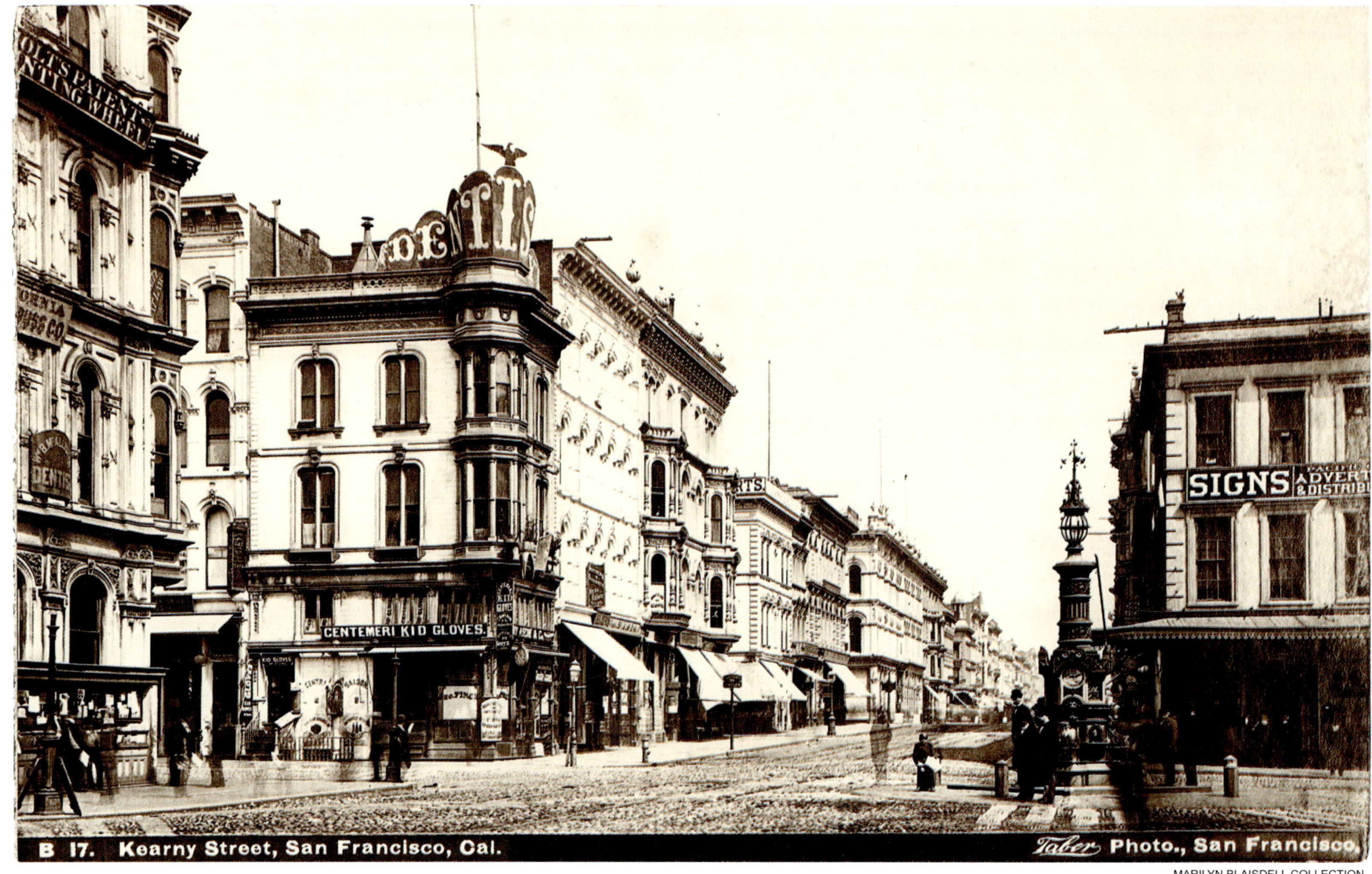

MARILYN BLAISDELL COLLECTION

Above: When dance-hall entertainer Lotta Crabtree donated a drinking fountain to San Francisco in 1875, it was installed in thebusy intersection of Market, Kearny and Geary Streets, creating a popular meeting place. This view, fountain at right, is from Market Street, looking up Kearny Street, with Geary on the left. The fountain, sometimes in early days derided as a Bavarian bedpost, has become a beloved San Francisco landmark.

Right: Isaiah Taber shot this view from the roof of his studio in the Hibernia Bank building at 8 Montgomery Street, probably in 1879 when he first moved in to his new quarters. The ornate gingerbread Grand Hotel on the left was overshadowed by the huge bulk of William Sharon's Palace Hotel, opened in 1875. Taber had direct telephone lines installed to both hotels so guests could arrange portrait appointments without venturing onto the street.

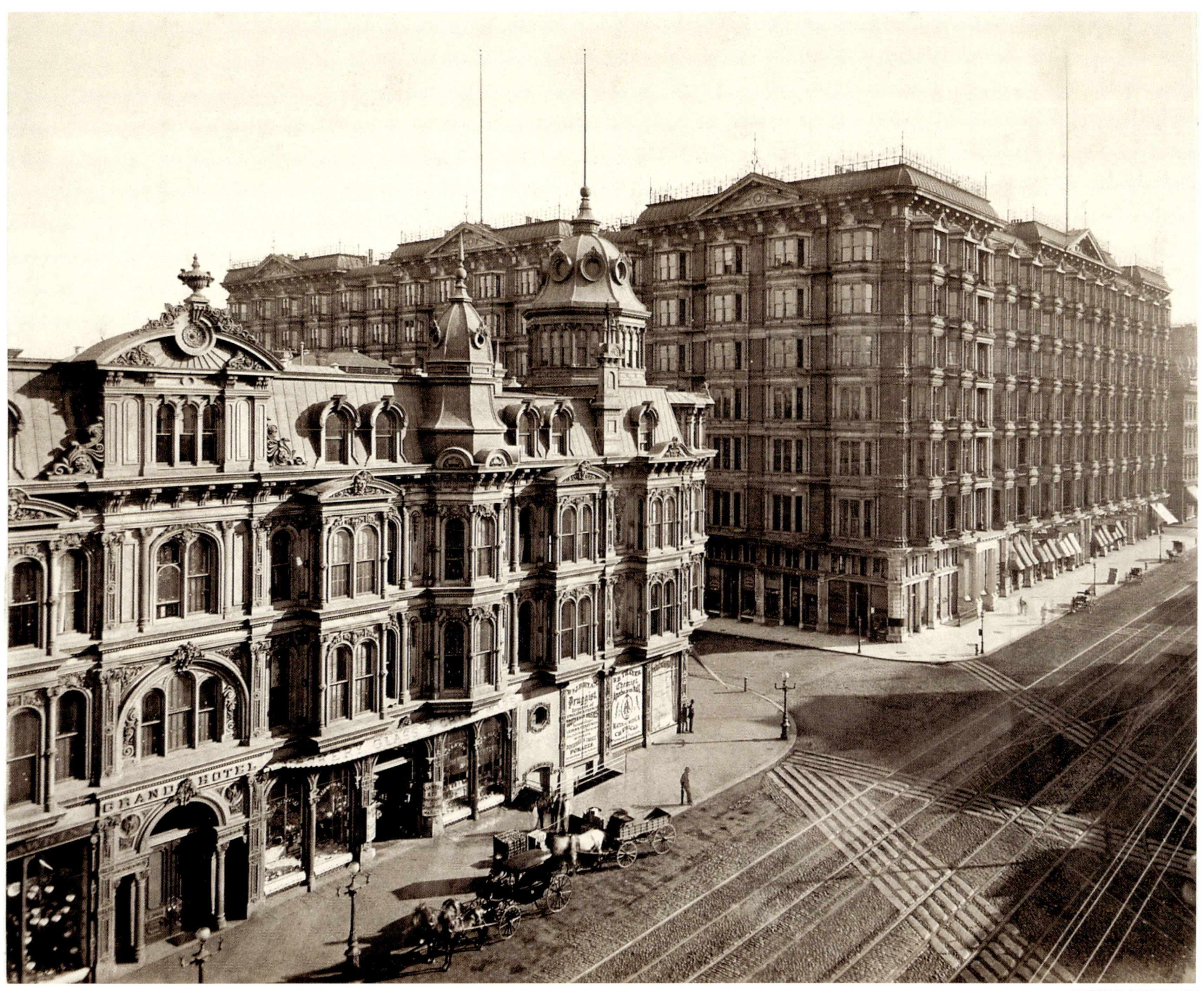

CALIFORNIA STATE LIBRARY

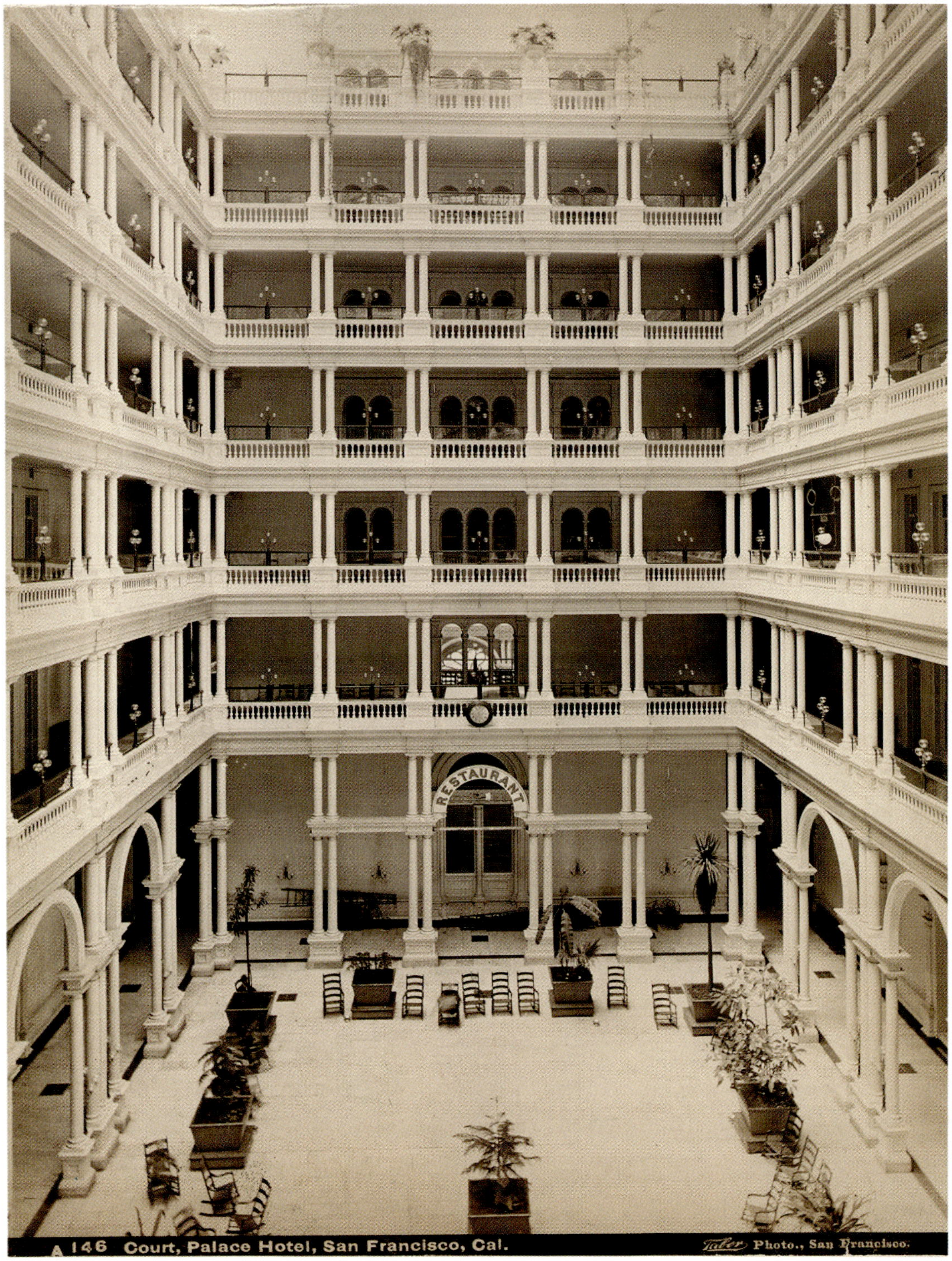

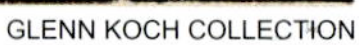

GLENN KOCH COLLECTION

CALIFORNIA STATE LIBRARY

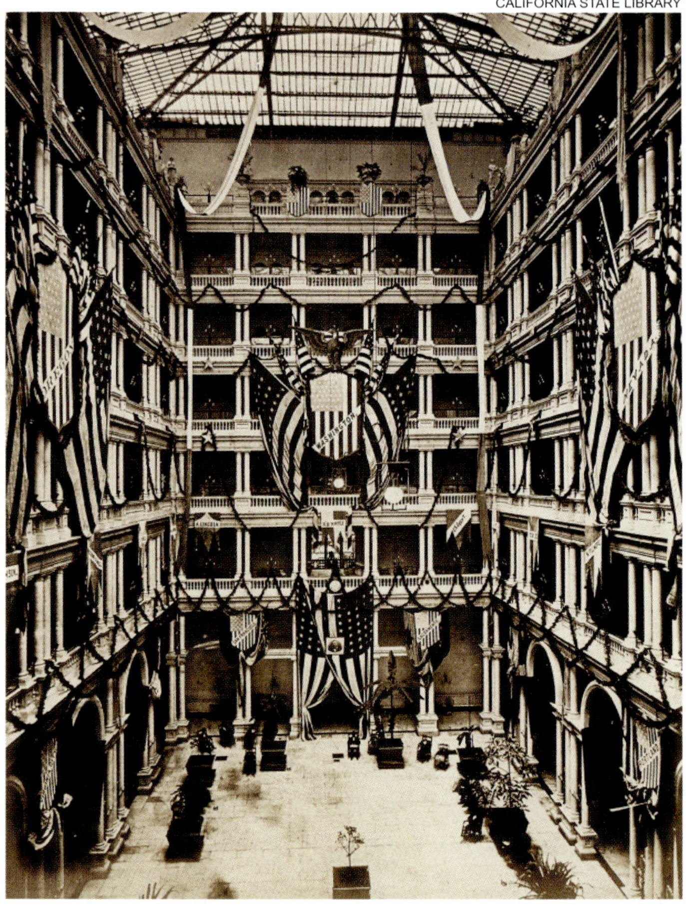

Above: The Palace Hotel interior court decorated for the visit of President Rutherford B. Hayes in September, 1880.
Left: The Palace court was originally a porte cochere *where horse-drawn carriages entered. Later it became a grand lobby leading to the dining room, and, after 1906, it became the dining room itself.*

If San Francisco was the queen city of the Pacific Coast. Market Street was its royal mall, and the Palace Hotel, aptly named, was the throne room. Perfectly situated on Market Street close to the business heart of the city, the Palace attracted a steady cortege of businessmen, political leaders, even foreign royalty. A guest could step from the Hotel onto Market Street and find himself facing an array of possibilities. To his left, a block away, the intersection of Market, Kearny, and Geary Streets crowned by Lotta's Fountain, was the closest thing San Francisco had to London's Piccadilly Circus. To the right, almost across the street, the visitor would see the intersection of Market, Montgomery, and Post Streets. Within two or three blocks of the Palace Hotel, San Francisco offered the visitor almost anything. Here were banks and eateries, legendary watering holes of the silver barons, theaters and fashionable shops. Chinatown was within walking distance. One could step into a street car at the hotel entrance and be whisked to the Ferry Building at the foot of Market Street and begin a journey to almost anywhere on earth. Nearby steamship and railroad offices offered excursions to the north and south where one could explore the scenic wonders of California.

Close by the Palace Hotel were the Grand Hotel across the street, and the Lick House, the Russ House, and "Lucky" Baldwin's impressive hotel and theater at Powell and Market Streets, giving the visitor a choice of fine accommodations. The hotels were magnets that drew not only visitors but merchants eager to cash in on the tourist trade and willing to pay high rents.

It had taken Isaiah Taber more than ten years from his arrival in San Francisco to reach the *crème de la crème* location he occupied at 8 Montgomery Street. It seemed every photographer in San Francisco wanted to be in the first two or three blocks of Montgomery Street, the closer to the Palace Hotel the better. Taber knew that visitors wanted to shop within walking distance of their hotels.

Women in particular wanted to shop in safety without having to climb onto street cars, dodge horses and climb flights of stairs. And women represented a major market for portrait photographers. They not only had their portraits taken but goaded or dragged their menfolk and children before the camera. Women, often responsible for maintaining family records, kept scrapbooks and albums. And they bought decorative and scenic photographs to display in the home.

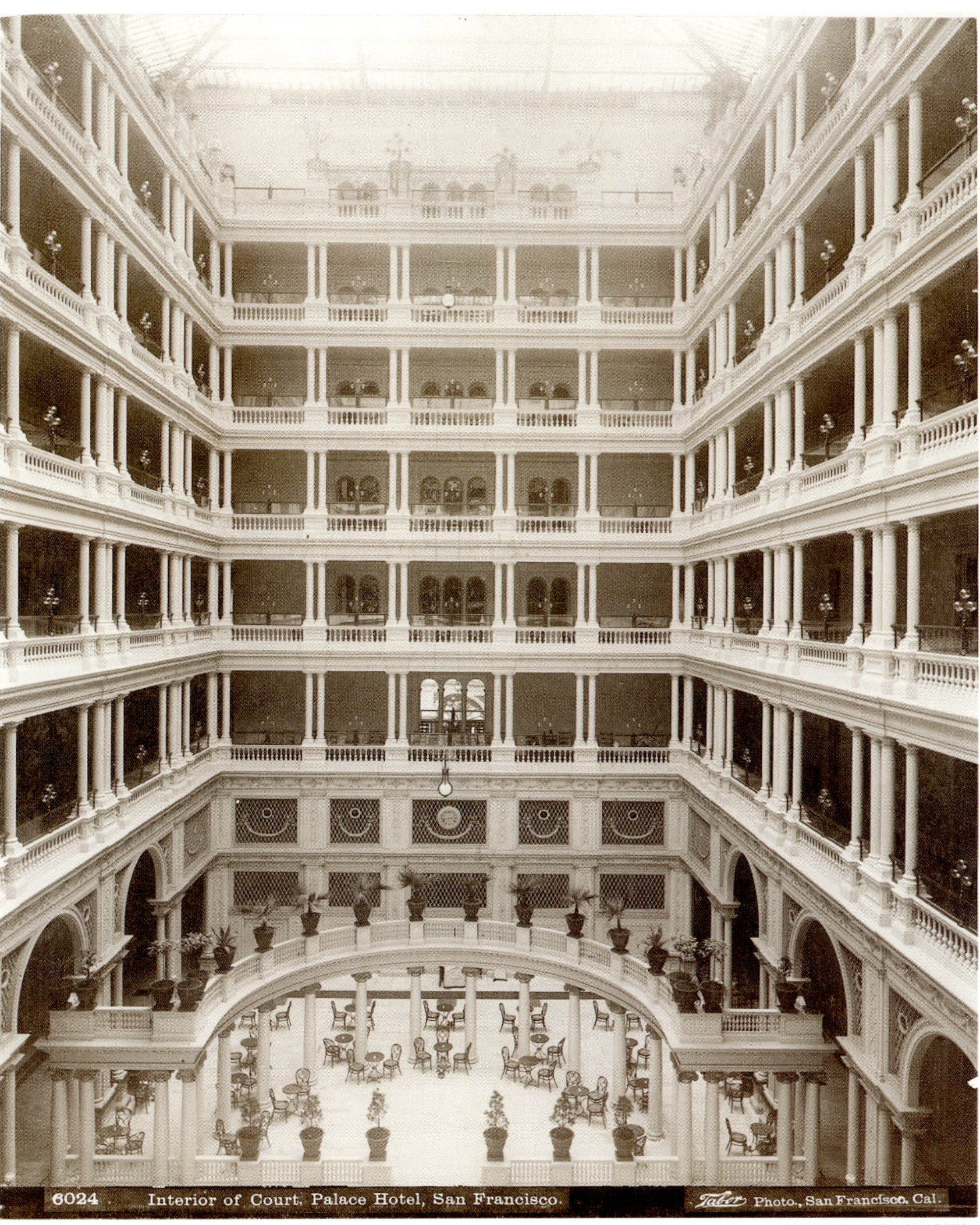

MARILYN BLAISDELL COLLECTION

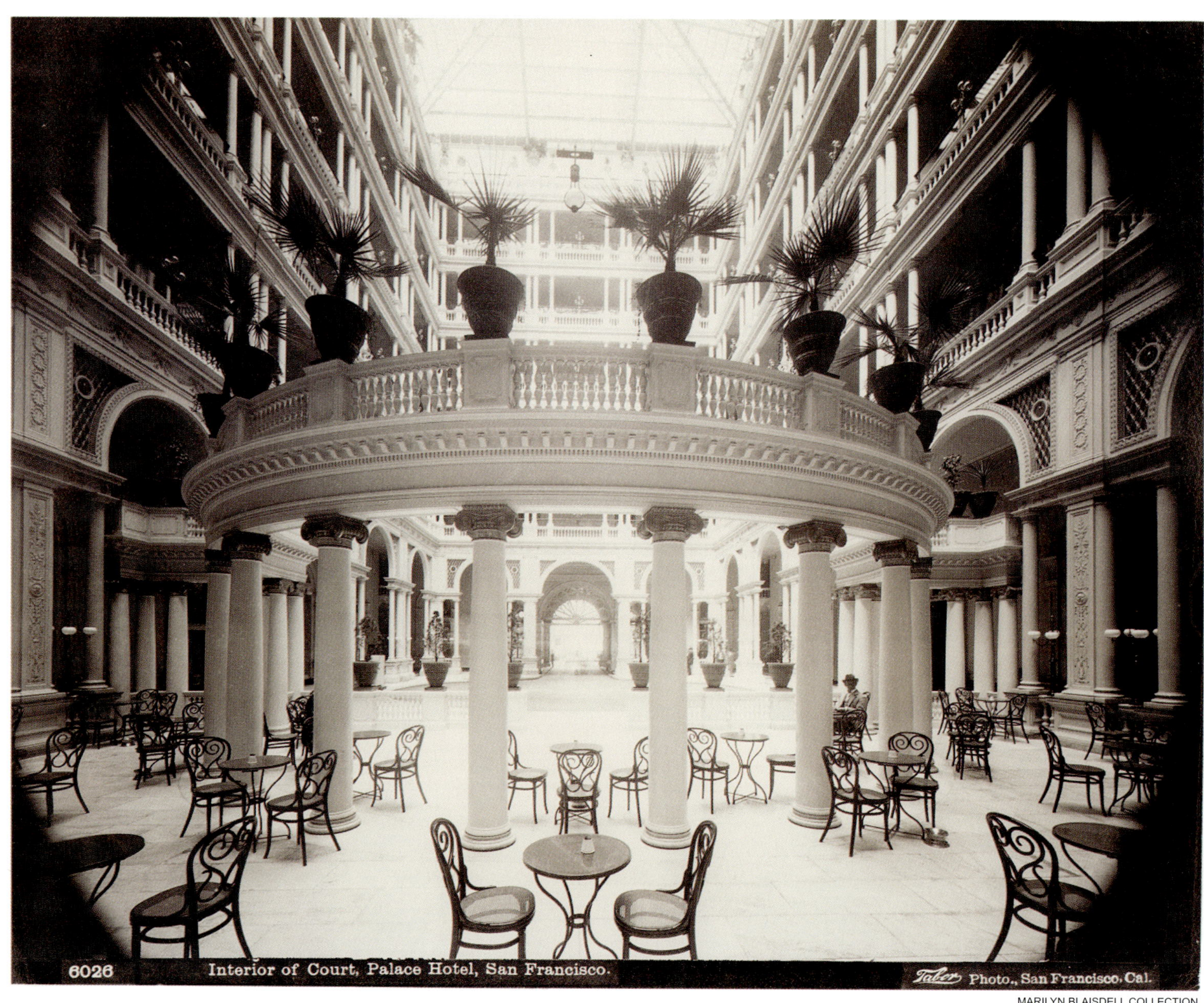

MARILYN BLAISDELL COLLECTION

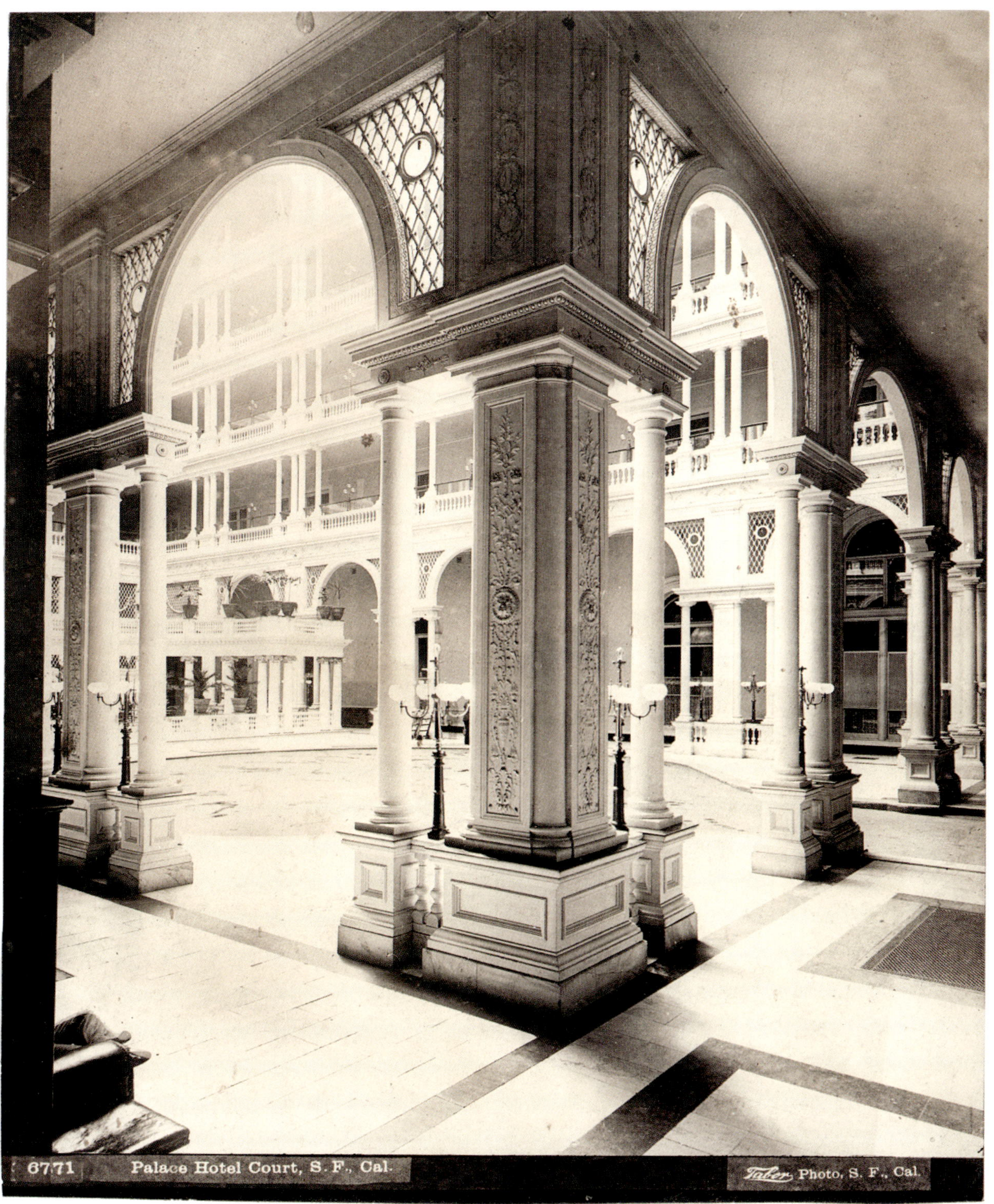

CALIFORNIA STATE LIBRARY

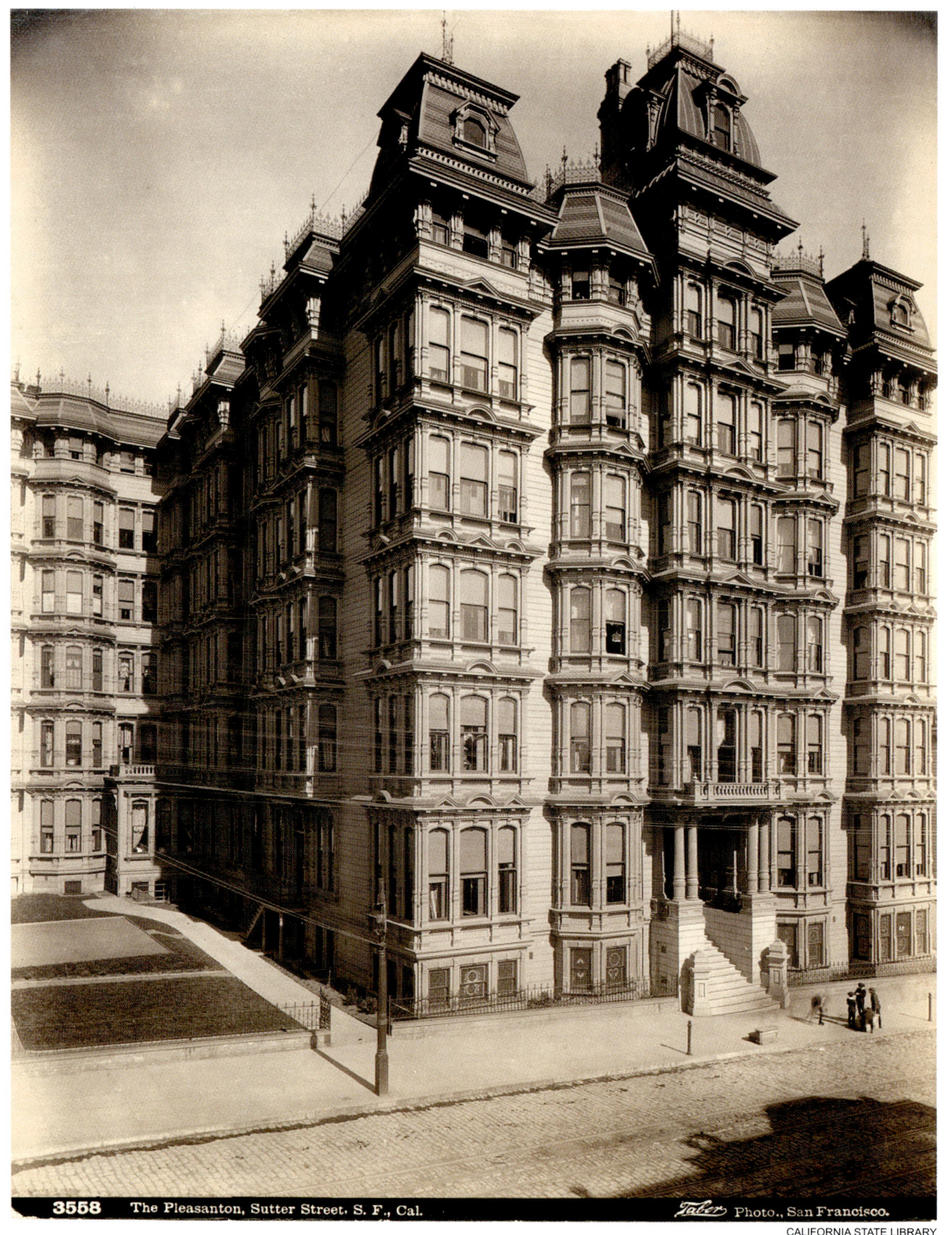

CALIFORNIA STATE LIBRARY

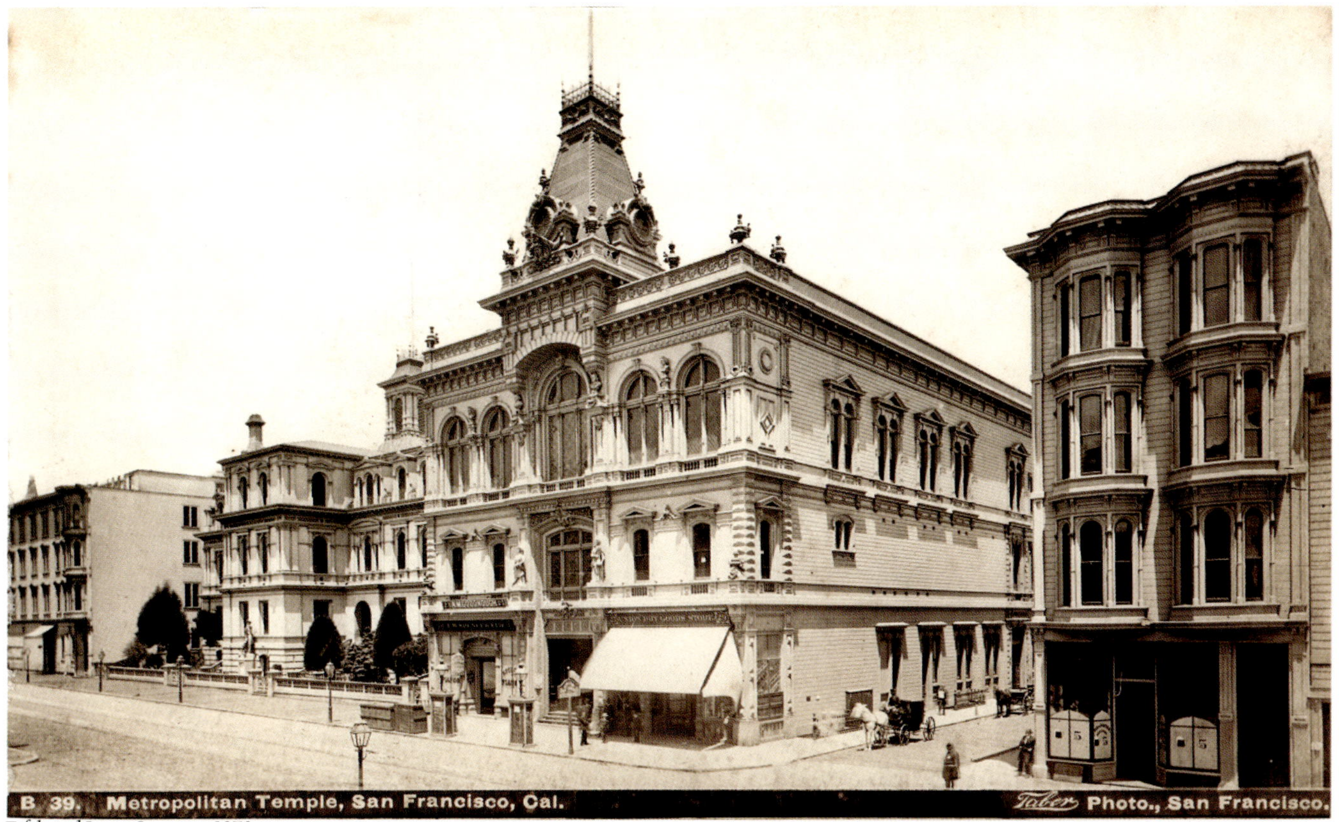

Fifth and Jessie Streets, c.1878

CALIFORNIA STATE LIBRARY

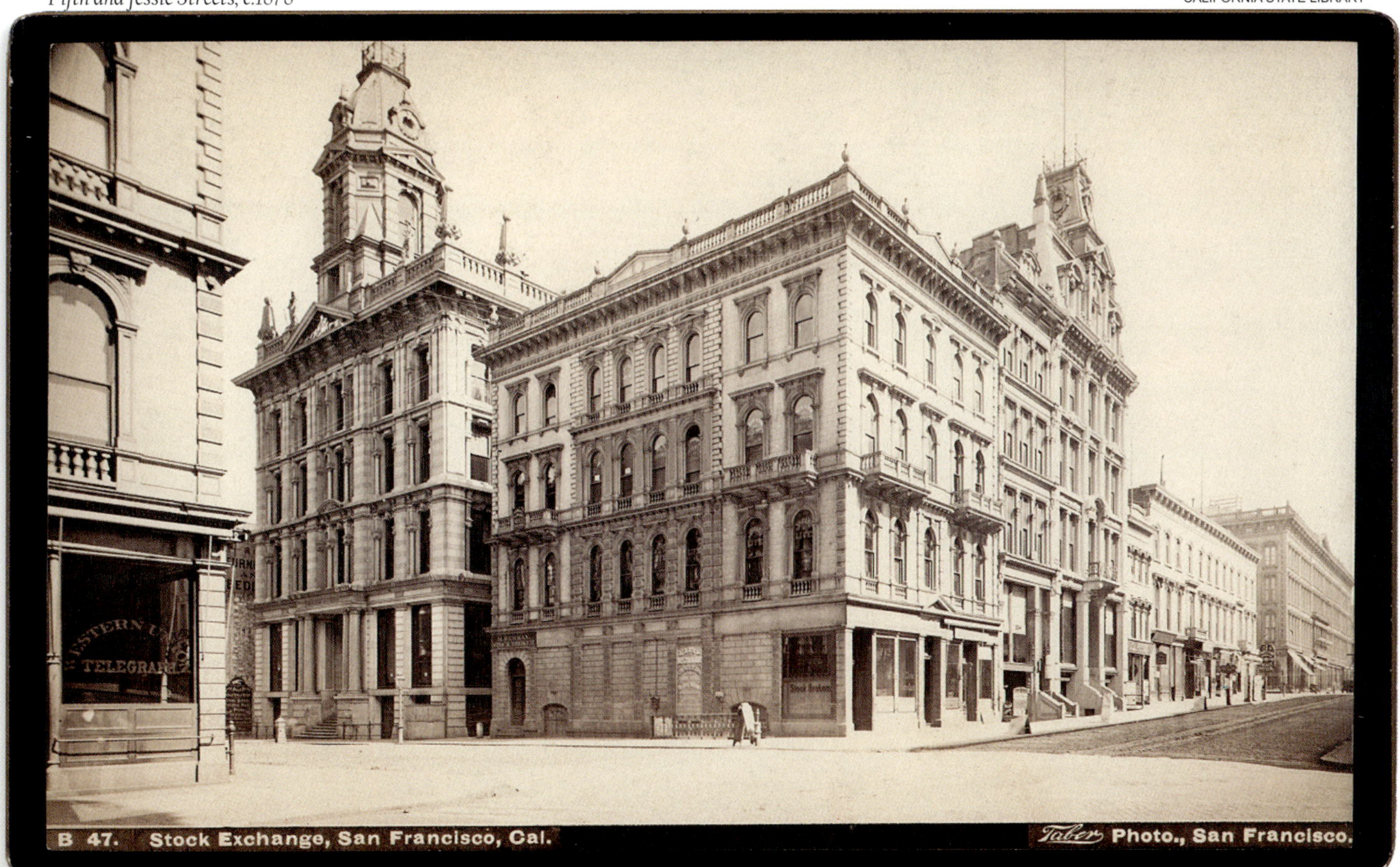

c. 1880

CALIFORNIA STATE LIBRARY

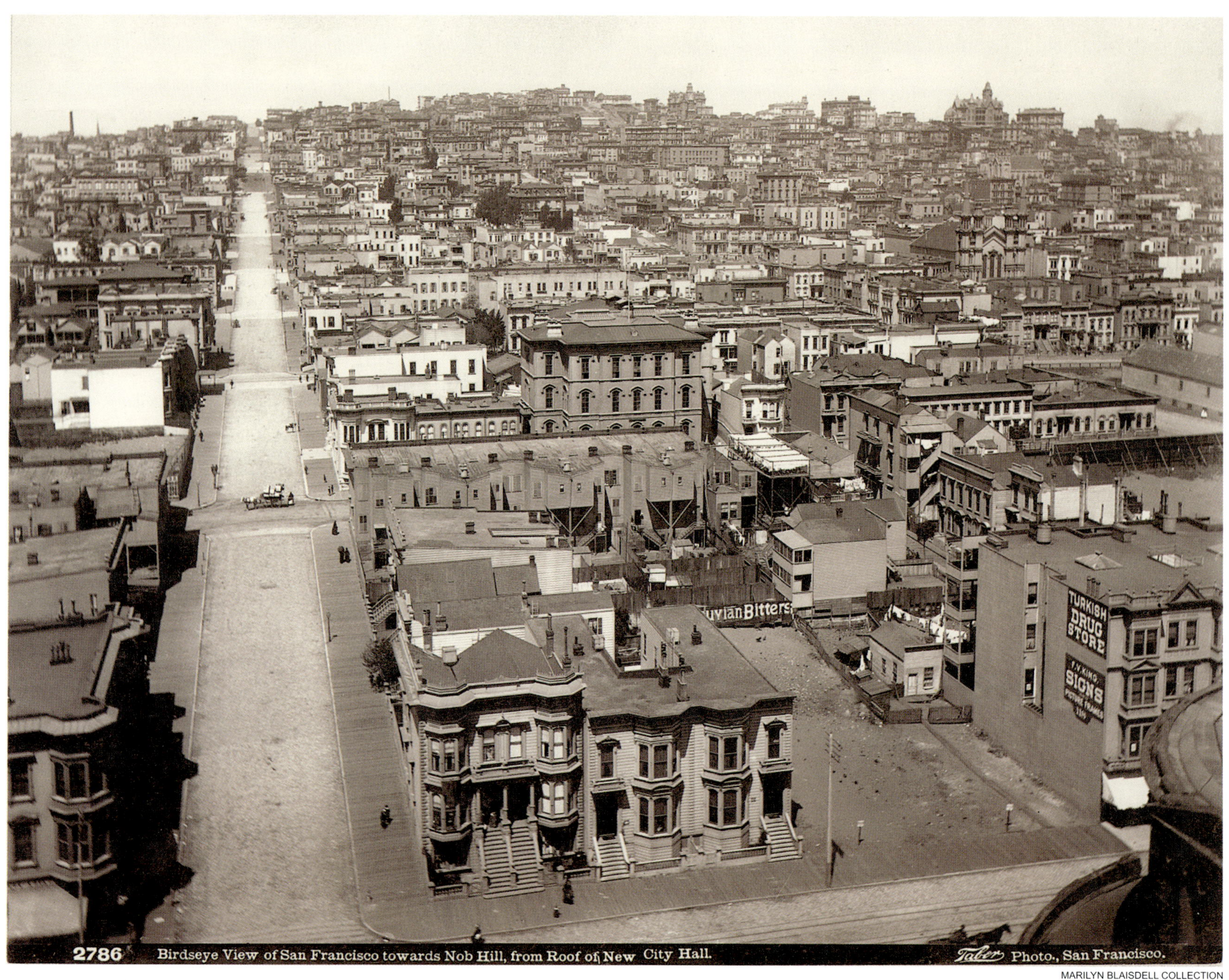

MARILYN BLAISDELL COLLECTION

Isaiah Taber climbed out on the roof of the Hall of Records at the new City Hall complex to make this shot looking north up Leavenworth Street from McAllister Street around 1878.

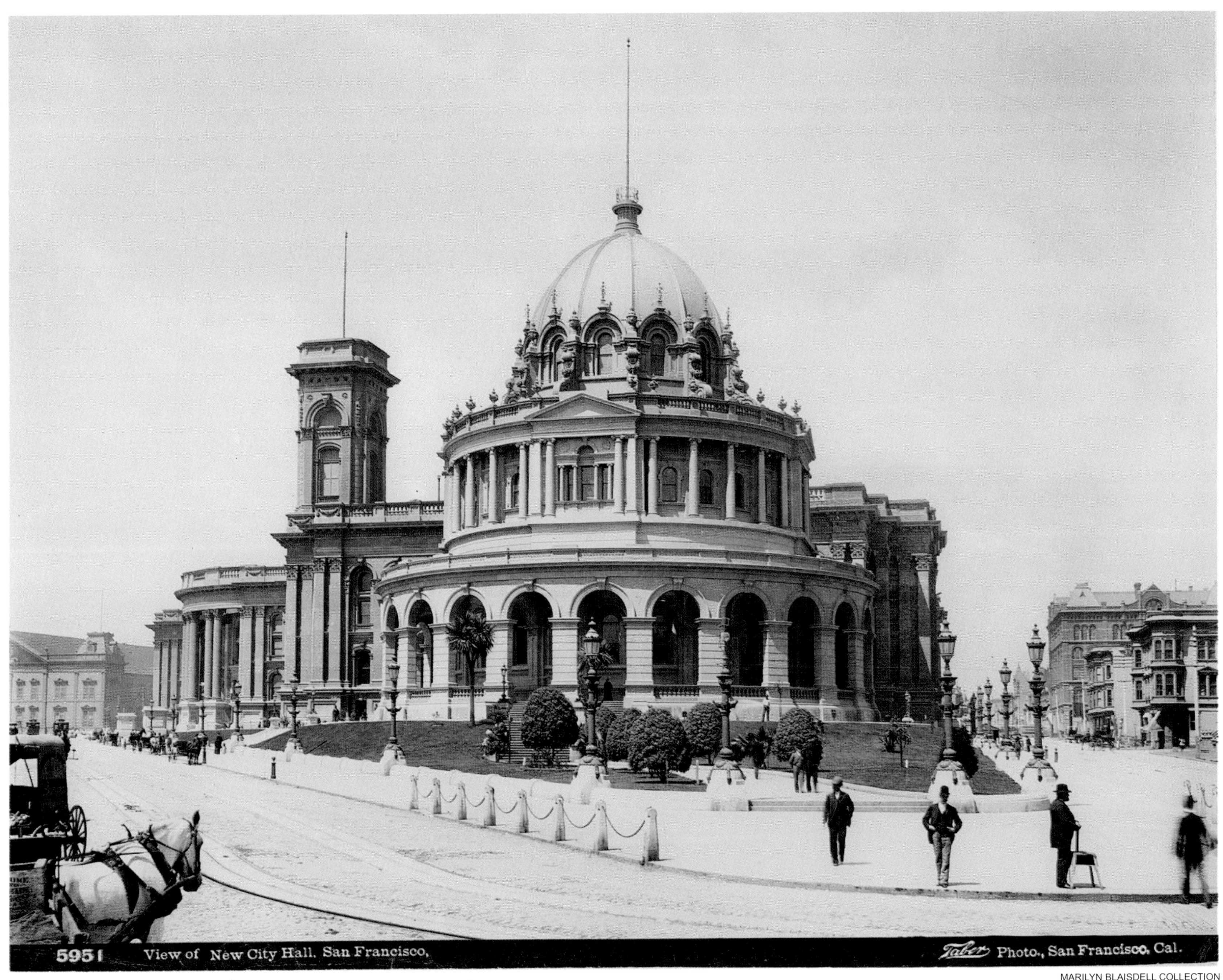

MARILYN BLAISDELL COLLECTION

The Hall of Records from Market Street, McAllister Street on the right.

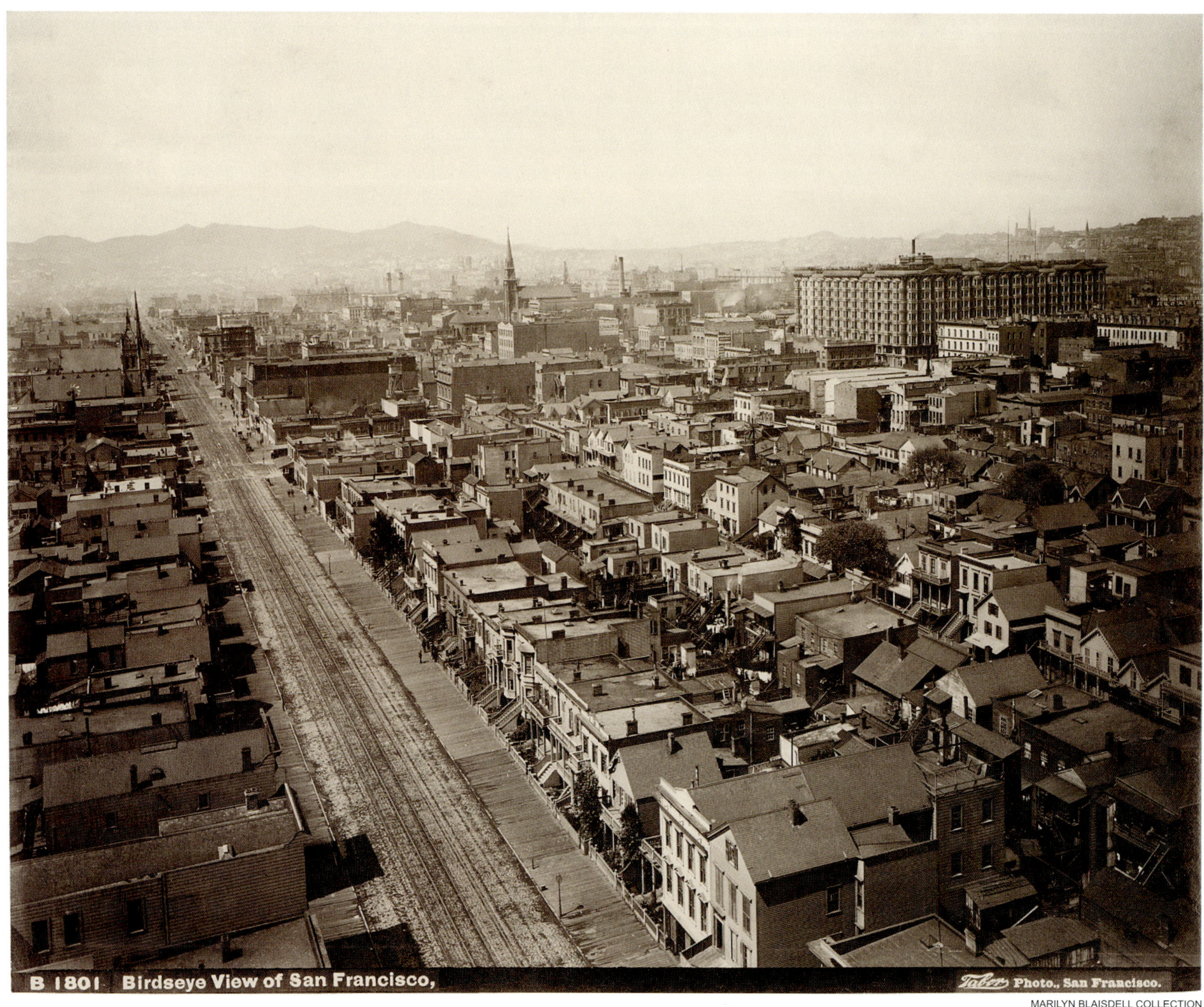

MARILYN BLAISDELL COLLECTION

Looking west along Howard Street around 1885, one of several views taken by Taber from this same vantage point. The sheer bulk of the Palace Hotel overwhelmed the surrounding South of Market homes and shops.

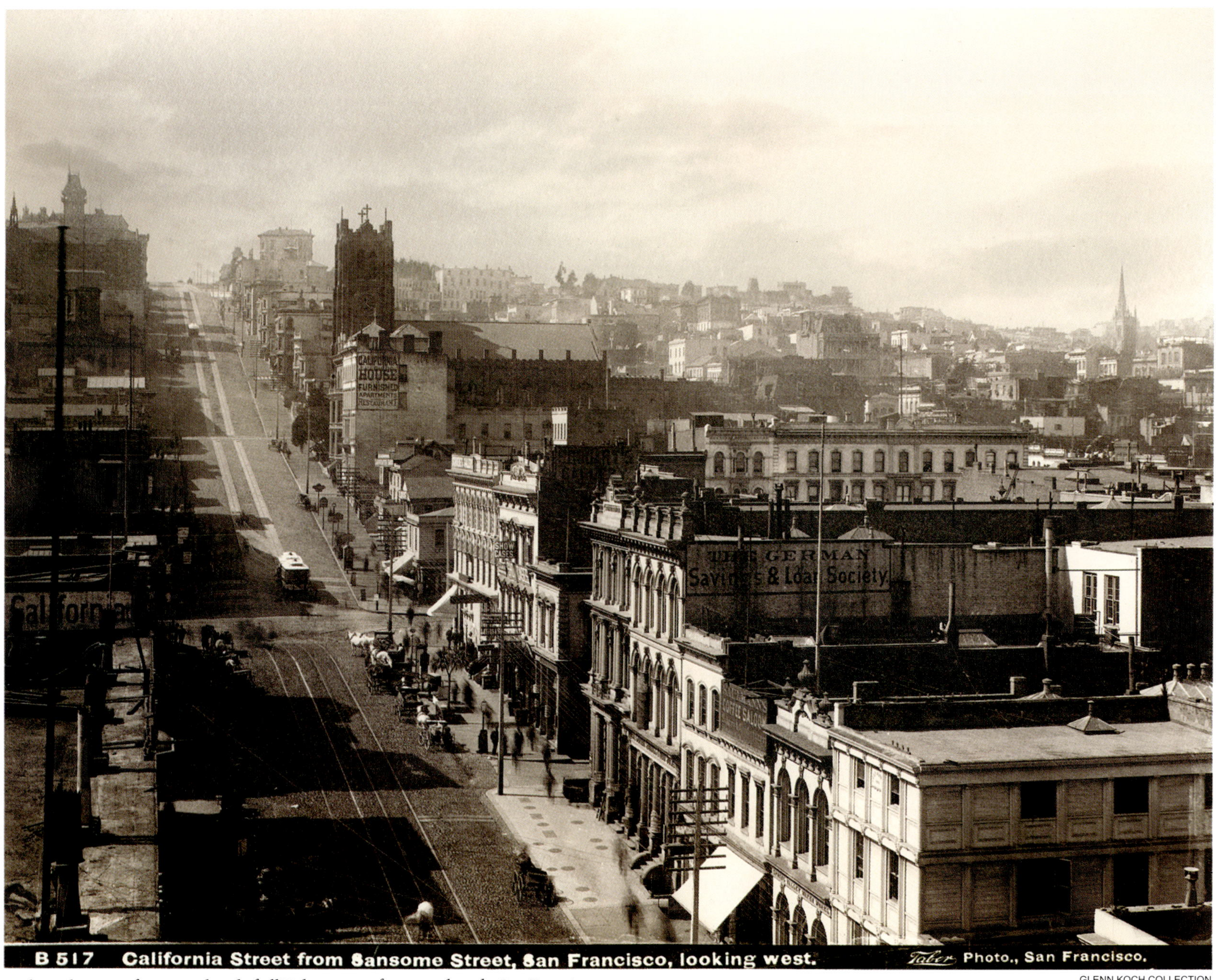

Perhaps the most often reproduced of all Taber views of pre-earthquake San Francisco.

GLENN KOCH COLLECTION

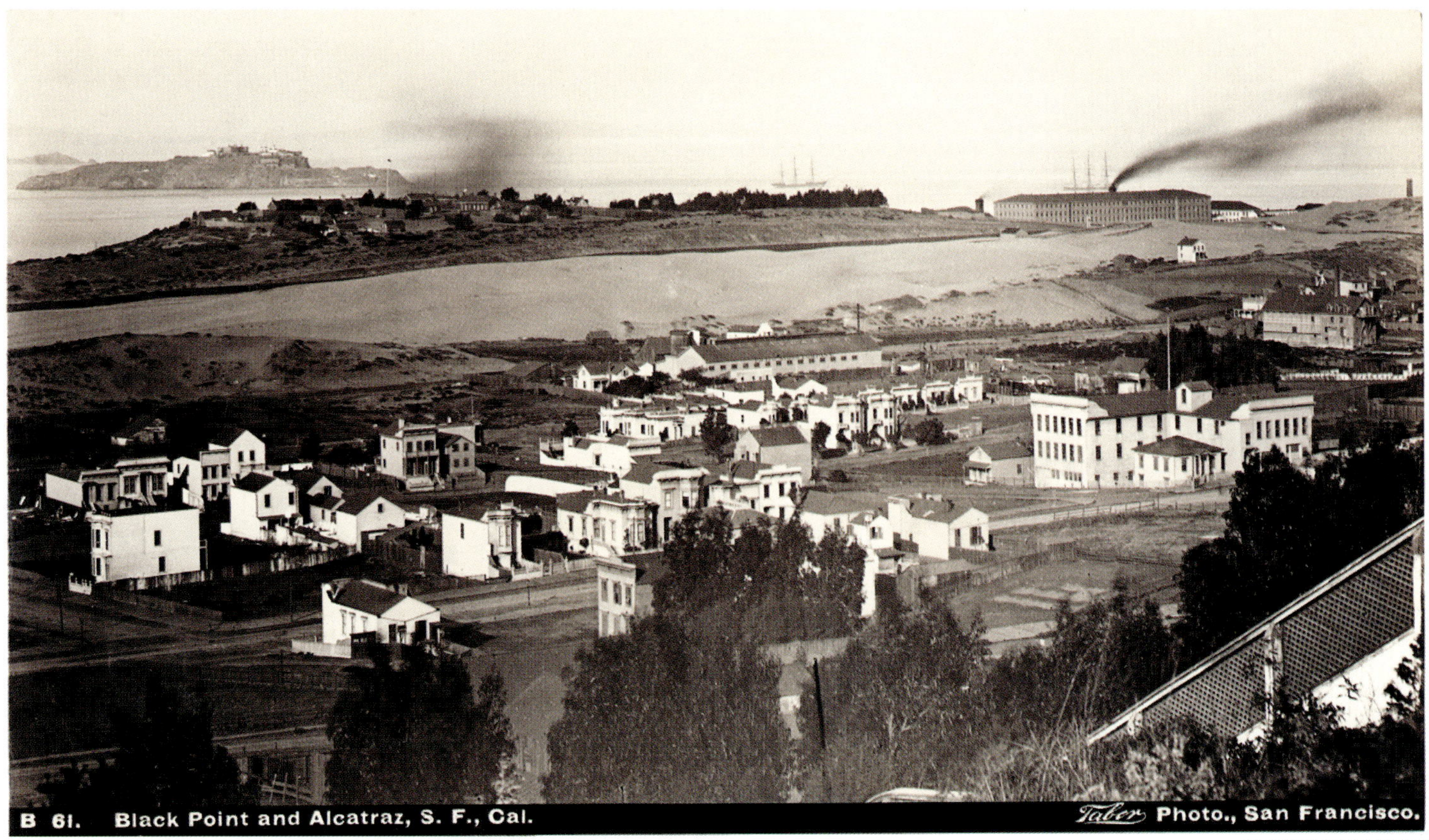

c. 1885

CALIFORNIA STATE LIBRARY

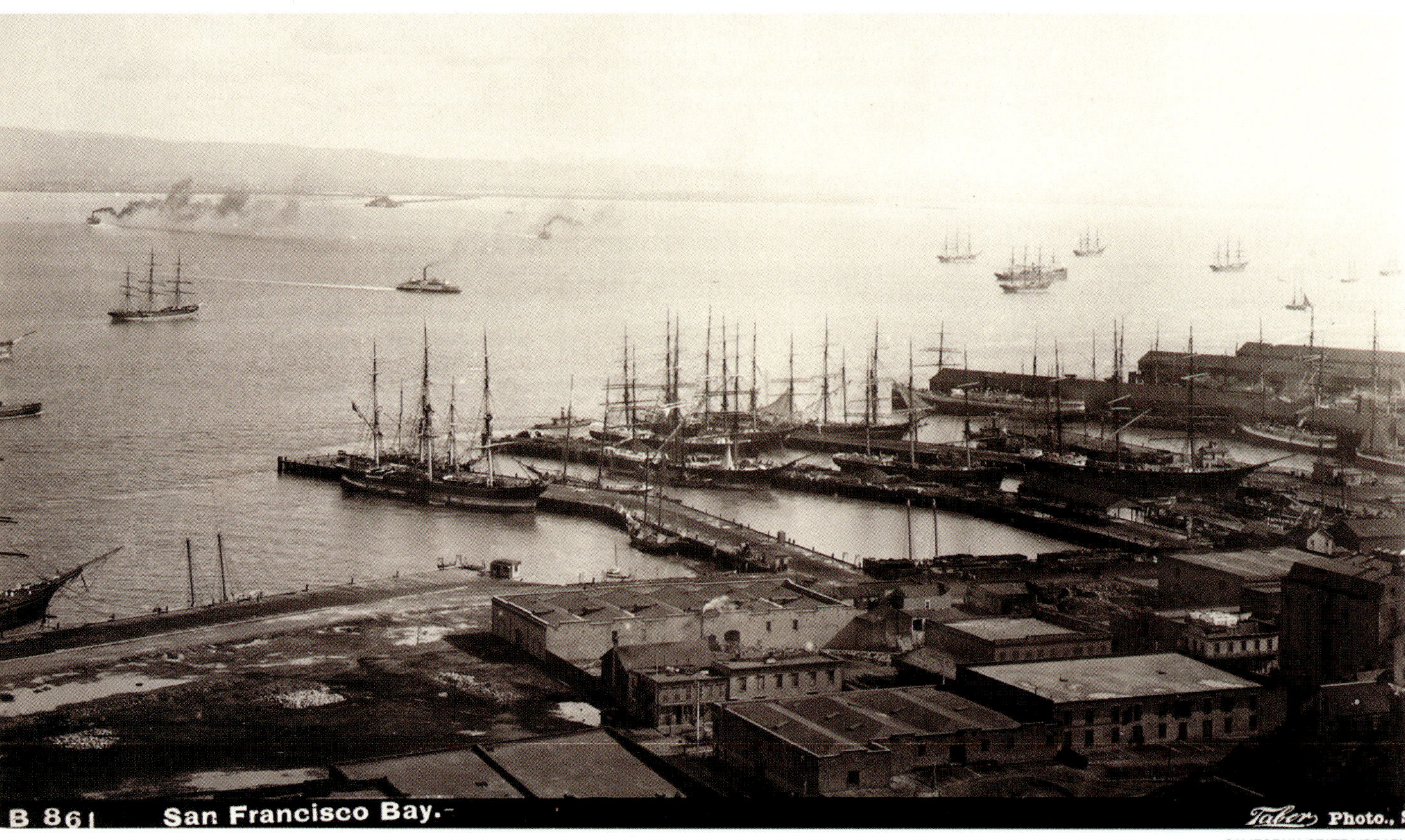

CALIFORNIA STATE LIBRARY

Looking east in the 1880s from above Front Street, Union Street Wharf, center.

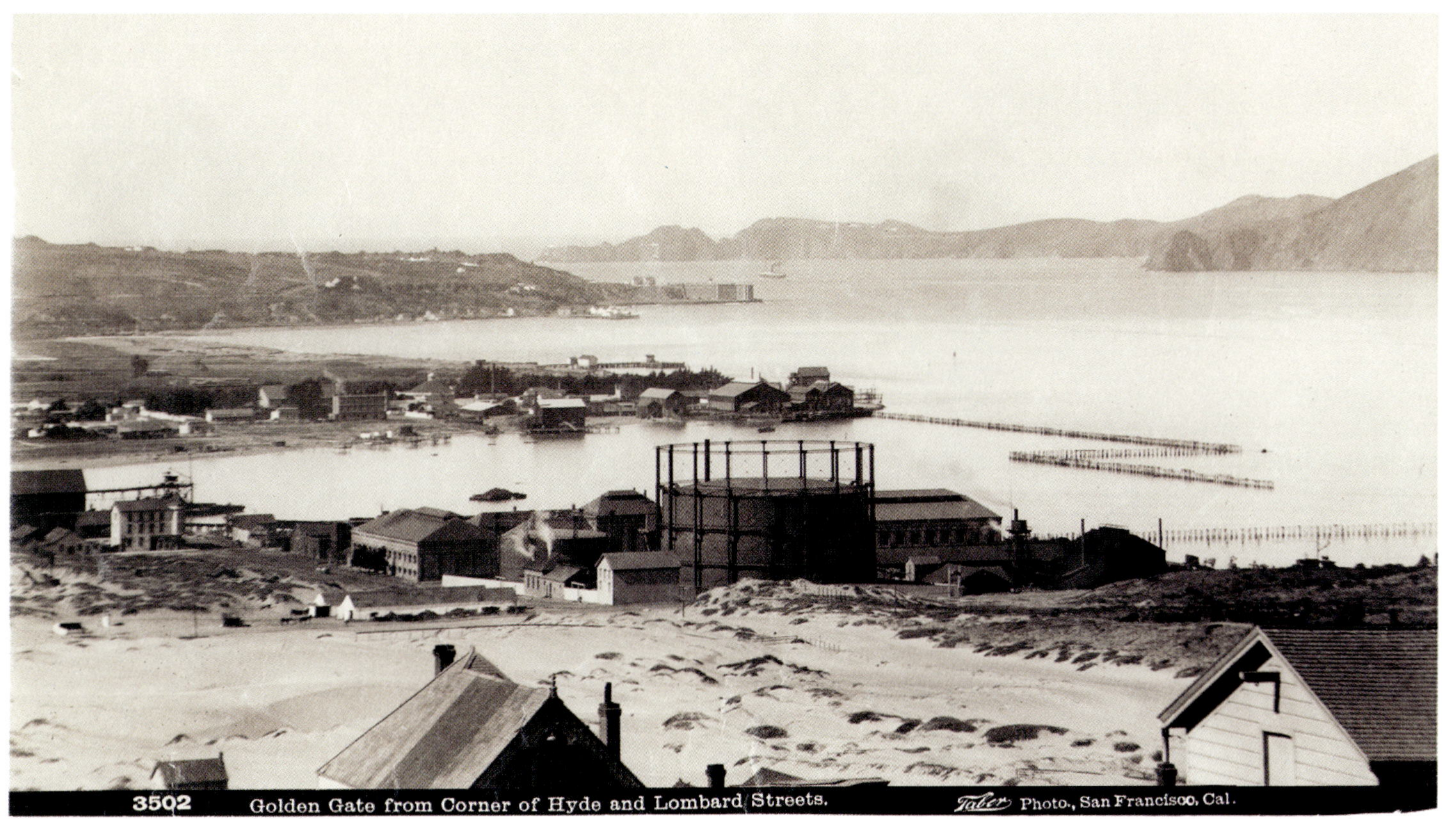

CALIFORNIA STATE LIBRARY

c.1880

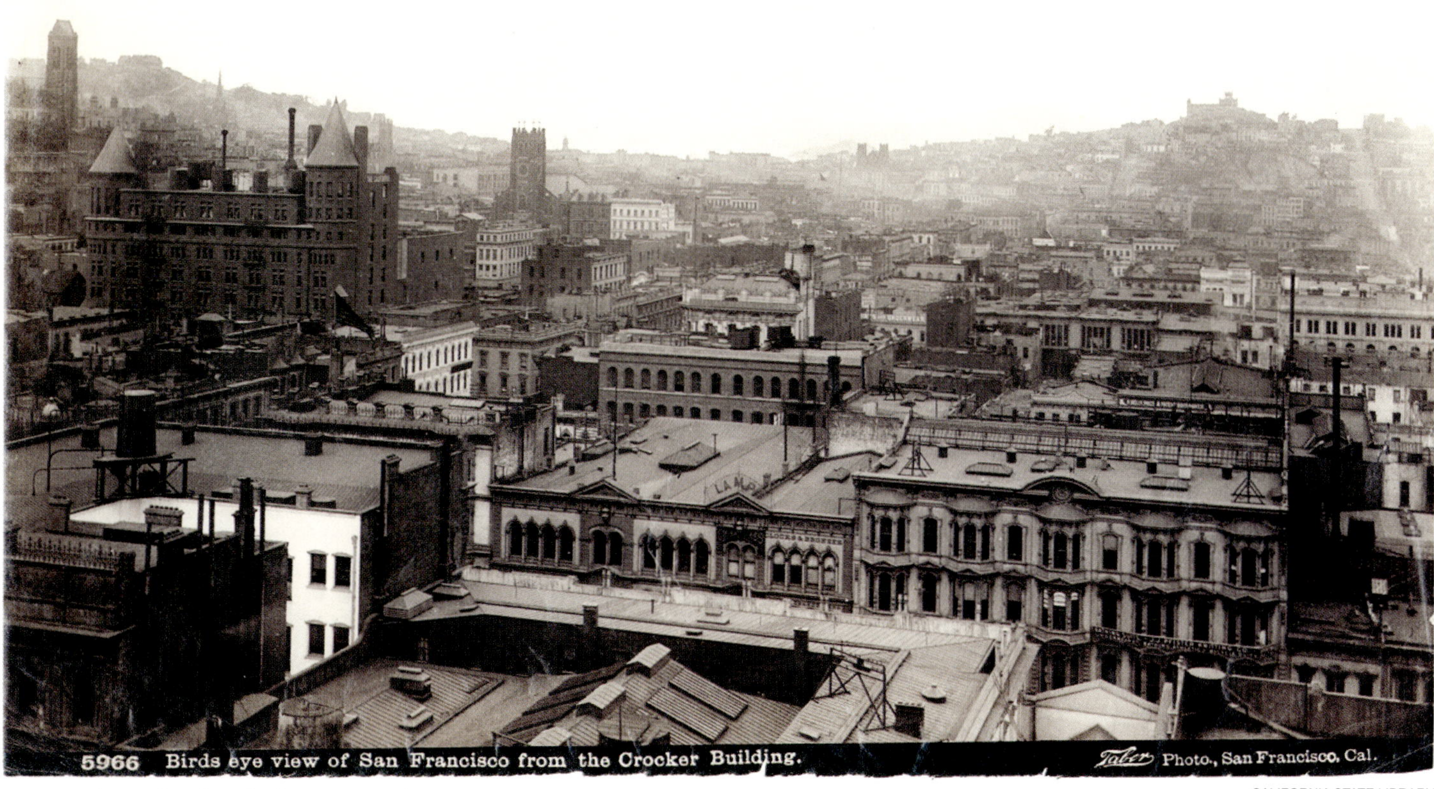

CALIFORNIA STATE LIBRARY

c.1885, Telegraph Hill in the distance at right.

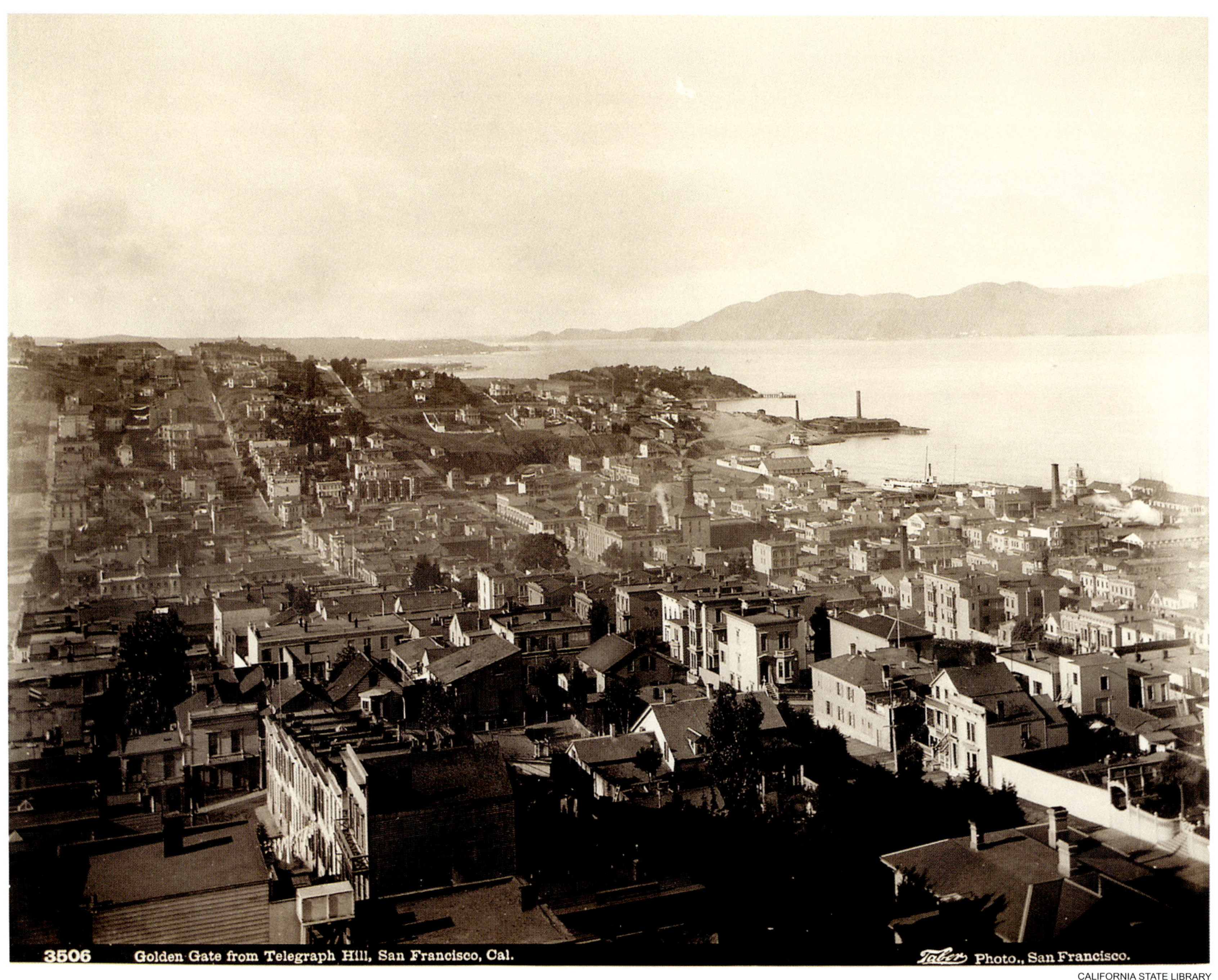

CALIFORNIA STATE LIBRARY

Taber would often return to good vantage points to record the changing city. Of necessity, some older views were dropped from his catalog as newer ones were added.
Above: Looking down Lombard Street, c.1884.

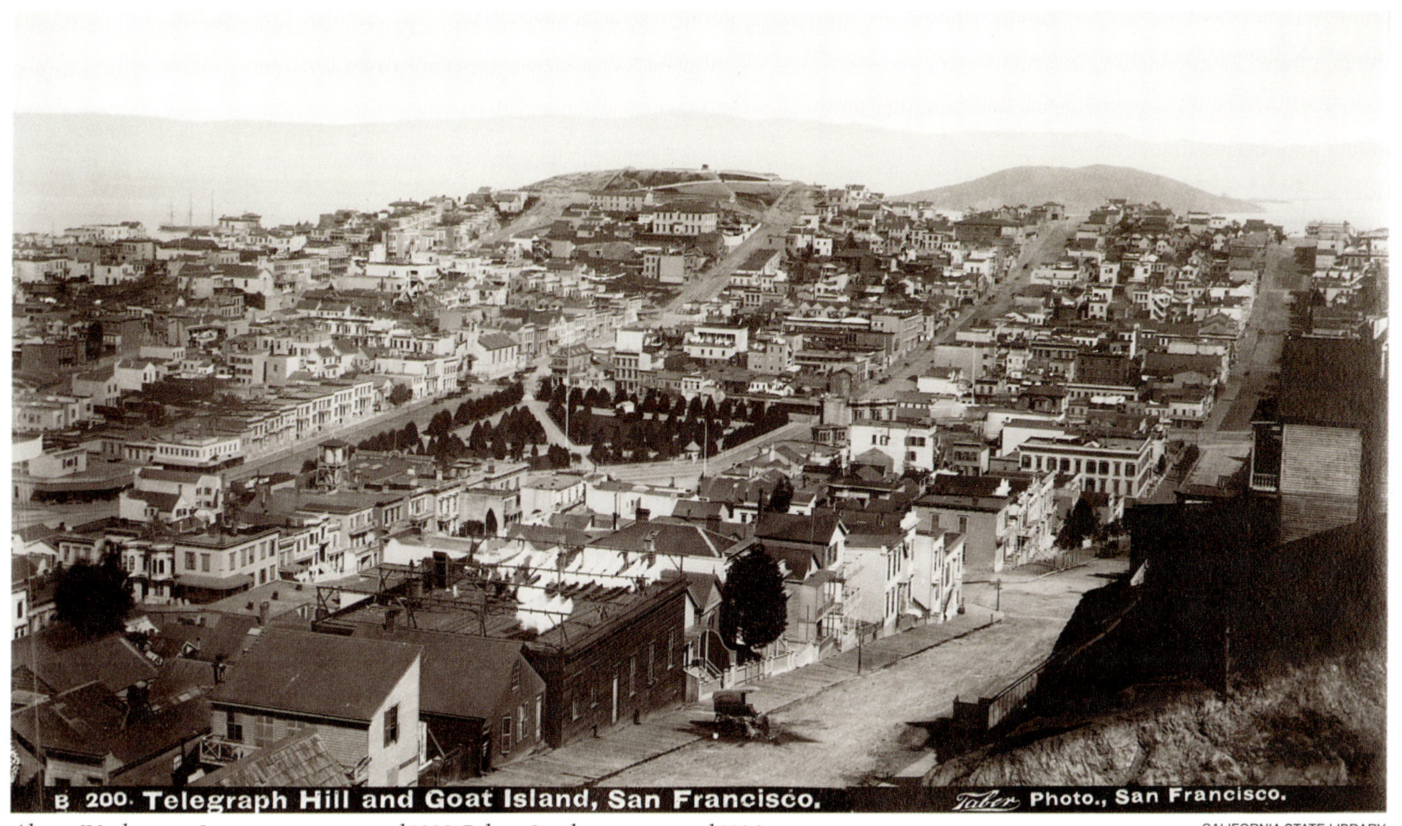

Above: Washington Square, center, around 1880. Below: Similar view around 1886.

CALIFORNIA STATE LIBRARY

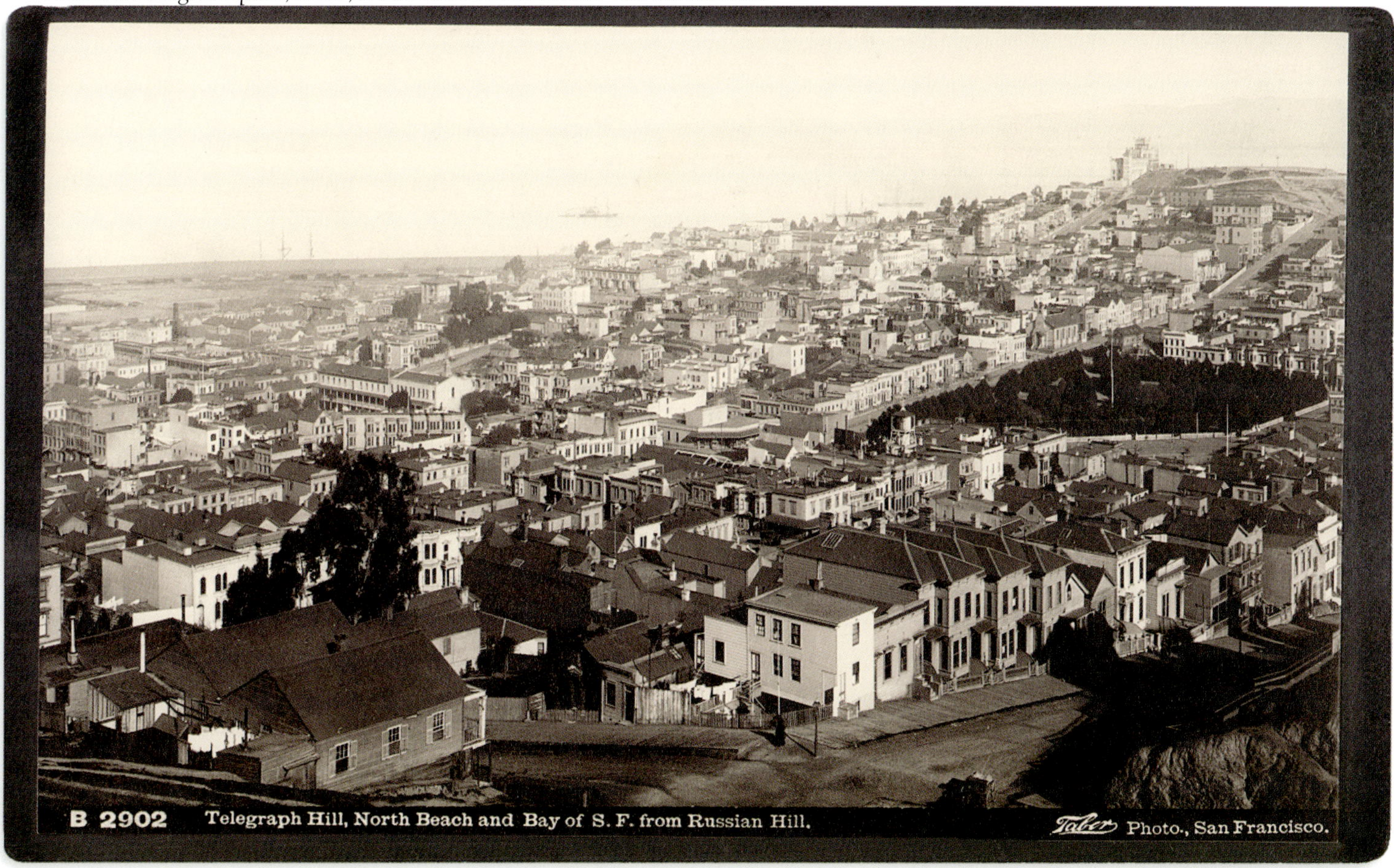

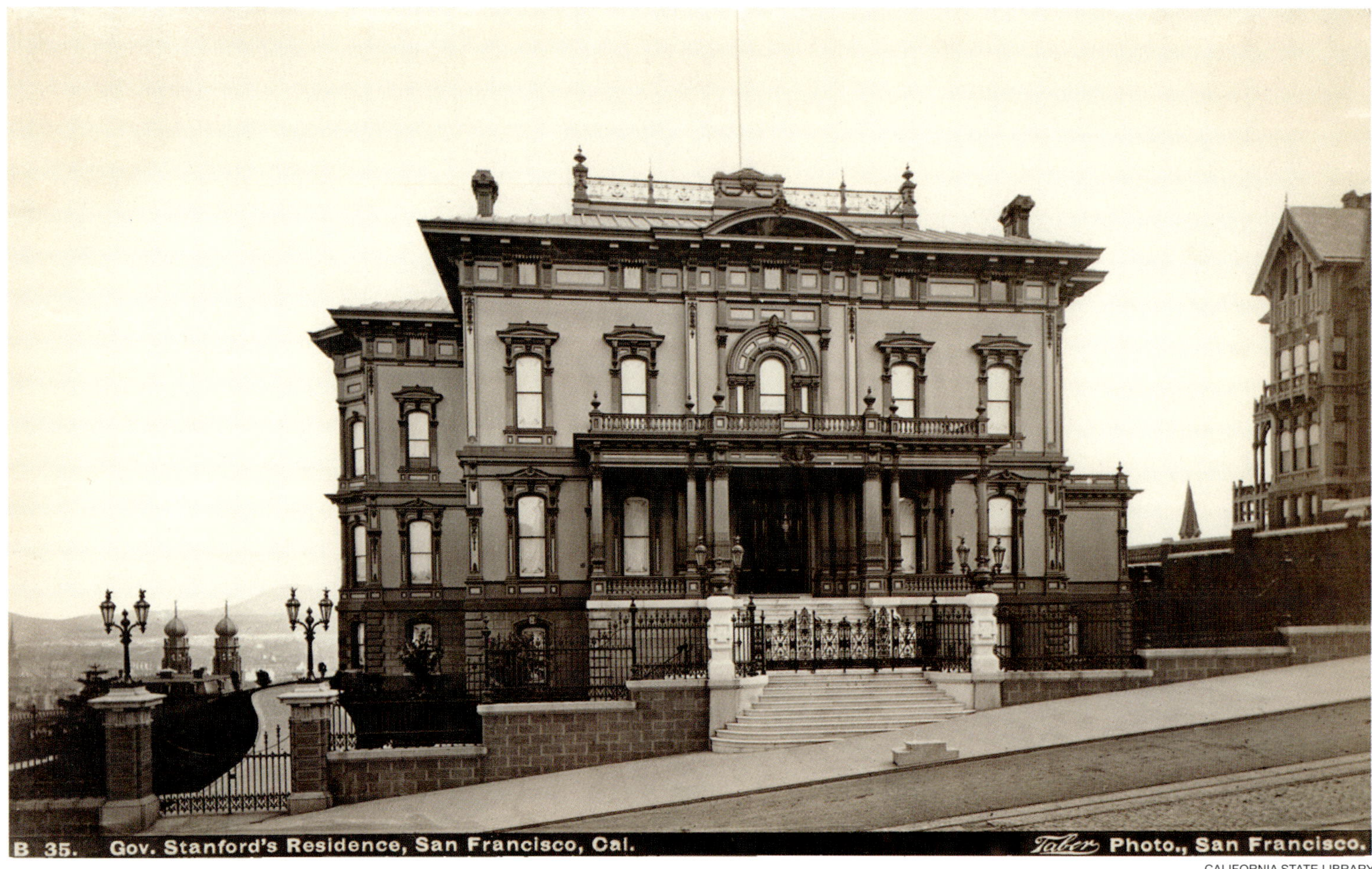

CALIFORNIA STATE LIBRARY

Above: California and Powell Streets. Photos of Nob Hill mansions, homes of legendary silver kings and gold rush millionaires, sold well to San Francisco visitors and residents alike. As each of the moguls tried to outdo each other with grandiose monuments to their financial success, Taber was there with his camera.

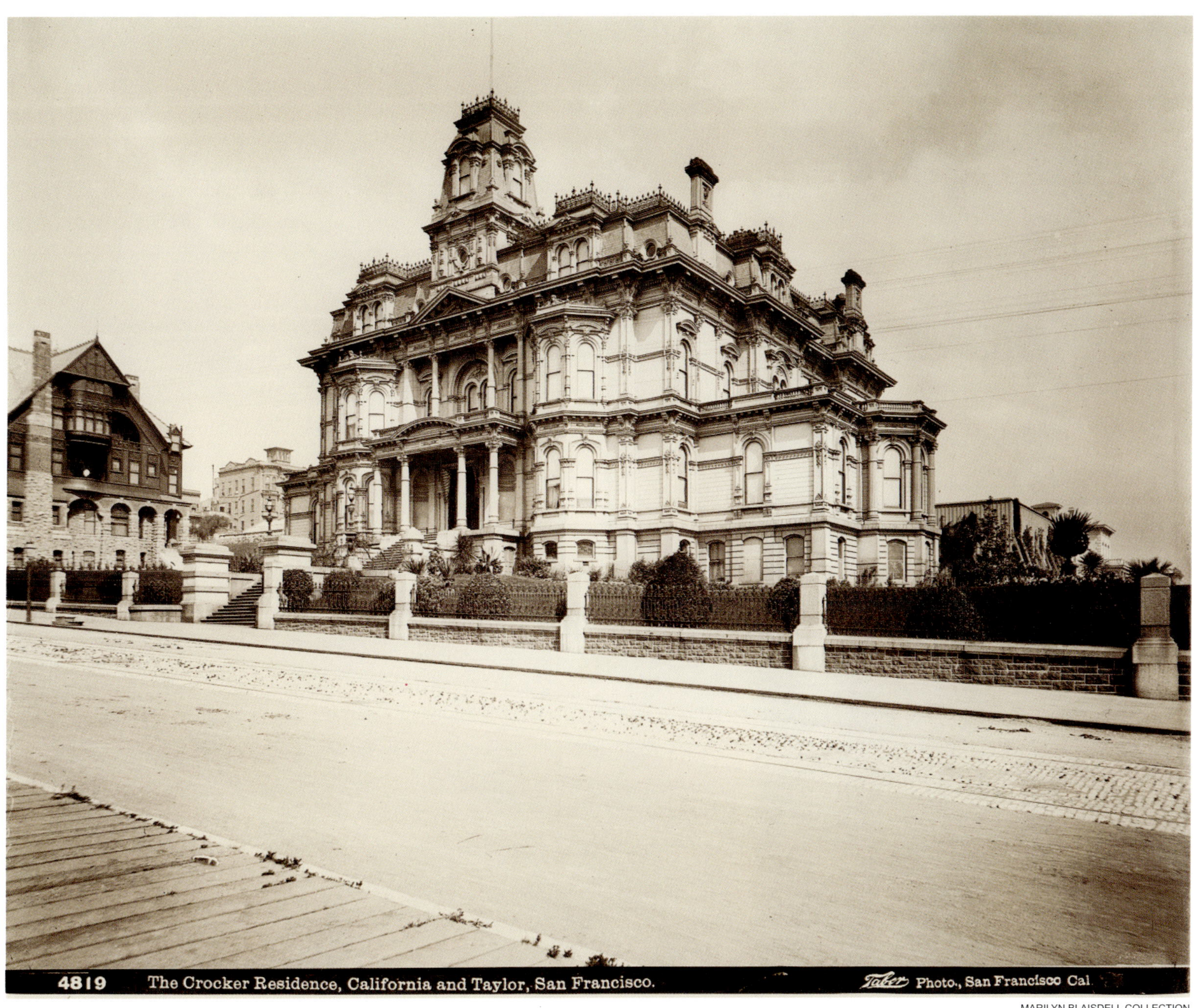

MARILYN BLAISDELL COLLECTION

The Charles Crocker mansion was considered by some critics a hideous example of ostentatious architecture, but it was breathtaking to behold. To the left is the home of William H. Crocker at California and Jones Streets.

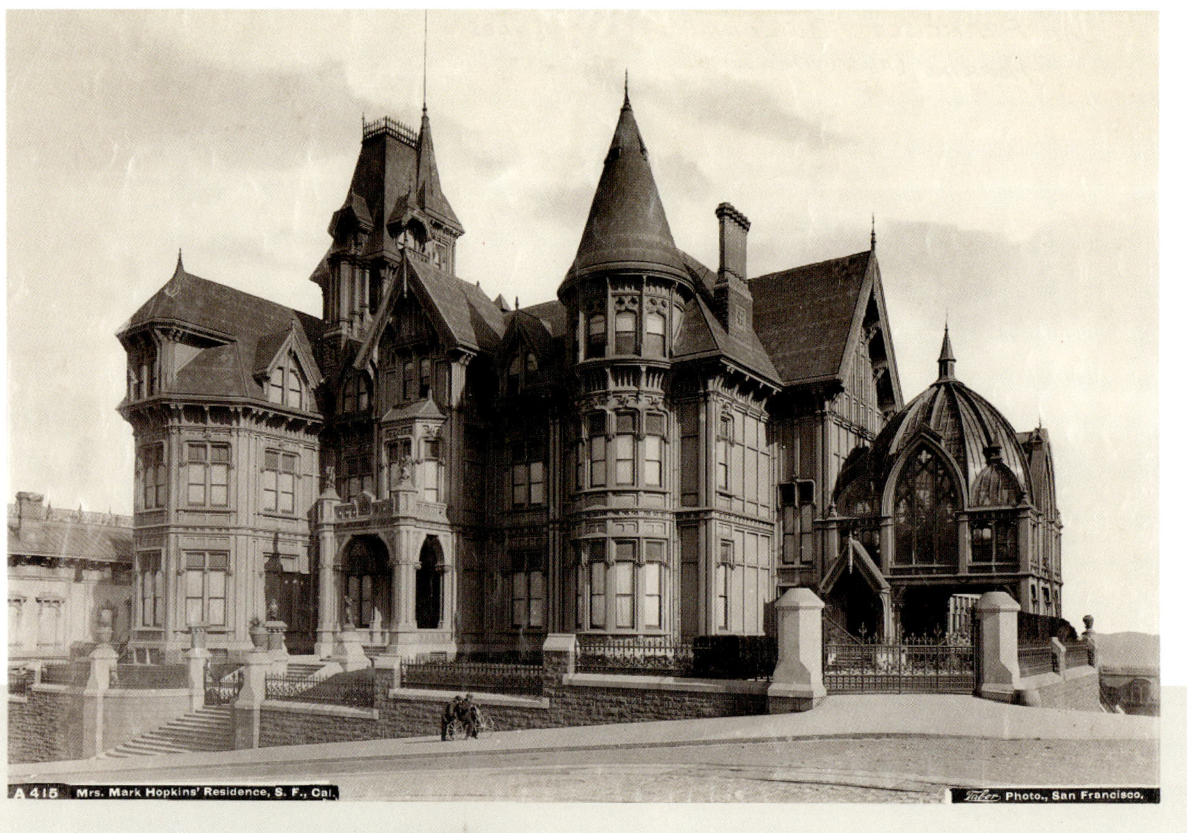

Of all the Nob Hill mansions, this baroque Norman-English extravaganza built by railroad tycoon Mark Hopkins was the most famous and recognizable. Taber sold at least a dozen views of it, including these. The mansion, with its 360-degree view of the city, bay, and ocean, remained popular even after Hopkins' death in 1879 and his widow's death in 1891. The structure became the first home of the San Francisco Art School (Hopkins Art Association). Along with almost all of the Nob Hill mansions, it burned in 1906. Today the Mark Hopkins Hotel stands on the site.

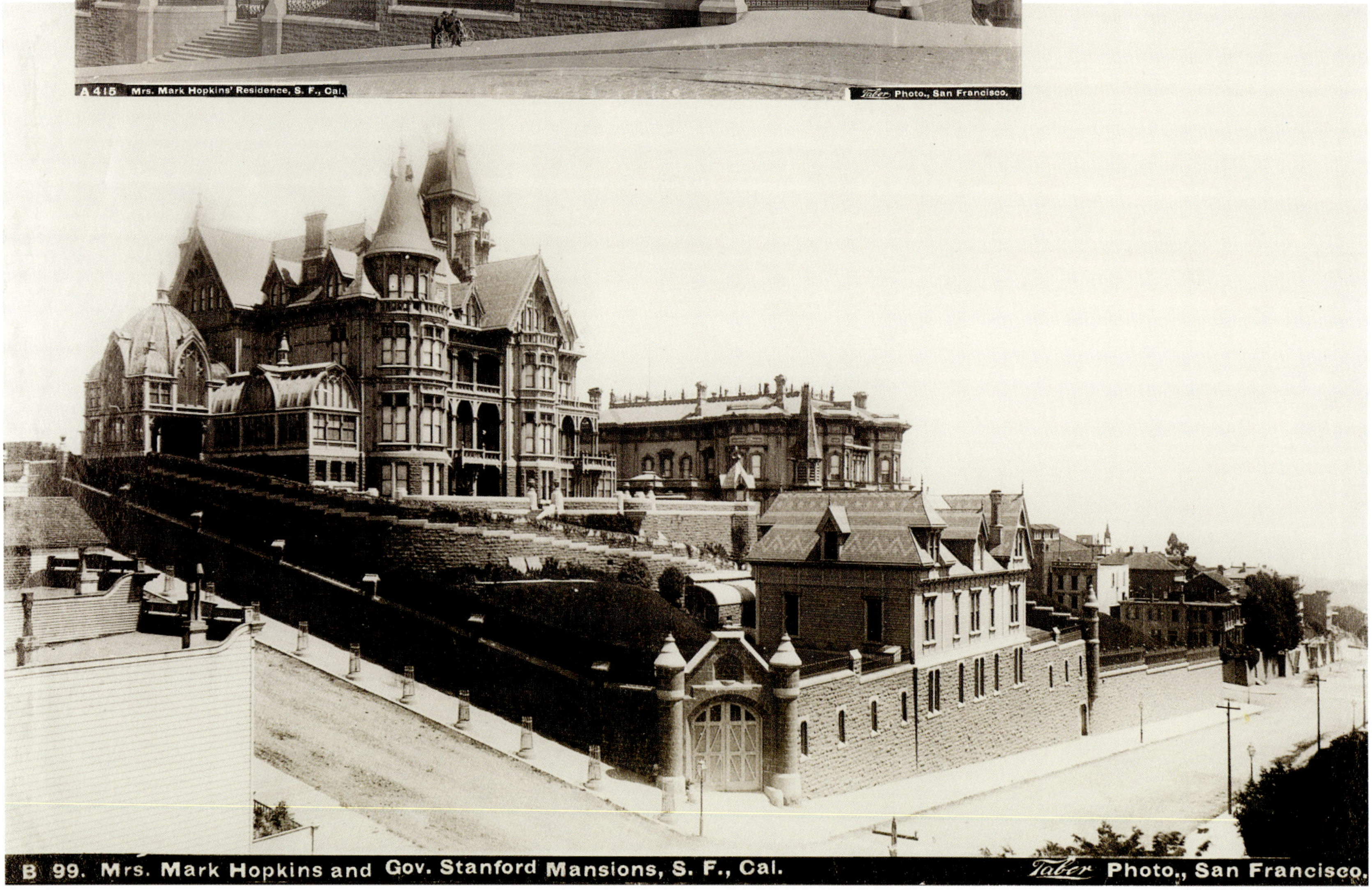

B 99. Mrs. Mark Hopkins and Gov. Stanford Mansions, S. F., Cal. Taber Photo., San Francisco.

MARILYN BLAISDELL COLLECTION

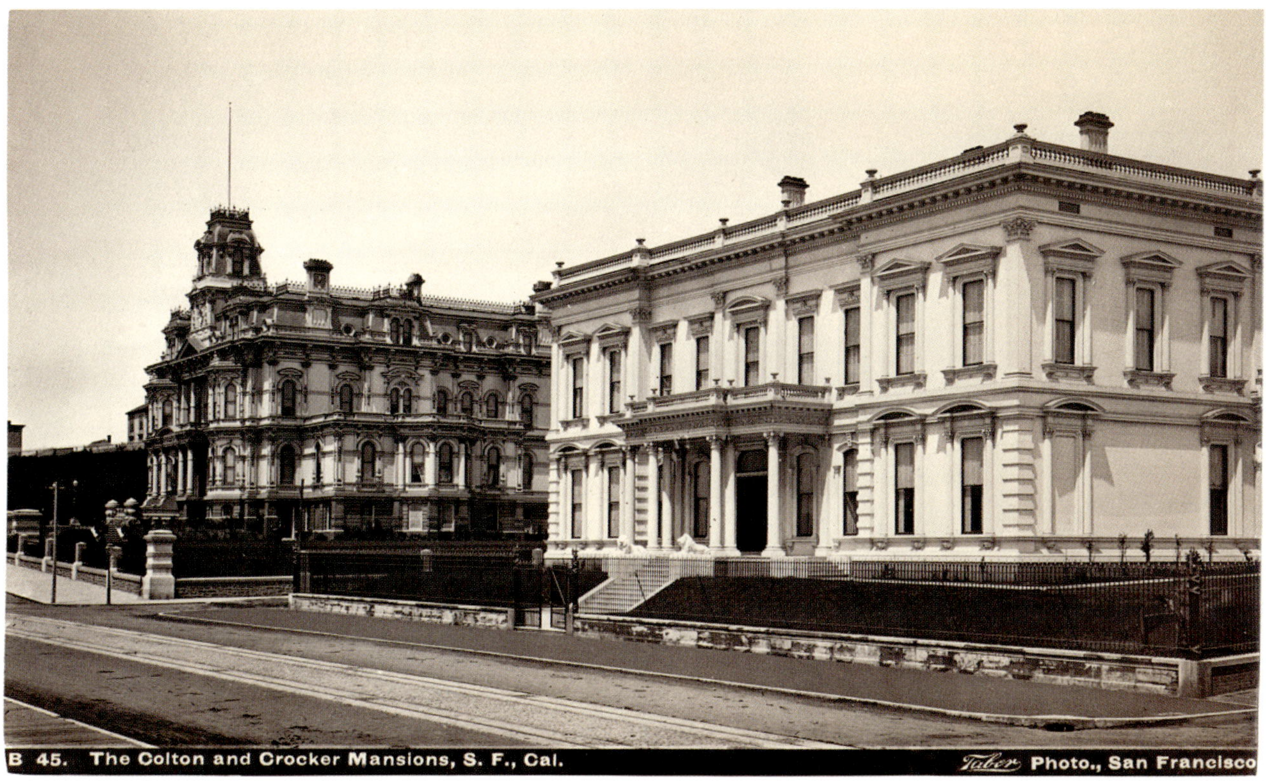

Above: California Street homes of David D. Colton, at right, and Charles Crocker, left.

CALIFORNIA STATE LIBRARY

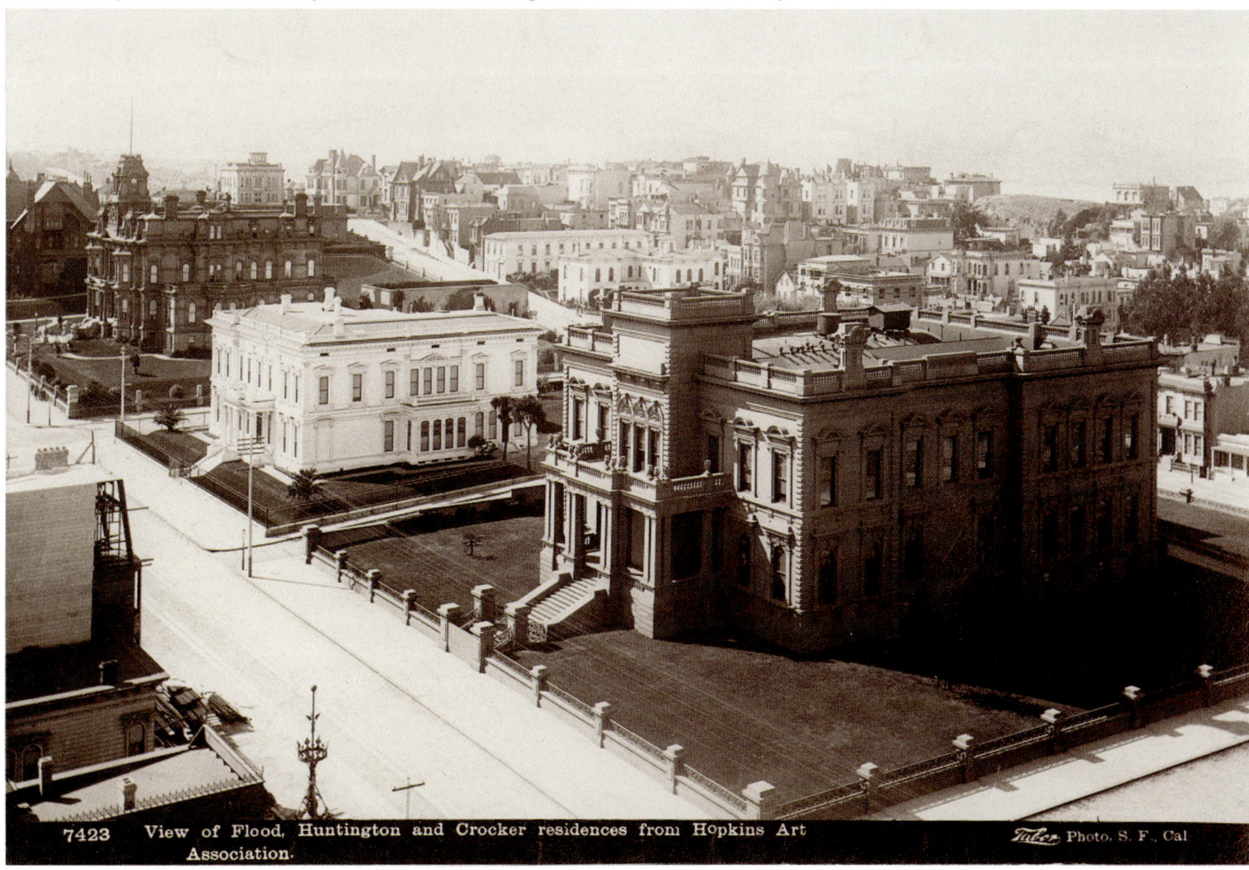

MARILYN BLAISDELL COLLECTION

The Flood mansion, right center, survived the fire and later became the Pacific Union Club.

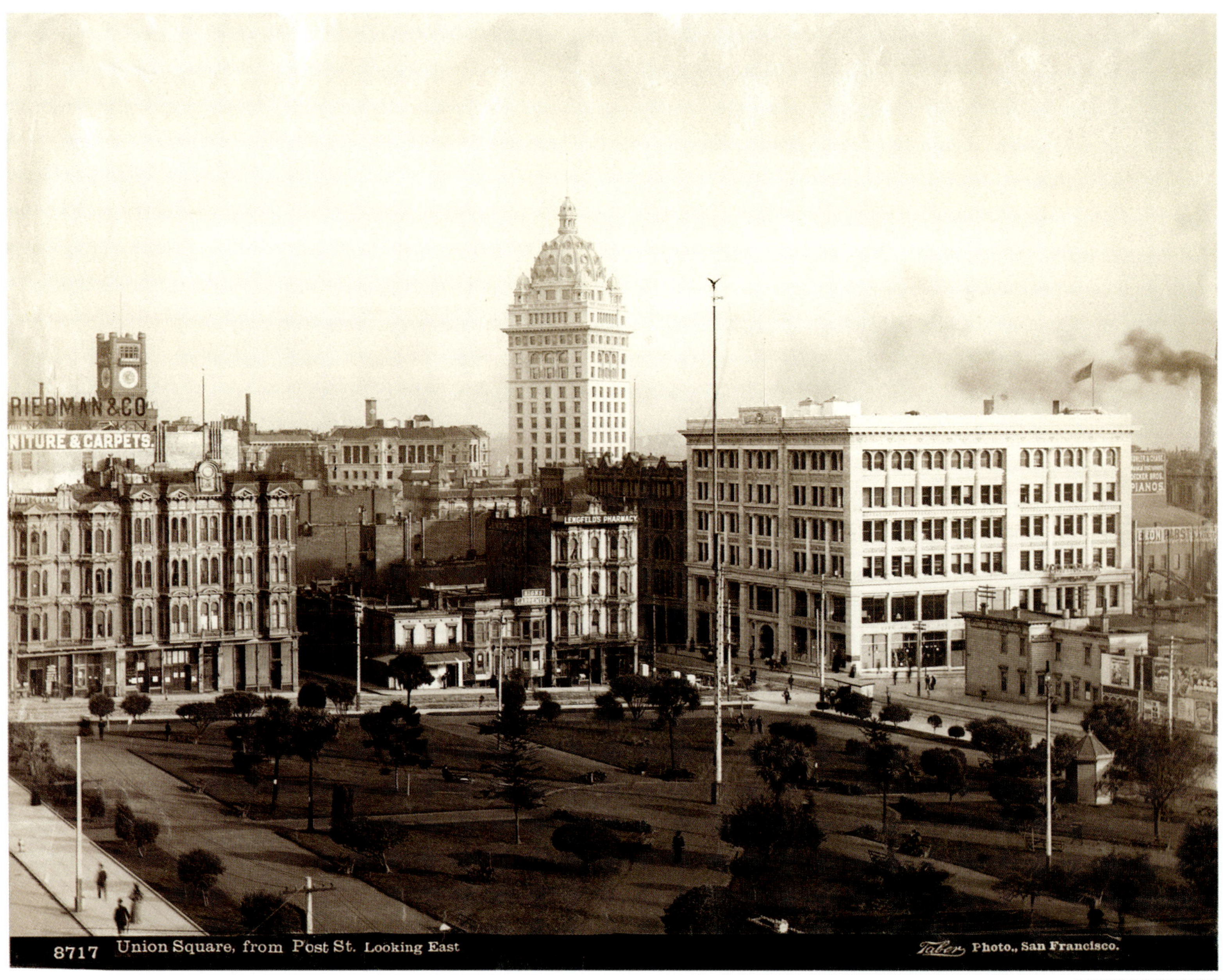

CALIFORNIA STATE LIBRARY

Two views of Union Square taken after 1897 when the Call Building on Market Street, above center, was completed, and before 1903, when the Dewey Monument replaced the flag pole at the center of the square. Post Street is on the left, Geary Street on the right.

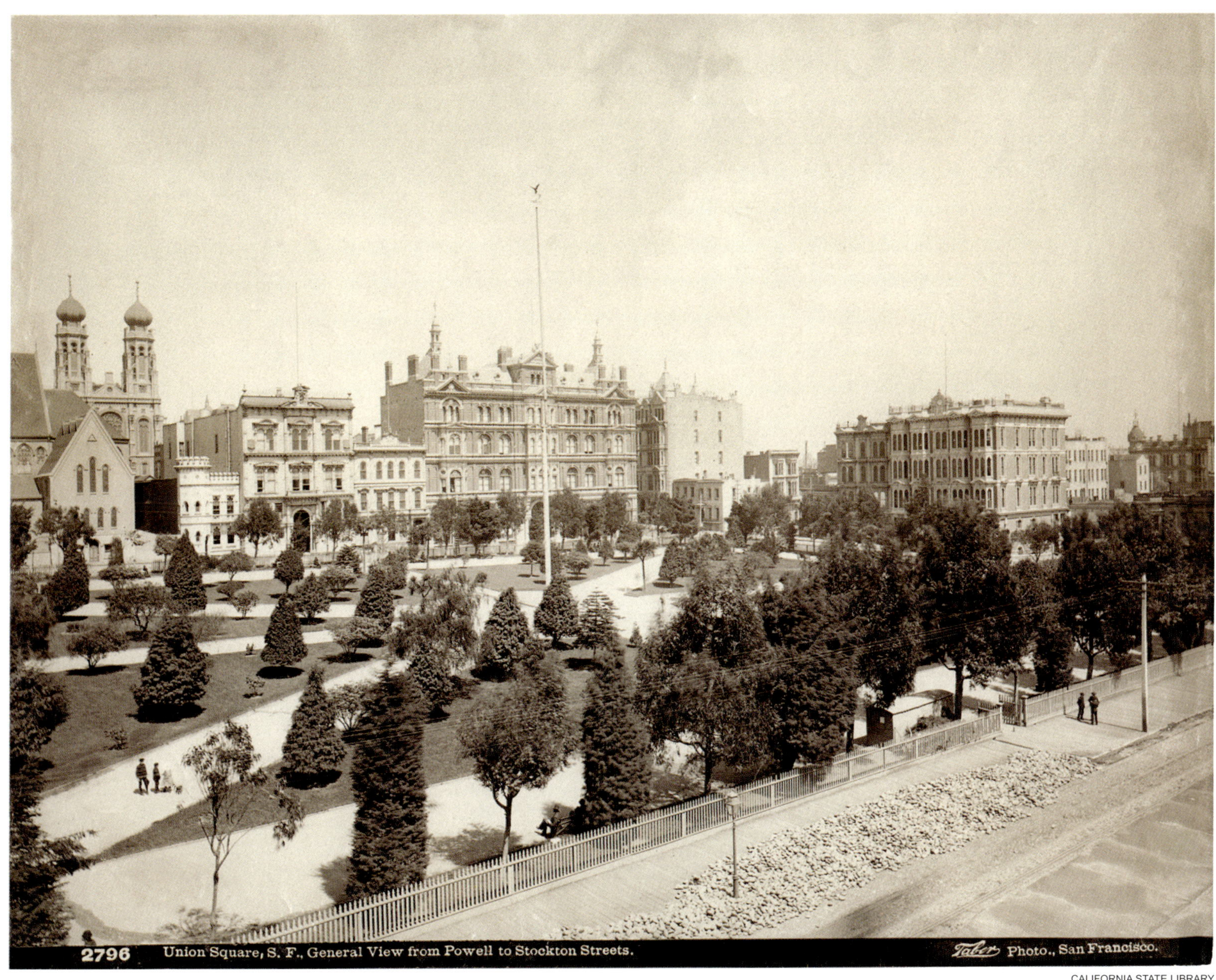

CALIFORNIA STATE LIBRARY

Above: Union Square looking north from Geary Street, Powell Street is out of sight to the left, Post Street is at the rear of the square.

CHINATOWN

Within a few blocks of Isaiah Taber's Montgomery Street studio and gallery was San Francisco's legendary Chinese quarter. Photographers including Taber recognized that visitors, with a seemingly insatiable curiosity about the place and its people, were eager to purchase photographs of Chinatown. Taber in the 1880s created a series of Chinatown photographs of the highest technical and aesthetic quality.

His photos reflect the prevailing late nineteenth-century attitude about San Francisco's Chinatown. The Chinese had first arrived in San Francisco during the gold rush. Since the 1860s, when large numbers of laborers immigrated to work on the railroads, the Chinese quarter had been part of the city's geography. It was seen grudgingly by non-Chinese as a permanent part of the city's cosmopolitan culture but its residents were subject to harsh and restrictive laws. The merchant class was viewed as benevolent, industrious, and commercially linked to Occidental business interests. The laboring class Chinese, however, were typically seen as sinister and wicked, the denizens of opium dens and mysterious narrow alleys where prostitution and gambling flourished. Both simplistic stereotypes, based on latent racism, nevertheless proved to be popular representations in photographs.

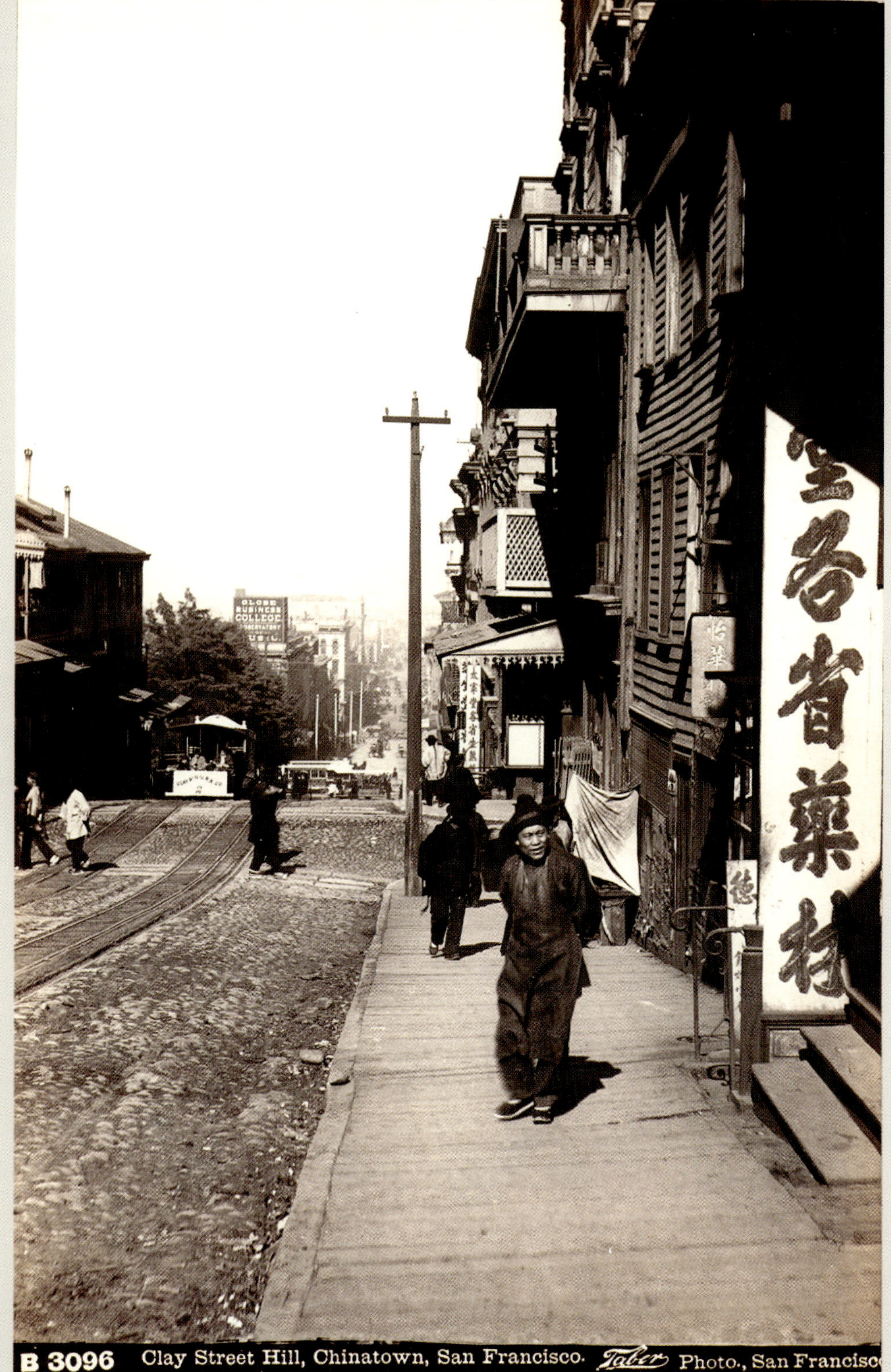

B 3096 Clay Street Hill, Chinatown, San Francisco. Taber Photo., San Francisco

CALIFORNIA STATE LIBRARY

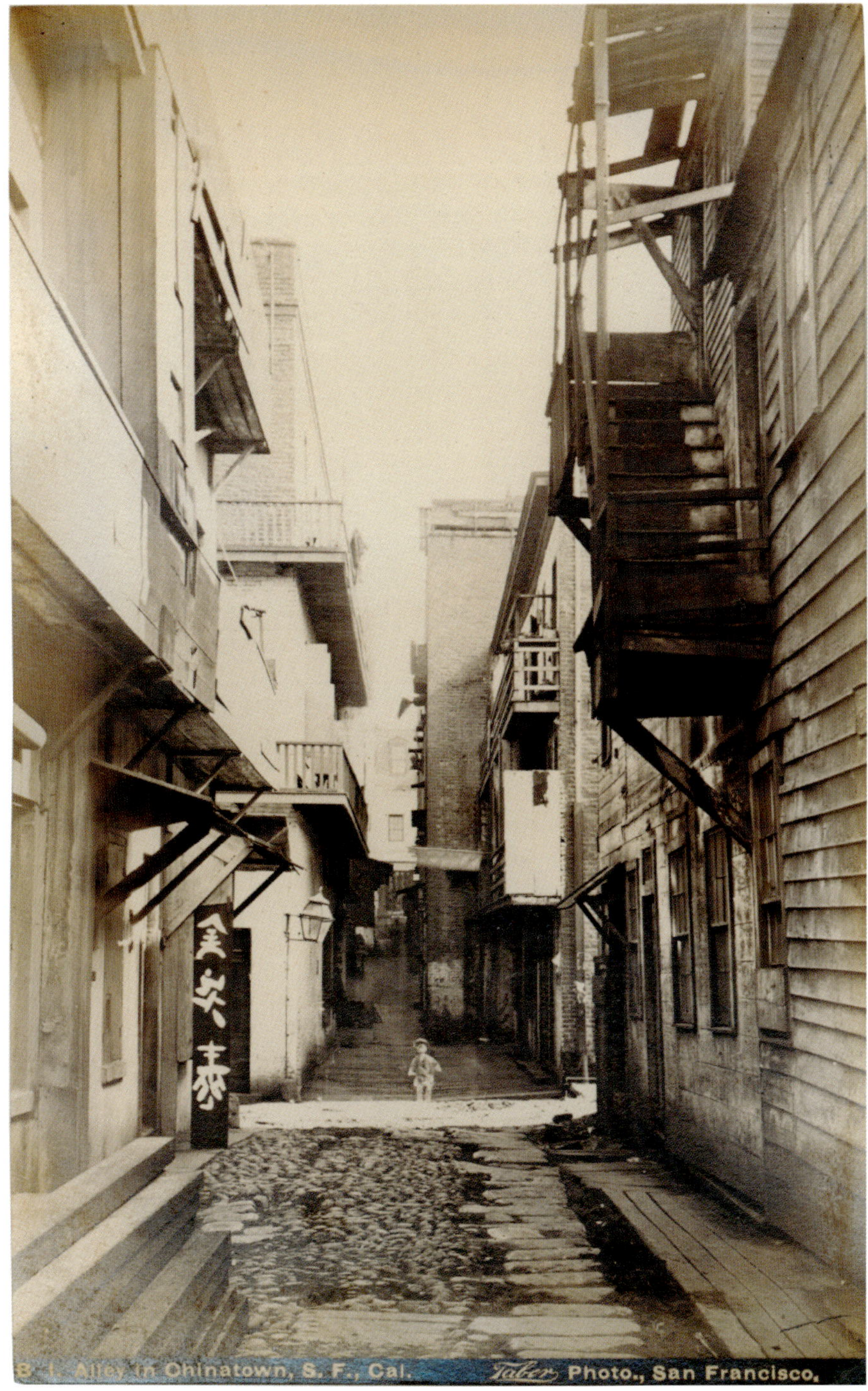

MARILYN BLAISDELL COLLECTION

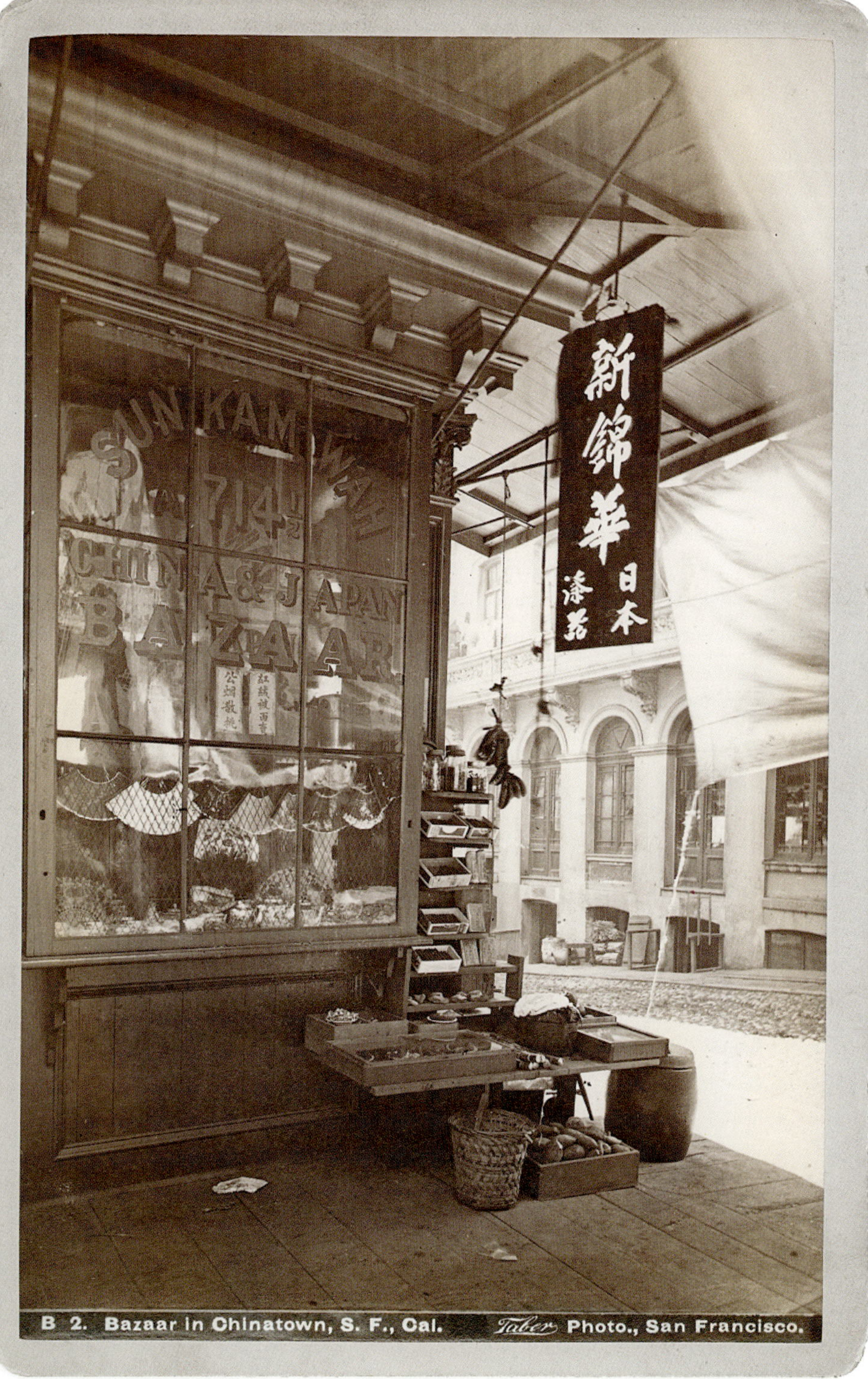

MARILYN BLAISDELL COLLECTION

Taber's Chinatown photos were widely copied as wood engravings in popular magazines of the 1870s and 1880s. The one above appeared in Harper's Weekly *with the child in the photo replaced by sinister figures.*

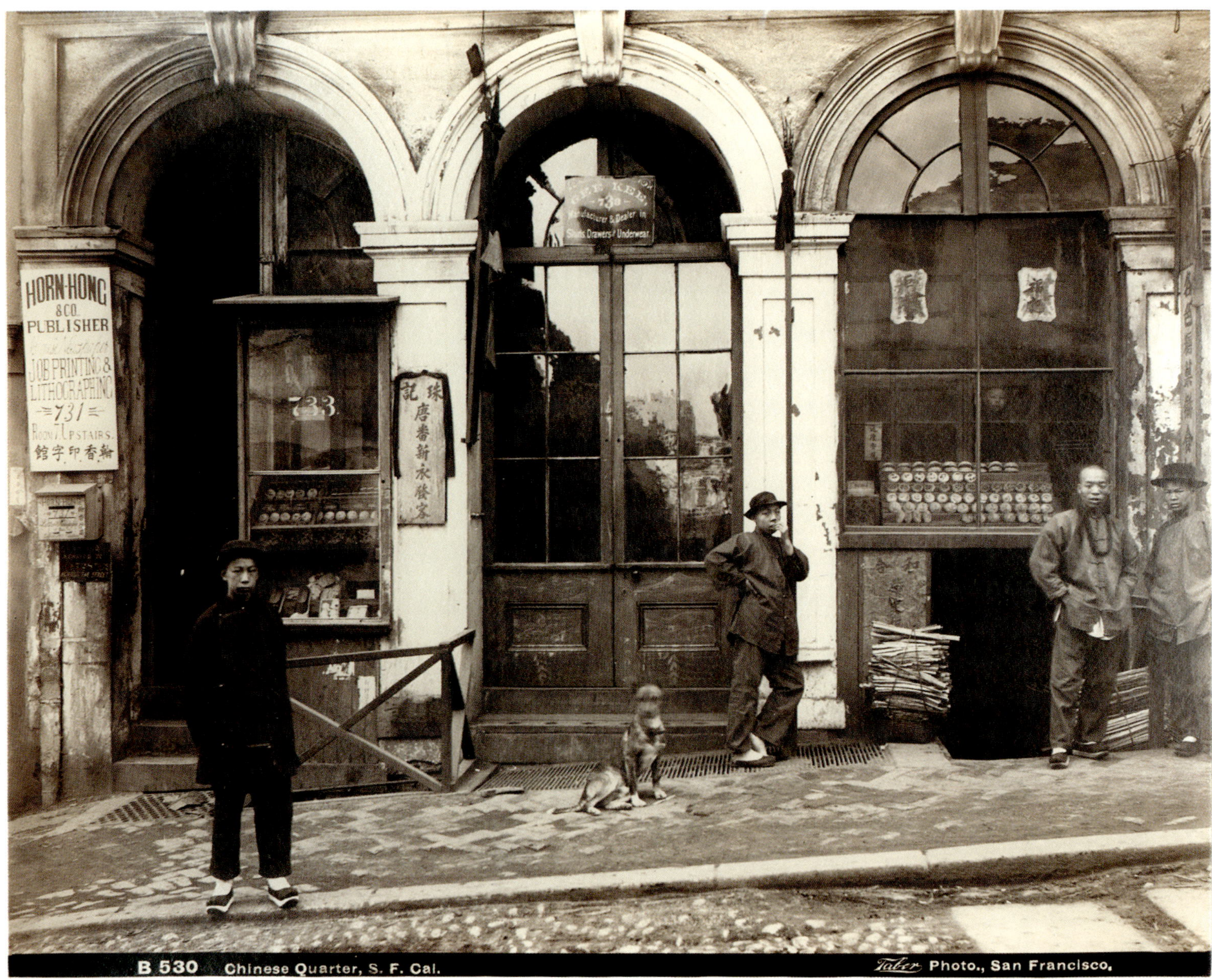

c. 1880

CALIFORNIA STATE LIBRARY

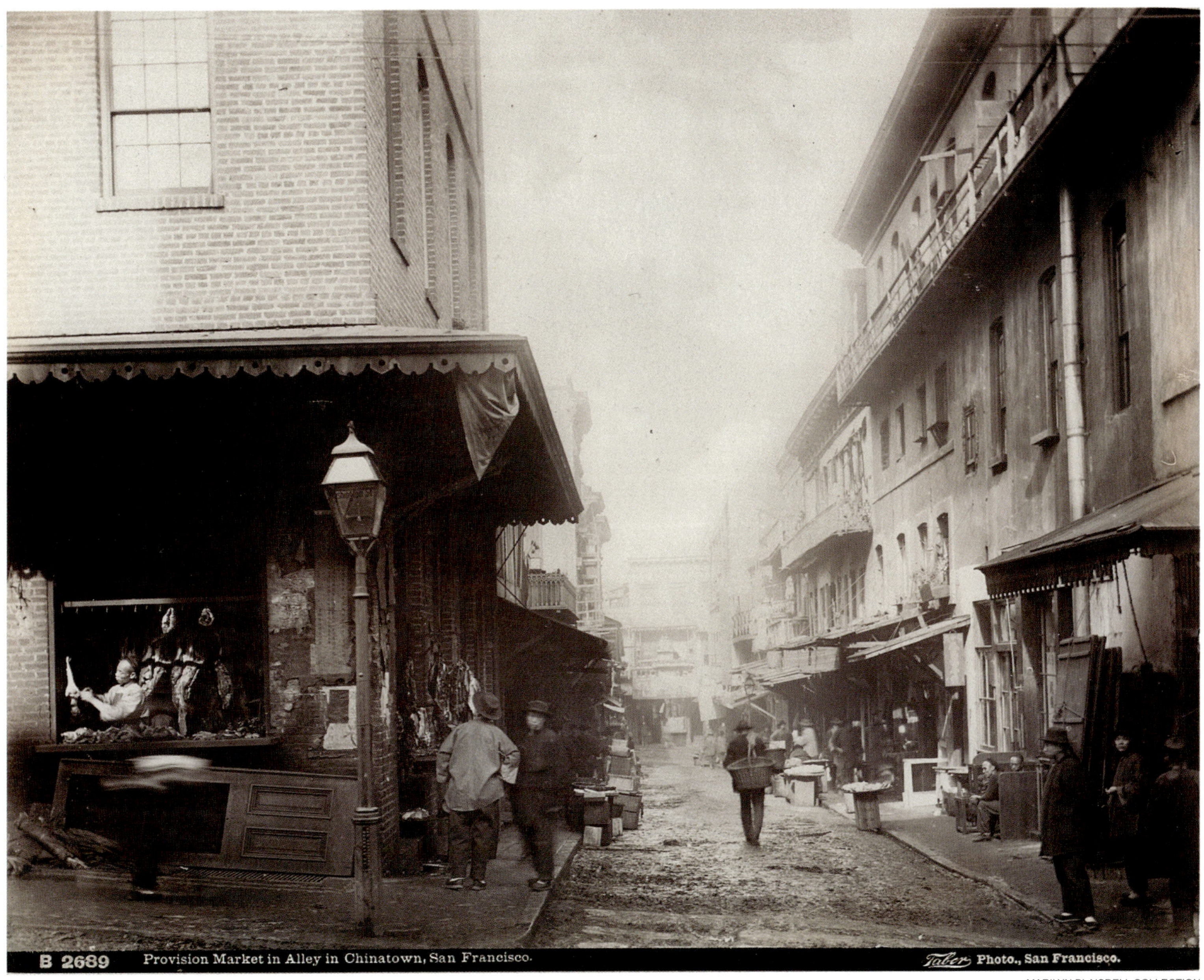

MARILYN BLAISDELL COLLECTION

Alley off Washington Street, c.1885.

Right: Opium dens, both fashionable as shown here, or squalid, either staged or authentic, were endlessly fascinating to Westerners. Taber allowed San Francisco newspapers free use of his photographs, and his Chinatown photos, usually unattributed, found their way into books and magazines such as Harpers Weekly *and* The Police Gazette.

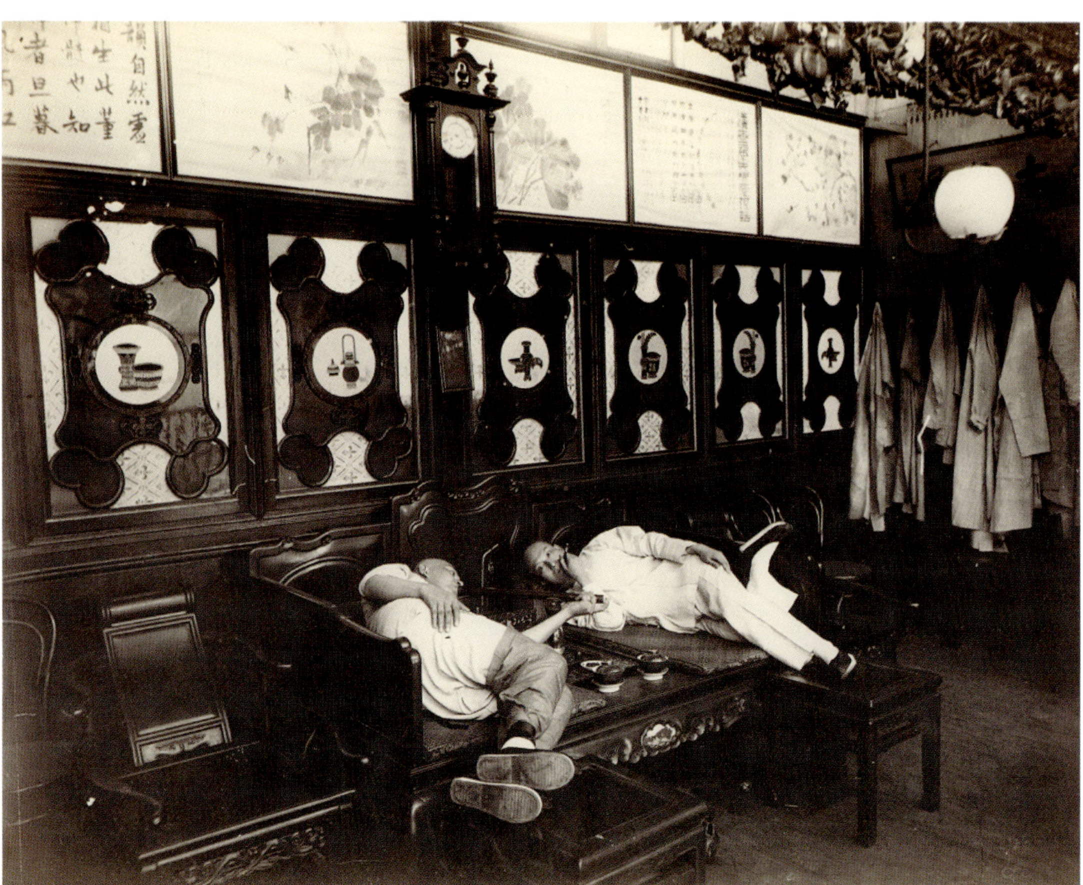

CALIFORNIA STATE LIBRARY

Left: This photo, purportedly of highbinders, was published by others as postcards with racist captions emphasizing its multi-racial composition. The highbinders were an alleged secret society of extortionists operating in San Francisco and in other American cities with Chinese populations. Highbinders supposedly offered protection for a price to Chinese merchants. The notion caught the American public's fancy much as the Mafia would a generation later, and the name highbinder entered the lexicon as a synonym for scoundrel.

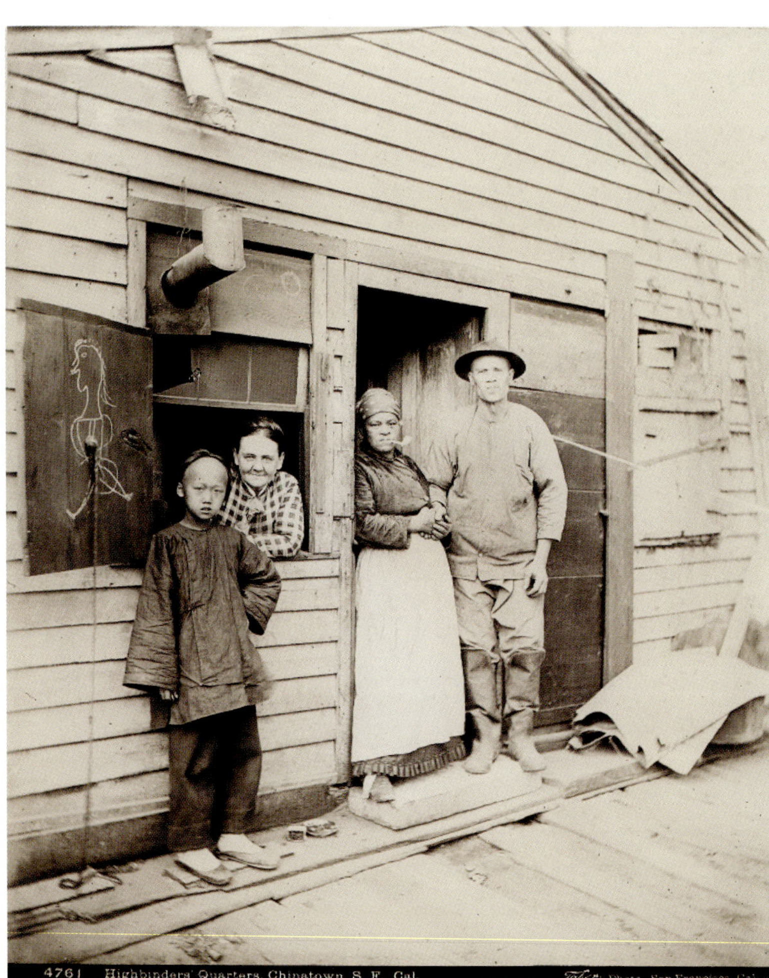

MARILYN BLAISDELL COLLECTION

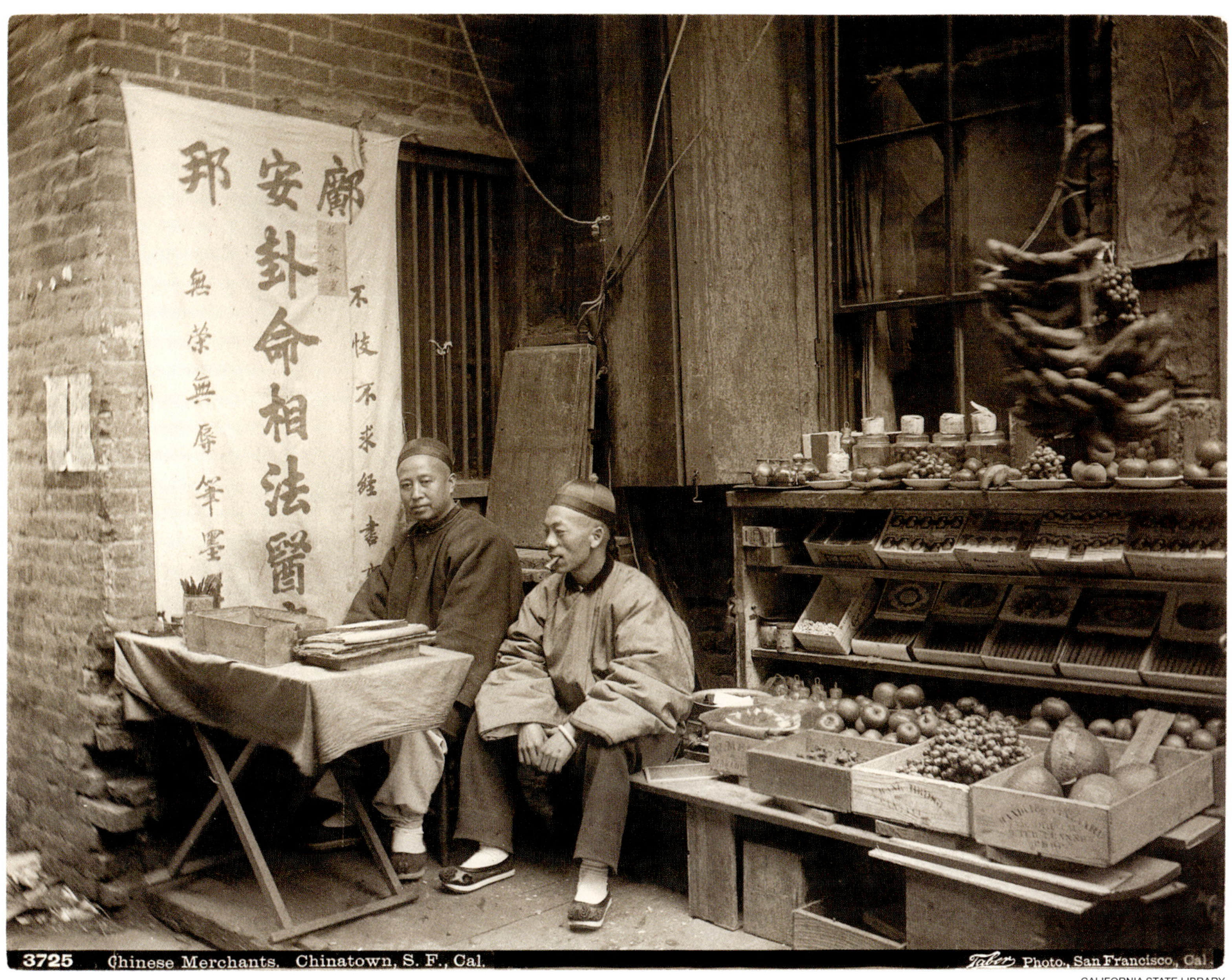

3725 Chinese Merchants. Chinatown, S. F., Cal. Taber Photo. San Francisco, Cal.

CALIFORNIA STATE LIBRARY

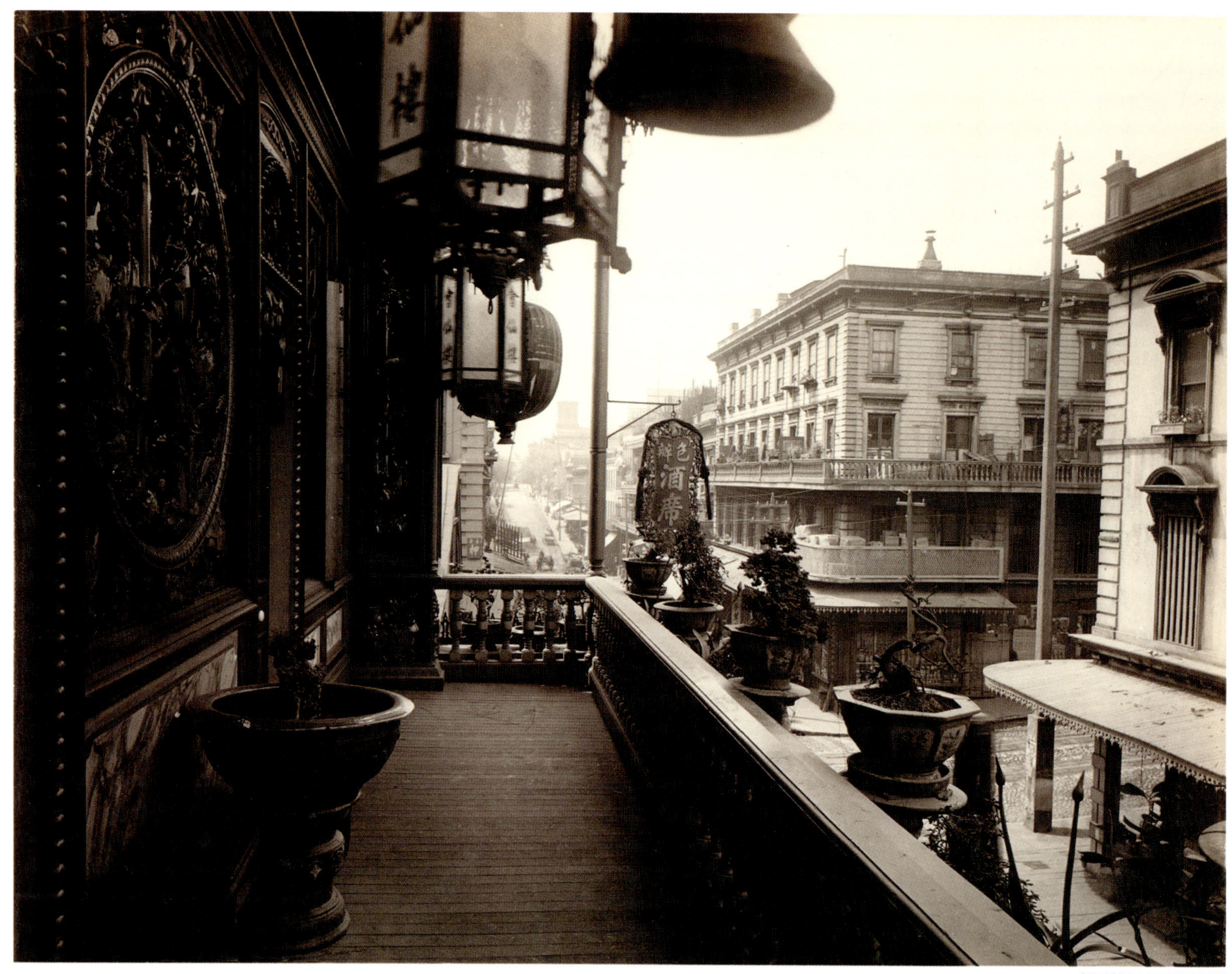

Balcony of the Woey Sin Lao restaurant, c.1886. CALIFORNIA STATE LIBRARY

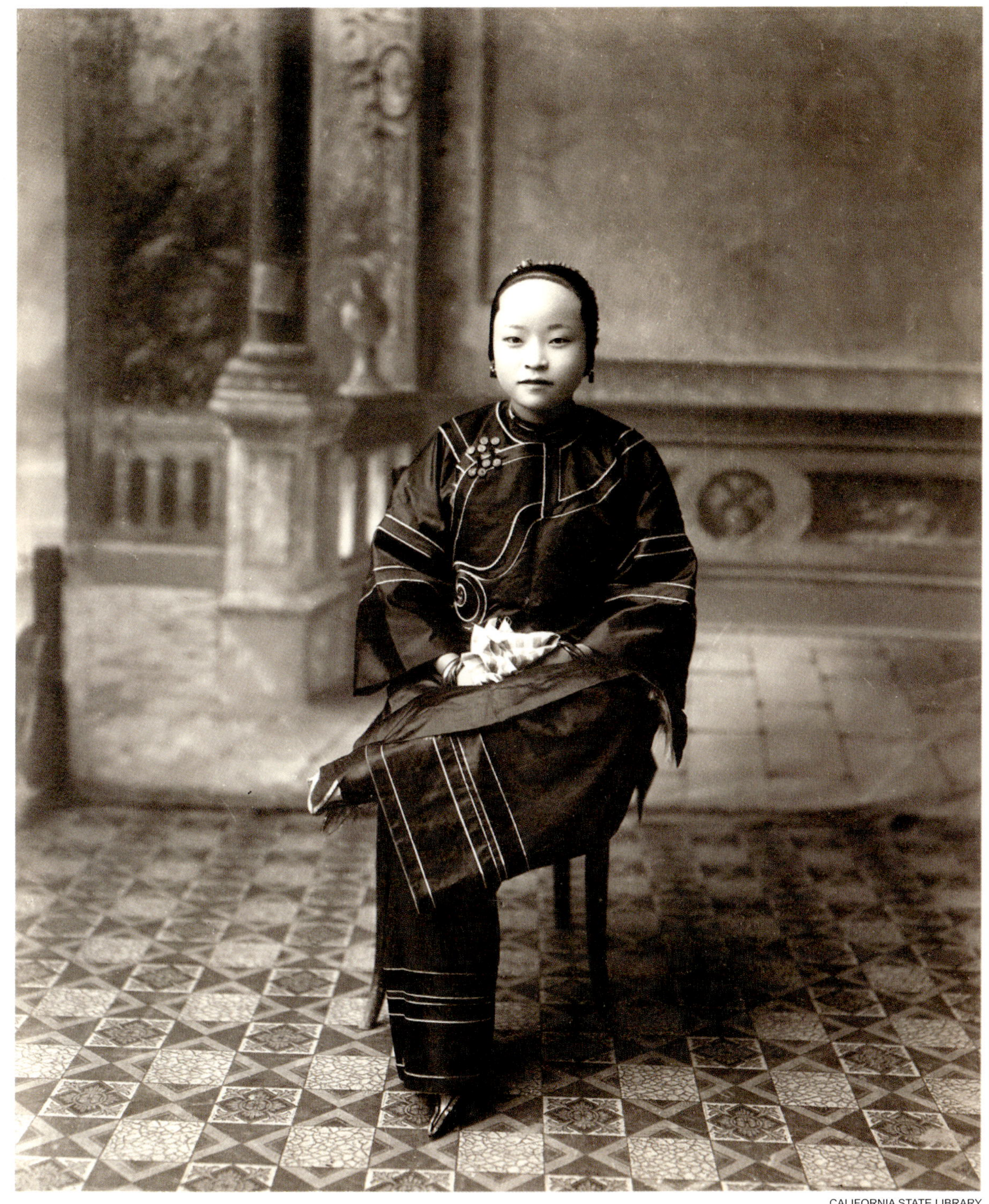

c.1886

CALIFORNIA STATE LIBRARY

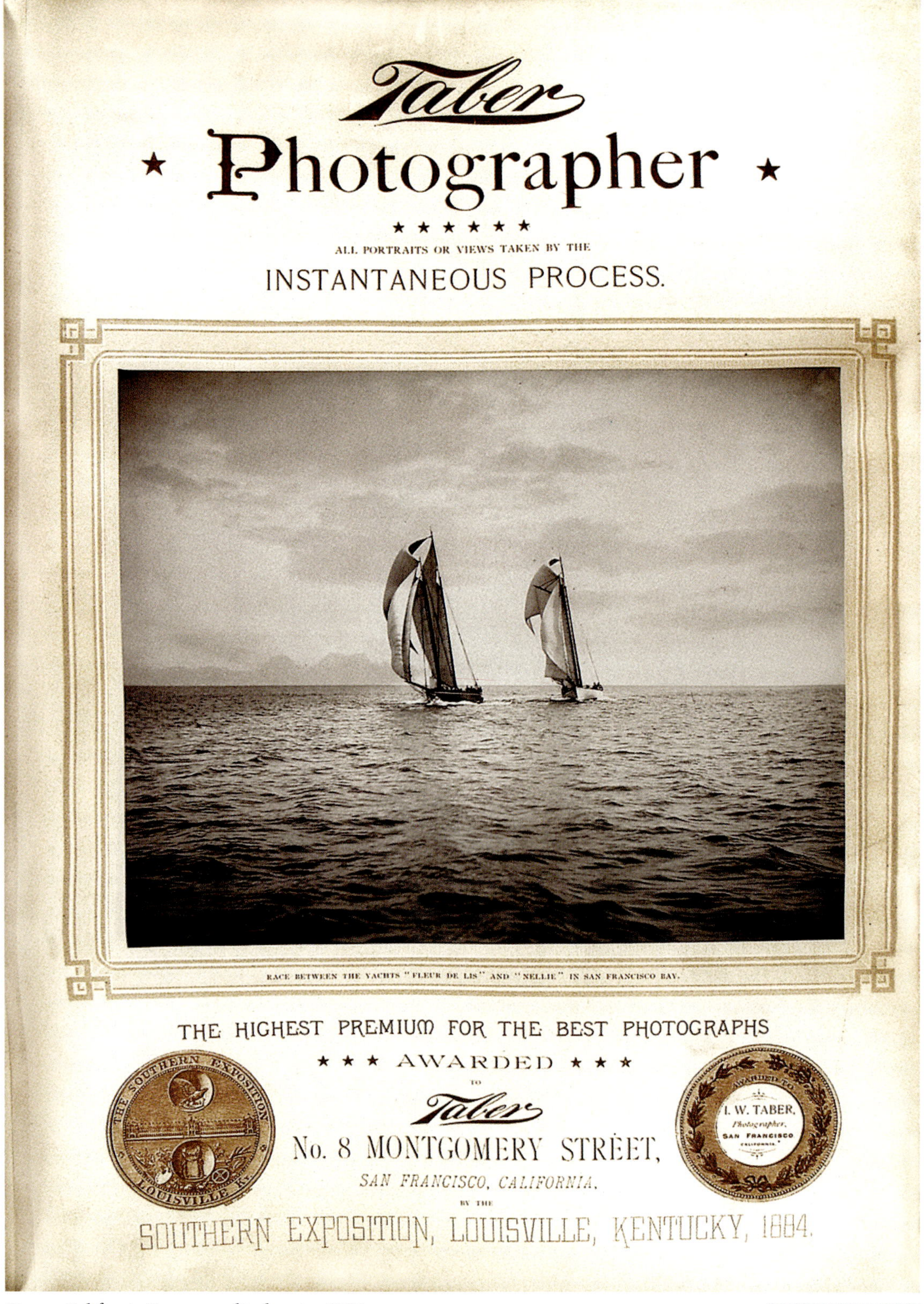

From *California Scenery and Industries, 1884.* CALIFORNIA STATE LIBRARY

SAN FRANCISCO BAY

Isaiah Taber descended from a long line of mariners. After three years at sea as a youth, he made at least three passages around Cape Horn aboard sailing vessels. In his later years he sailed to Hawaii and the South Pacific and journeyed to Alaska and Europe by steamer. His work kept him ashore for most of his career but he never lost his love of the sea. Although generally not known as a maritime photographer, Taber captured some remarkable scenes of San Francisco Bay as part of his documentation of his adopted city. When shortened exposure times made instantaneous photographs possible in the late 1870s, Taber took his camera to sea and along the lengthy San Francisco shoreline with its myriad maritime activity. He was particularly proud of the photos he made from the decks of moving vessels, quite an accomplishment with a clumsy 8 x 10-inch glass-plate view camera.

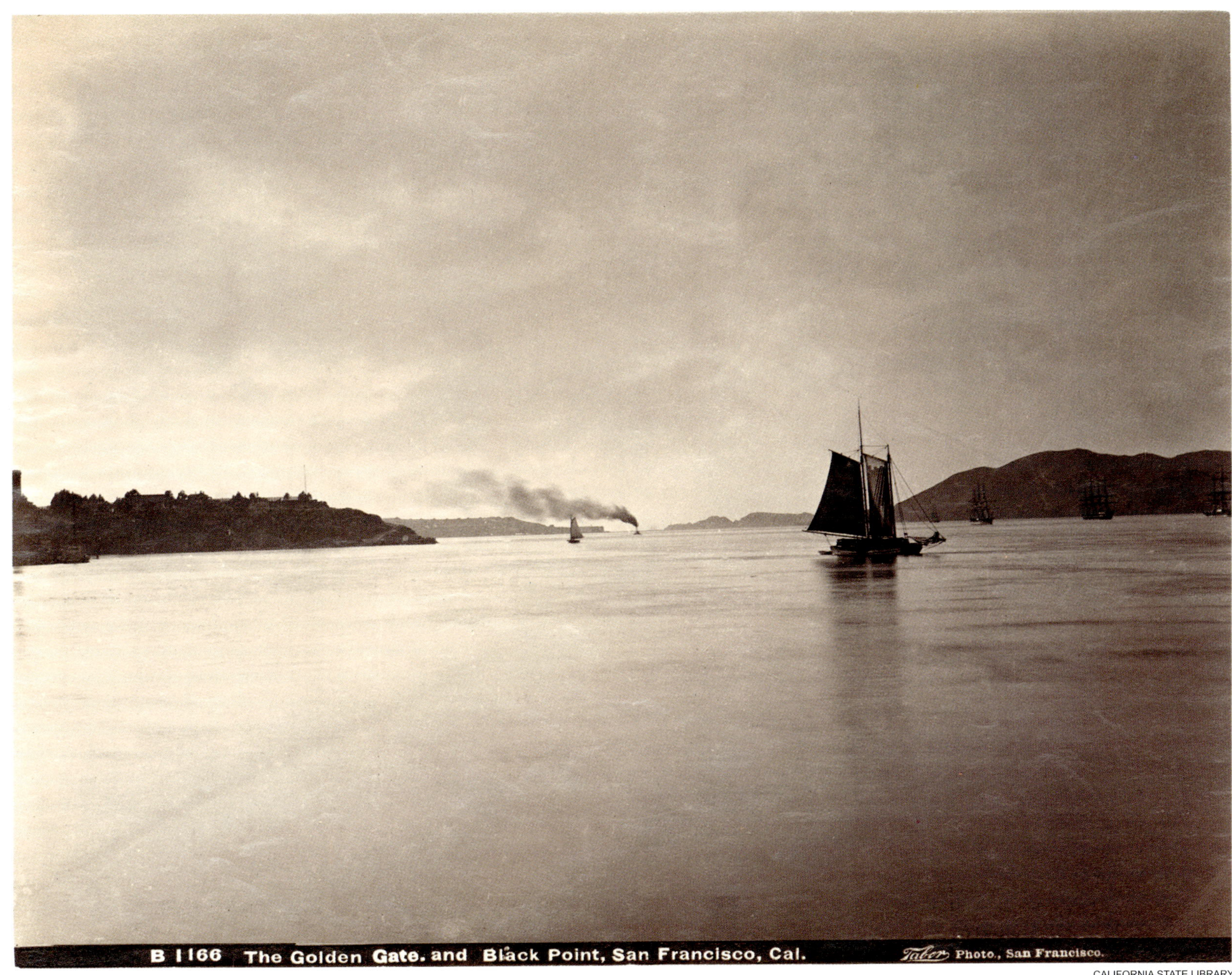

CALIFORNIA STATE LIBRARY

c. 1881

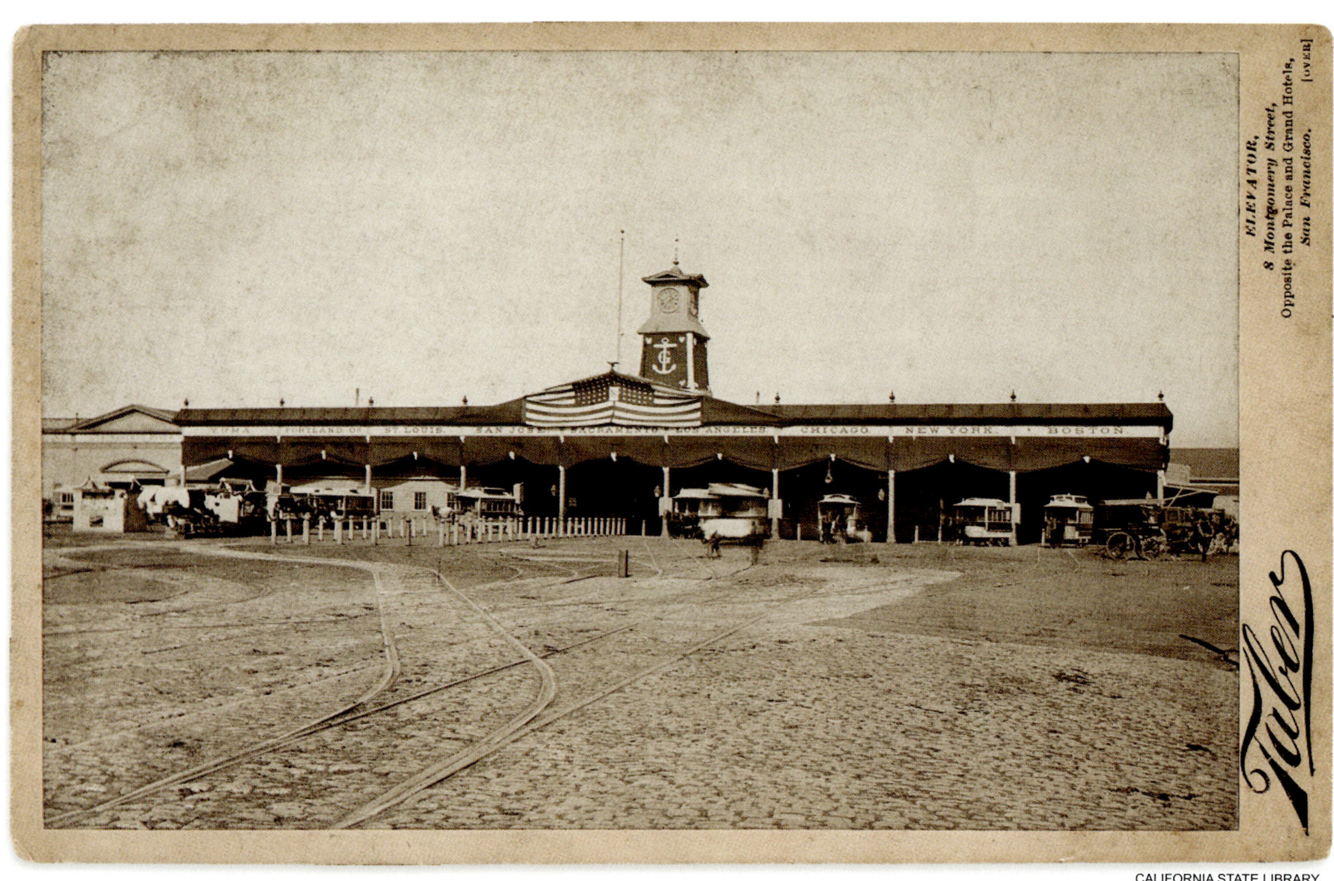

Old ferry house at the foot of Market Street, c.1882.

CALIFORNIA STATE LIBRARY

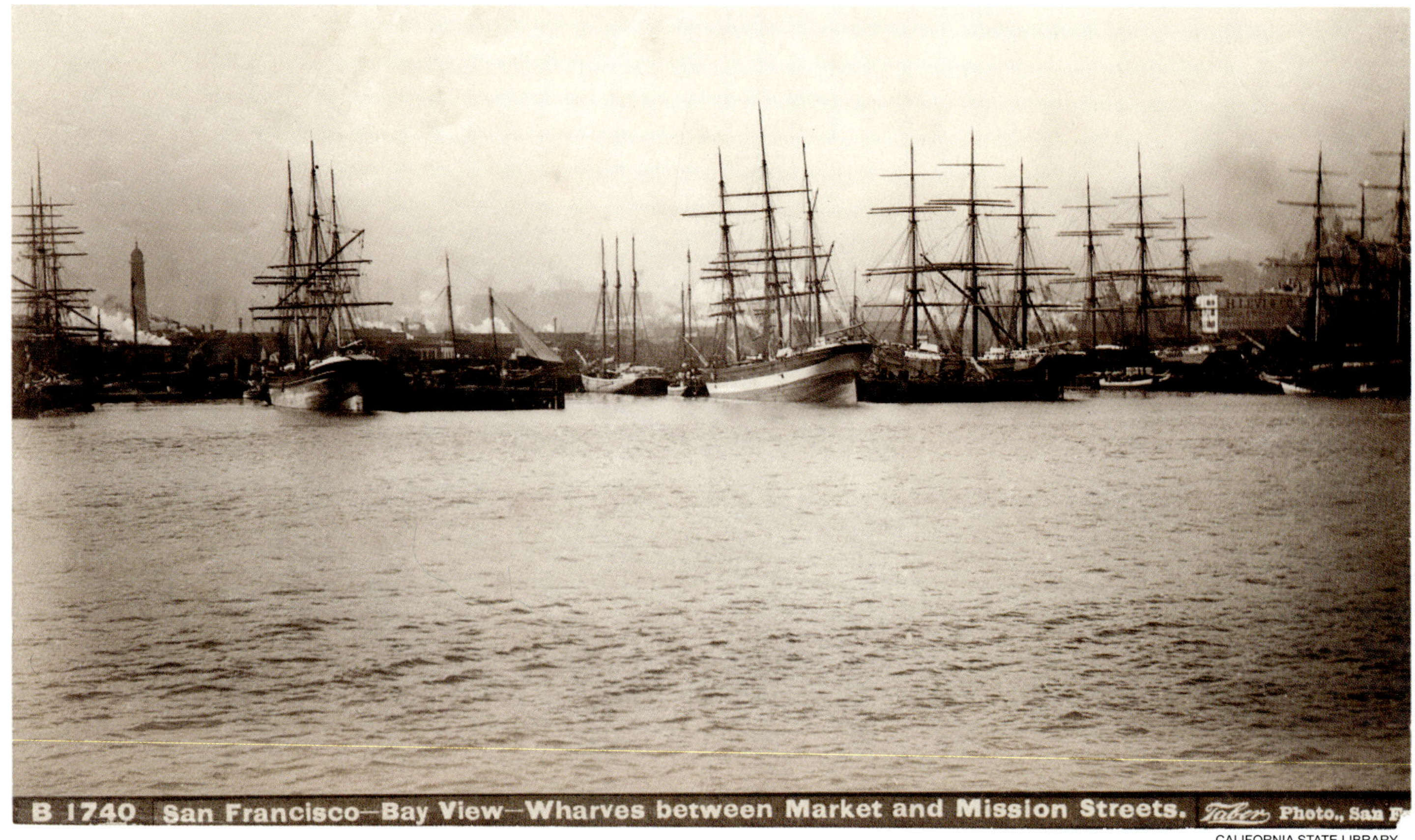

CALIFORNIA STATE LIBRARY

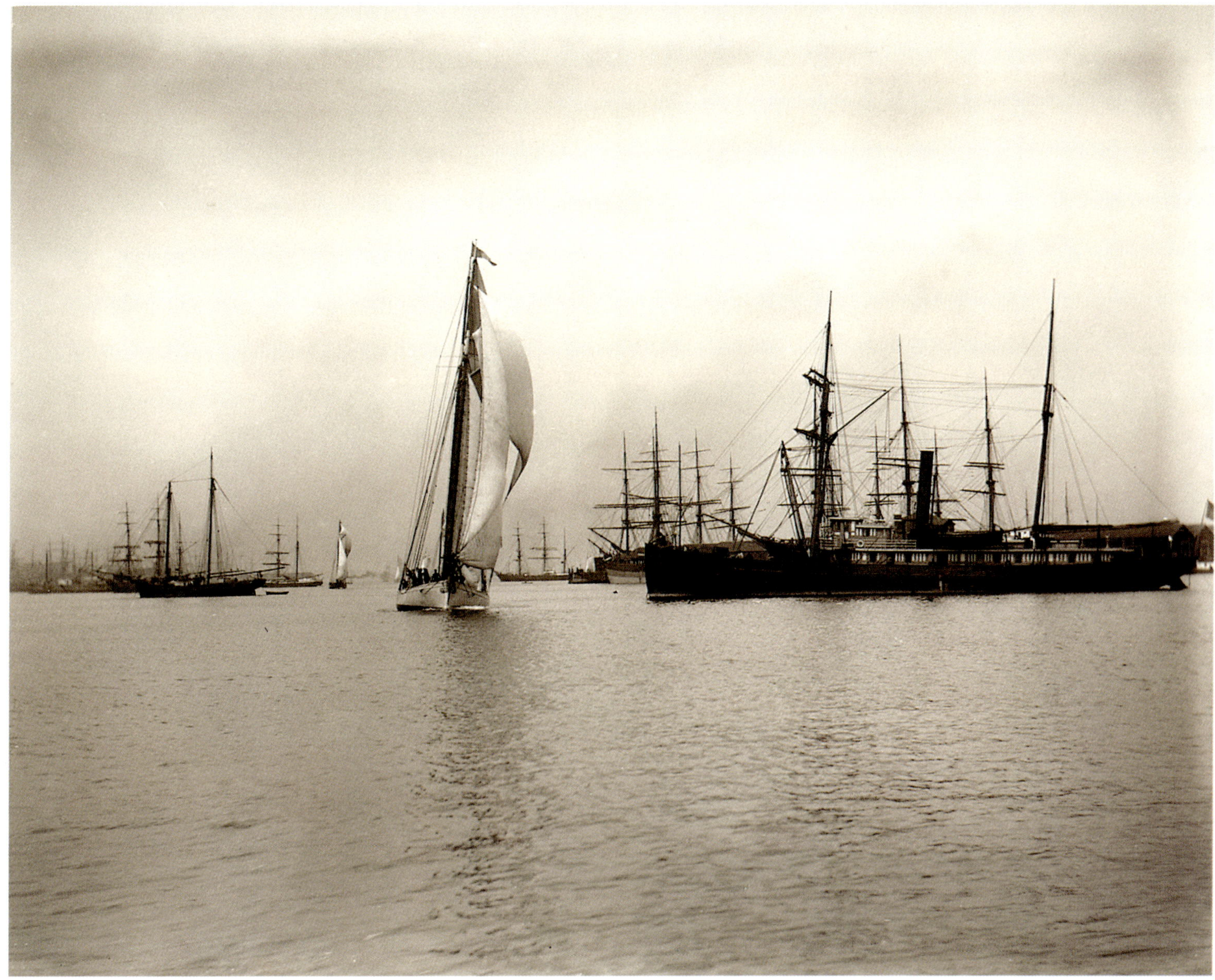

CALIFORNIA STATE LIBRARY

San Francisco Bay, c.1884.

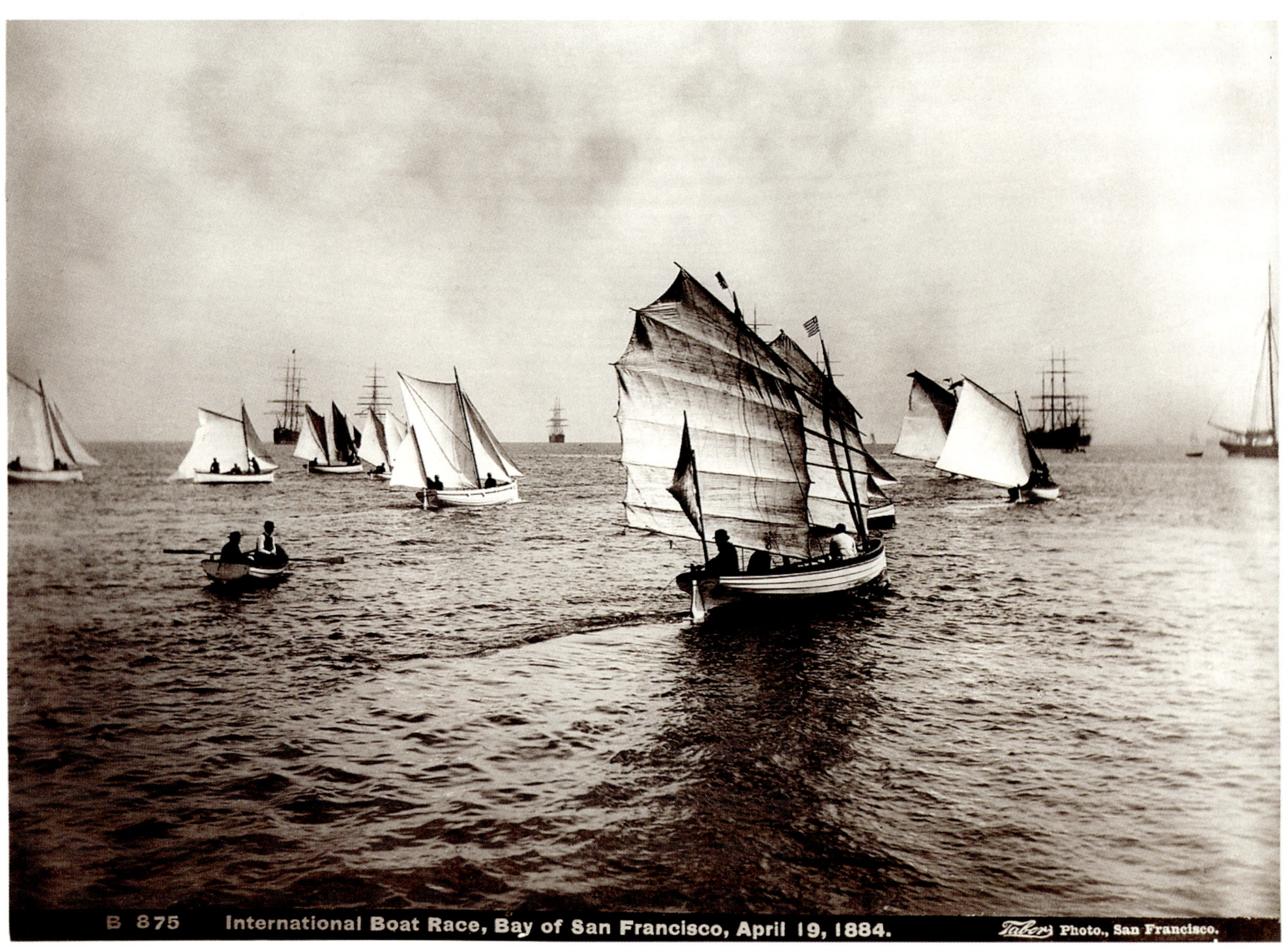

CALIFORNIA STATE LIBRARY

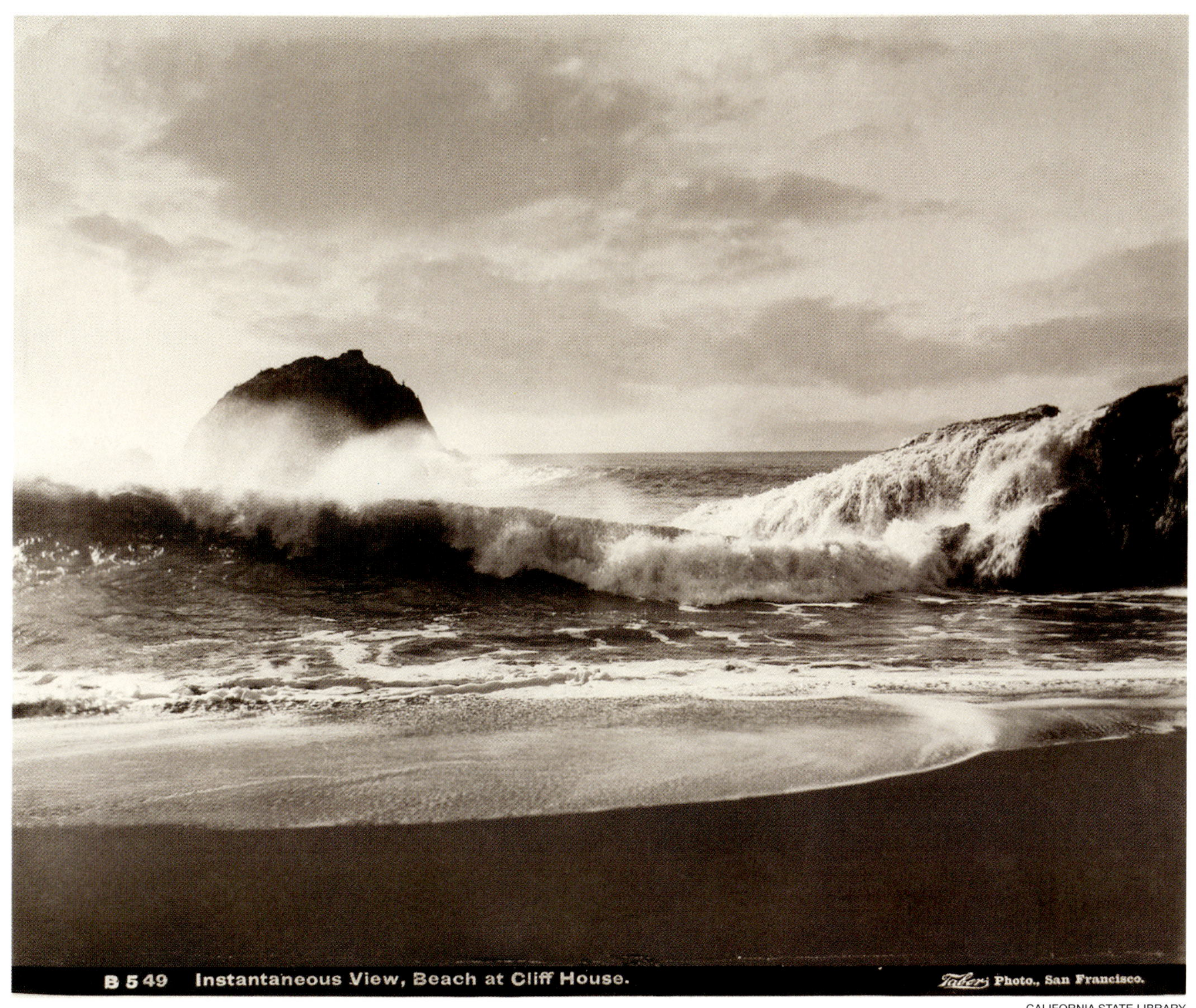

CALIFORNIA STATE LIBRARY

c.1882

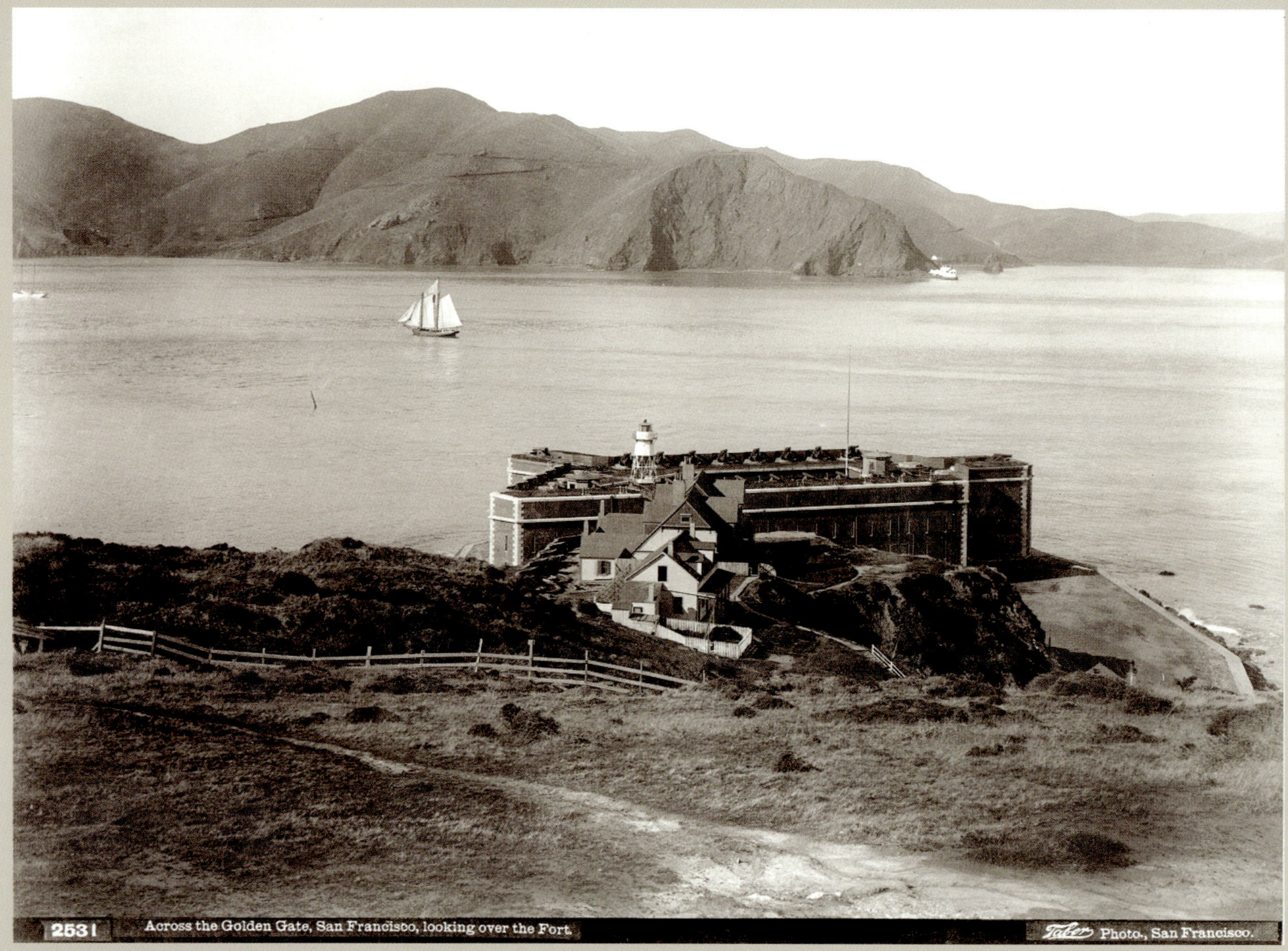

MARILYN BLAISDELL COLLECTION

Fort Point, guarding the Golden Gate, was completed in 1861 in time for the Civil War. The fort's guns, however, were never fired in defense of San Francisco Bay. Renamed Fort Winfield Scott in 1882, the fort became obsolete yet remained a popular photographic attraction. When engineers in the 1930s proposed it be demolished to make way for the Golden Gate Bridge, San Franciscans demanded the old brick fort be spared. The bridge was redesigned to arch over Fort Point. Taber made these shots around 1884, when Fort Point was still garrisoned. Another Civil War era fort in New Bedford, Massachusetts, is called Fort Taber in honor of Isaiah Taber's cousin, Isaac Congdon Taber.

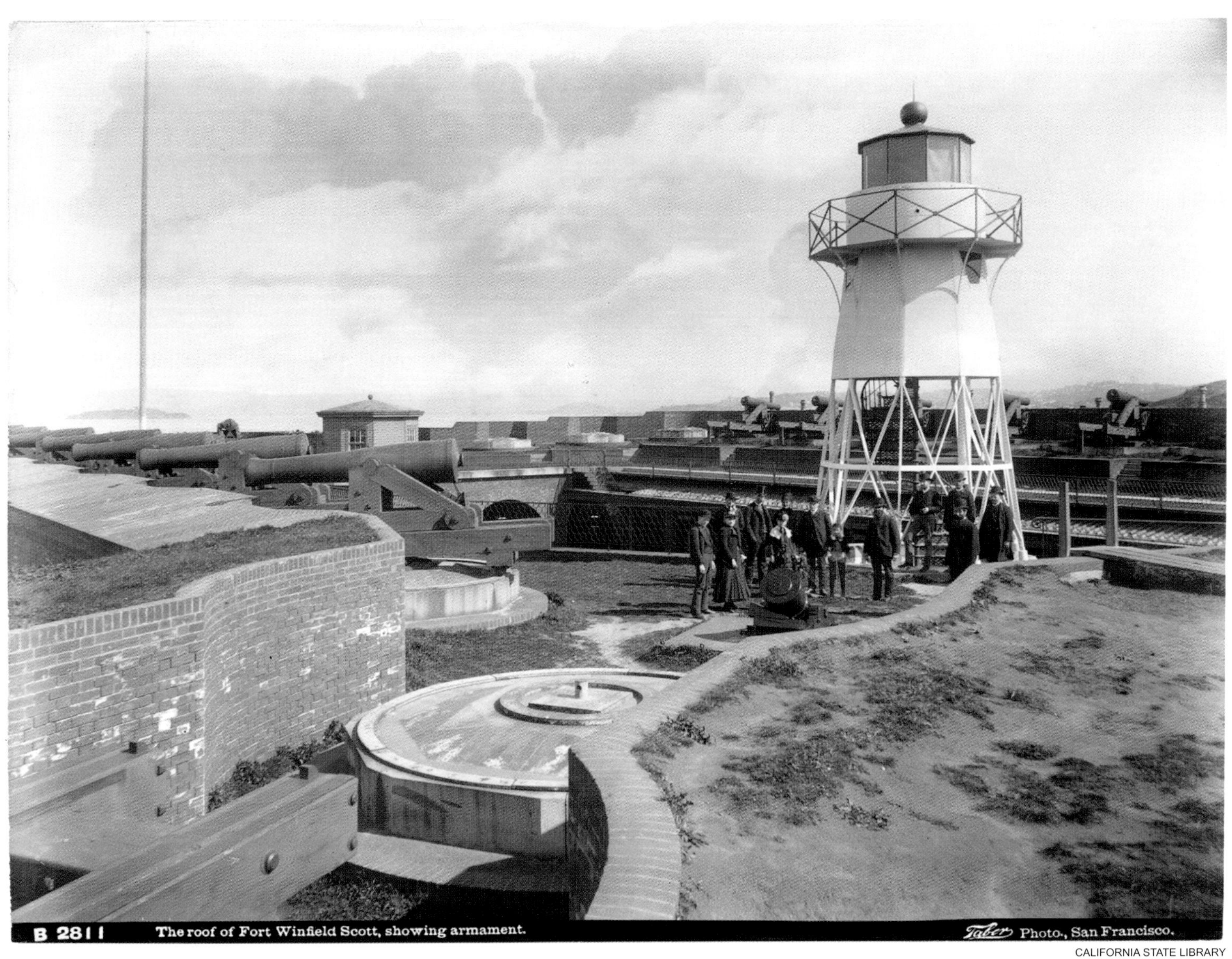

B 2811 The roof of Fort Winfield Scott, showing armament. Taber Photo., San Francisco.

CALIFORNIA STATE LIBRARY

MARILYN BLAISDELL COLLECTION

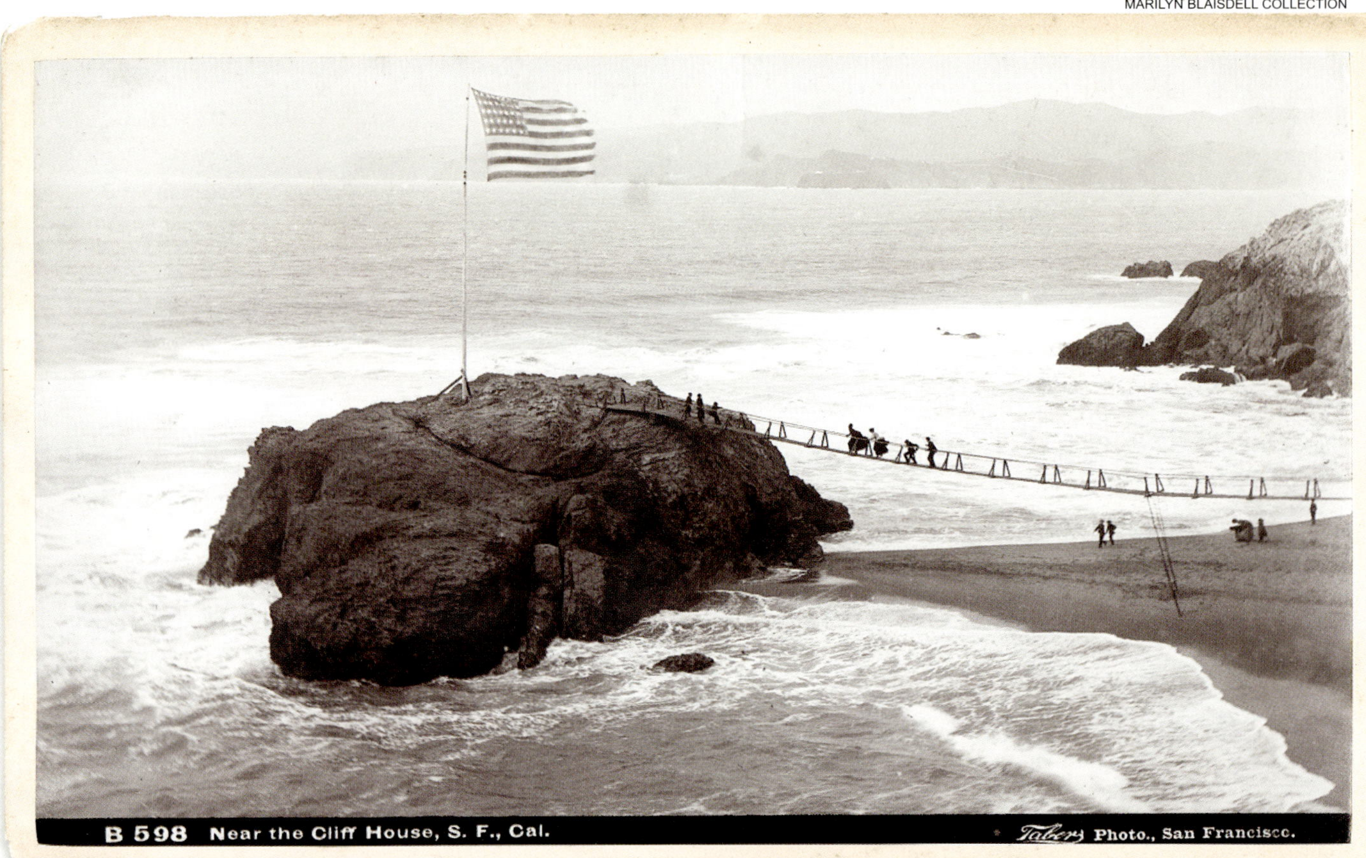

Above: Suspension bridge to Flag Rock below Sutro Baths, c. 1886.

Below: Western entrance to Golden Gate Park at Ocean Beach, c. 1880.

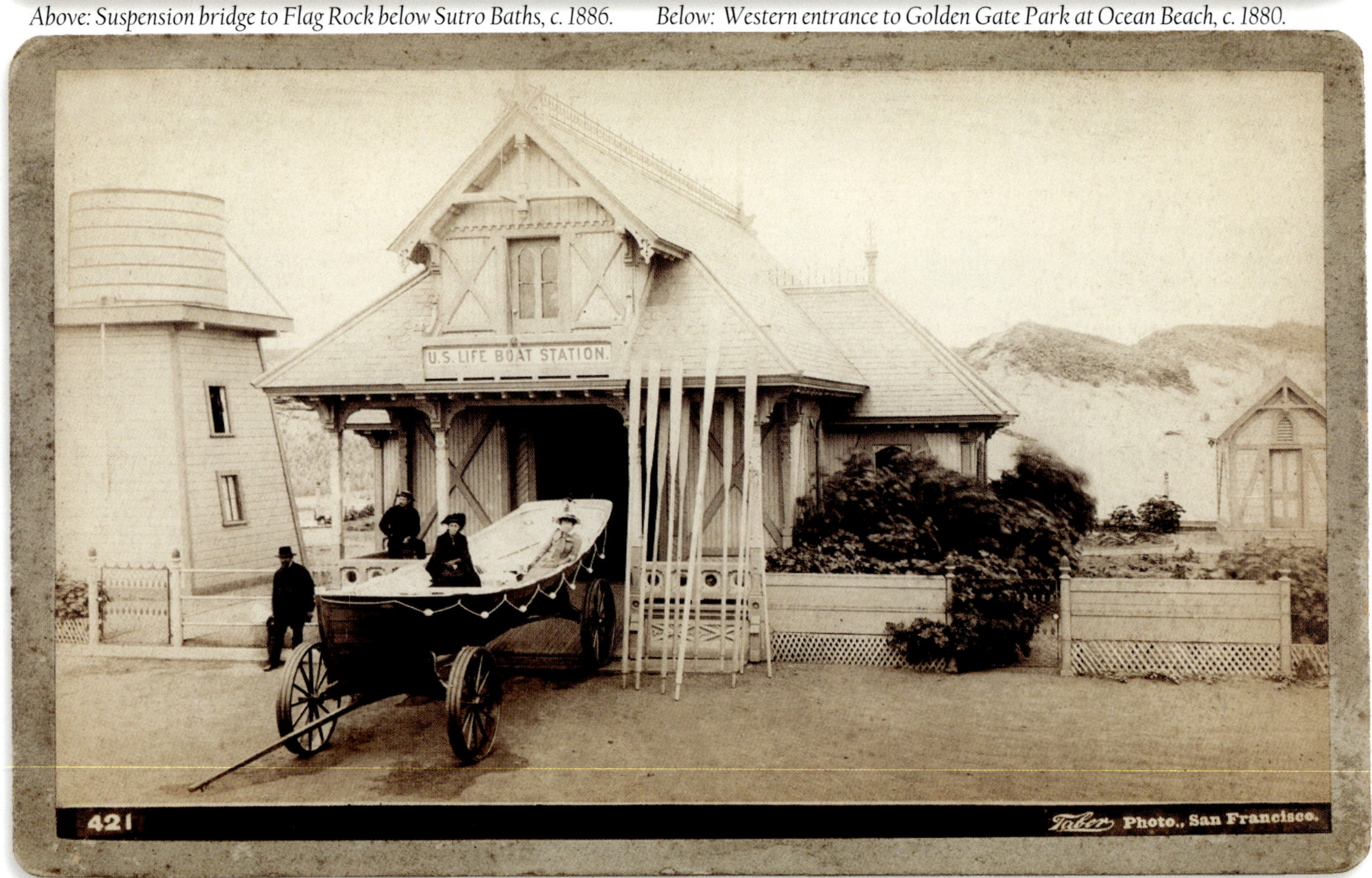

CALIFORNIA STATE LIBRARY

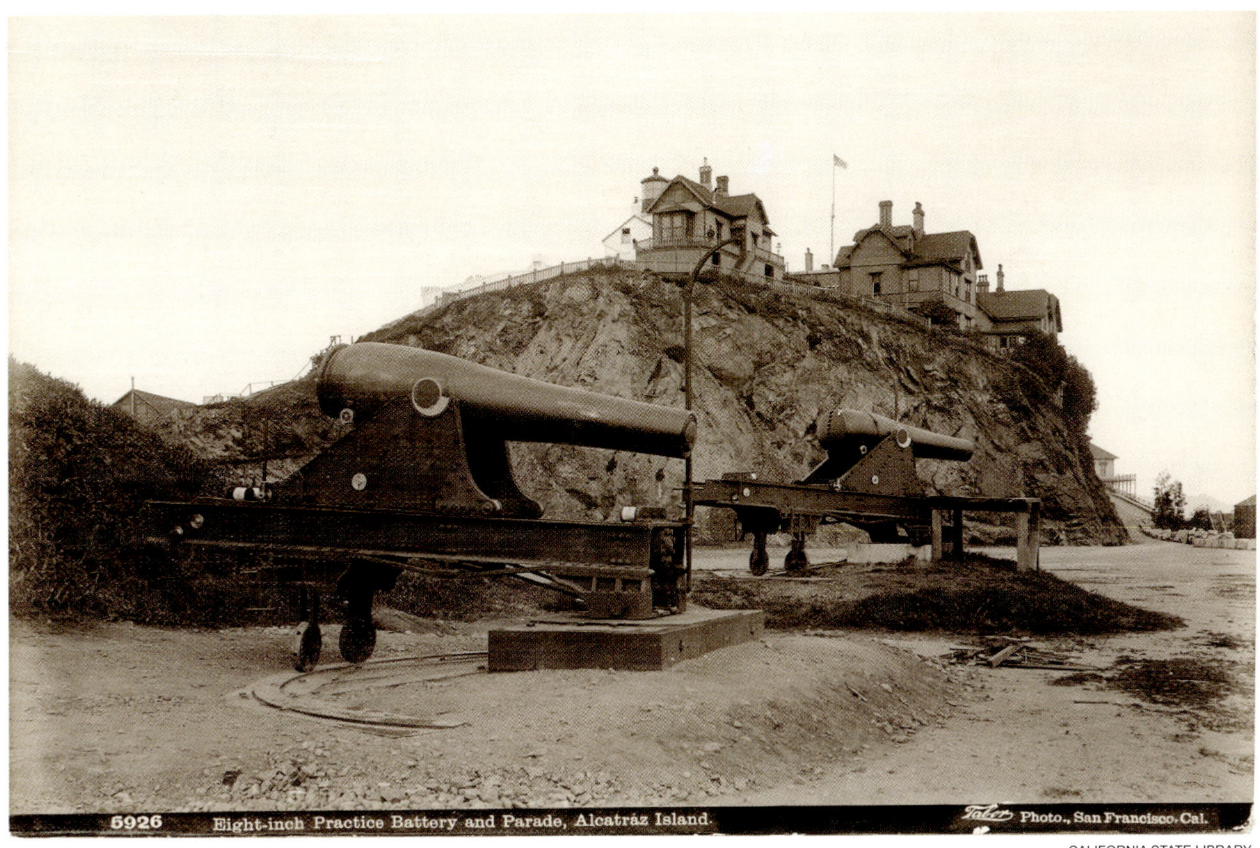

CALIFORNIA STATE LIBRARY

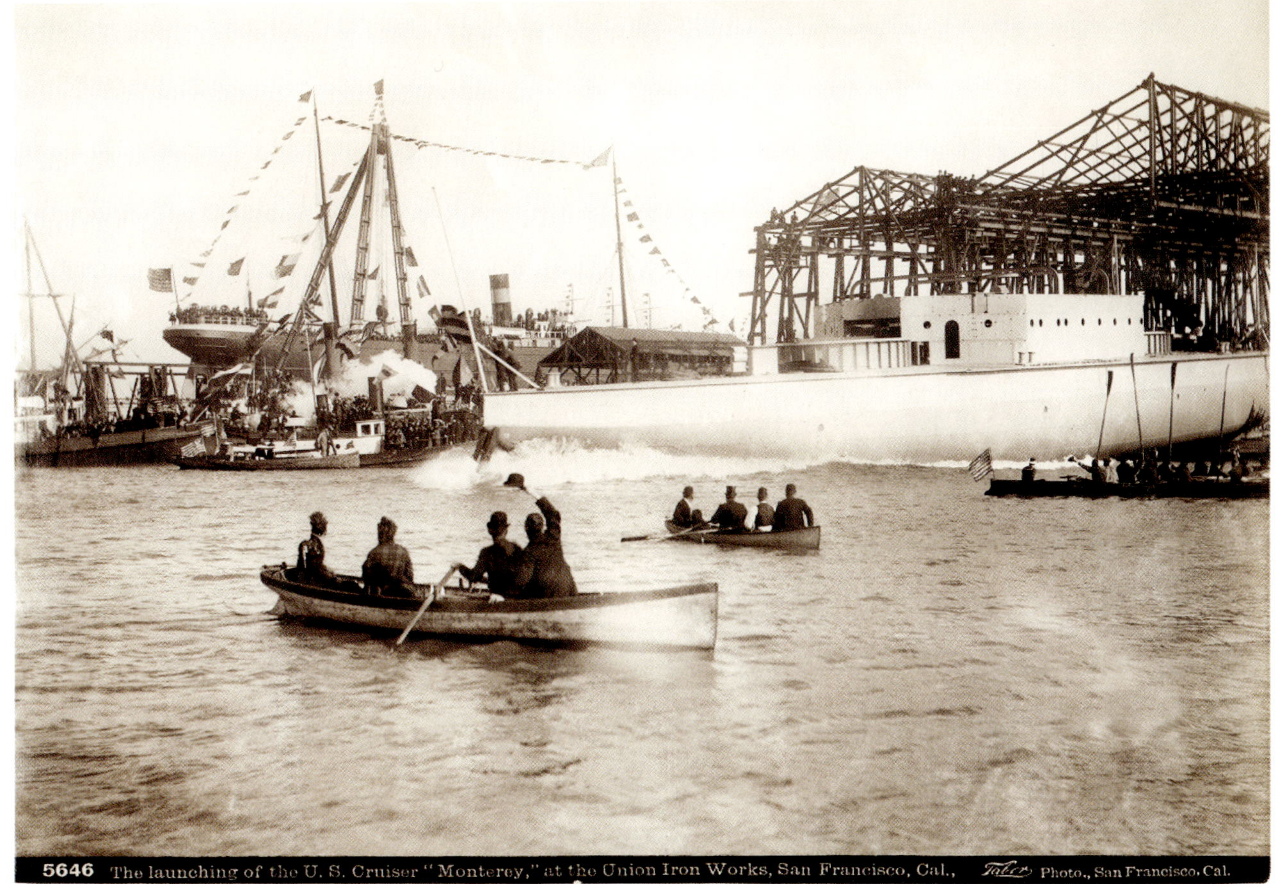

CALIFORNIA STATE LIBRARY

Photos by Taber of current events are rare because Taber generally stuck to themes and scenes that could be sold over several years. Photo-journalistic shots quickly became dated and difficult to sell. The launch of the monitor Monterey, *April 28, 1891, created a stir in the local press because few warships were built in San Francisco at that time.*

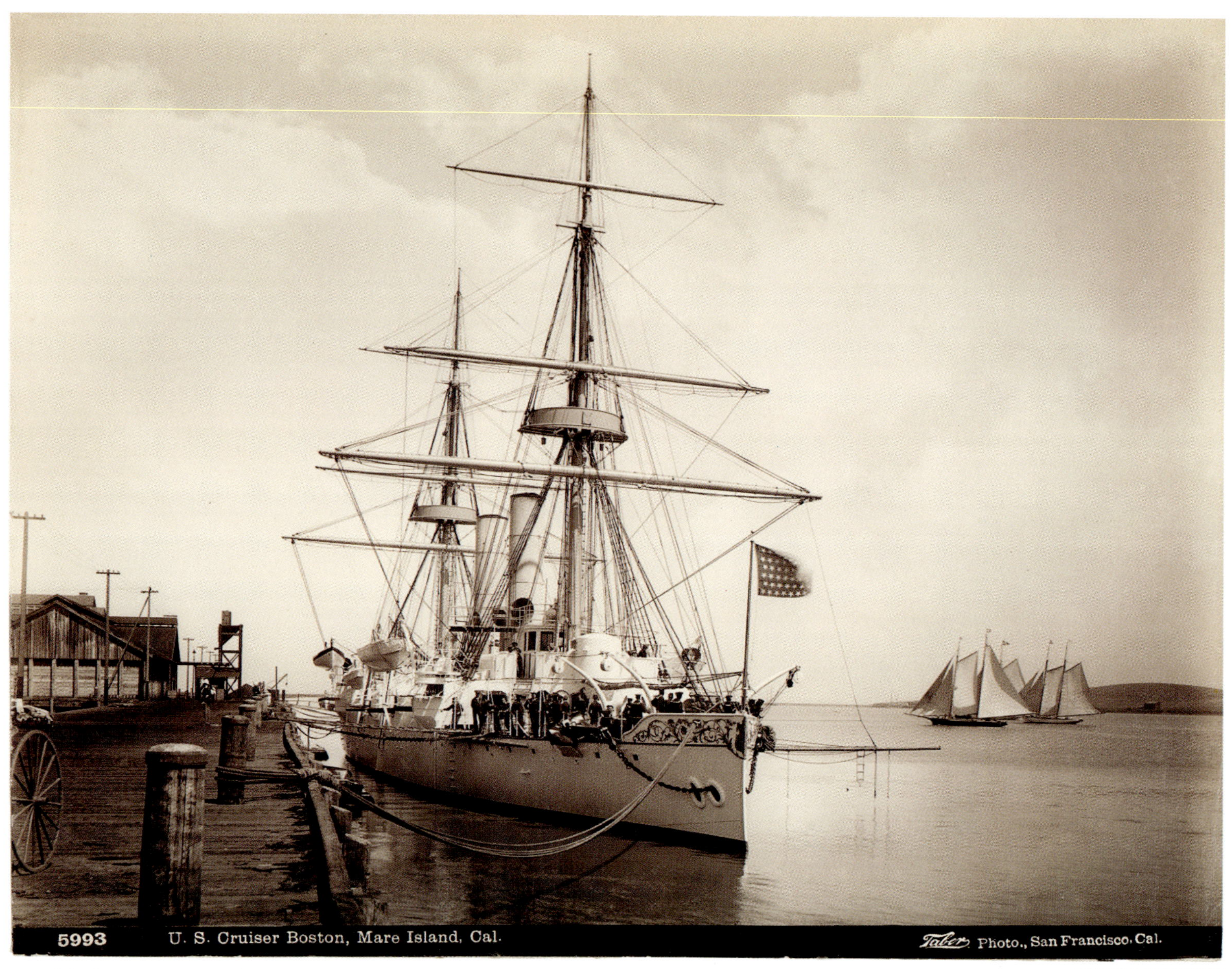

CALIFORNIA STATE LIBRARY

One of the first steel ships built for the "new" Navy in the late 1880s, Boston *still carried a full suit of sails in addition to steam propulsion. Seen here around 1890,* Boston *spent most of her life as a receiving ship, or floating barracks, at Mare Island.*

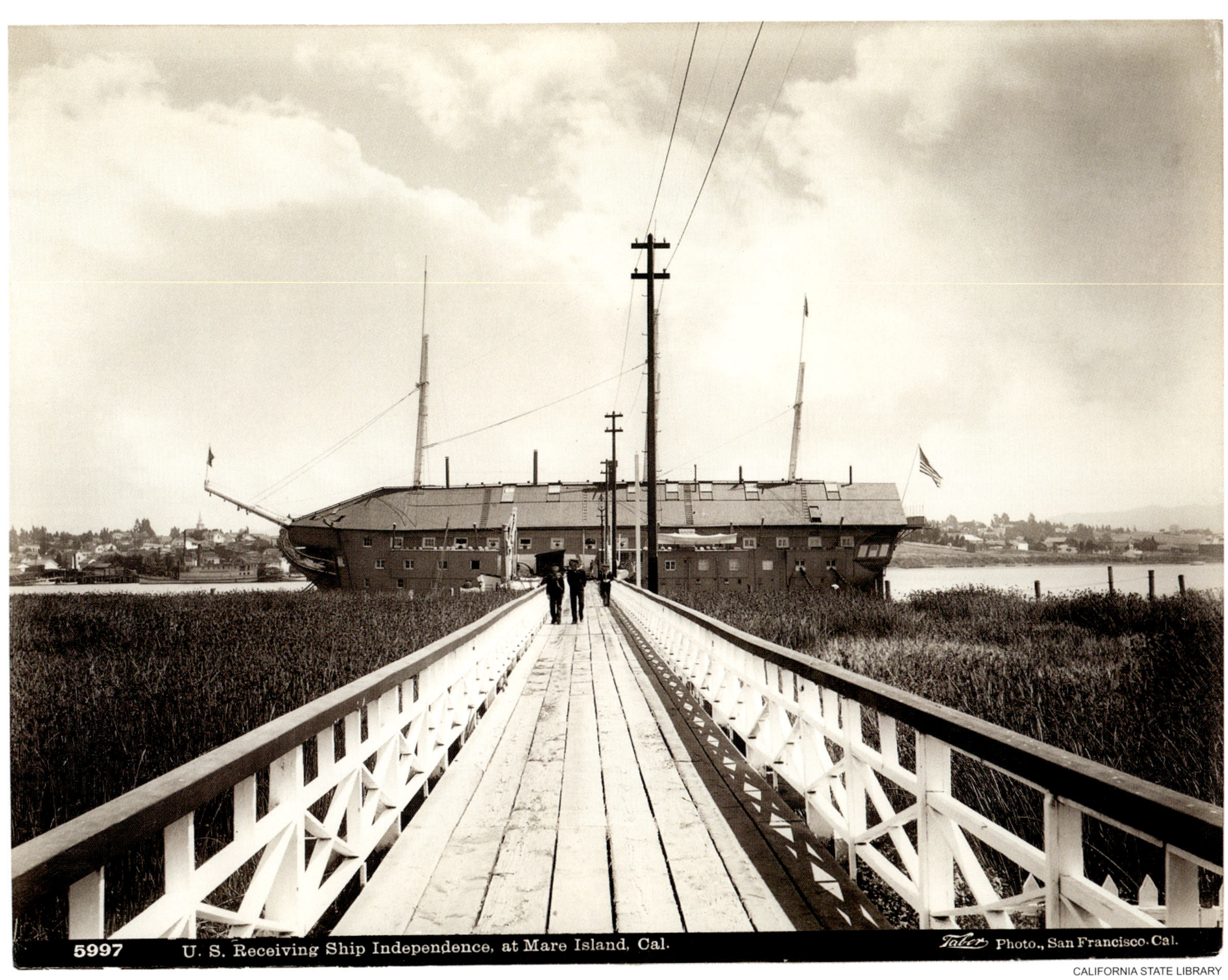

CALIFORNIA STATE LIBRARY

An even older warship serving at Mare Island was the old frigate Independence, *built for the War of 1812.*

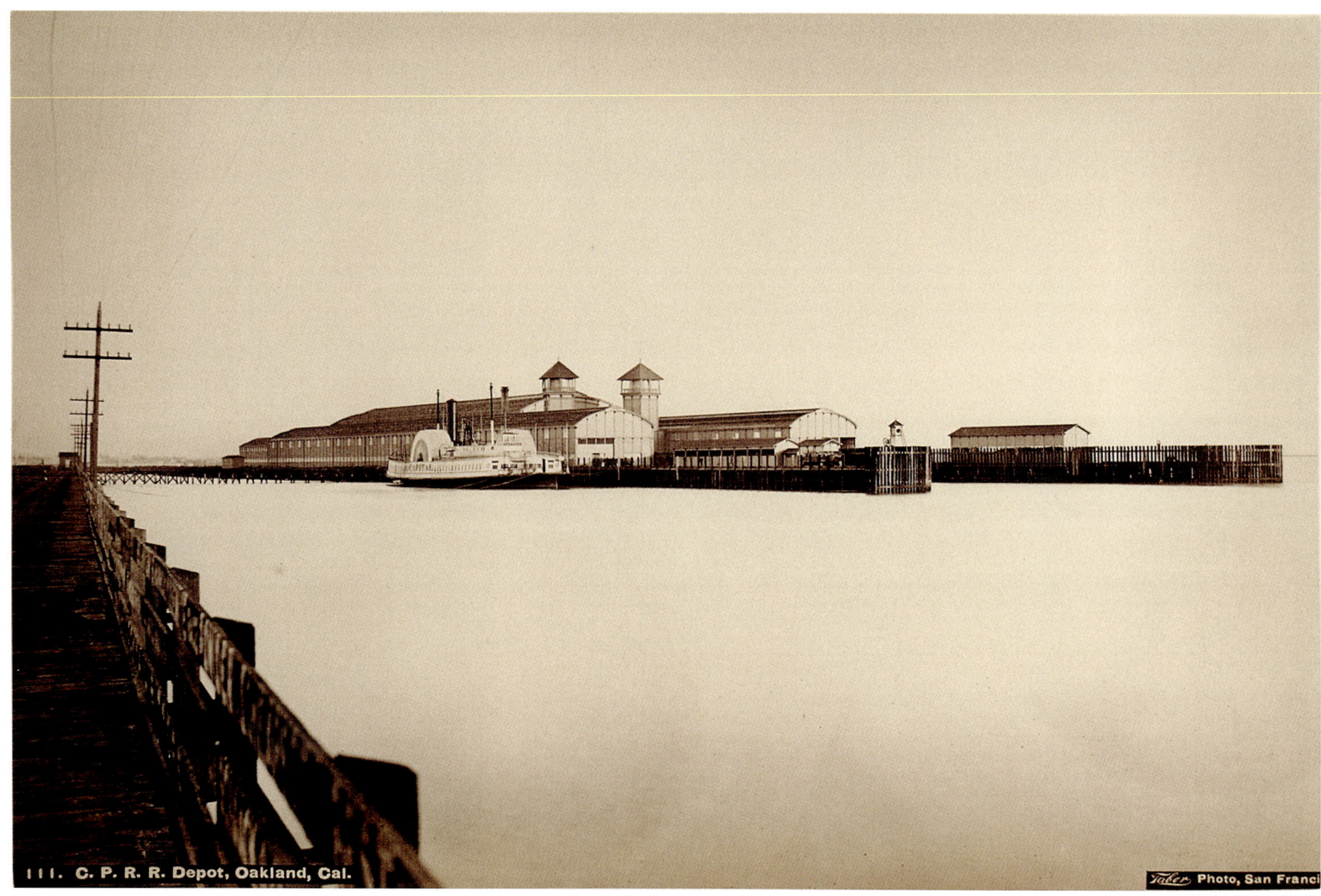

CALIFORNIA STATE LIBRARY

Taber commuted by ferry from Oakland to San Francisco from 1875 to 1891, and used the ferries as a platform for his camera. The photo above, however, was taken from the railroad mole in Oakland leading to the Central Pacific Railroad ferry terminal. The sidewheeler ferry Capital *lies alongside the wharf.*

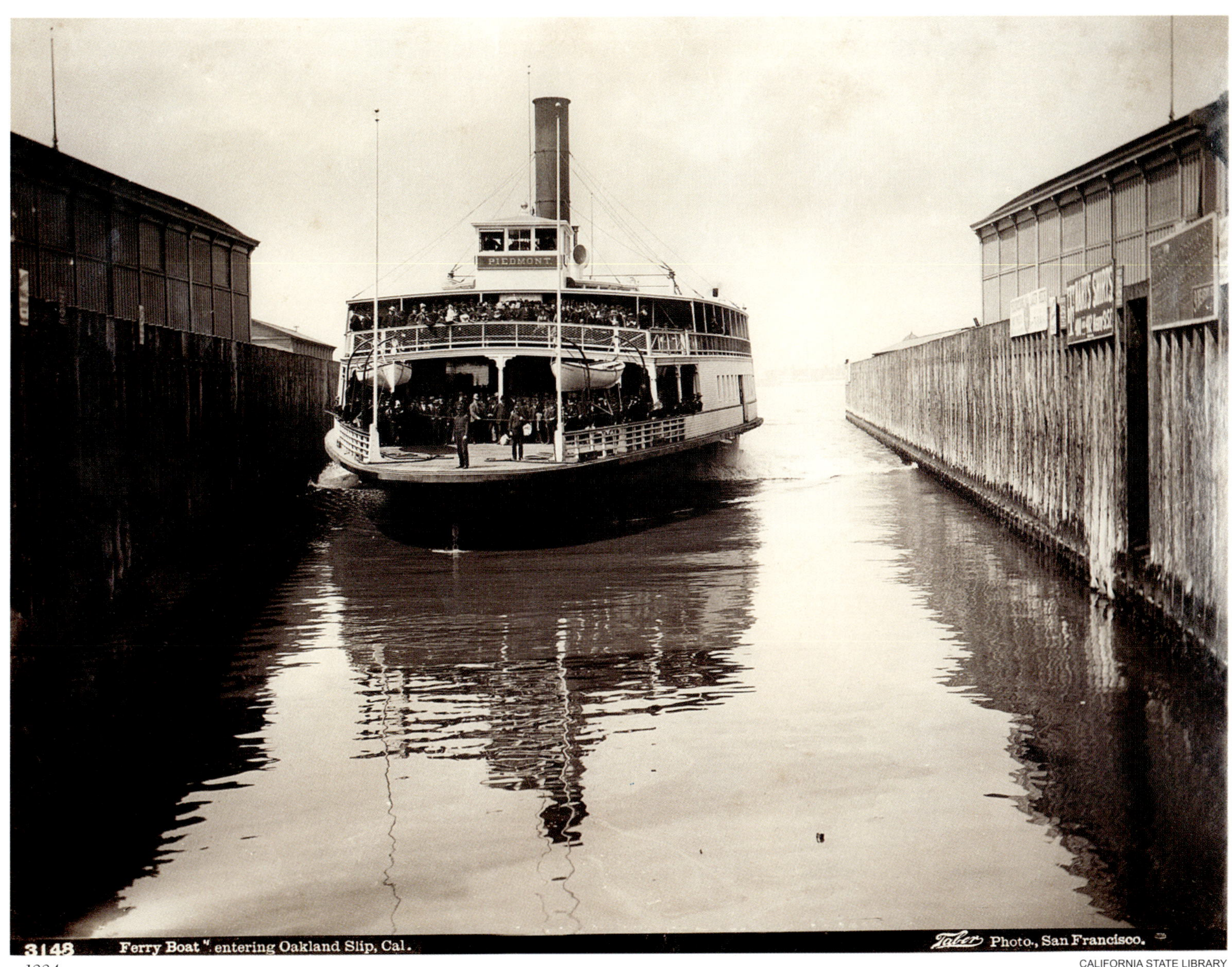

c. 1884

CALIFORNIA STATE LIBRARY

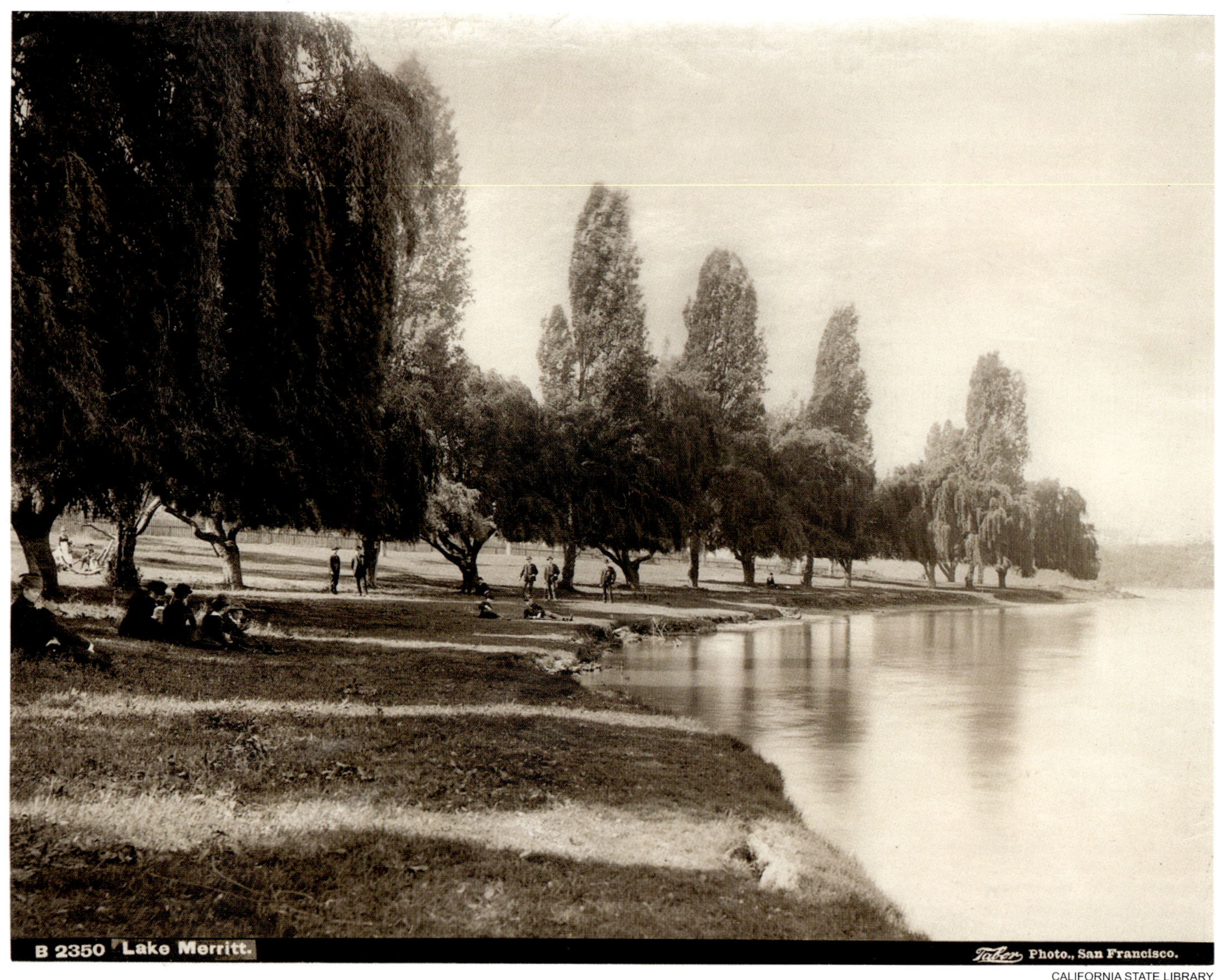

CALIFORNIA STATE LIBRARY

Oakland, California, c.1884, a scene near Taber's home. His friend and neighbor Dr. Samuel Merritt developed the lake as part of a fashionable residential neighborhood.

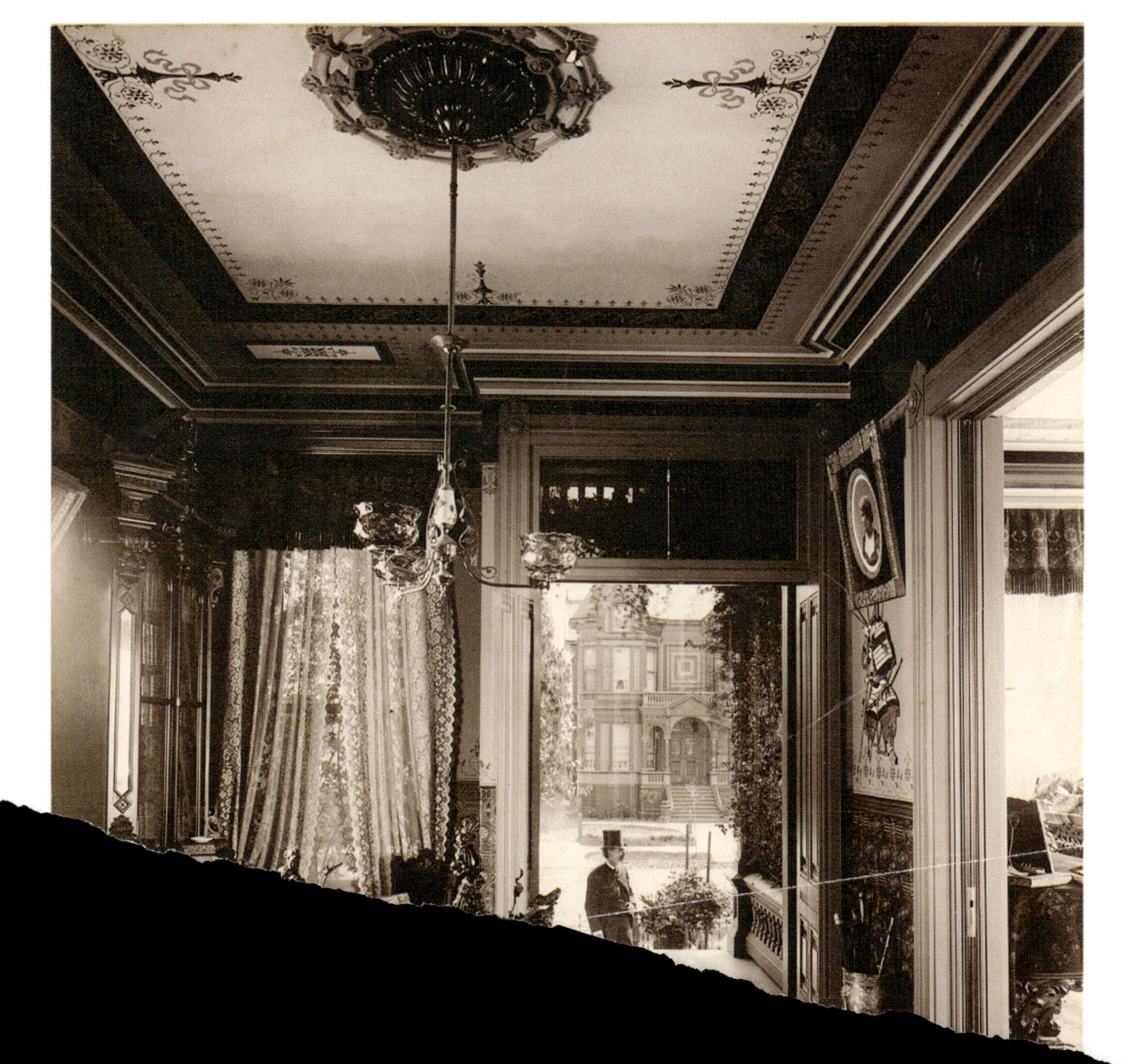

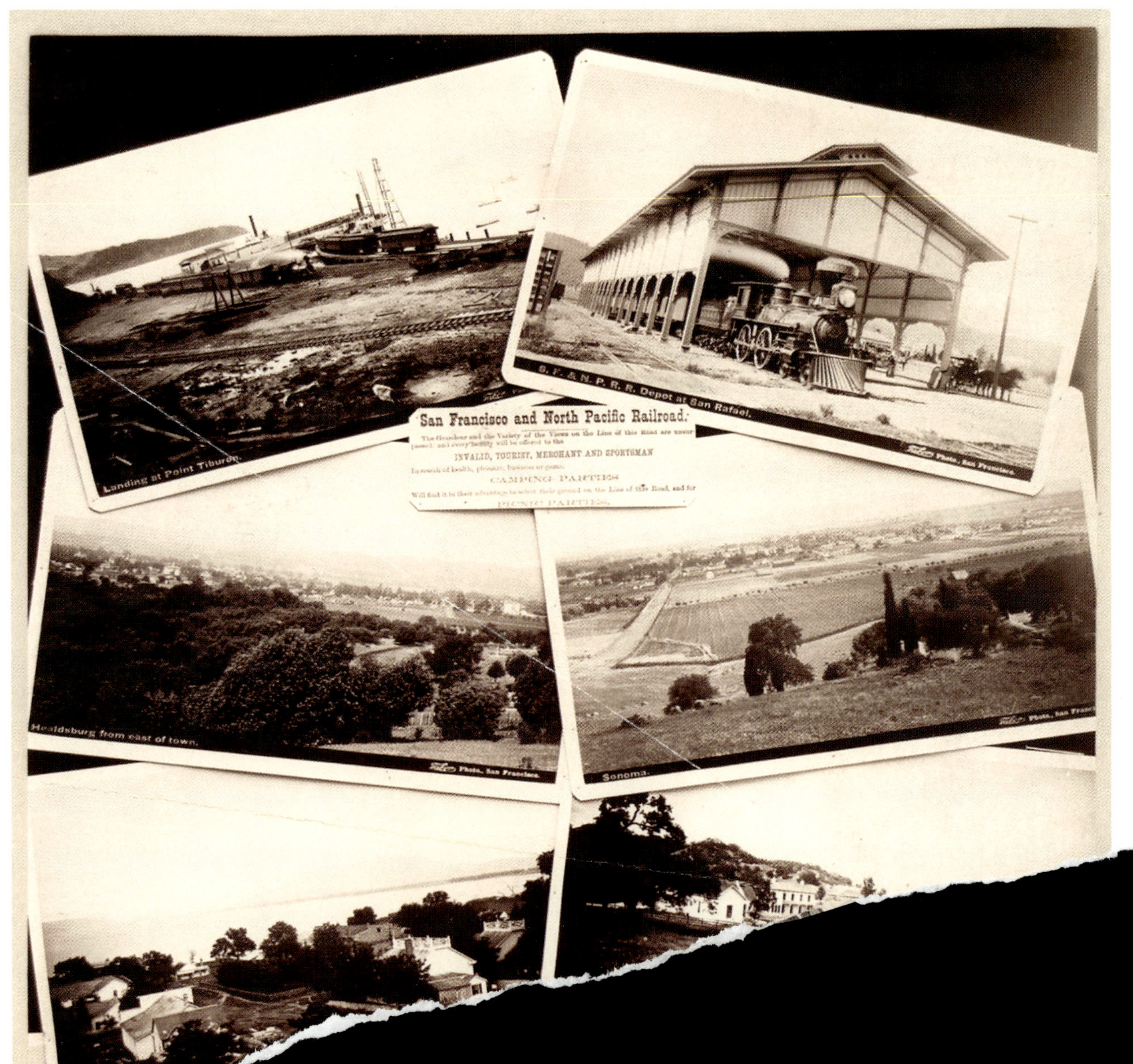

WINE COUNTRY

Whenever time permitted or necessity dictated, Isaiah Taber would journey out of San Francisco to enhance his catalog of scenic views. And California had much to offer, both north and south. He followed the principal routes of the California tourists since these were his main customers. On days trips he probably managed with a single assistant, but longer trips to the Sierra Nevada, Los Angeles, or San Diego required additional help and careful planning. He had to ship his glass plate unexposed negatives by rail, unless he purchased them on location. Exposed plates had to be packed carefully and shipped by rail back to San Francisco for processing or printing. Side trips had to be arranged, and guides hired to accompany him to remote sites such as Indian rancherias or old adobe ruins. On th doubt met wi acqui

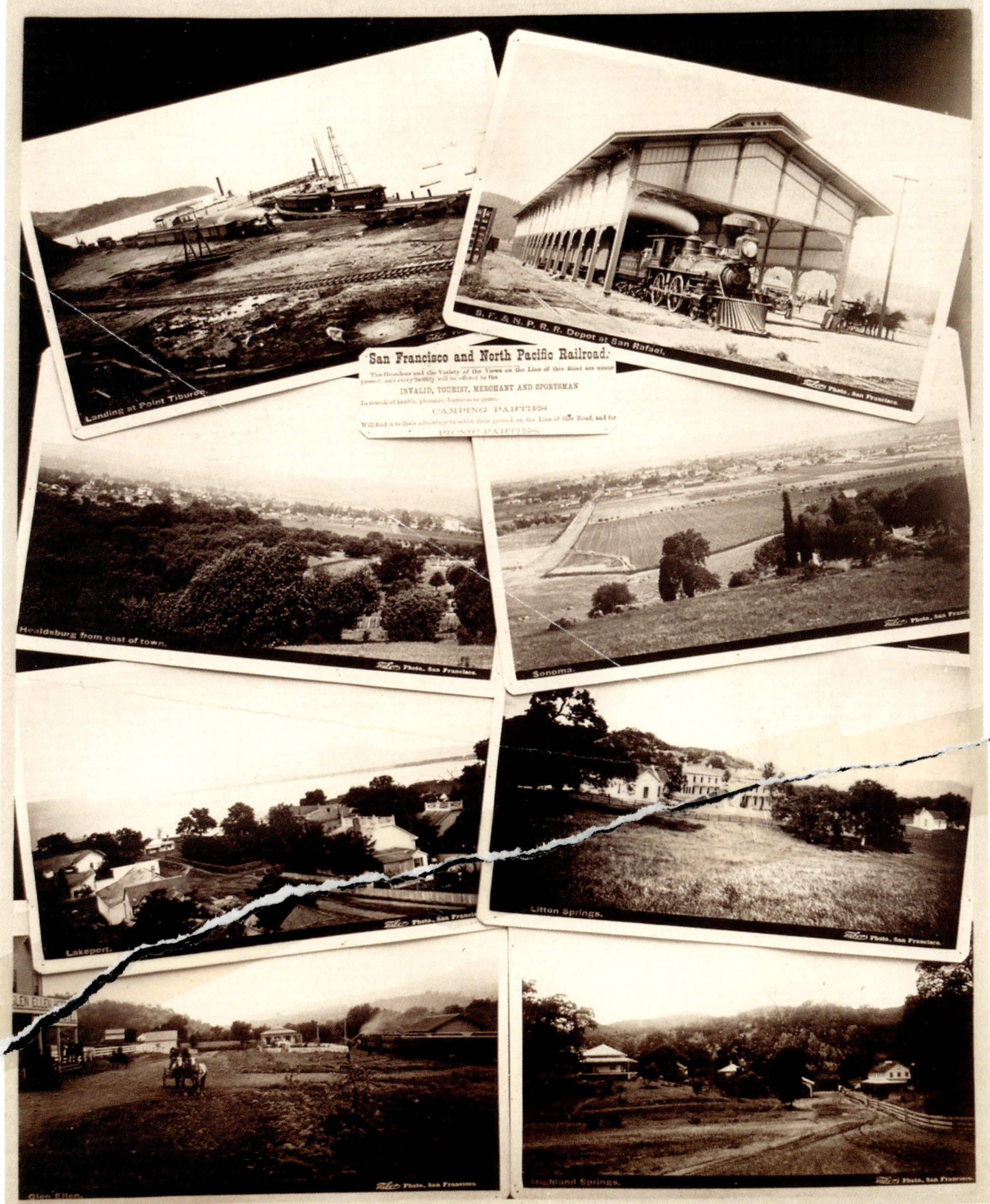

CALIFORNIA STATE LIBRARY

WINE COUNTRY

Whenever time permitted or necessity dictated, Isaiah Taber would journey out of San Francisco to enhance his catalog of scenic views. And California had much to offer, both north and south. He followed the principal routes of the California tourists since these were his main customers. On days trips he probably managed with a single assistant, but longer trips to the Sierra Nevada, Los Angeles, or San Diego required additional help and careful planning. He had to ship his glass plate unexposed negatives by rail, unless he purchased them on location. Exposed plates had to be packed carefully and shipped by rail back to San Francisco for processing or printing. Side trips had to be arranged, and guides hired to accompany him to remote sites such as Indian rancherias or old adobe ruins. On these trips Taber no doubt met with other photographers and acquired negatives to add to his offerings.

Convenient to San Francisco in Taber's day as it is now, the lush wine country had irresistible appeal. A short ferry ride across San Francisco Bay, and he could catch a train north through Marin County and on to Sonoma, Mendocino or Napa County. In an advertisement, left, for the San Francisco and North Pacific Railroad in his 1884 photographic album, *California Scenery and Industries*, Taber included eight views of some of the attractions on the line. Clockwise from upper left are the landing at Point Tiburon, the depot at San Rafael, the town of Sonoma, Litton Springs, Highland Springs, Glen Ellen, Lakeport, and Healdsburg.

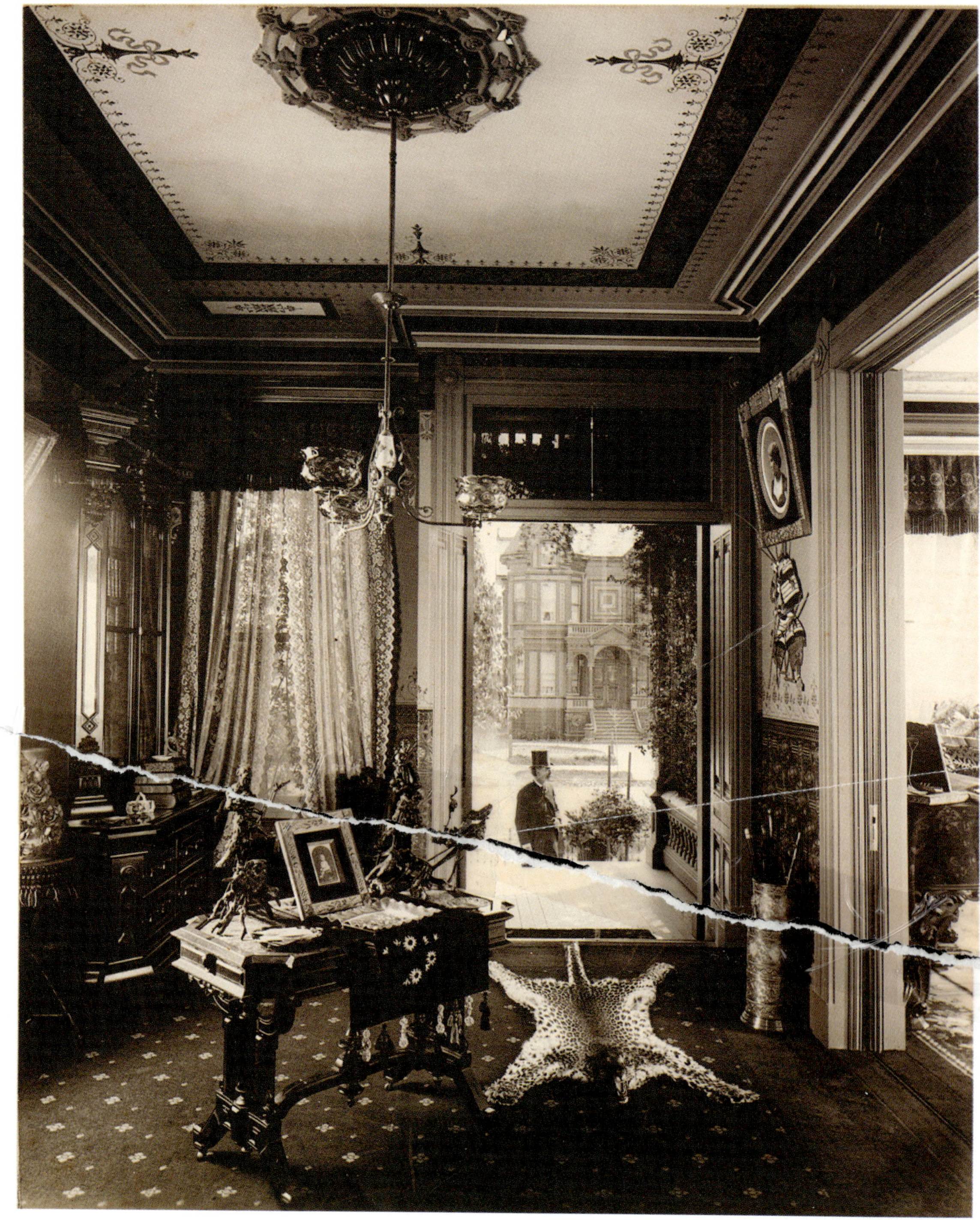

Isaiah Taber outside his front entry hall, 1351 Madison Street, Oakland, c.1884.

CUNEO COLLECTION

MARILYN BLAISDELL COLLECTION

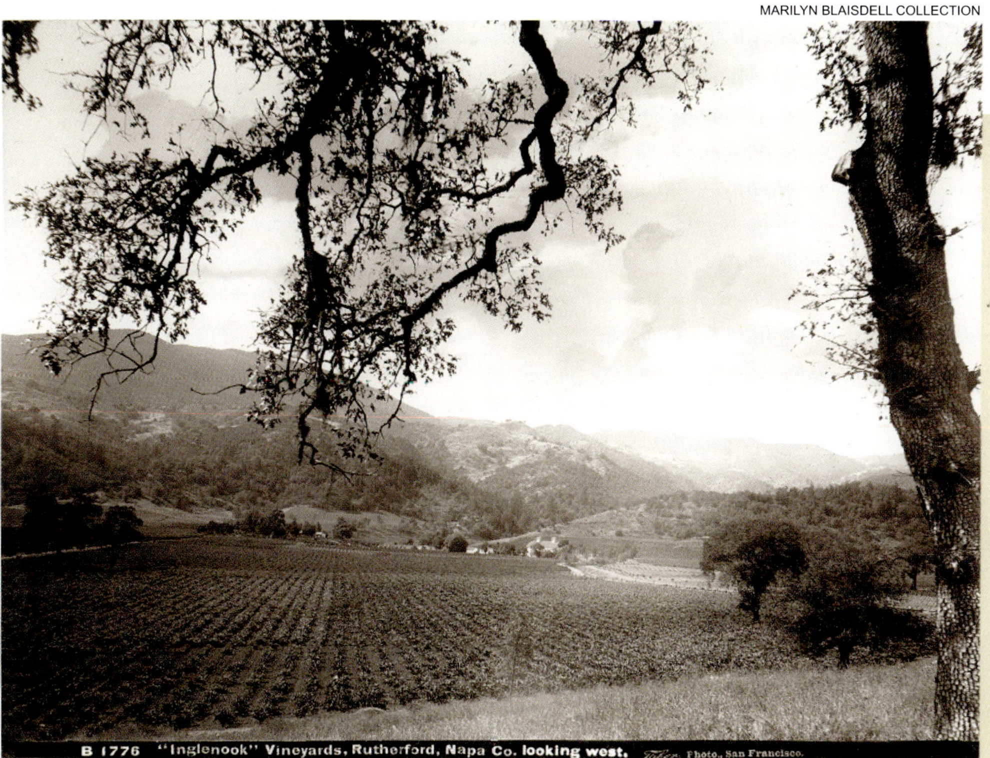

The wineries and vineyards, then as now, reminded visitors of European countrysides. Taber's photographs made ideal souvenirs to take back home. For visitors with little time to take in the sights for themselves, Taber would gladly produce a custom album of scenic views right in his San Francisco gallery.

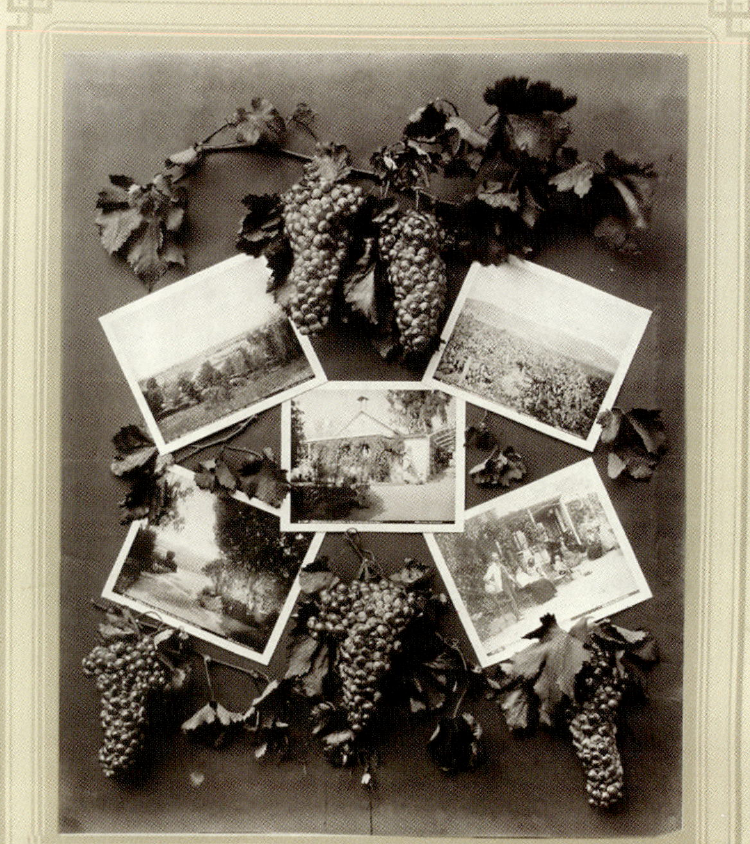

Page from *California Scenery and Industries*, 1884.

CALIFORNIA STATE LIBRARY

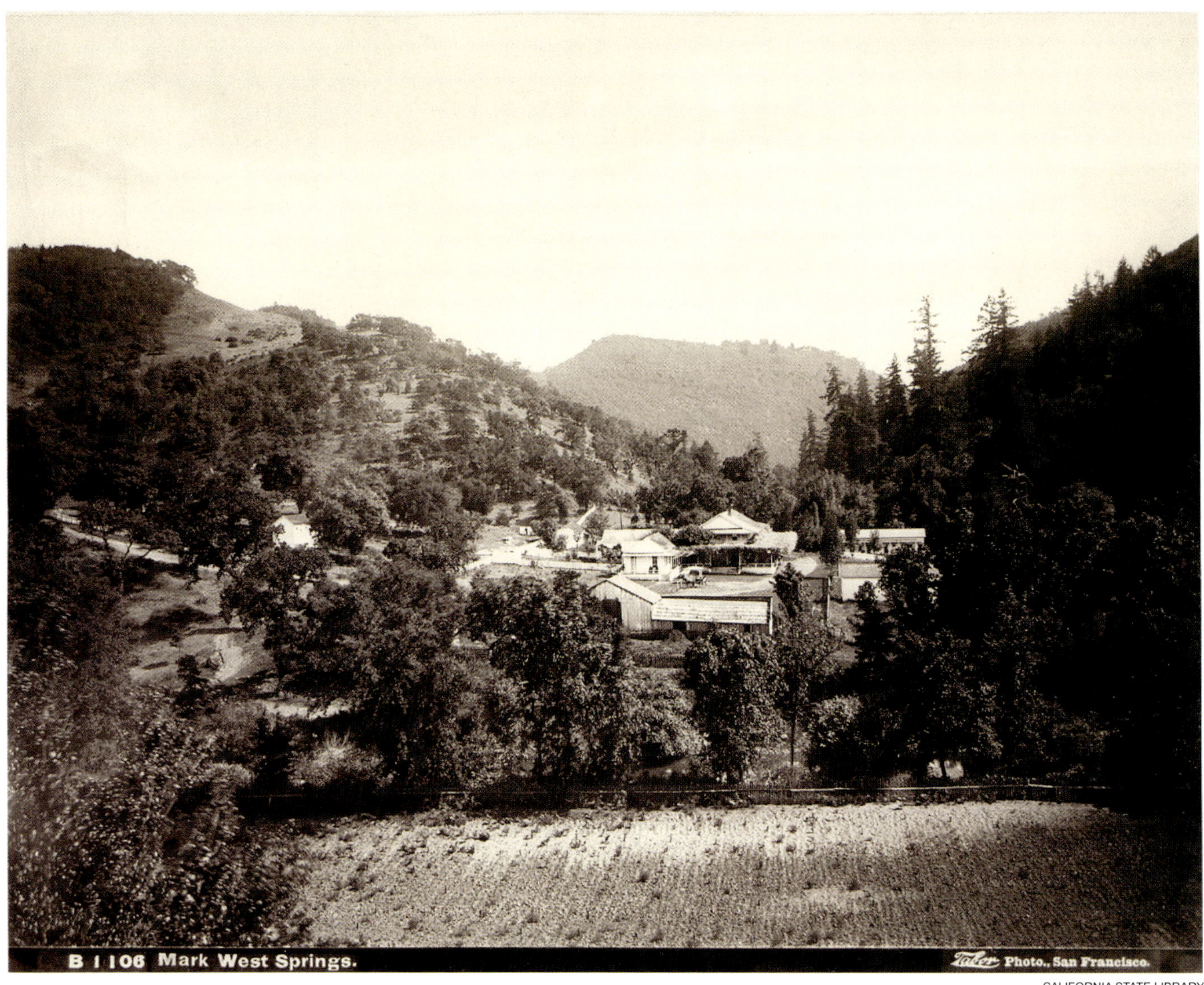

CALIFORNIA STATE LIBRARY

Sonoma County, c. 1883.

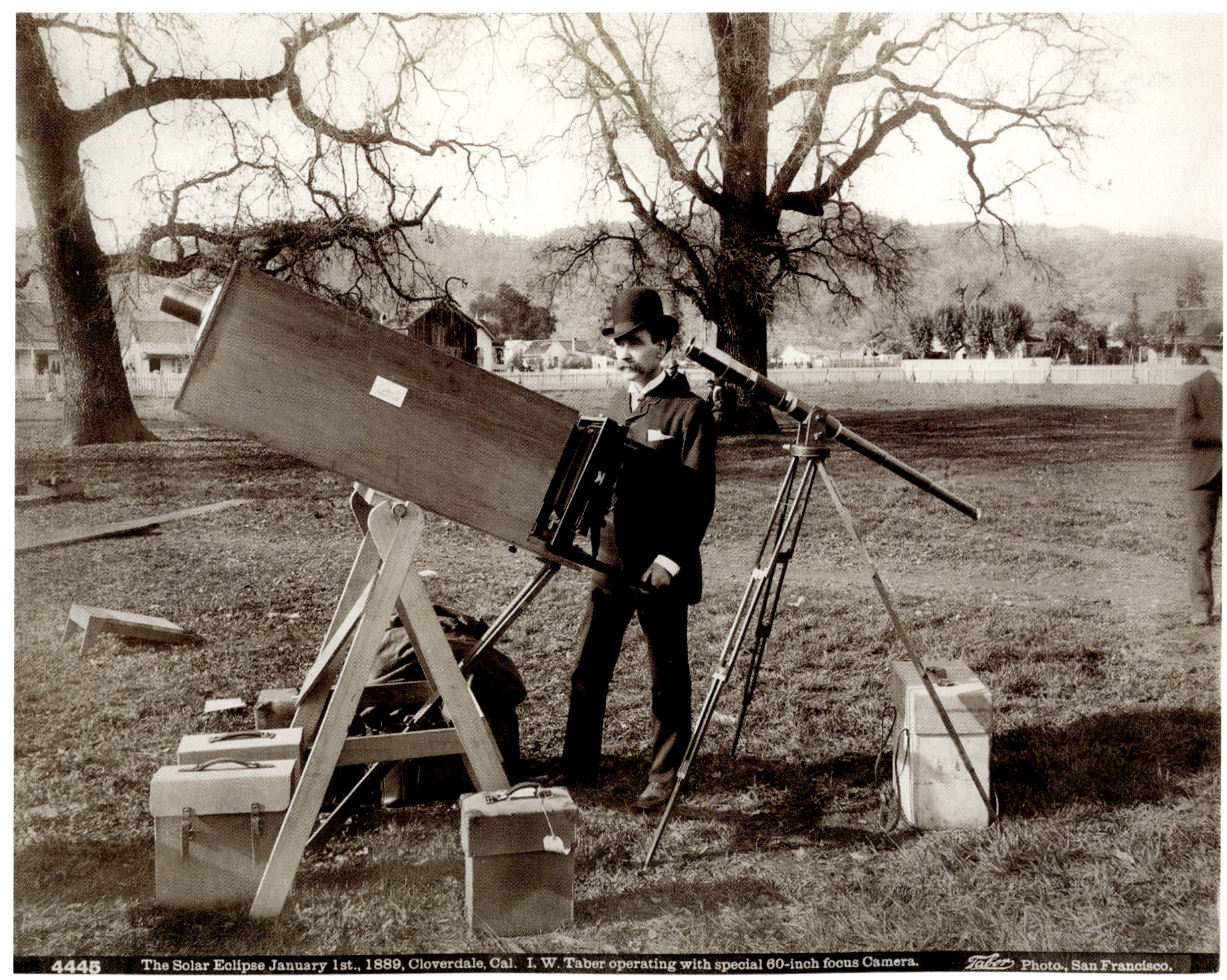

Sonoma County.

CALIFORNIA STATE LIBRARY

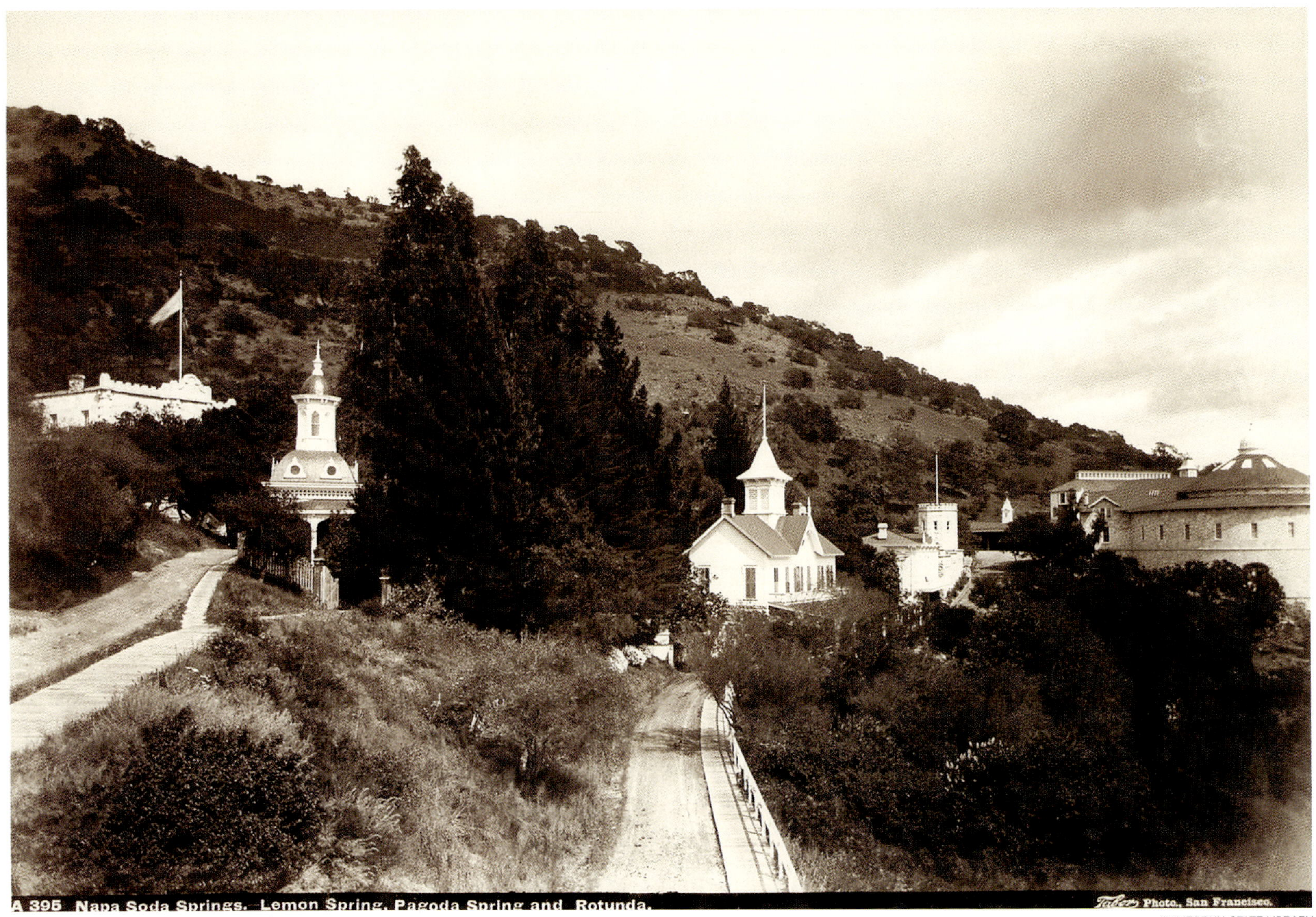

CALIFORNIA STATE LIBRARY

c. 1884

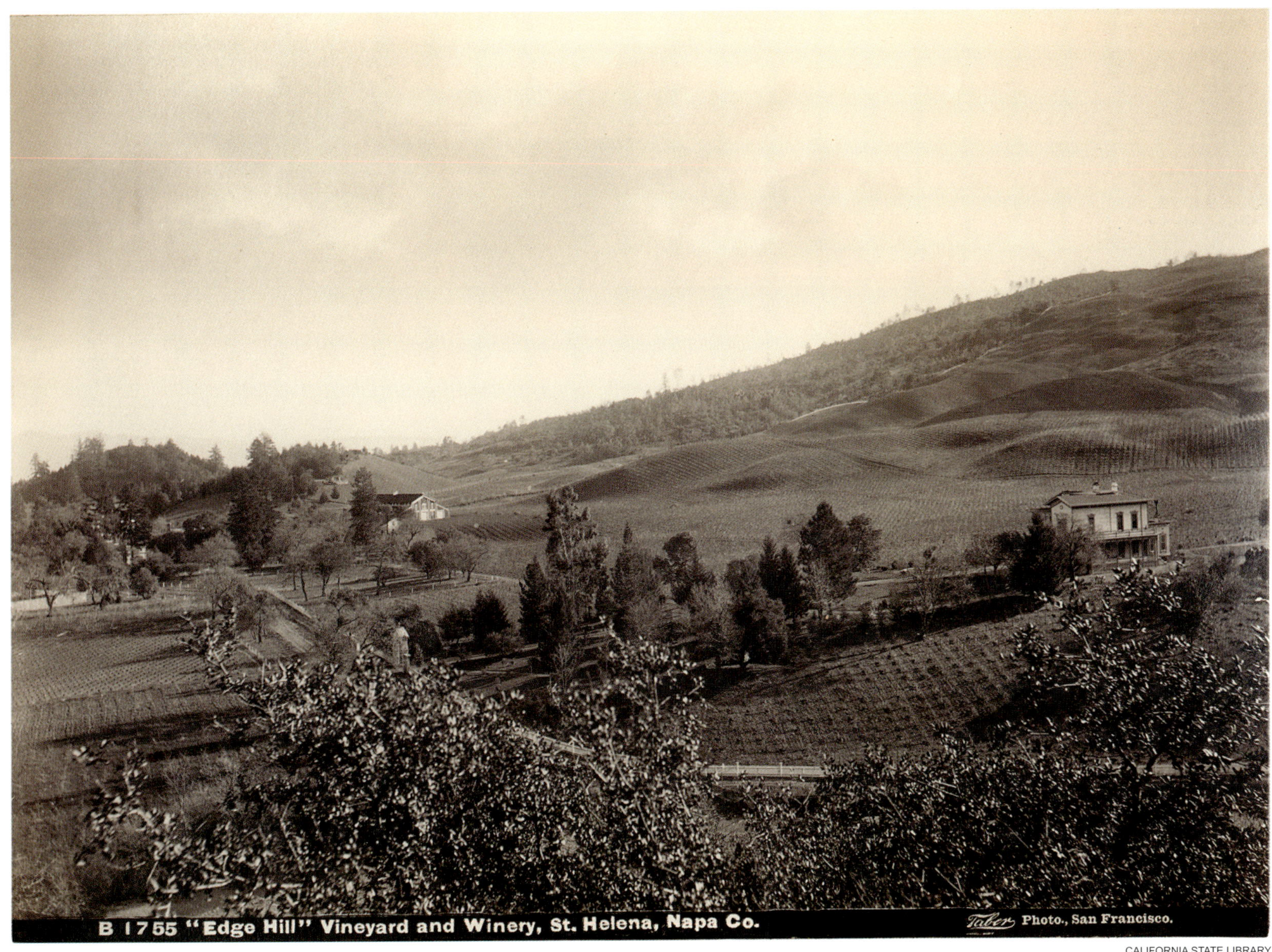

CALIFORNIA STATE LIBRARY

c. 1884

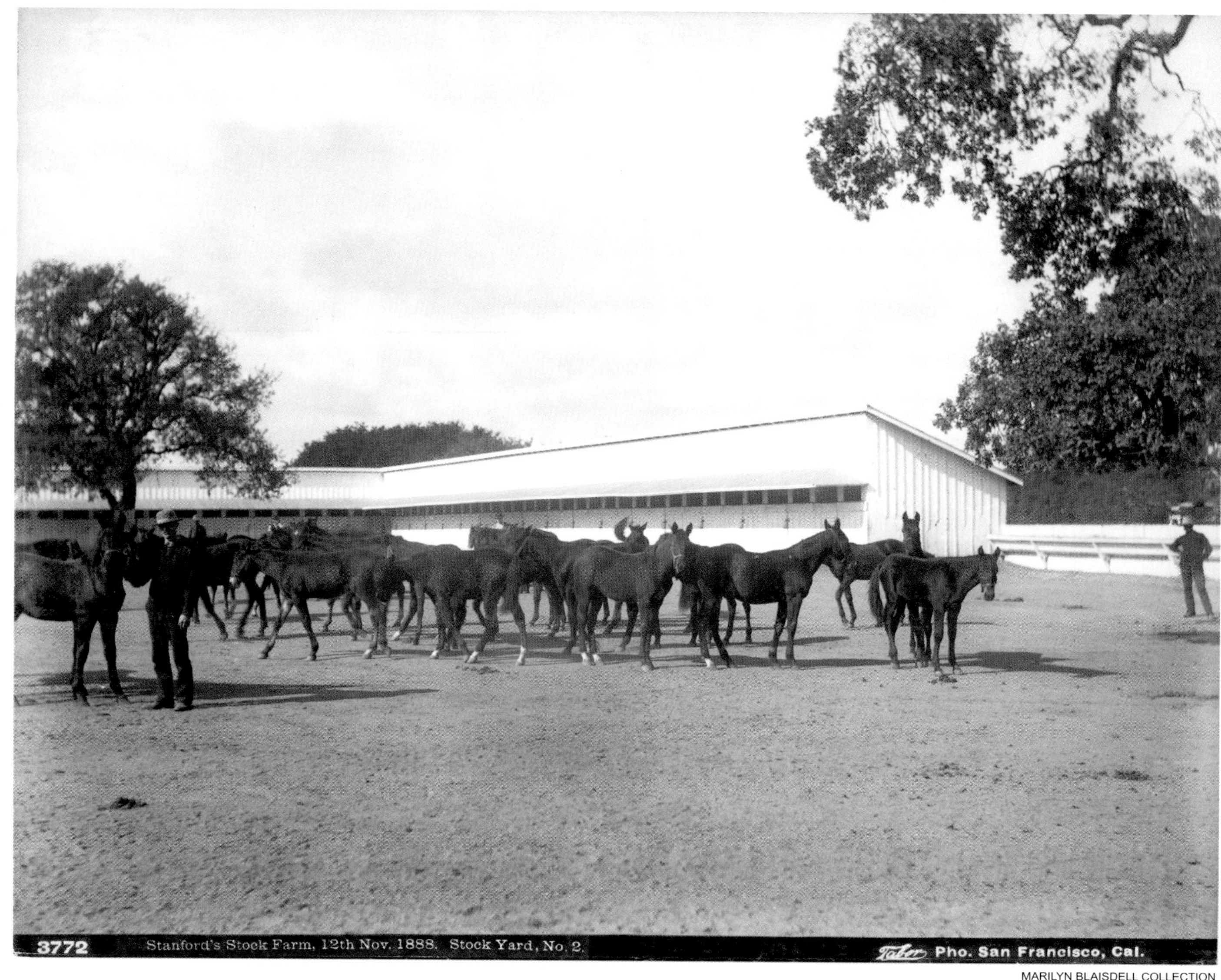

MARILYN BLAISDELL COLLECTION

California's millionaire senator and ex-governor Leland Stanford, president of the Central Pacific Railroad and Southern Pacific Railroad, was also California's leading horse breeder. Fascinated by photography as well as trotting horses, Stanford commissioned Eadweard Muybridge in the late 1870s to devise a way to shoot stop-action photos of his champion racers. The results advanced the science of photography, making stop-action or "instantaneous" photos practical. In the late 1880s after photographing Stanford's home, Taber was invited to photograph Stanford's stock farm, Mayfield Grange, near Palo Alto. The farm later became the site of Stanford University.

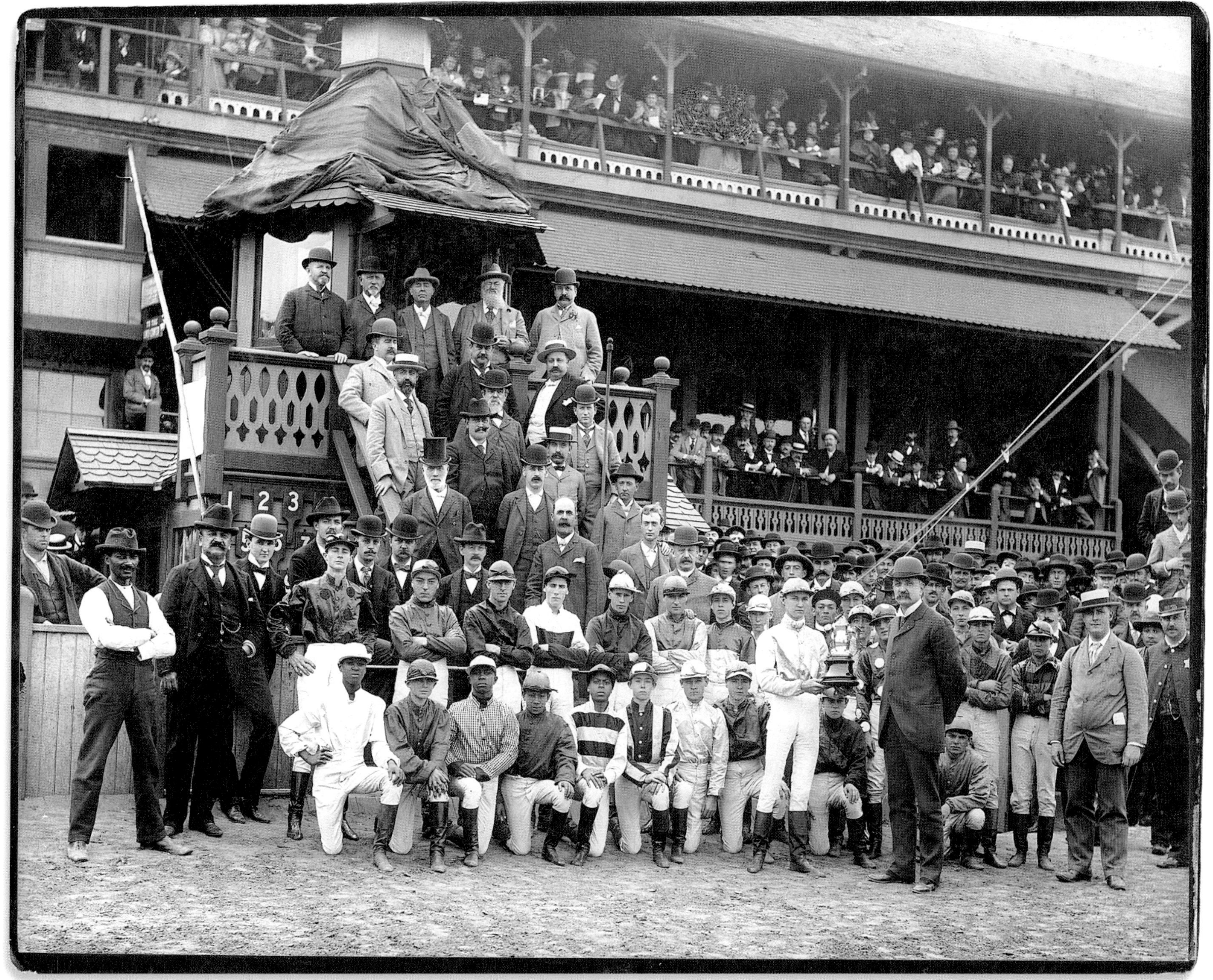

MARILYN BLAISDELL COLLECTION

Portrait of jockeys, track officials and racing fans at the Bay District race track located between First and Fifth Avenues, Anza and Fulton Streets, San Francisco. The popular track opened in 1873 and closed May 27, 1896, the day Taber made this photograph. An intriguing mystery: Two figures in upper balcony, center, have been obliterated by a retoucher, presumably so they cannot be recognized.

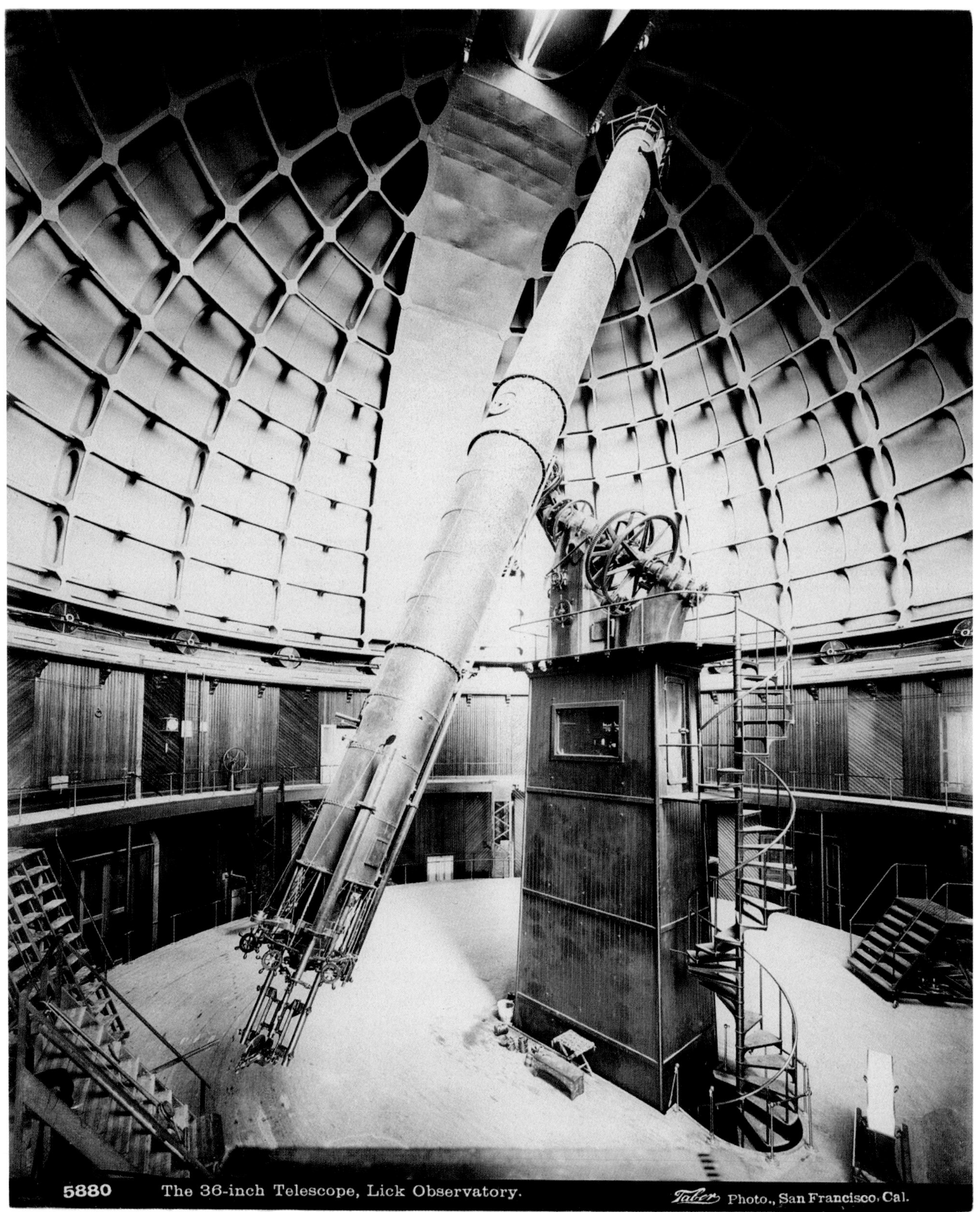

MARILYN BLAISDELL COLLECTION

Taber's interest in all things mechanical led him in 1887 to Mount Hamilton above San Jose for installation of the 36-inch telescope at Lick Observatory. The observatory was financed by San Francisco real estate tycoon James Lick, a notorious tightwad, who in his old age became a generous benefactor. Lick is entombed beneath the telescope's concrete foundation.

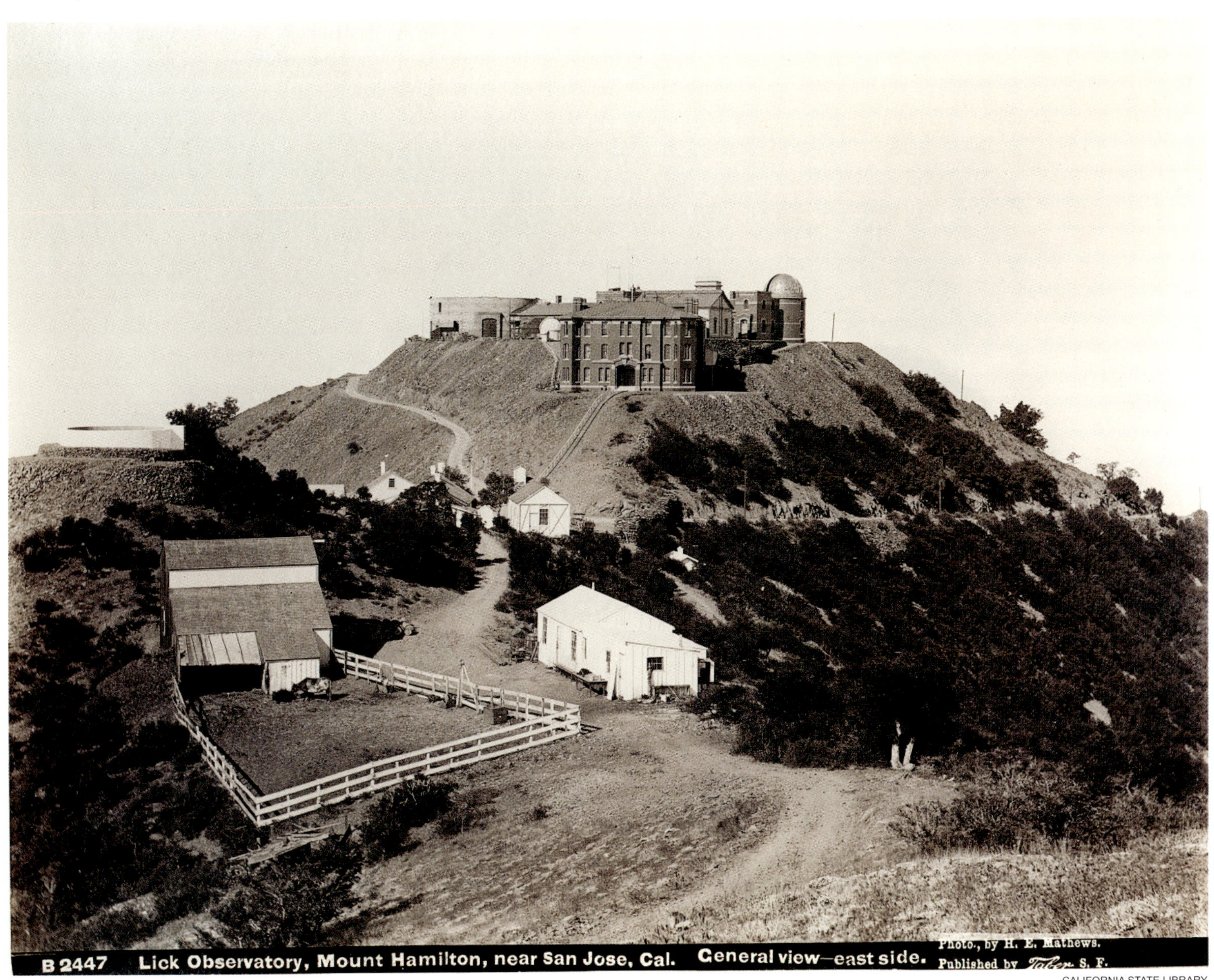

CALIFORNIA STATE LIBRARY

A rare example of photograph published by Taber Photographic Art Gallery with a credit line by another photographer. C.1886.

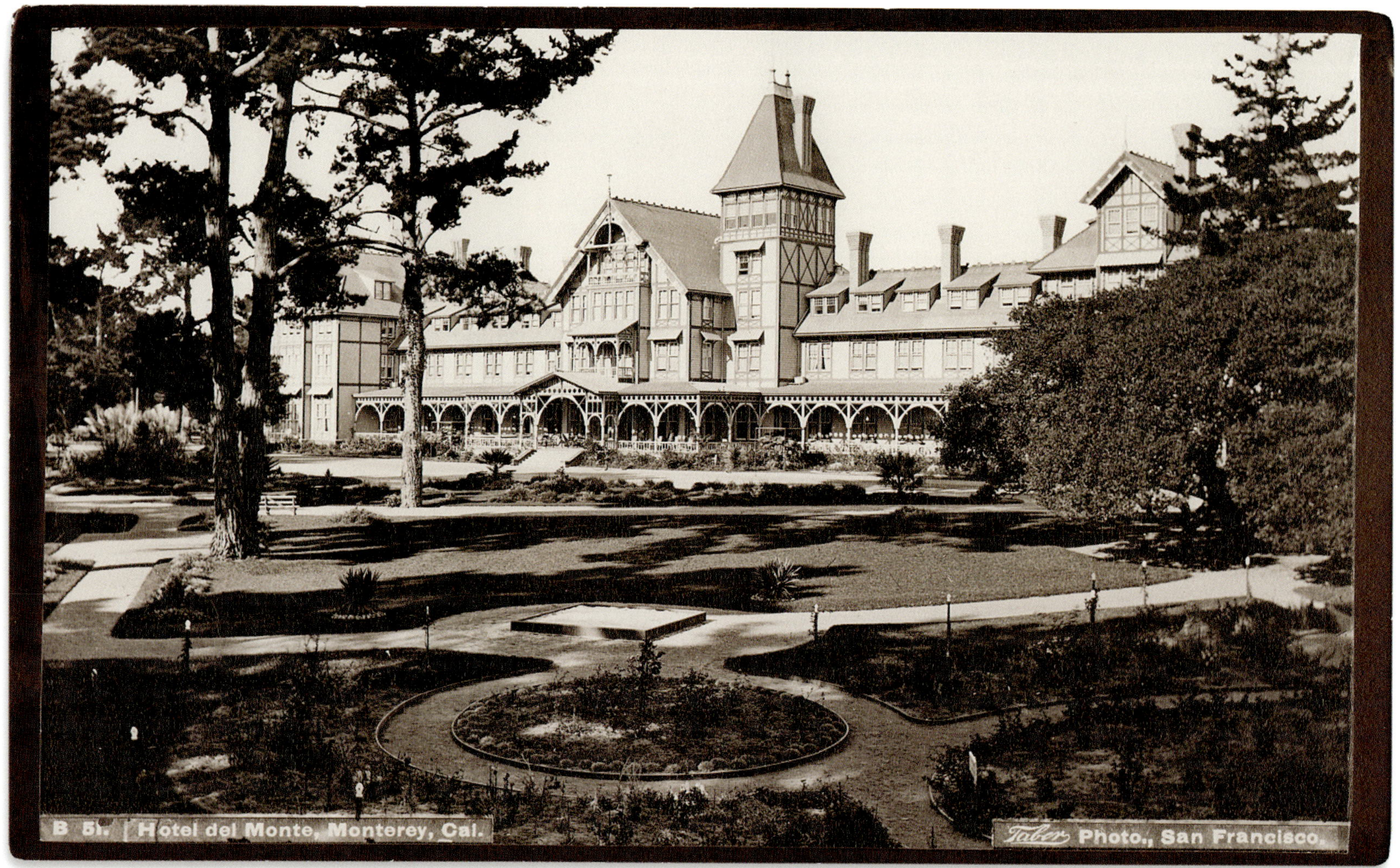

MARILYN BLAISDELL COLLECTION

Taber offered current photos of the major resort hotels in California. Monterey's Del Monte Hotel, built in 1880 by the Southern Pacific Company, was perhaps the most famous, and Taber made repeated visits. He photographed not only the hotel and grounds but made portraits on the spot of visiting celebrities, some of whom arrived by private railway car.

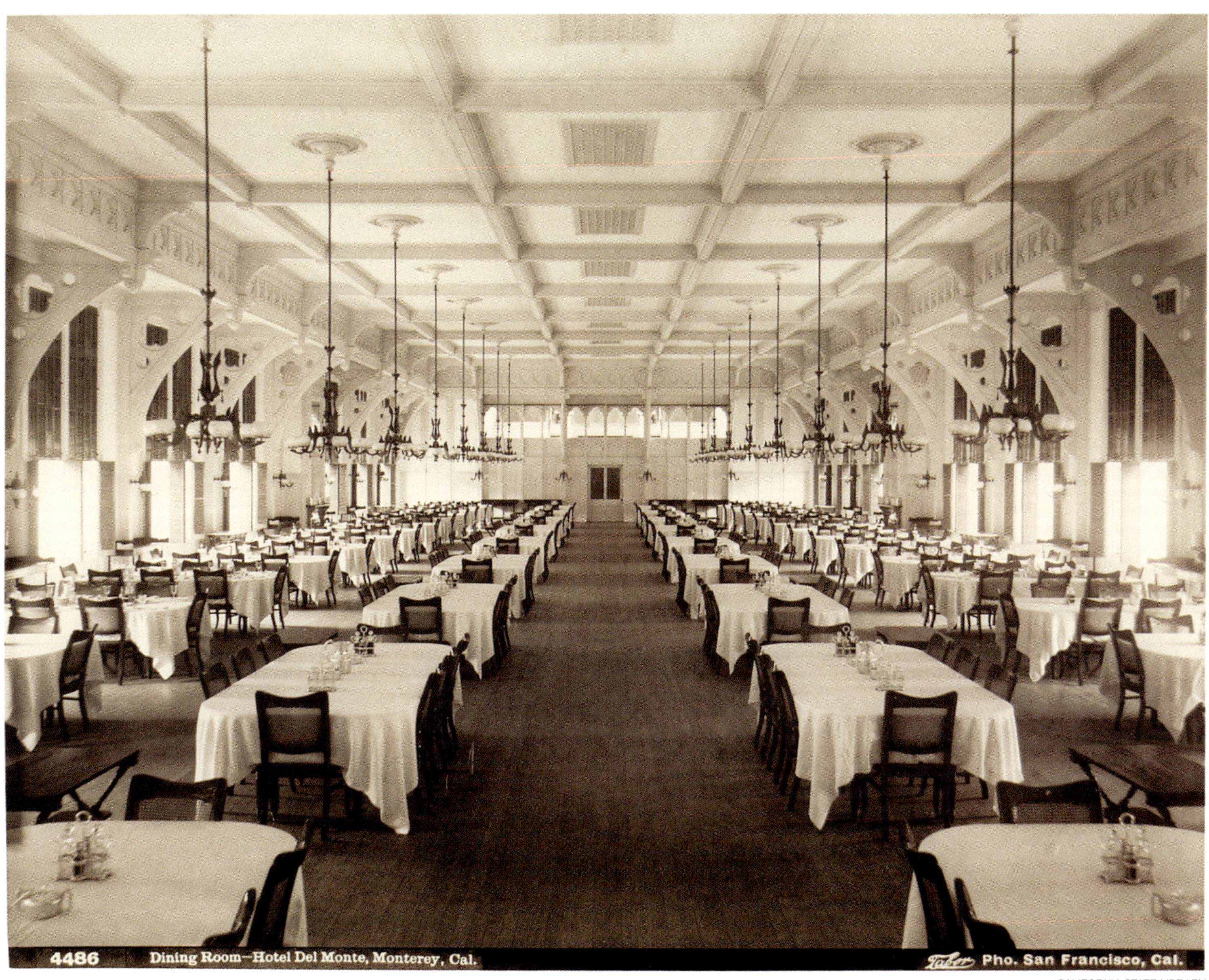

c. 1884

CALIFORNIA STATE LIBRARY

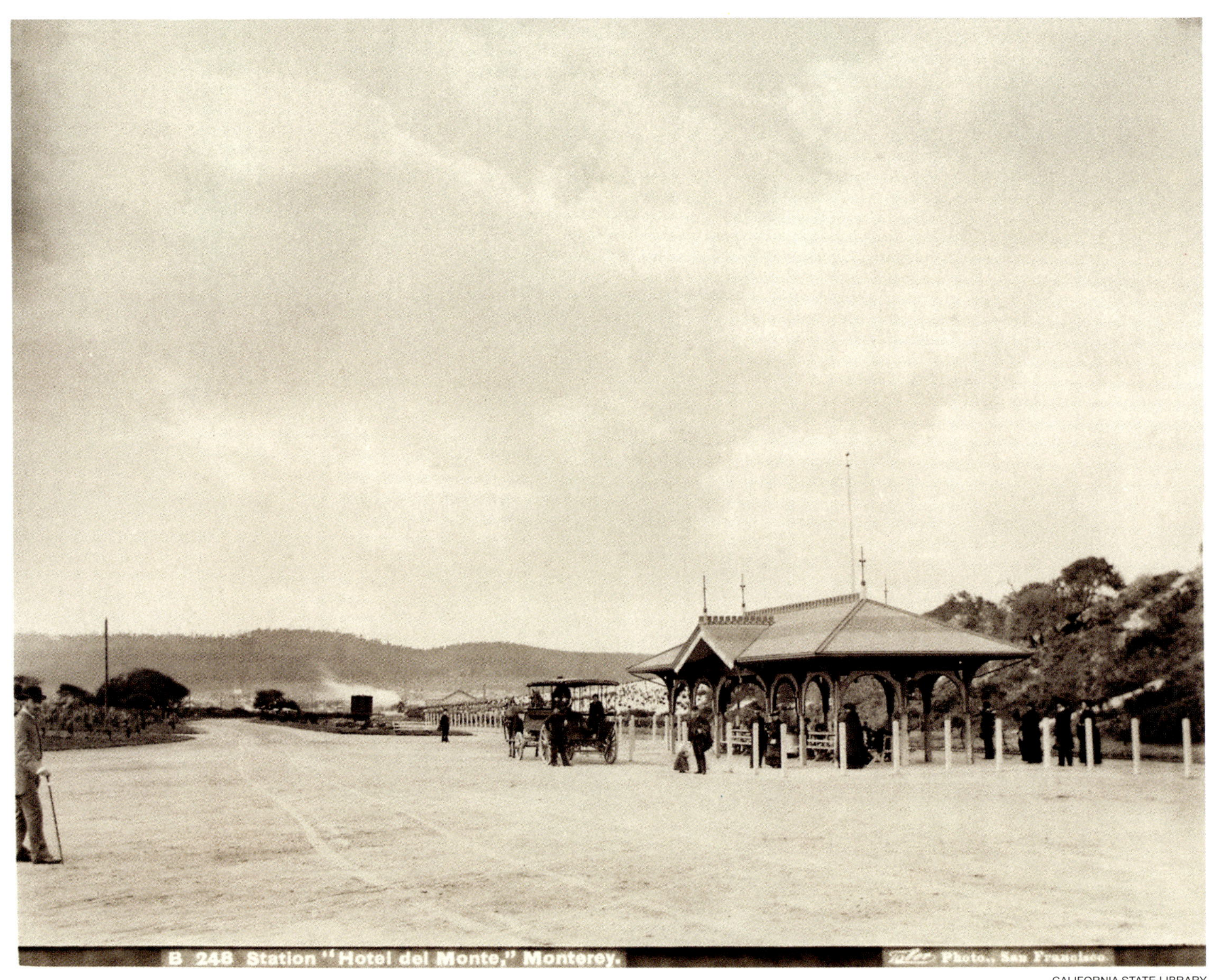

CALIFORNIA STATE LIBRARY

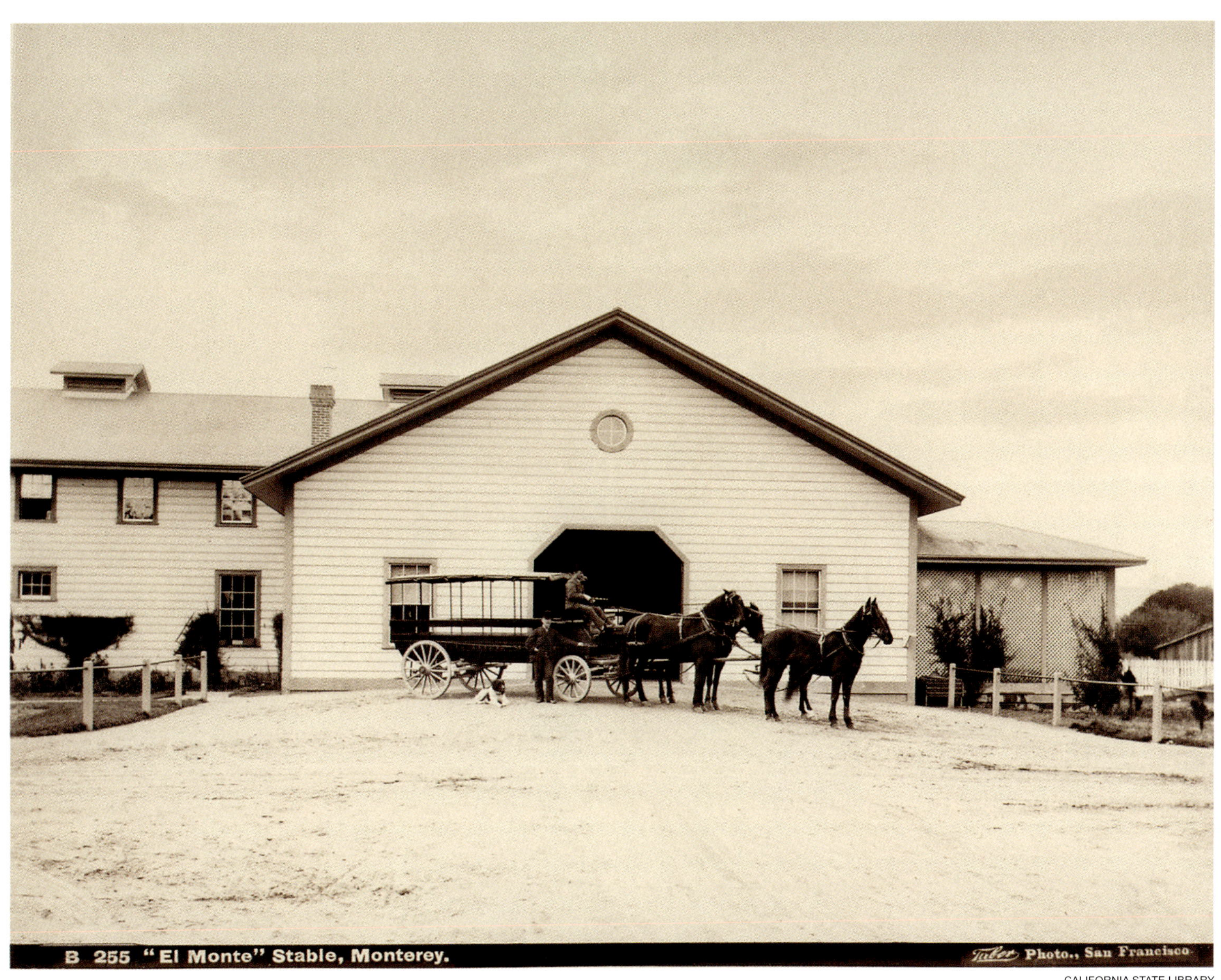

CALIFORNIA STATE LIBRARY

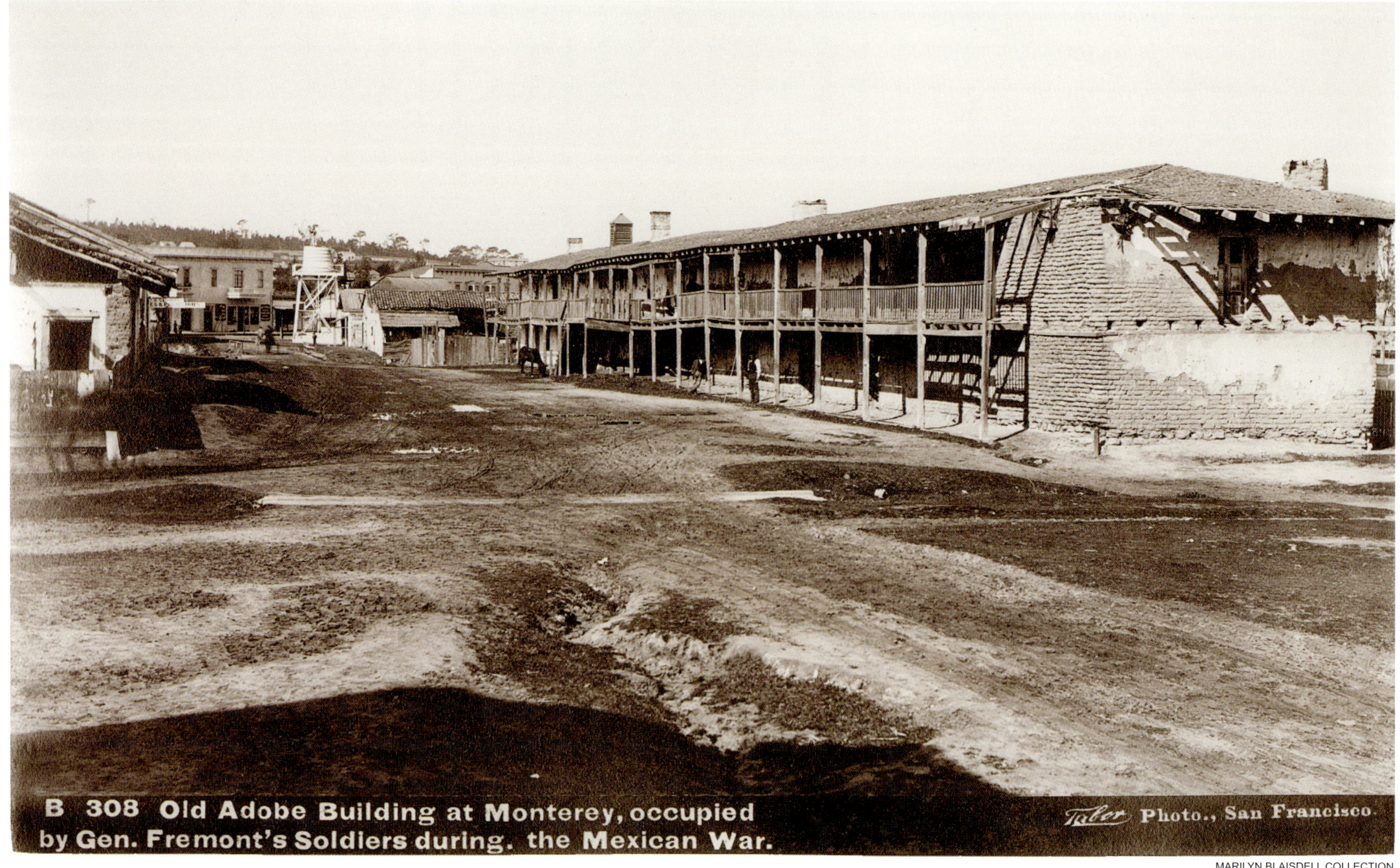

MARILYN BLAISDELL COLLECTION

El Cuartel, or military barracks, above, was built in 1840 by the governor of Mexican California, Juan Bautista Alvarado. The Monterey peninsula abounded in historic sites and Isaiah Taber, keen on California history, found them irresistible. Many of the old buildings and Spanish missions had fallen into picturesque decay, and, as such, became popular subjects for artists and photographers. Renewed interest in the 1880s led to protection and restoration of the old landmarks.

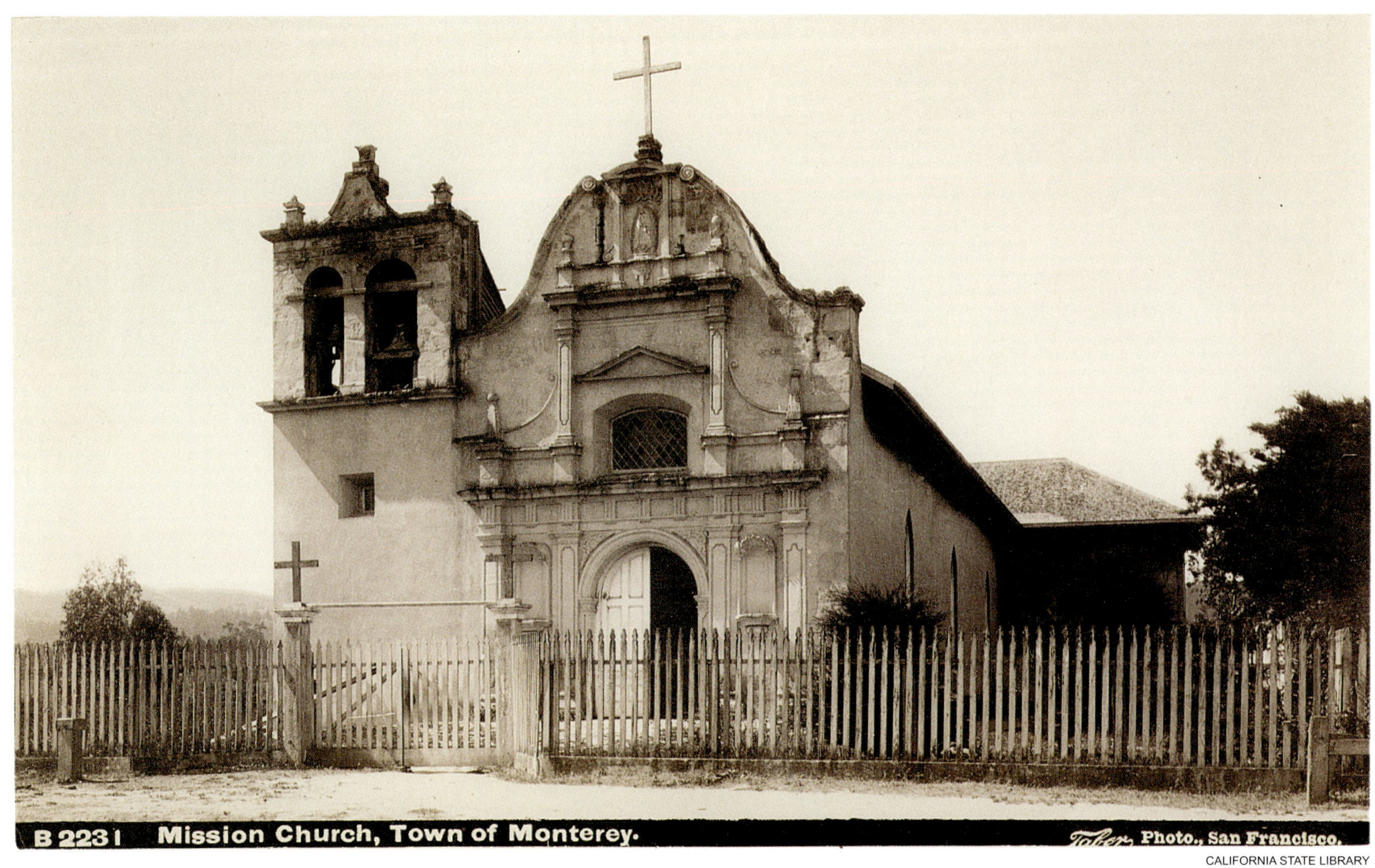

CALIFORNIA STATE LIBRARY

Royal San Carlos Chapel, designed in 1791, photographed by Taber around 1885.

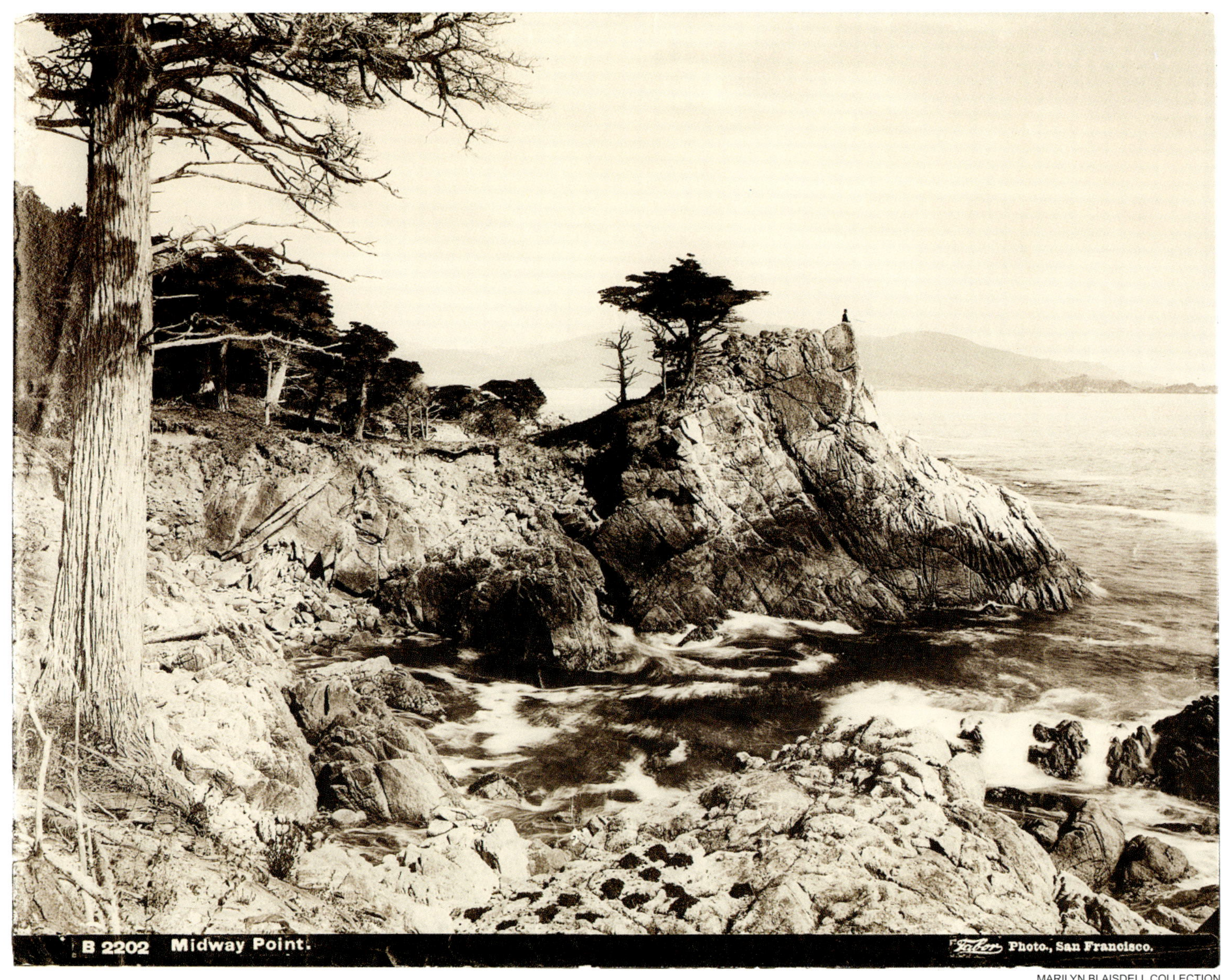

MARILYN BLAISDELL COLLECTION

c. 1884

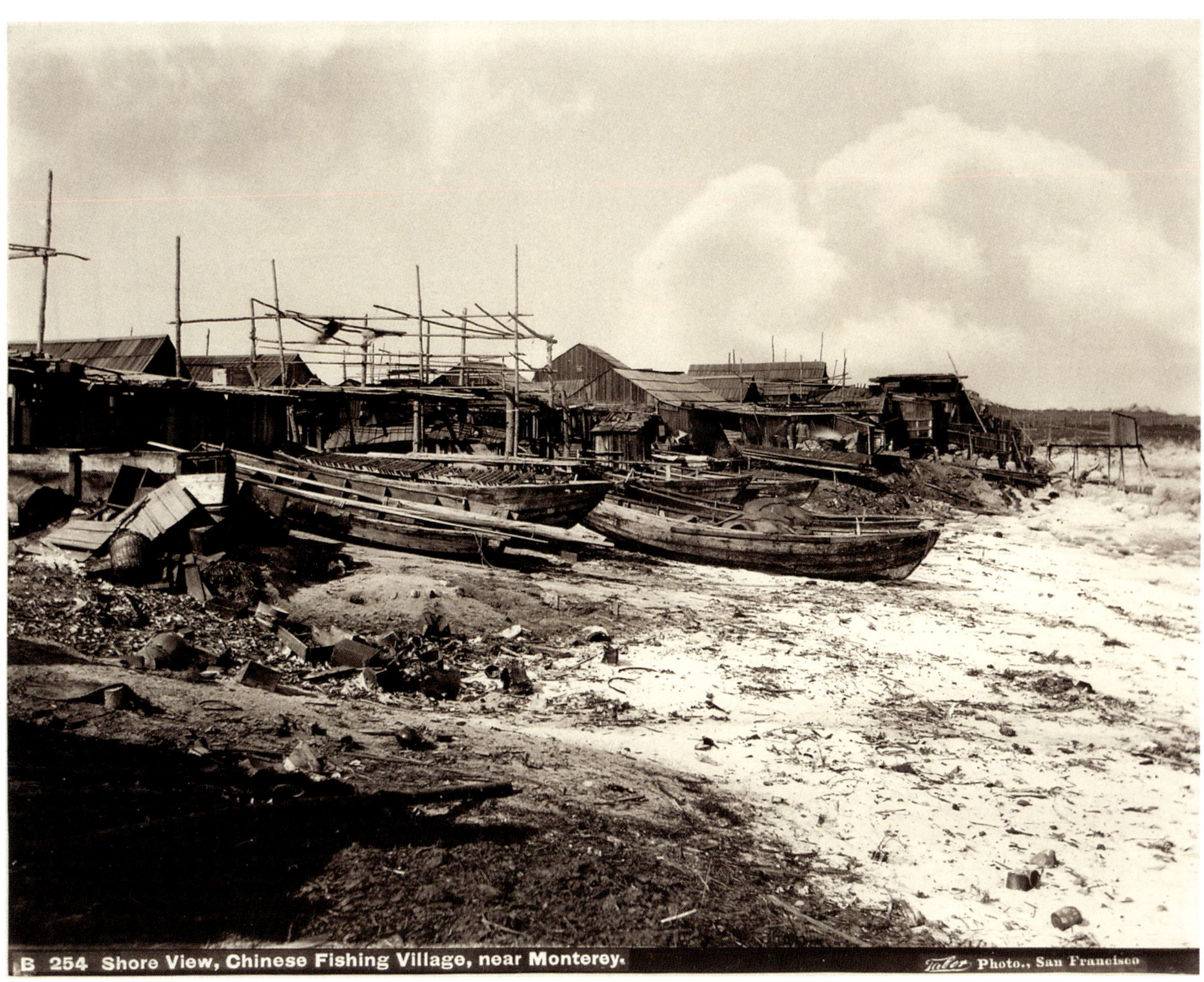

c. 1884

CALIFORNIA STATE LIBRARY

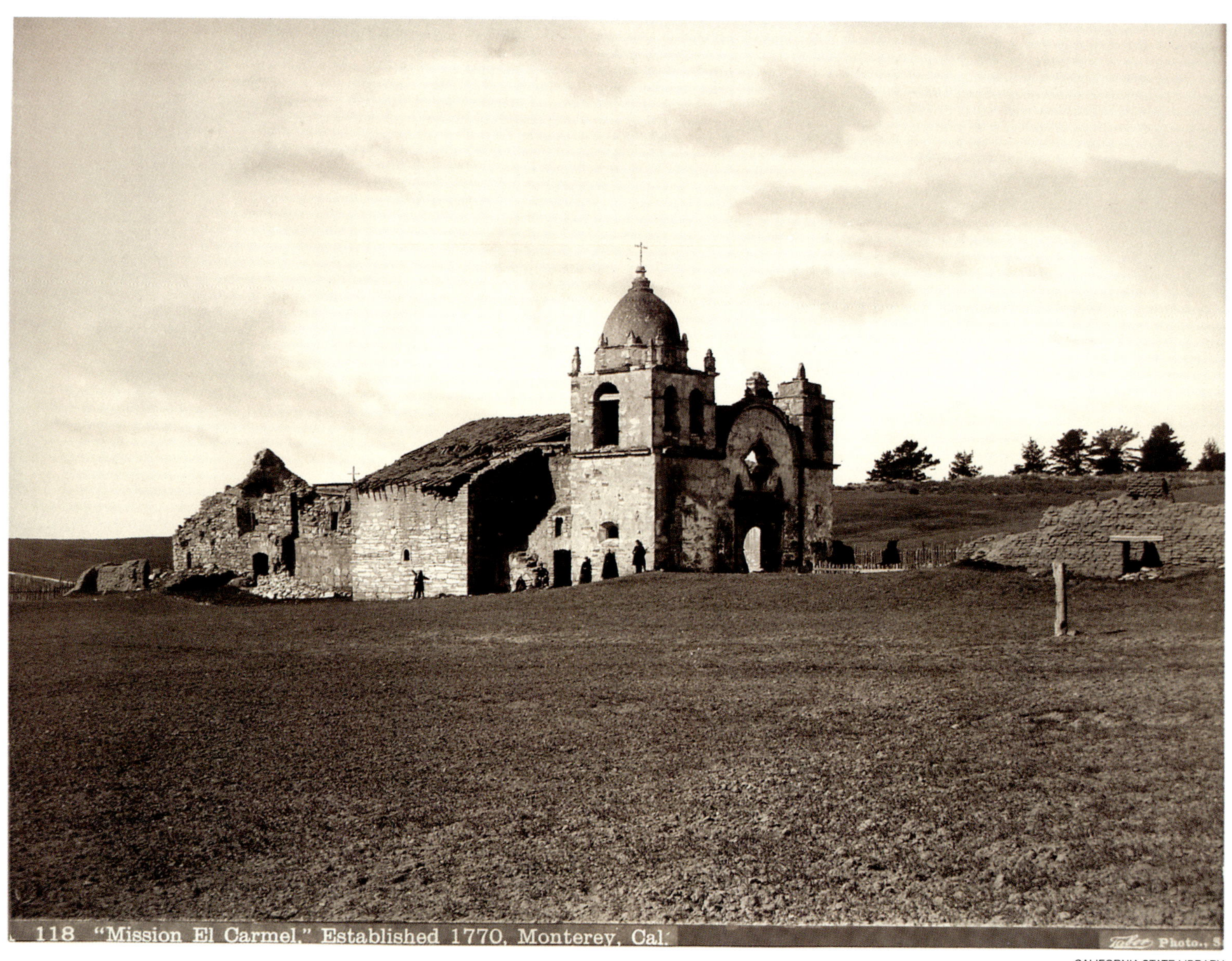

CALIFORNIA STATE LIBRARY

Mission San Carlos Borromeo de Carmelo, around 1882 before a new roof was added to protect the ruins. The church and sacristy shown above were built between 1793 and 1798.

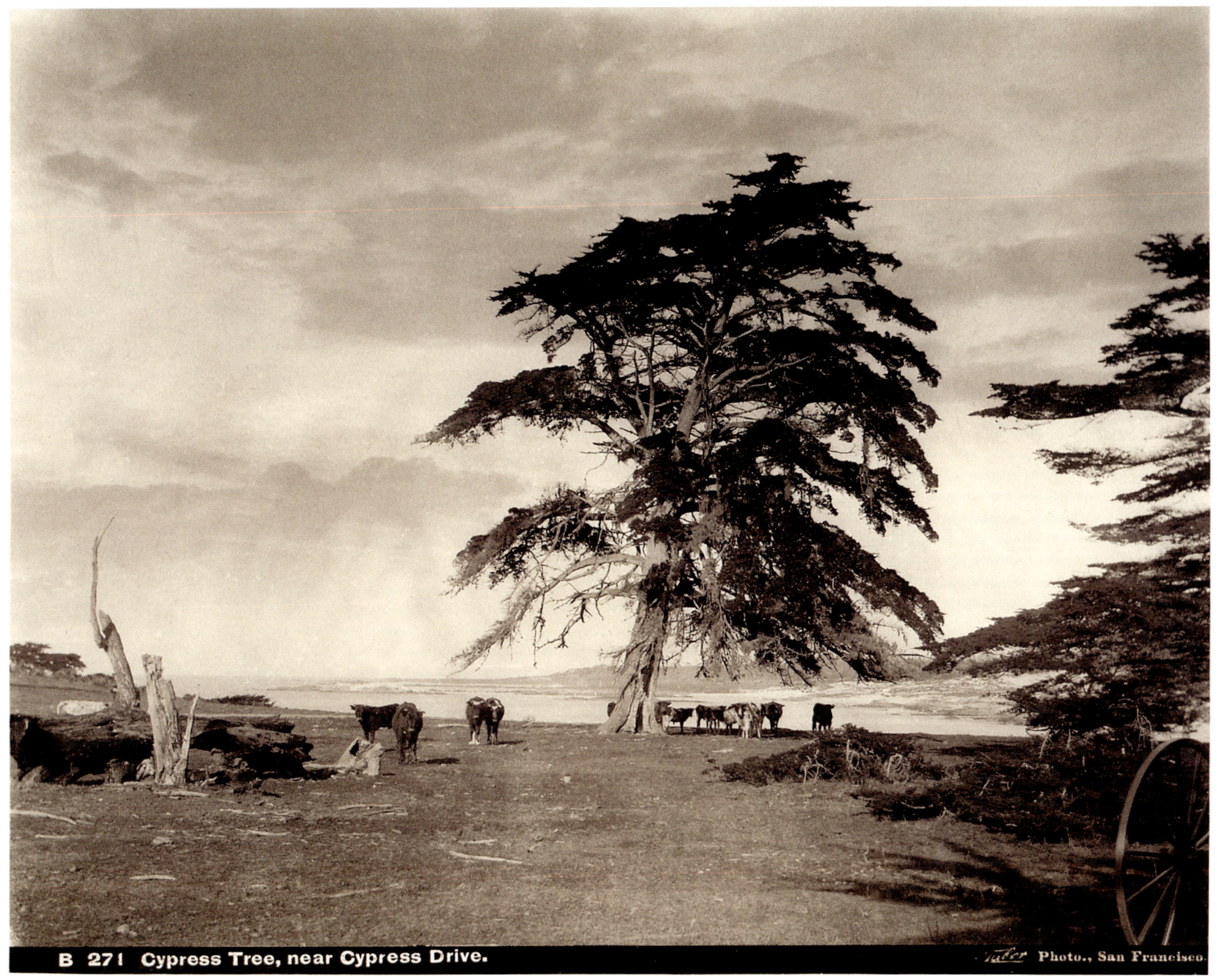

c. 1885

CALIFORNIA STATE LIBRARY

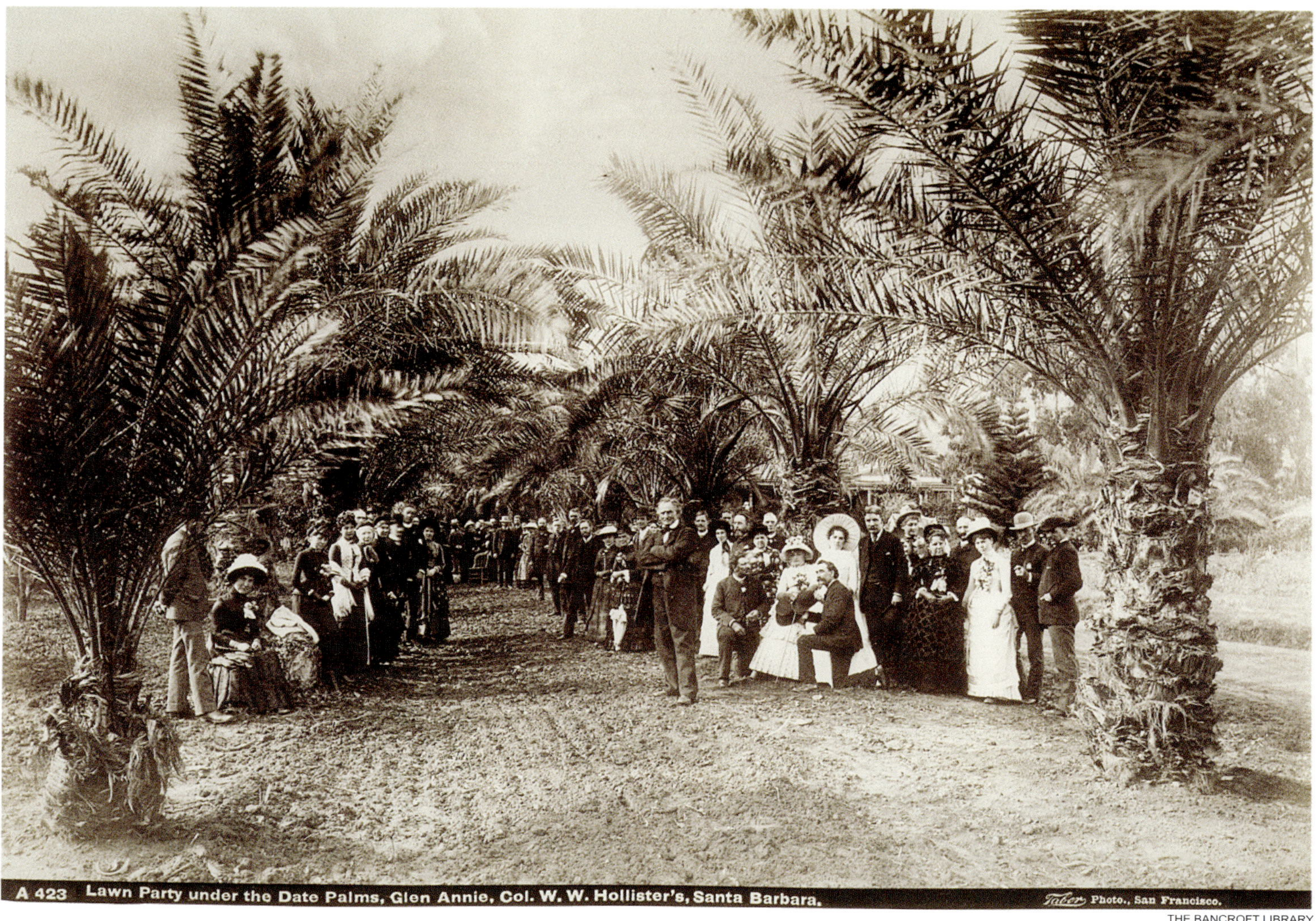

THE BANCROFT LIBRARY

While on a photo excursion to Southern California in April, 1885, Isaiah Taber was invited to stay with William Hollister at Glen Annie, his home near Gaviota in Santa Barbara County. Hollister, a pioneer rancher and namesake of the town of Hollister in San Benito County, is the tall man at center. Taber is kneeling to his left in front of the voluminous-skirted lady in white. He is holdinga remote cable release, partially visible on the ground, leading to his camera. Hollister, besides raising sheep and fruit trees, built a vacation resort at Santa Barbara, the Arlington House, shown at right.

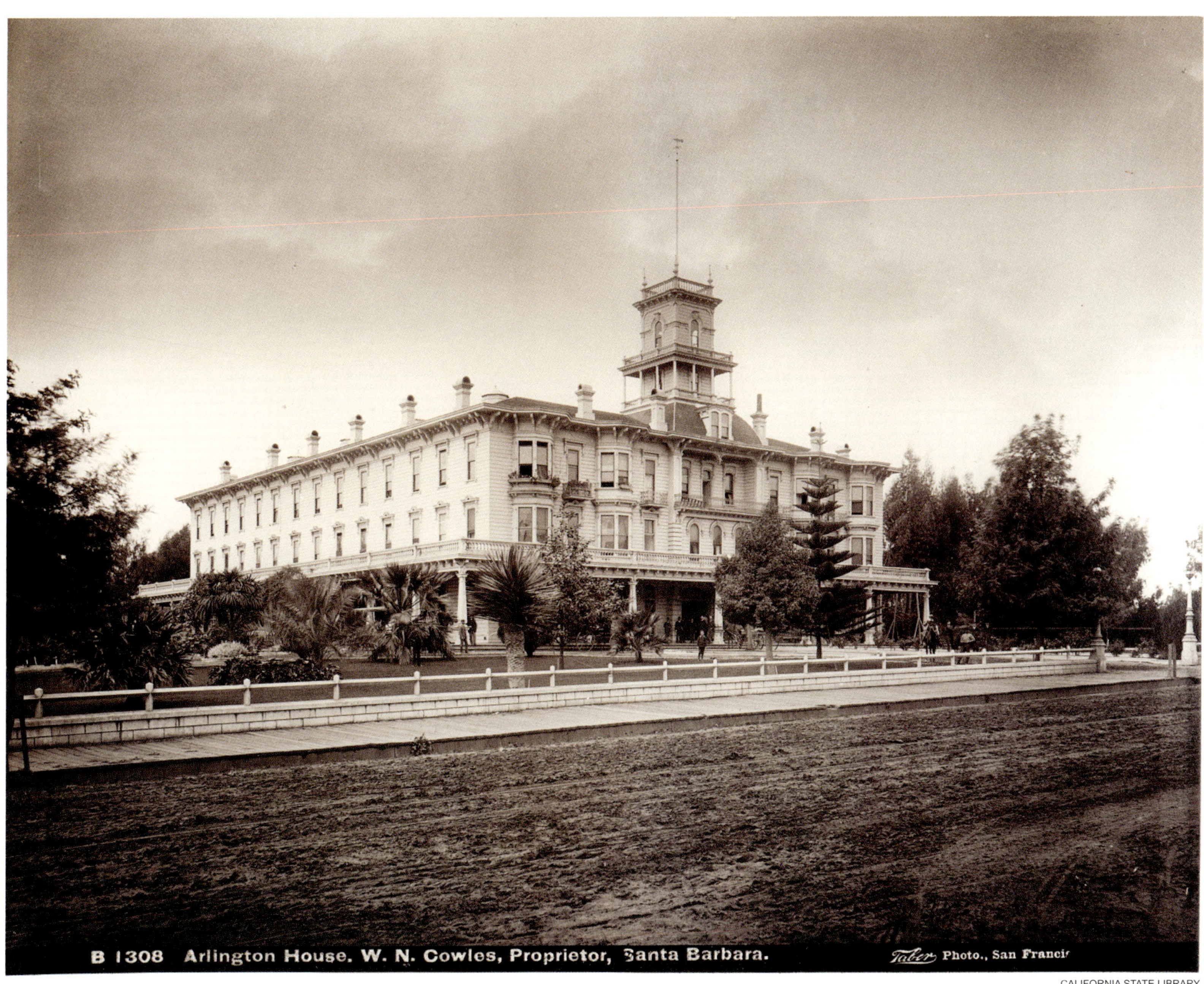

CALIFORNIA STATE LIBRARY

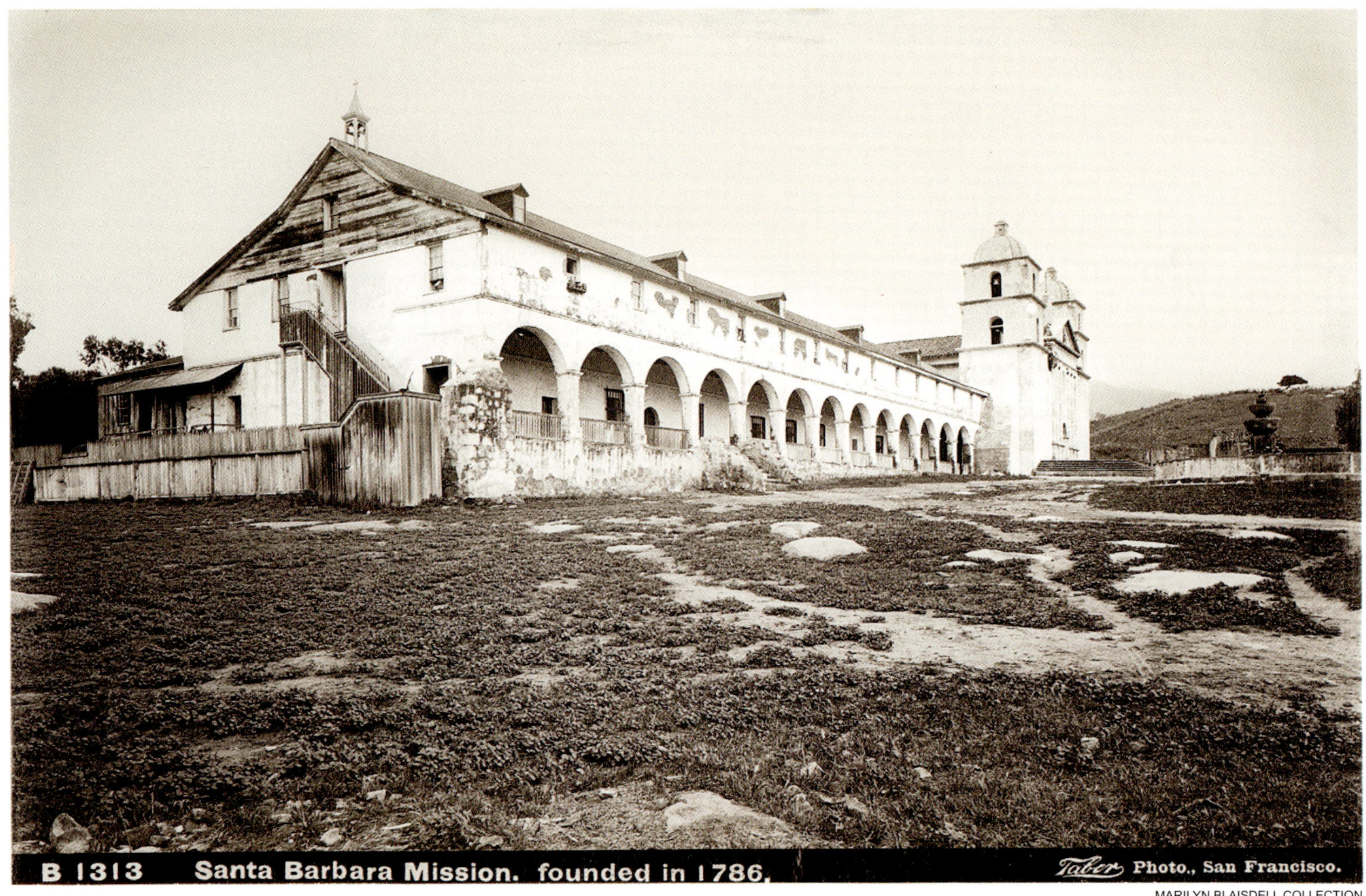

MARILYN BLAISDELL COLLECTION

The monastery wing of Mission Santa Barbara, c.1885.

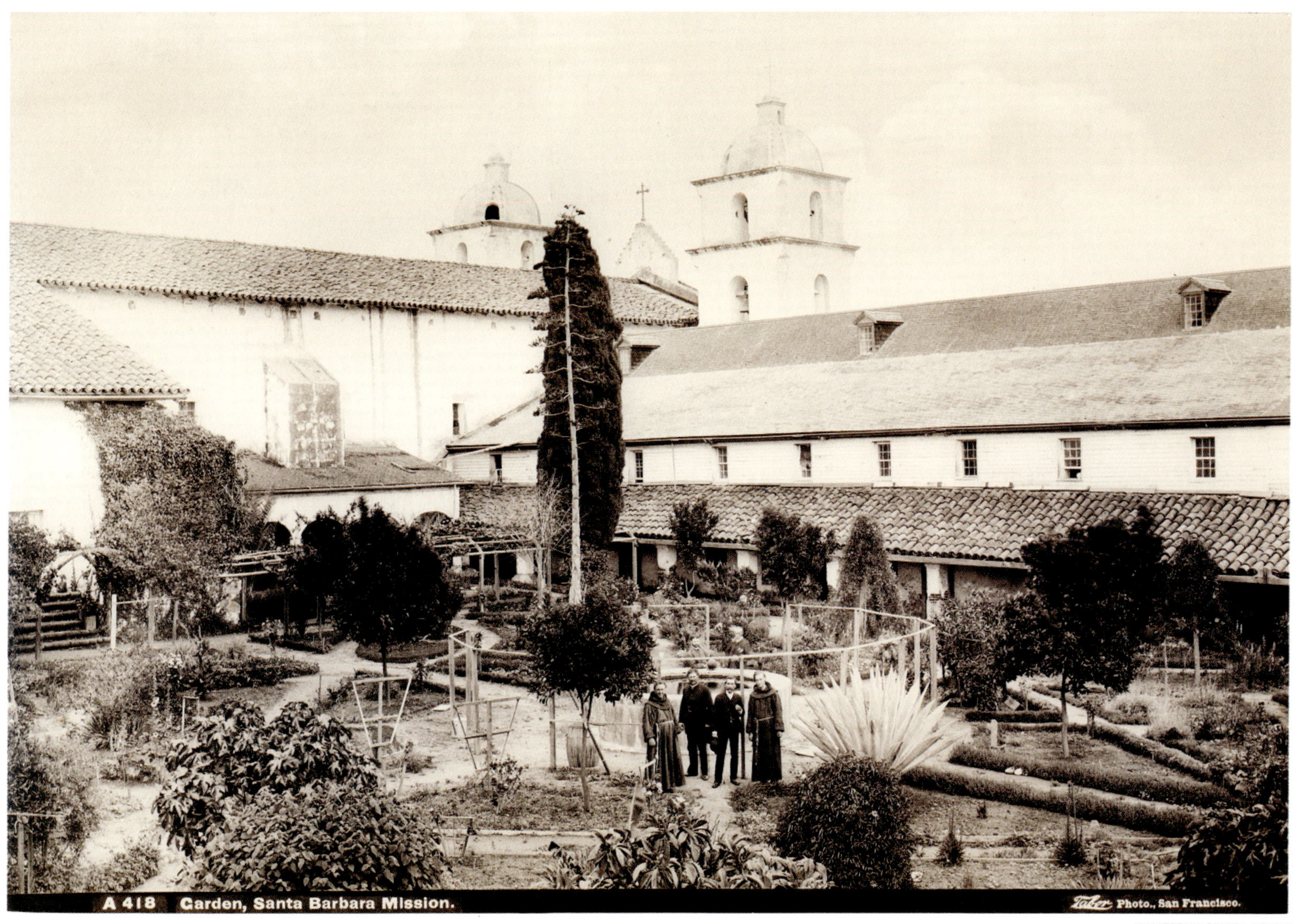

CALIFORNIA STATE LIBRARY

Isaiah Taber, second from right, with church officials, c.1885. Wherever Taber traveled in California, he sought out and photographed pioneers. Often he wrote biographical sketches or persuaded the pioneers to write details in their own hand.

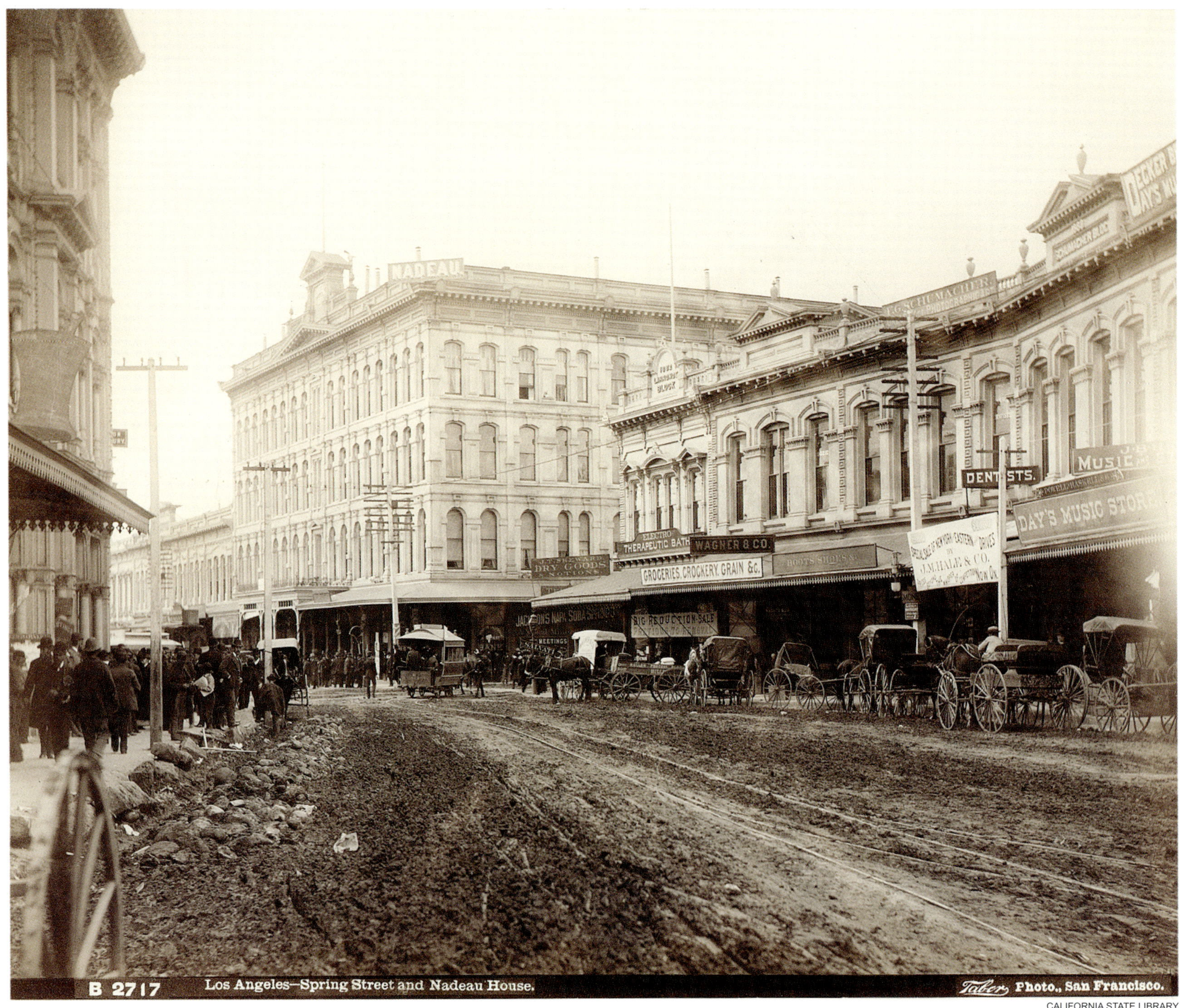

CALIFORNIA STATE LIBRARY

Two views of Los Angeles in the mid-1880s, when Spring Street was the commercial heart of the city. In the scene above, taken when street improvements were under way, a temporary horsecar track sprawls across the muddy street.

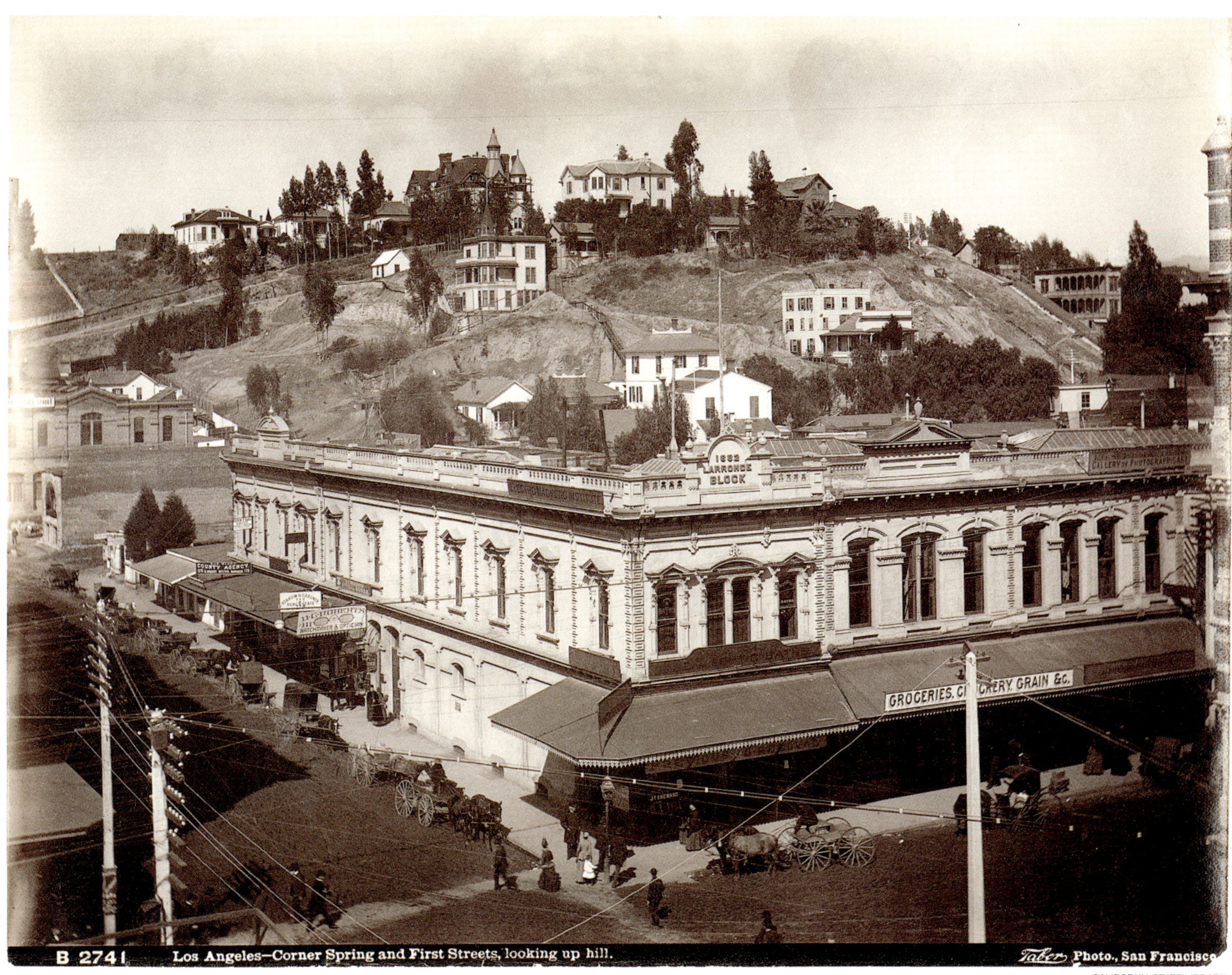

B 2741 Los Angeles—Corner Spring and First Streets, looking up hill. Taber Photo., San Francisco

CALIFORNIA STATE LIBRARY

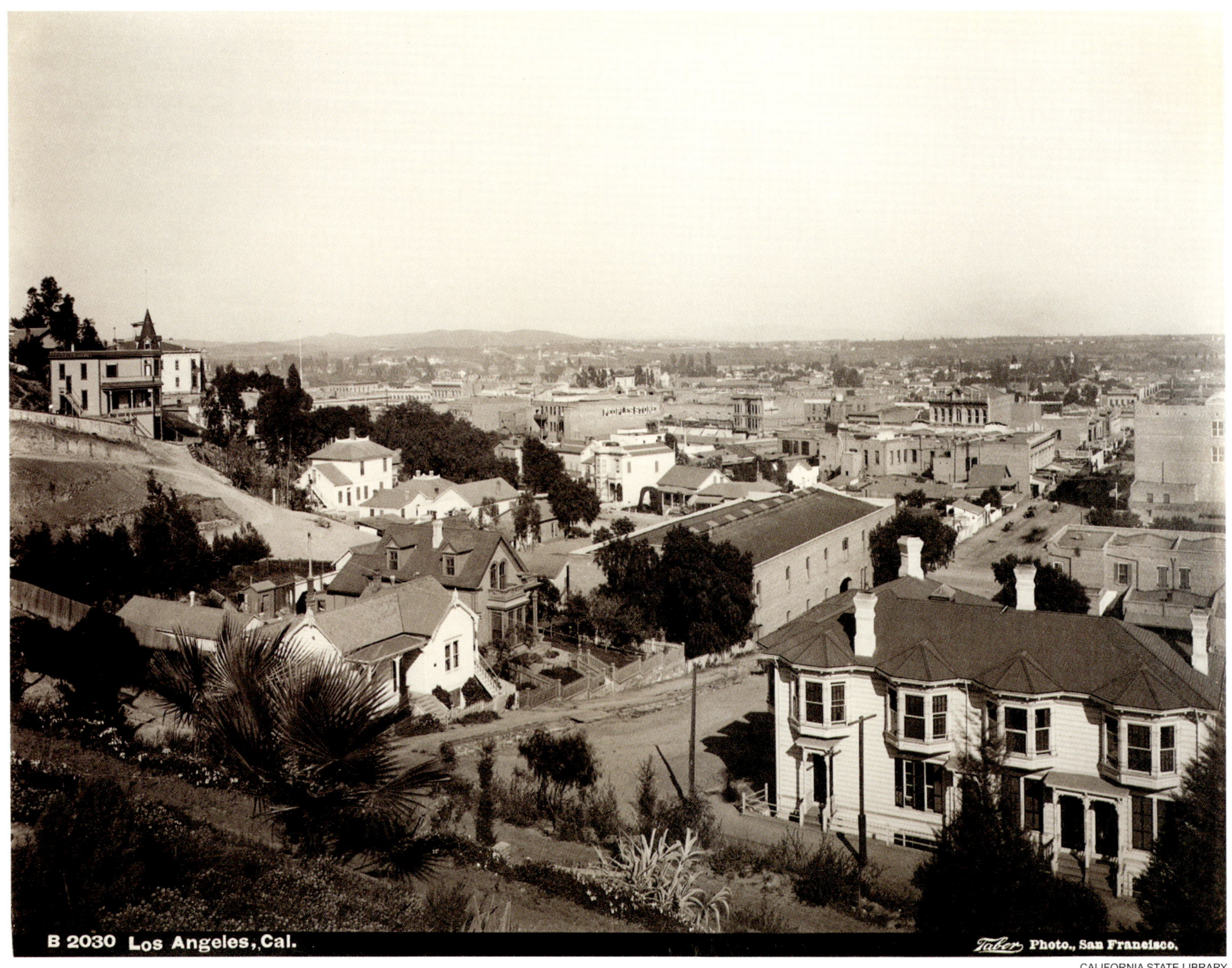

CALIFORNIA STATE LIBRARY

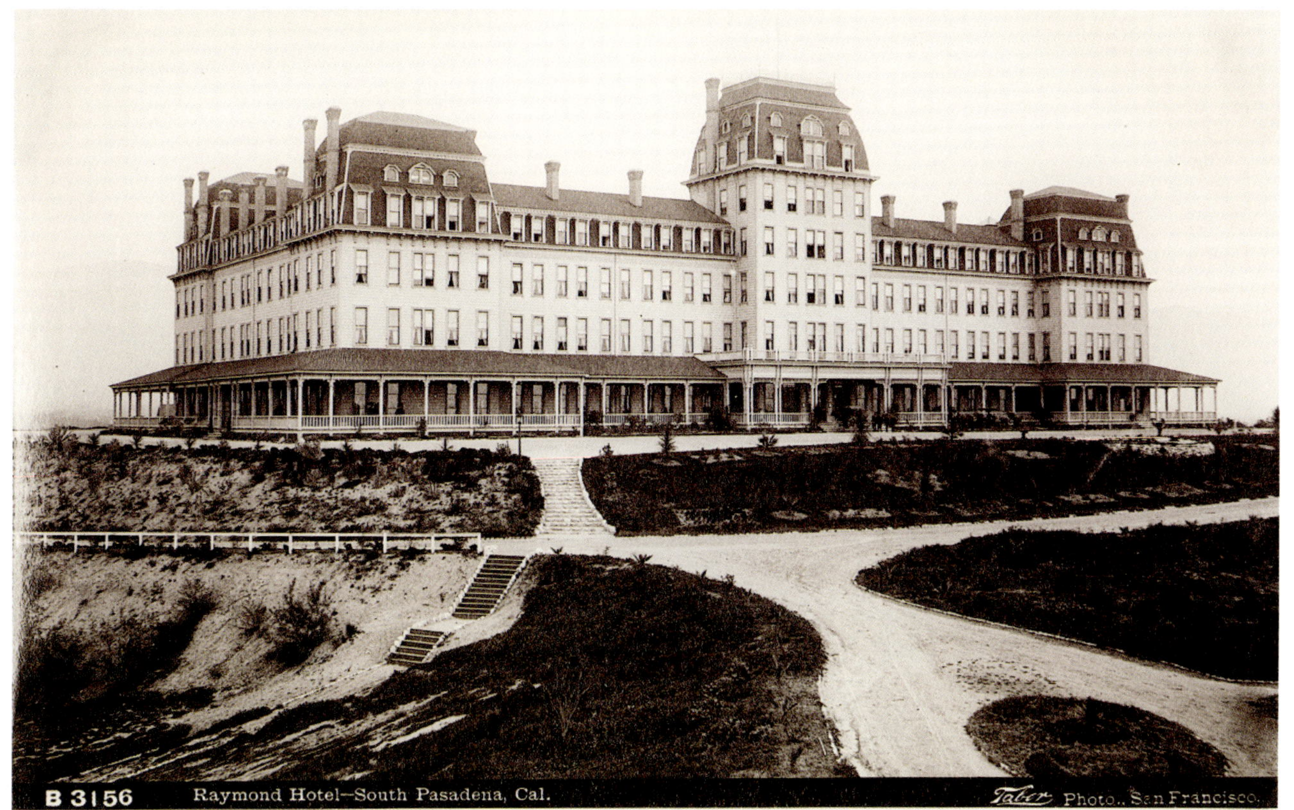

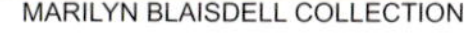
MARILYN BLAISDELL COLLECTION

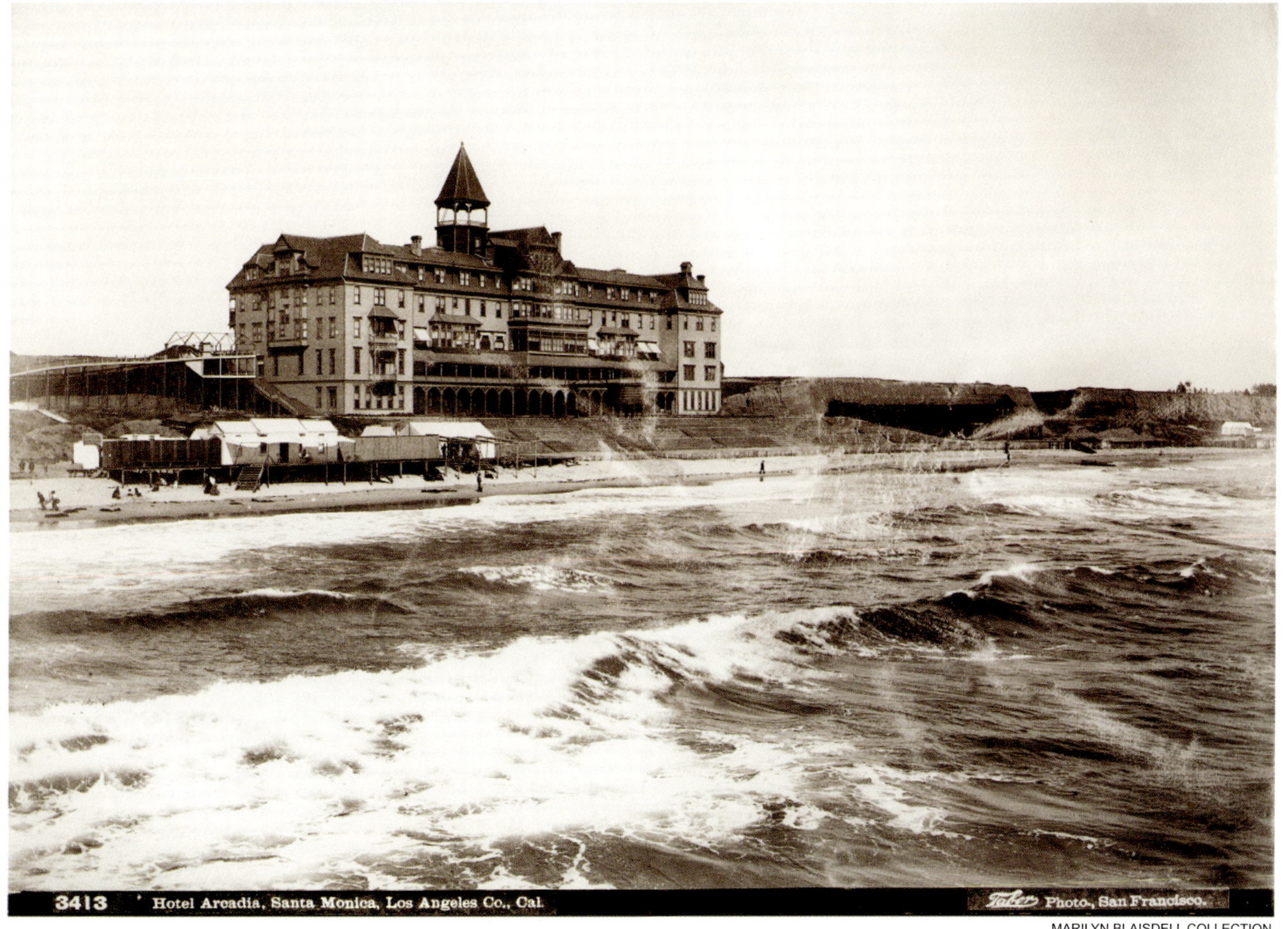

MARILYN BLAISDELL COLLECTION

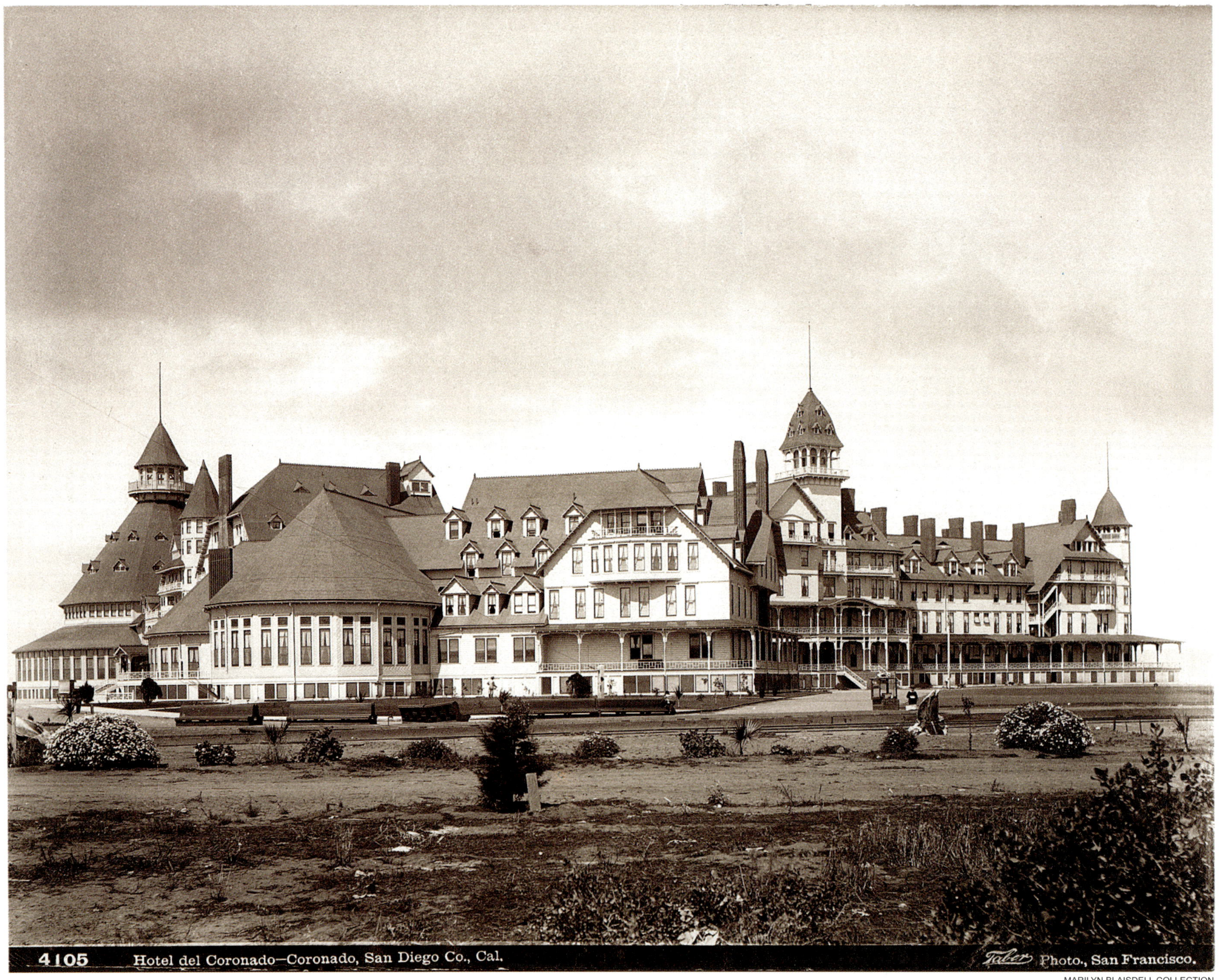

MARILYN BLAISDELL COLLECTION

The Hotel del Coronado, built in 1888 by Elisha Babcock, became the queen of California's beach-front luxury hotels. Babcock ran the Coronado Beach Company, San Diego water company, the gas and electric company, the salt works, and the Coronado railroad and ferry companies. Through his efforts the former barren sandy Coronado peninsula became a thriving resort.

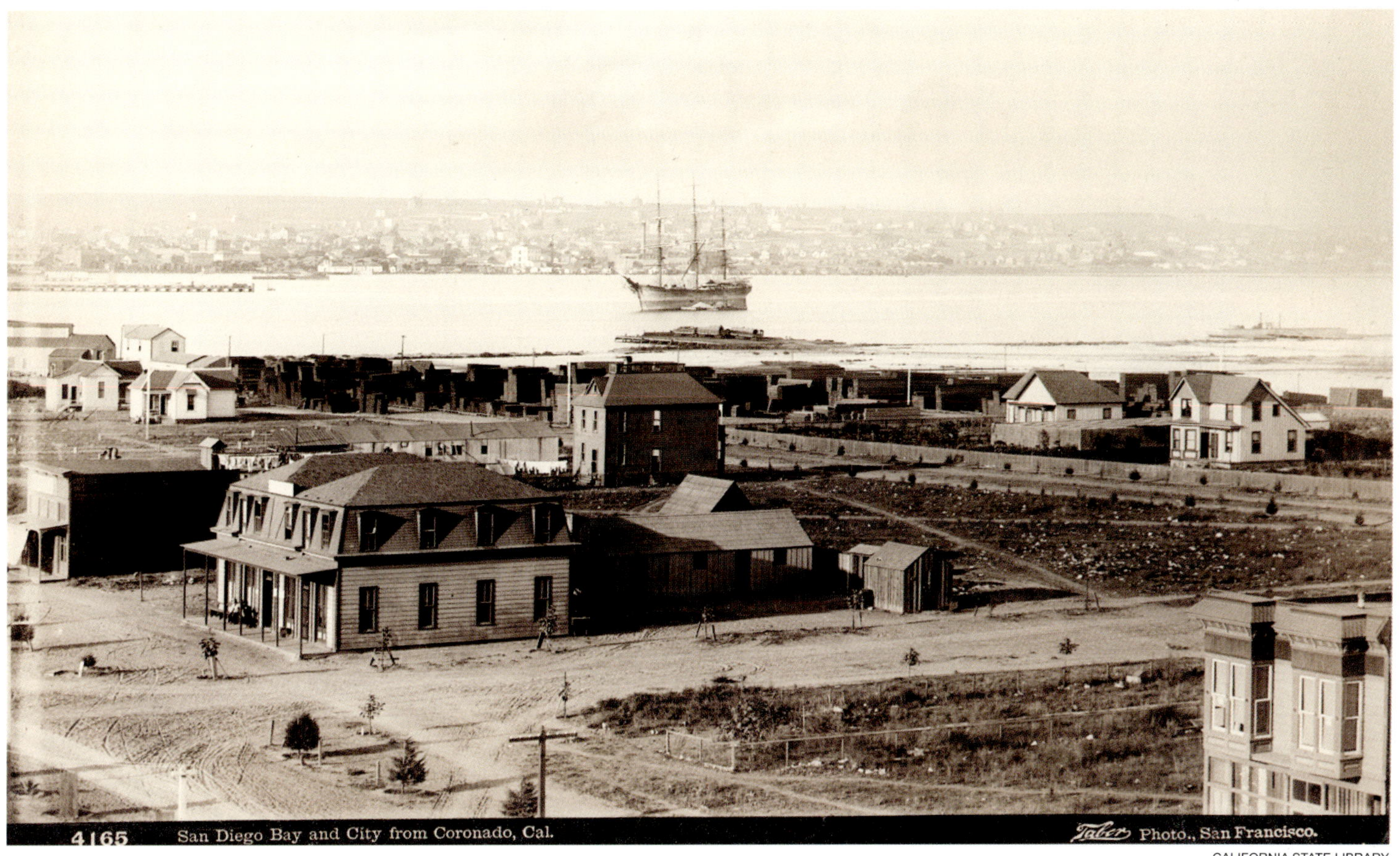

CALIFORNIA STATE LIBRARY

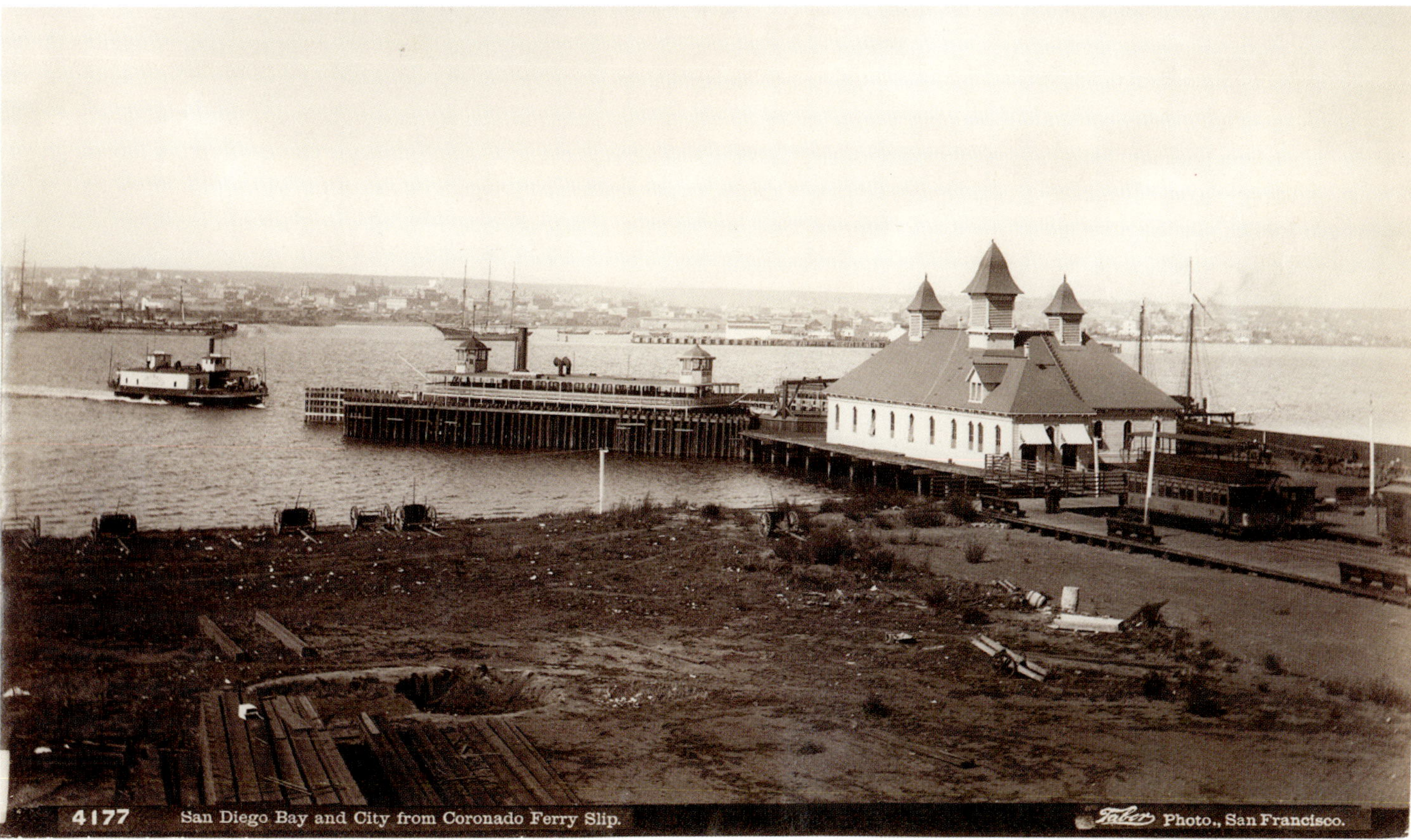

CALIFORNIA STATE LIBRARY

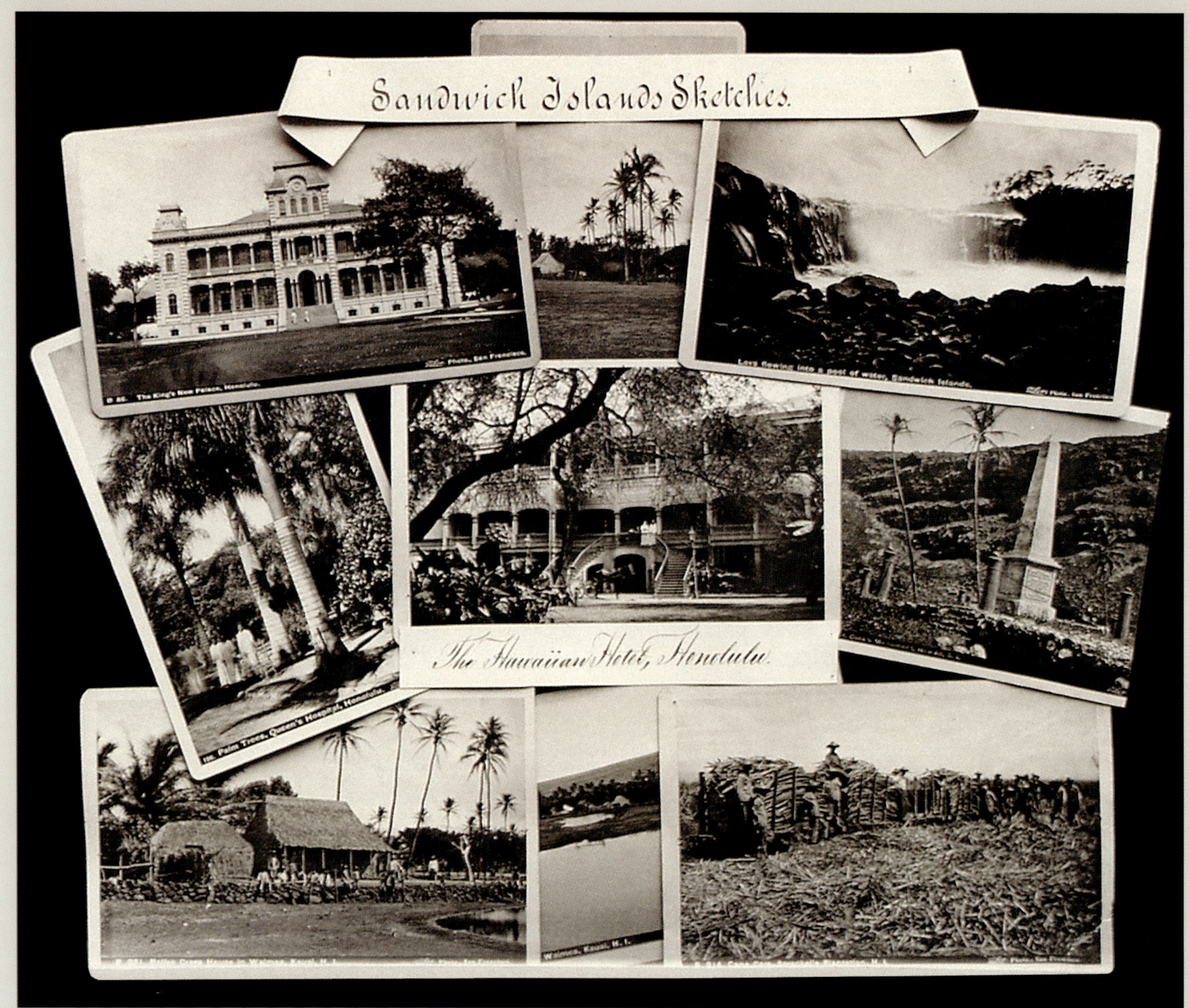

CALIFORNIA STATE LIBRARY

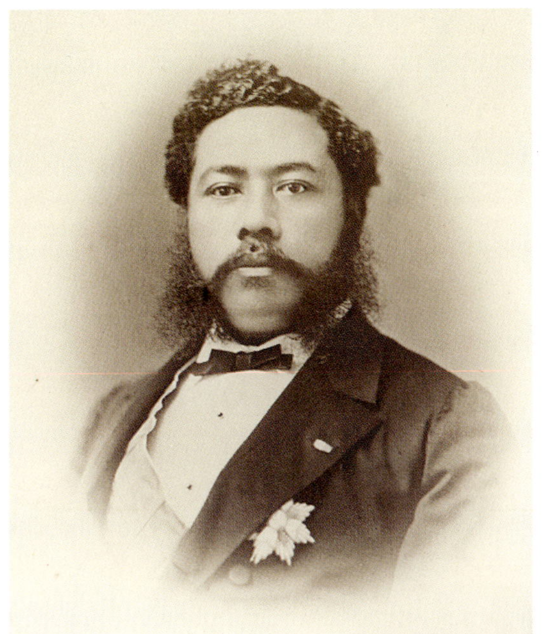

CALIFORNIA STATE LIBRARY

HAWAII

Isaiah Taber instinctively knew that the Sandwich Islands caught the interest of Californians and visitors to the state. When, in 1880, he was invited to sail to Hawaii and the South Pacific with his friend and Oakland neighbor Dr. Samuel Merritt, he jumped at the chance. During the six-week cruise, Taber photographed landmarks and attractions including an active volcano, becoming the first San Francisco photographer to offer Hawaiian scenic views. While in Honolulu, he met and made portraits of King Kalakaua. The king, on a round the world tour in 1881, visited Taber in San Francisco and had more portraits made. Taber so impressed the king that Kalakaua invited him and his wife to the king's belated coronation to be held at the Iolani Palace in 1883. The Taber's attended as guests of King Kalakaua and Queen Kapiolani.

Above: King of the Sandwich Islands, Kingdom of Hawaii, Col. David Kalakaua, 1882.

Right: A souvenir montage assembled by Isaiah Taber for his companions on his voyage to the Sandwich Islands and the South Pacific in 1880. The voyagers were, clockwise from top, Dr. Samuel Merritt, Isaiah Taber, Miss Nellie Knowles, Miss Alice Dyer, Mrs. Dr. Garcelon, Miss Minnie Dyer, Miss McLellan, and T.T. Dargle. Dr. Merritt's schooner yacht Casco was chartered in 1888 by Robert Louis Stevenson to take him to Tahiti.

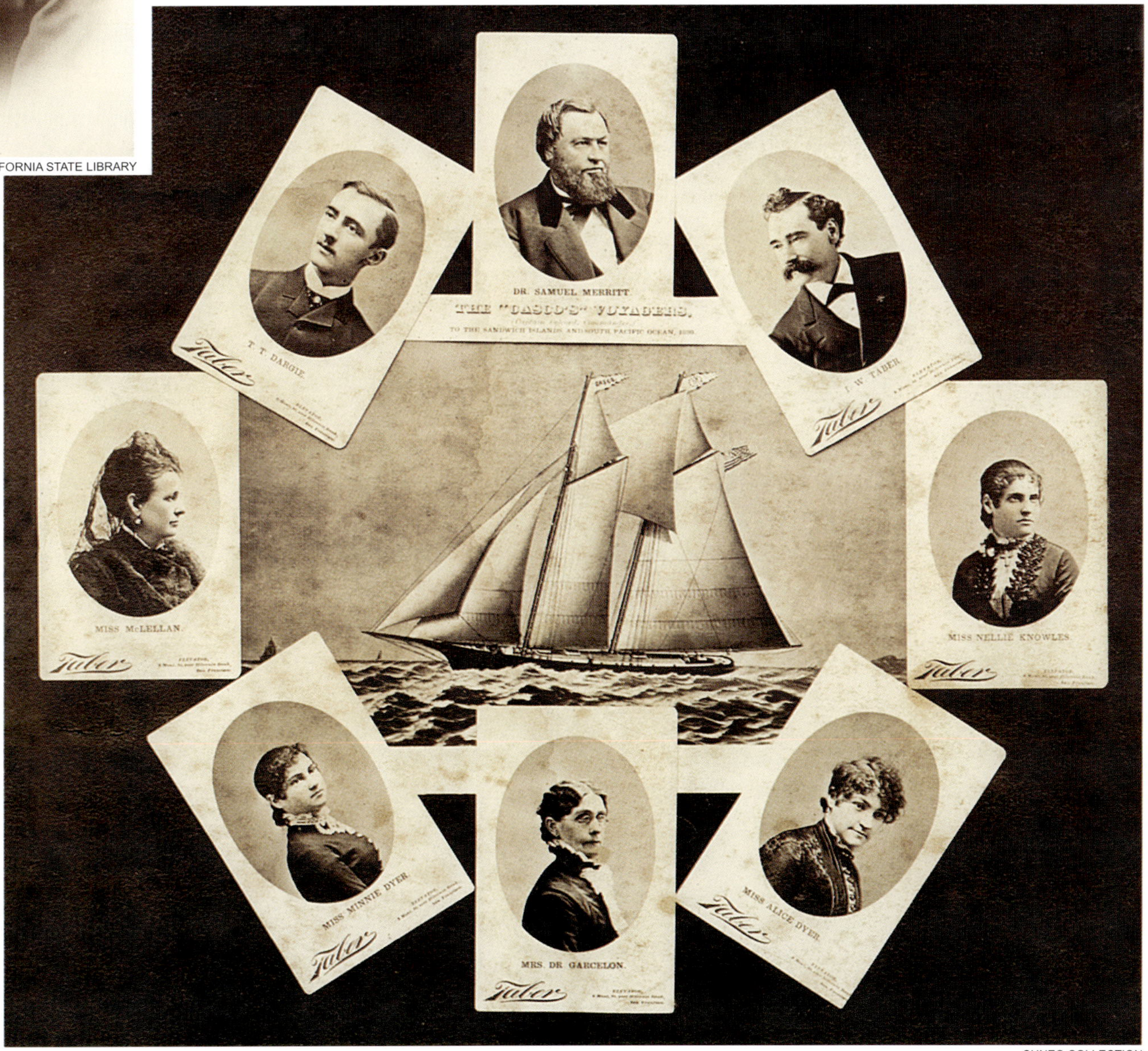

CUNEO COLLECTION

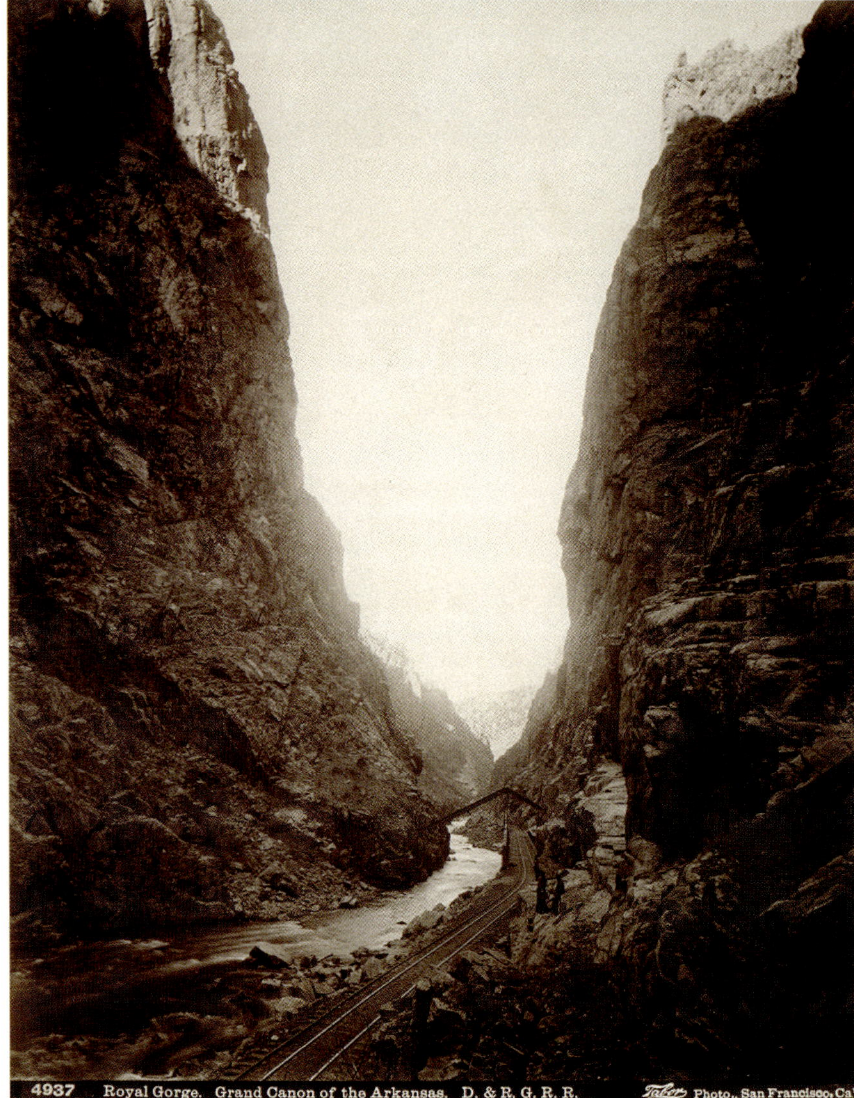

THE BANCROFT LIBRARY

By the 1890s railroad travel in the west had opened new horizons for photographers by making spectacular scenery more accessible. Isaiah Taber made several trips by rail, sometimes in the company of other photographers, north to Oregon and Washington, and east to Utah, Wyoming, and Colorado.

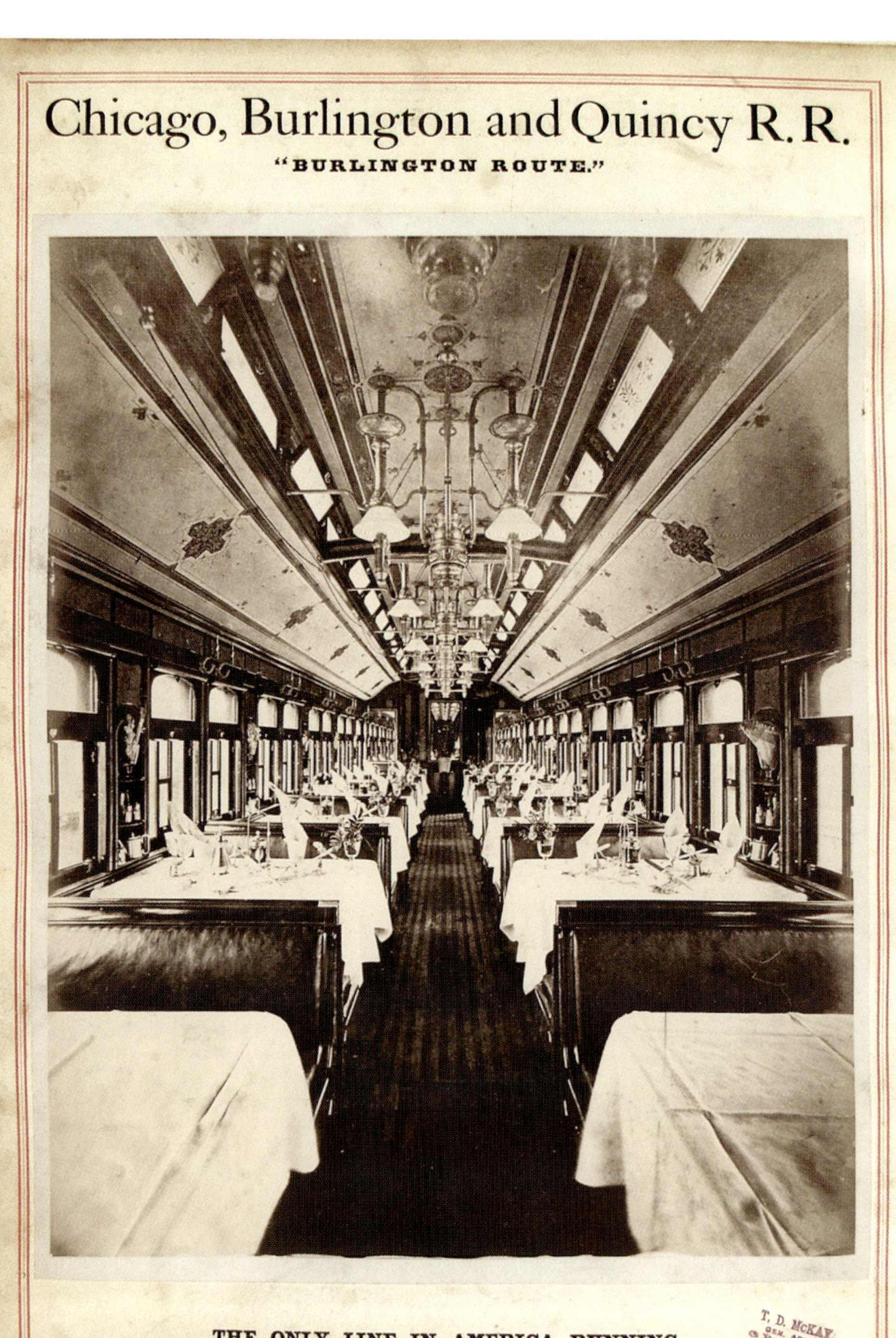

From the Taber Photographic Album, *1880.*

CALIFORNIA STATE LIBRARY

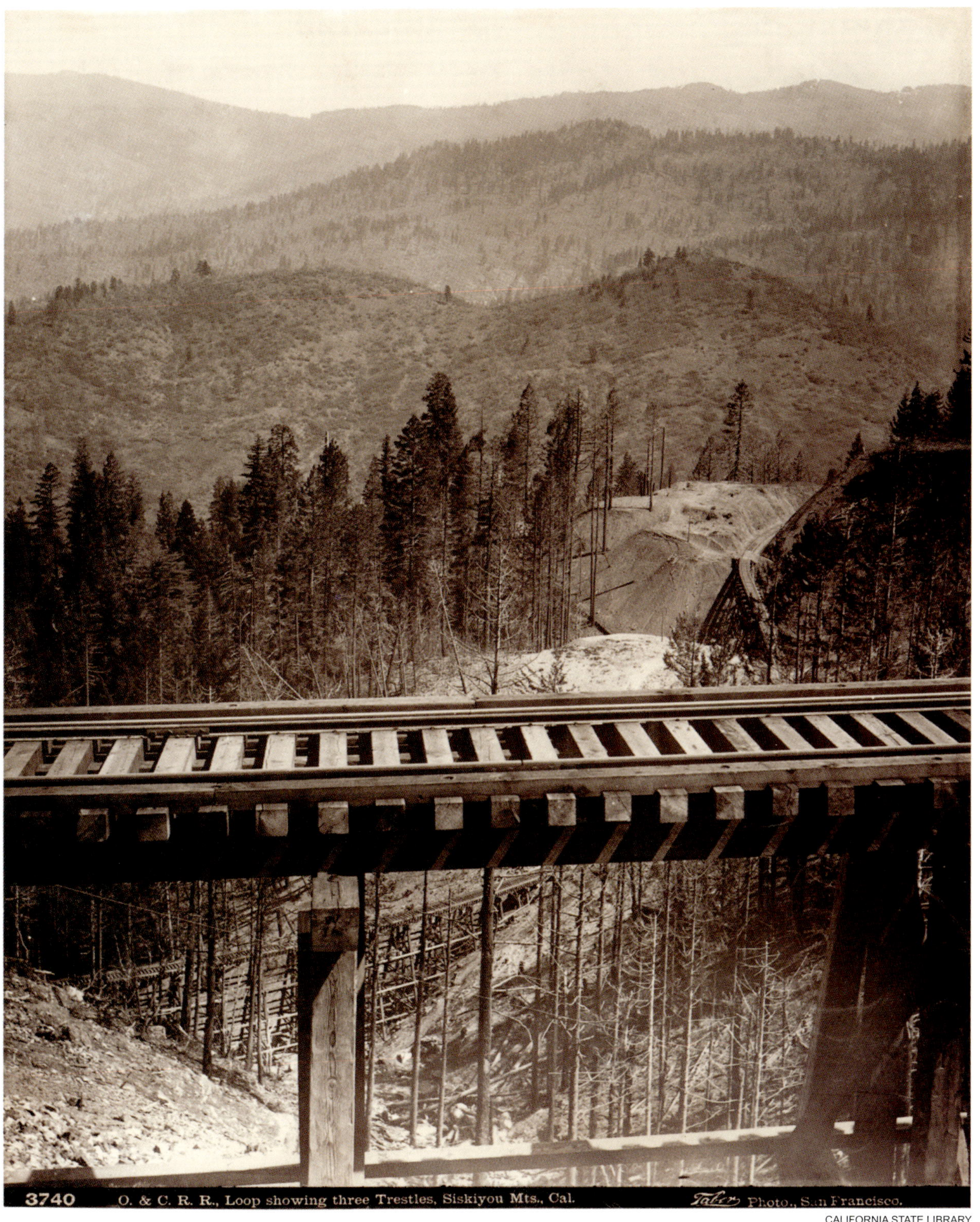
3740 O. & C. R. R., Loop showing three Trestles, Siskiyou Mts., Cal. Taber Photo., San Francisco.

CALIFORNIA STATE LIBRARY

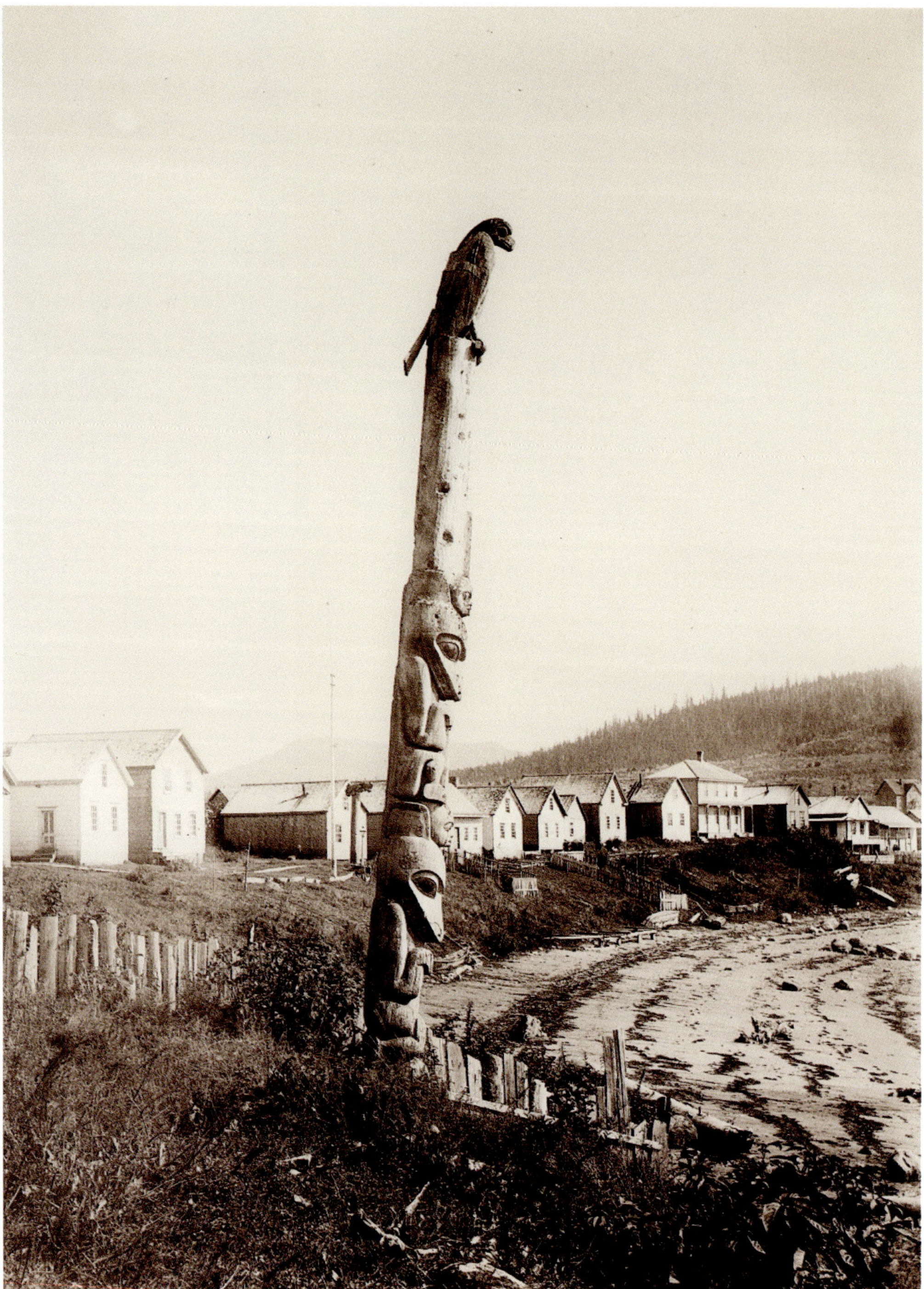

MARILYN BLAISDELL COLLECTION

Native village near Juneau, 1889.

ALASKA

In the late 1880s, prospectors were finding gold in Alaska and the Yukon, and the possibility of a major gold strike equal to the California mother lode caught the public fancy. Photographs of this strange land and its native inhabitants sold well in the East as well as the West. Isaiah Taber, alert as always to popular interests, journeyed north to Juneau in the spring of 1889. There he photographed native villages and the spectacular face of Muir Glacier, trying to capture the breath-taking translucence and shimmering reflections of glacial ice.

He heard the legend of ghost cities seemingly suspended in the sky. These apparitions, sworn to by prospectors and natives, were explained as distant cities reflected off glacial ice. Isaiah Taber's sea-caption brother Charles, always interested in geological and atmospheric phenomena, probably told Isaiah about the stories years earlier. Isaiah Taber himself had seen the Northern Lights and glacial ice from the deck of a whaling vessel in 1846.

During Taber's 1889 visit to Alaska, a sensational version of the legend was circulating that a prospector named Willoughby had seen a ghostly city in the sky that looked like the city of Bristol, England. Willoughby had photographed it, but those who had seen the photo declared it was not mirage-like, but a detailed city, and appeared to be a fraud.

Another story at the same time told of two prospectors near Muir Glacier who had seen a strange city reflected in a pan of quicksilver. They concluded that the ancient city was buried in the ice and shone up through it at various times and the reflection somehow appeared on the mirror-like surface of the quicksilver in the pan. Alexander Badham, in his 1890 book, *Wonders of Alaska,* said that "I. W. Taber, the reliable photographer" had taken a picture of the reflected scene. Badham published the Taber photo along with another sketch of Muir Glacier with seemingly architectural "gothic" spires in the distance. He concluded that the Taber photo, with its fantastic unknown city, was a composite photo of the pan superimposed with a photo of a painted city.

Would Isaiah Taber have perpetrated such a fraud? Yes, if he did it with a wink. It was the type of preposterous story he would find amusing, a fitting subject for a practical joke.

In 1893 Taber and Alexander Badham became acquainted when Taber was named official photographer for the upcoming Midwinter Exposition at San Francisco. Badham, a controversial local politician and nephew of San Francisco pioneer Sam Brannan, became secretary of the Midwinter Exposition. One wonders if the Alaskan ghost city ever came up in conversations between them.

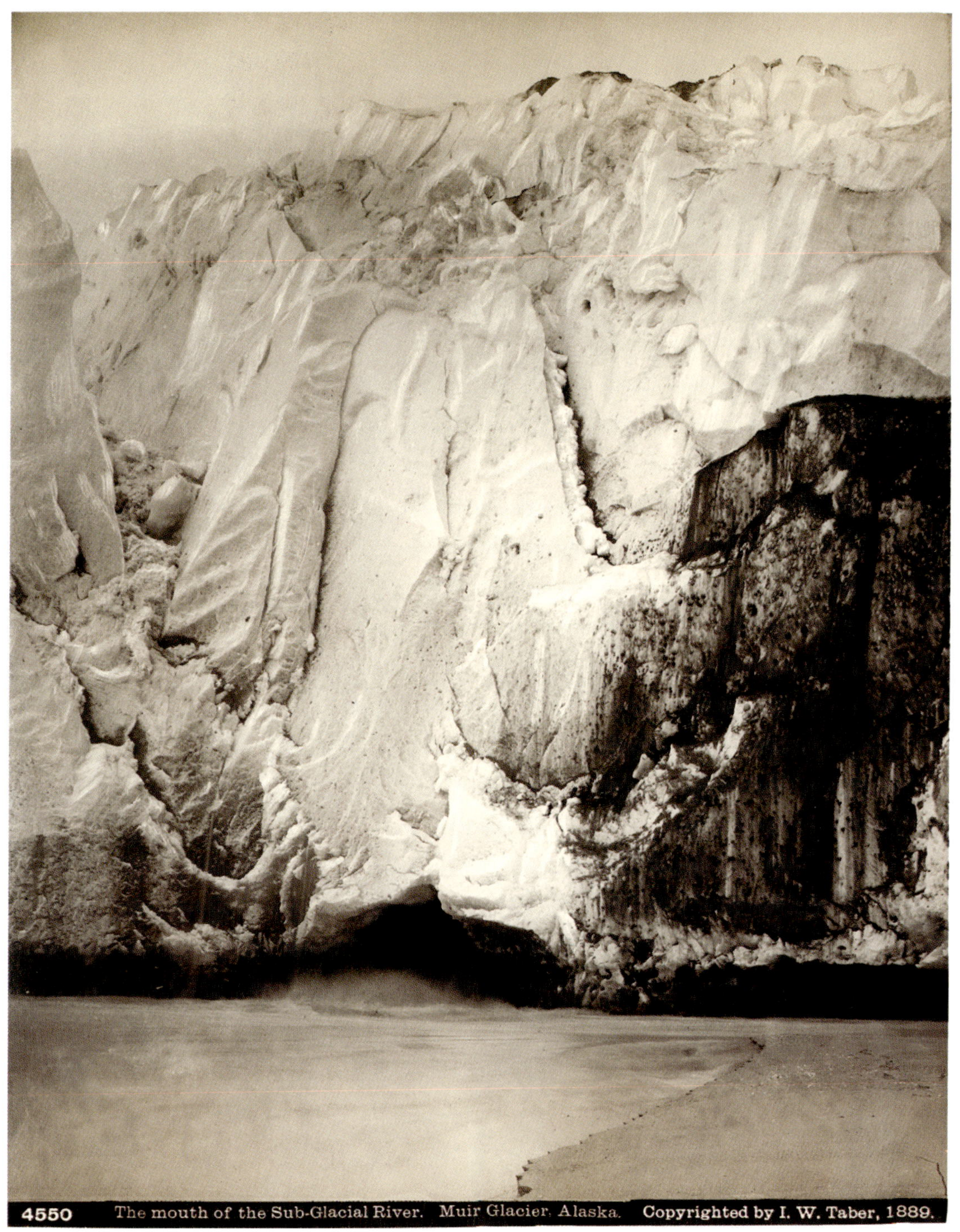
4550 The mouth of the Sub-Glacial River. Muir Glacier, Alaska. Copyrighted by I. W. Taber, 1889.

The Yosemite Falls

HEIGHT, ABOUT 2550 FEET.

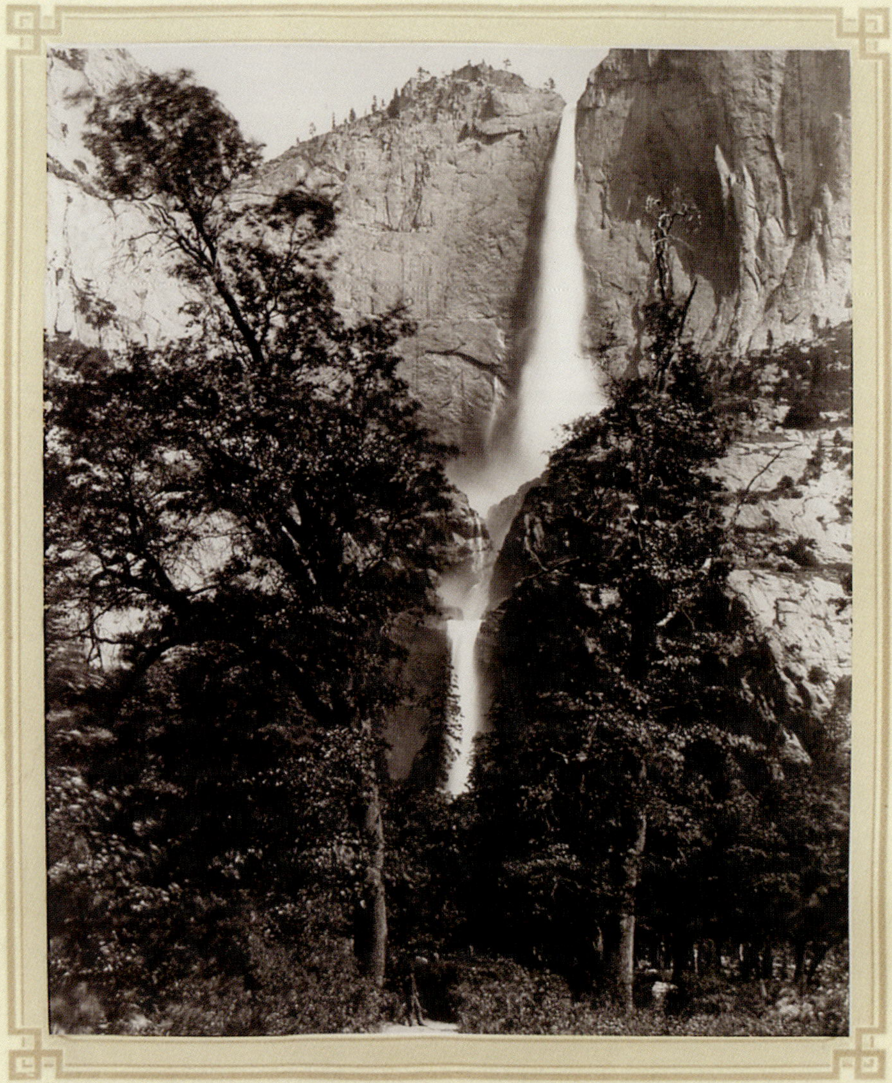

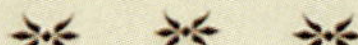

The above is a view of the Yosemite Falls taken from the best point for general observation, distant about one mile from the base of the falls. The upper part is a vertical fall of 1502 feet, then there is a series of cataracts equal to about 559 feet plumb, and the final plunge to the base of the precipice measures about 400 feet.

These falls are generally considered the chief wonder of the valley, and excel in height, and in combined grandeur and beauty, any other known natural wonders of the kind.

This photograph was taken during the month of May—in ordinary seasons the best time to visit the valley, as there is then the greatest volume of water in all the falls.

The Three Brothers' Trail, by way of Columbia Rock, affords a rather difficult means of ascent to the extreme summit of the falls, whence there is a superb view of the valley and its surroundings, which will well repay the hardy and adventurous climber.

From California Scenery and Industries, *1880.* CALIFORNIA STATE LIBRARY

Isaiah Taber had a special affinity for Yosemite Valley. When he returned to San Francisco in 1864 to work for Bradley and Rulofson as a portrait artist, he had his first opportunity to visit Yosemite and see its already legendary grandeur. That same year President Abraham Lincoln signed into law an act granting "Yo-Semite" and the Mariposa big-tree grove to the State of California to preserve in perpetuity. Public awareness of the extraordinary valley was due in part to the photographs made in the early 1860s by Charles Leander Weed and Carleton E. Watkins. It is unrecorded when Taber made his first journey to the valley, but given his determination and boundless energy, it was probably soon after he got settled in San Francisco.

Taber's arrival on the California scene corresponded to the beginning of a golden age of landscape photography, roughly from the end of the Civil War to 1900. Advancements in photographic technology ushered in the era. Daguerreotype cameras were eclipsed by glass-negative cameras capable of producing large highly-detailed photographs in natural outdoor light. More importantly, the new process allowed multiple prints to be made from a single negative. Watkins' instantly popular mammoth-plate photographs of scenic views made San Francisco a focal point for photographers and galleries specializing in landscape photography. Taber, sensing an expanding market, became a publisher of photographic prints as well as a photographer.

Yosemite became a lucrative part of Taber's scenic view collection. Judging from the sheer number of Yosemite scenes offered over the years by Taber beyond those he acquired from others, he made numerous photographic forays into the valley and the surrounding region.

The Stoneman House under the shadow of Half Dome in Yosemite Valley, built by the State in the late 1880s, contained 92 rooms and most of the amenities of a first-class San Francisco hotel. The Yosemite commissioners leased the hotel to James Jay Cook, Mariposa businessman and Yosemite entrepreneur. Cook had financed Carleton Watkins' Yosemite Art Gallery, seized it when Watkins apparently was unable to repay him, and arranged, in 1876, to have Taber publish Watkins' scenic photographs. Taber's continuing interest in Yosemite led to him being appointed to the Yosemite Commission in 1888. He served in that capacity for four years.

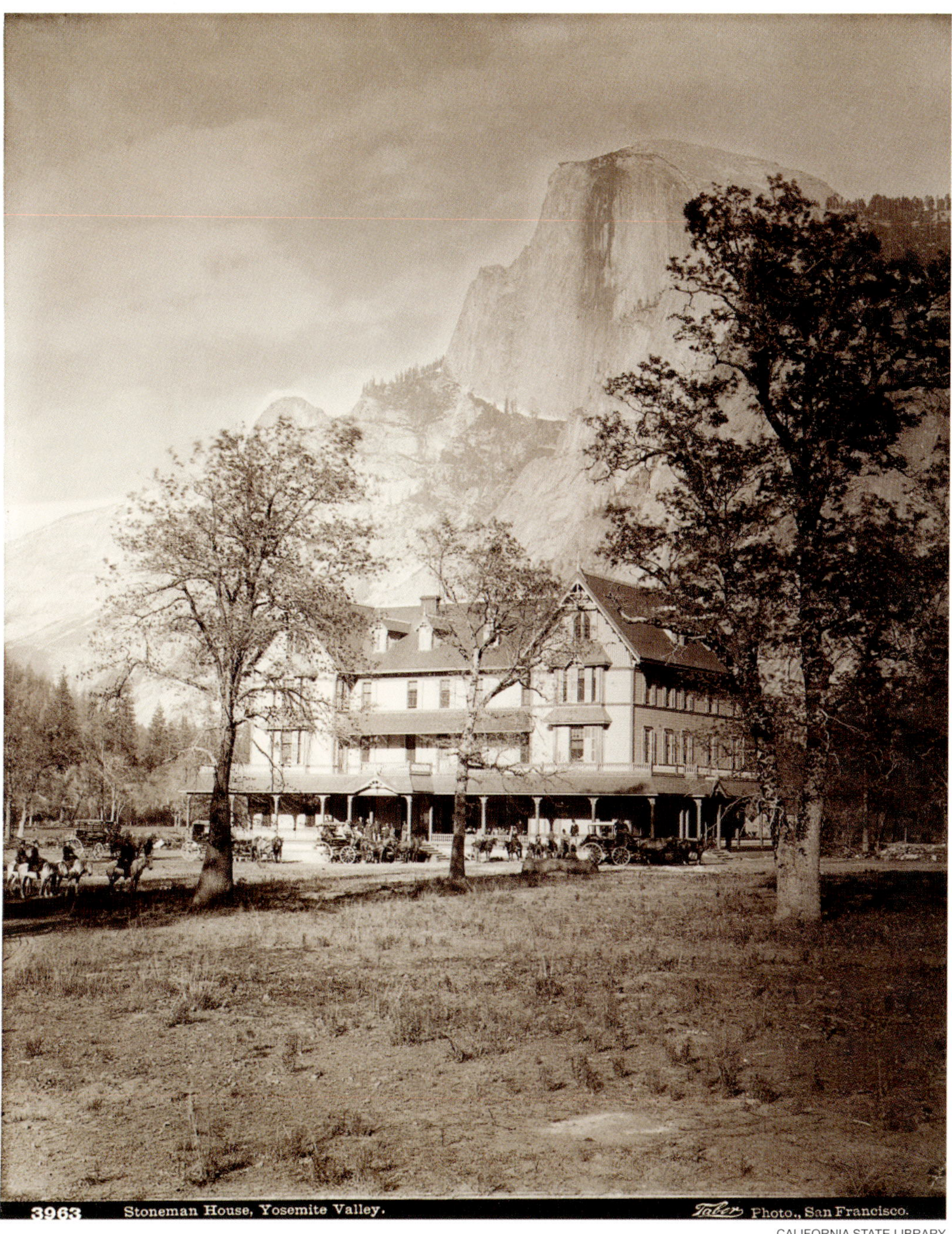

CALIFORNIA STATE LIBRARY

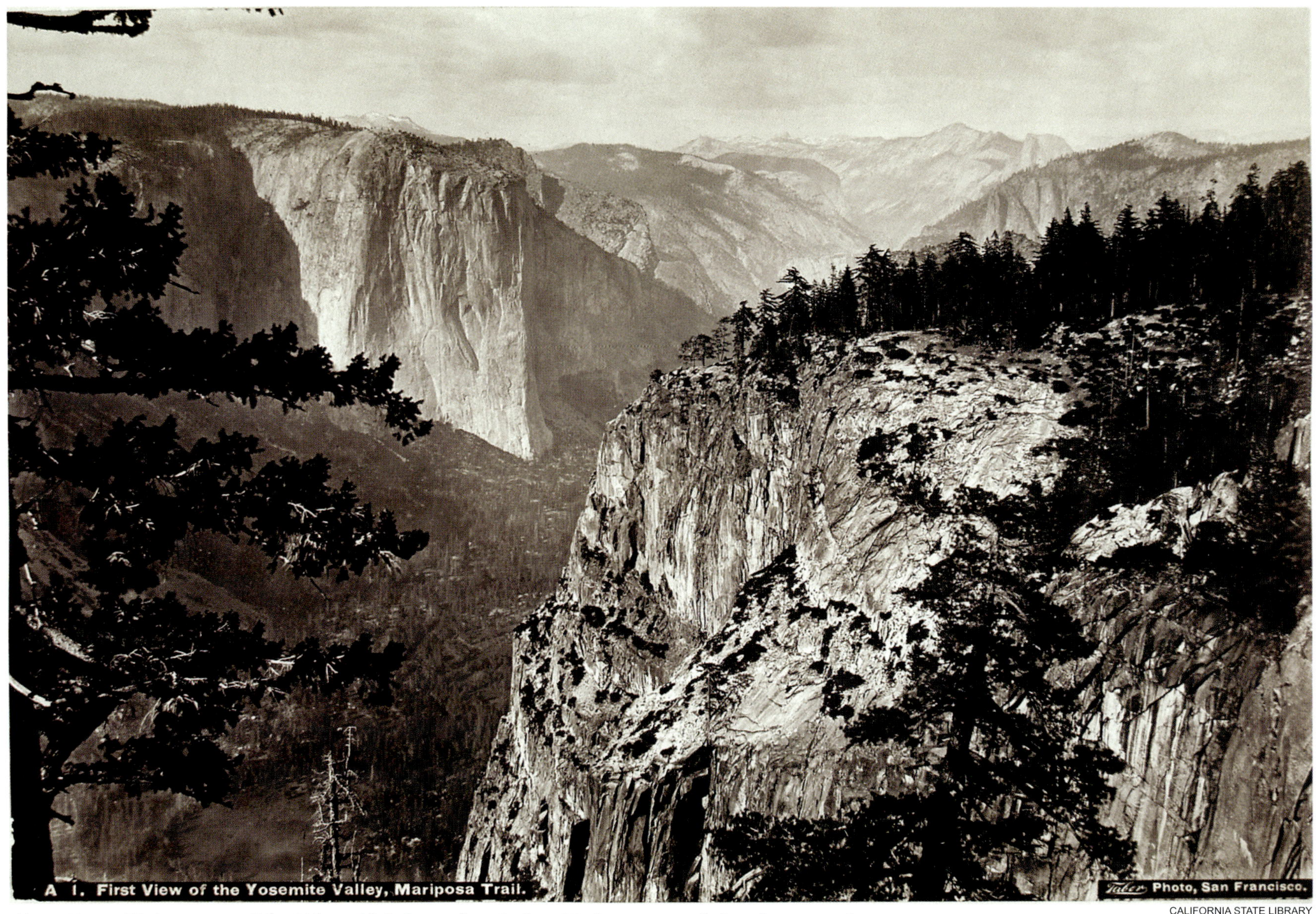

CALIFORNIA STATE LIBRARY

Above: From a Watkins negative. When Taber published prints from Carleton Watkins' negatives, he kept the same numbers.

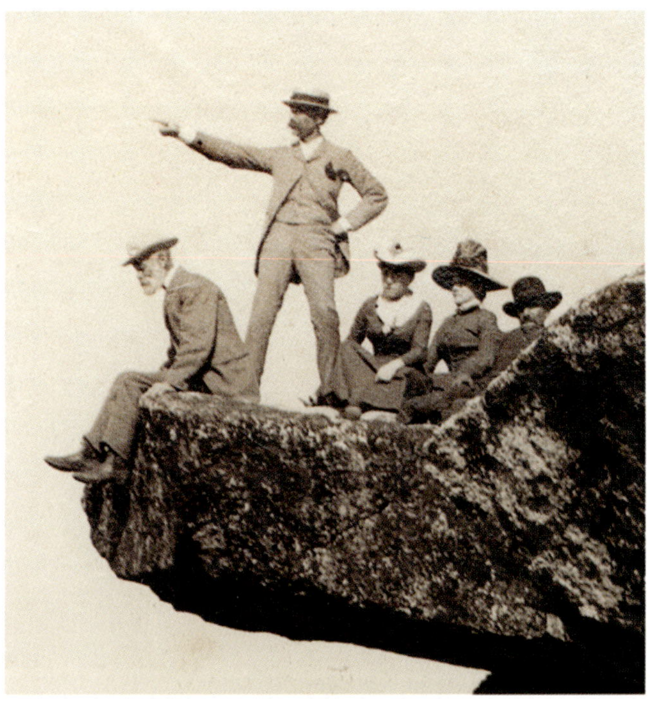

Isaiah Taber, above and at right, standing at Glacier Point in 1887. With Taber are Lily Langtry, seated in tall hat, and her traveling companions. The man seated on the lip of the rock may be Lily's husband, Edward Langtry. Taber escorted Langtry and her party around Yosemite Valley, pointing out its scenic wonders. In those days, every visitor to the valley had to be photographed on the overhanging rock on Glacier Point. Langtry, celebrated British actress and mistress of the Prince of Wales, later King Edward VII, toured the United States extensively in the 1880s. She purchased a 6,500-acre ranch in Lake County where she bred horses.

Taber used a cropped version of this photo as a promotional card by adding a flag bearing the legend "Taber" to his outstretched hand. The photo was taken by an assistant.

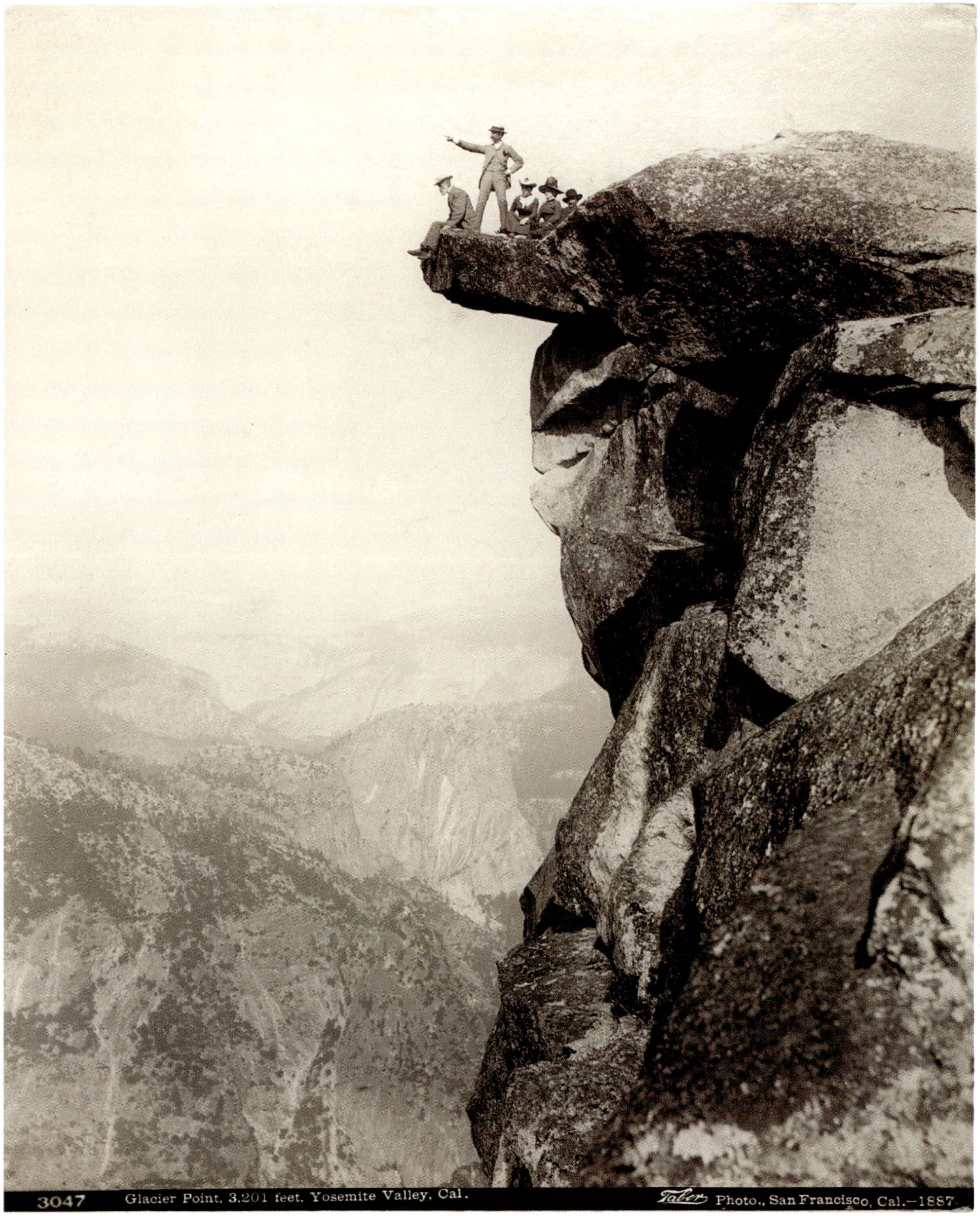

3047 Glacier Point, 3,201 feet. Yosemite Valley, Cal. Taber Photo., San Francisco, Cal.—1887

CALIFORNIA STATE LIBRARY

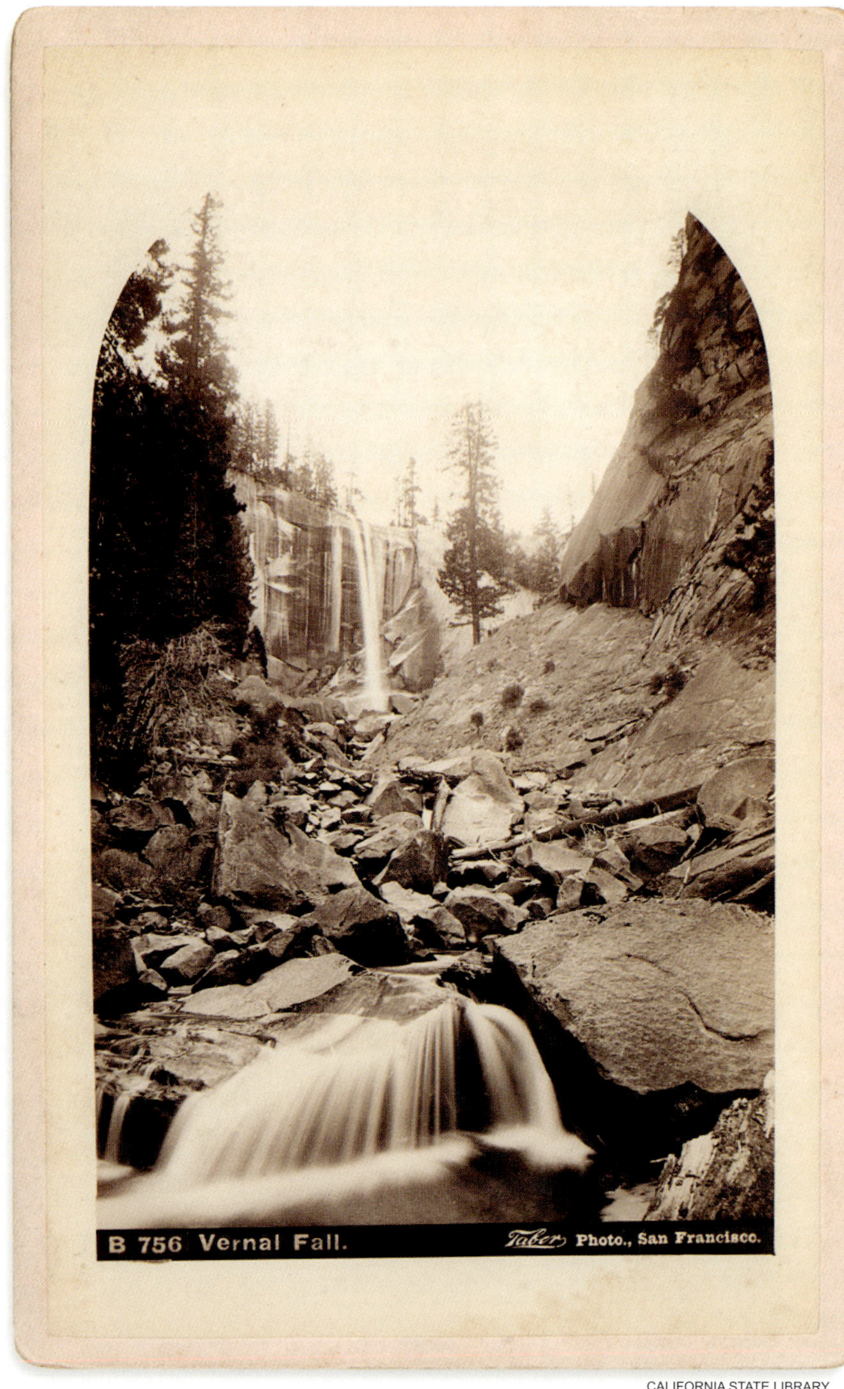

CALIFORNIA STATE LIBRARY

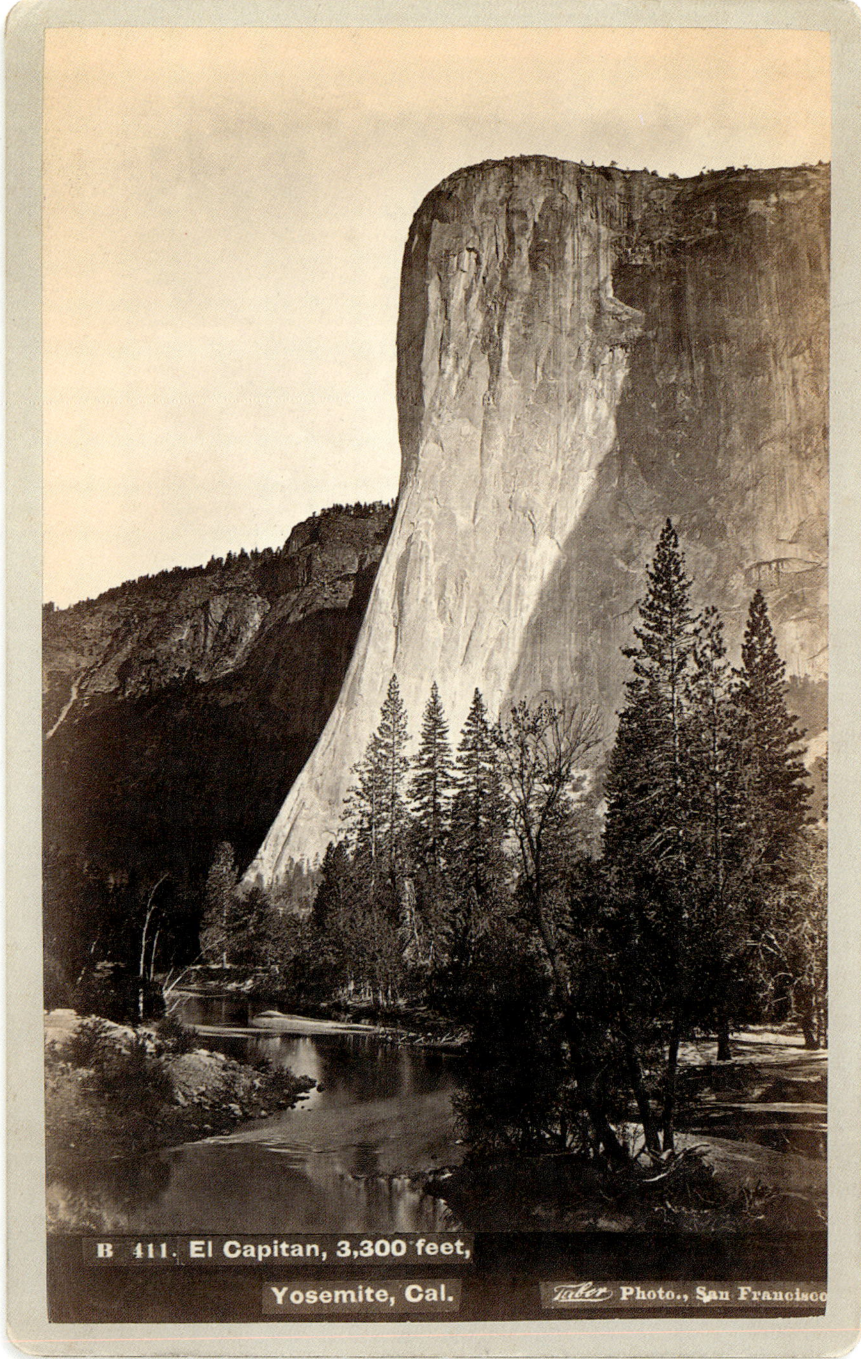

CALIFORNIA STATE LIBRARY

These four prints were published by Taber in the late 1870s or early 1880s. The cabinet card second from left, opposite page, is from a Watkins negative. Taber offered in addition to his standard print sizes, stereographs of Yosemite and other locales. Stereopublishing, a complex, demanding business, never became a major part of Taber's publishing enterprise. Taber had seen the stereograph market suffer a sales slump during the Civil War and again in the early 1870s, due to a general business depression. The instability of stereograph prices plus increasing competition may have made Taber leery of stereopublishing.

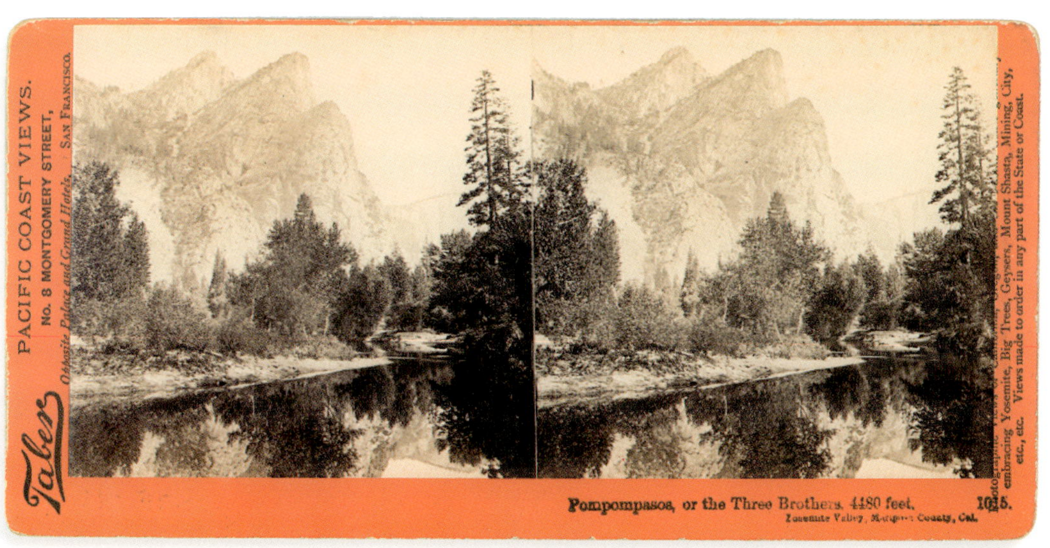

WINDGATE PRESS

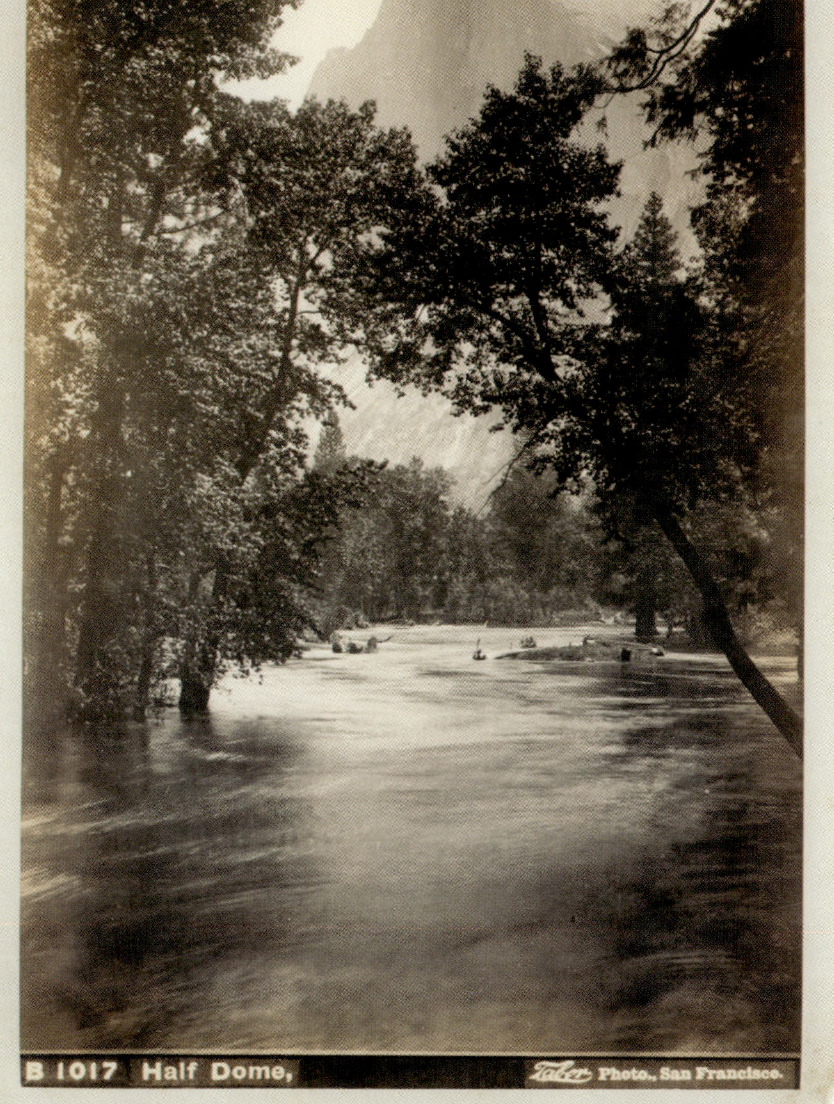

CALIFORNIA STATE LIBRARY

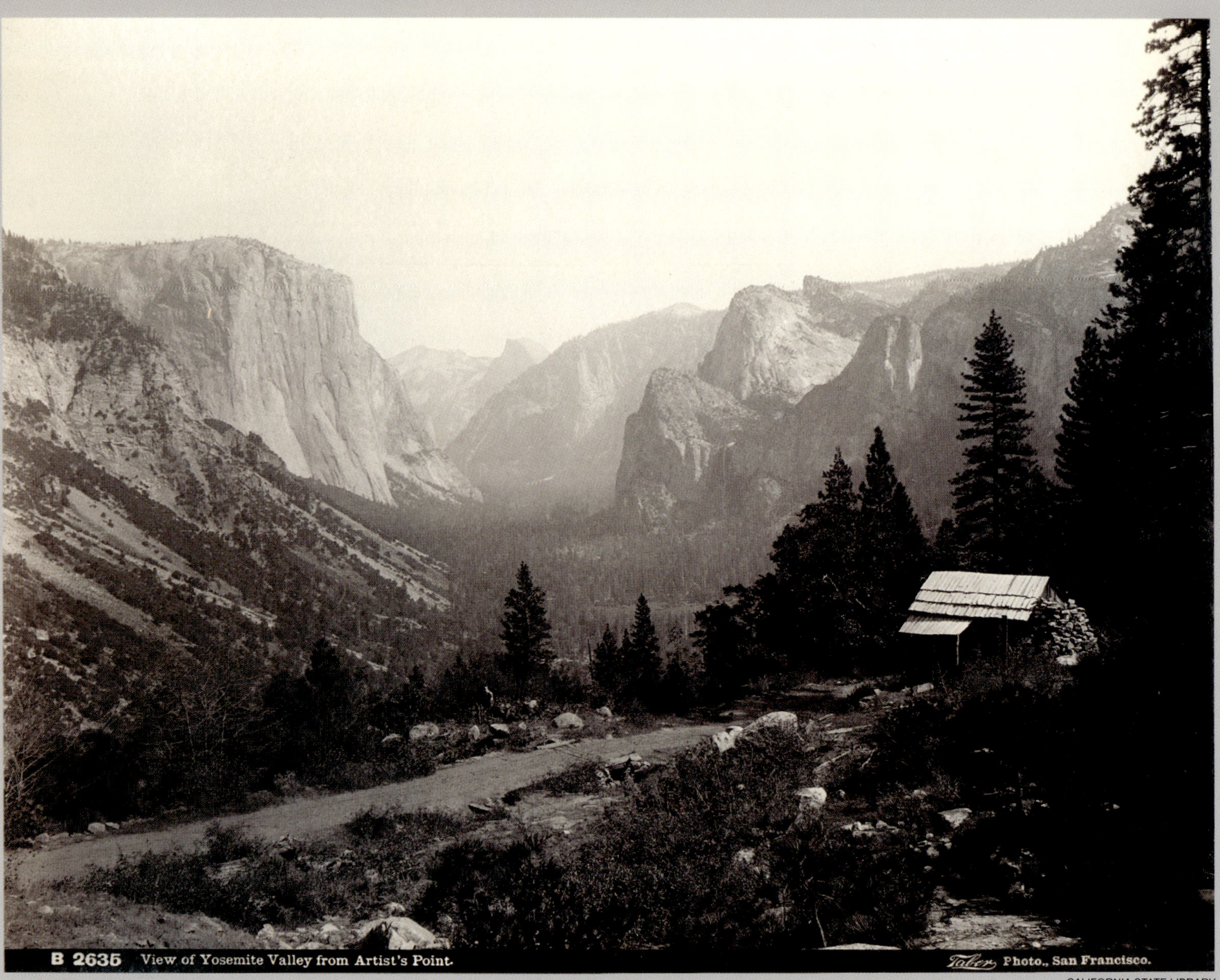

CALIFORNIA STATE LIBRARY

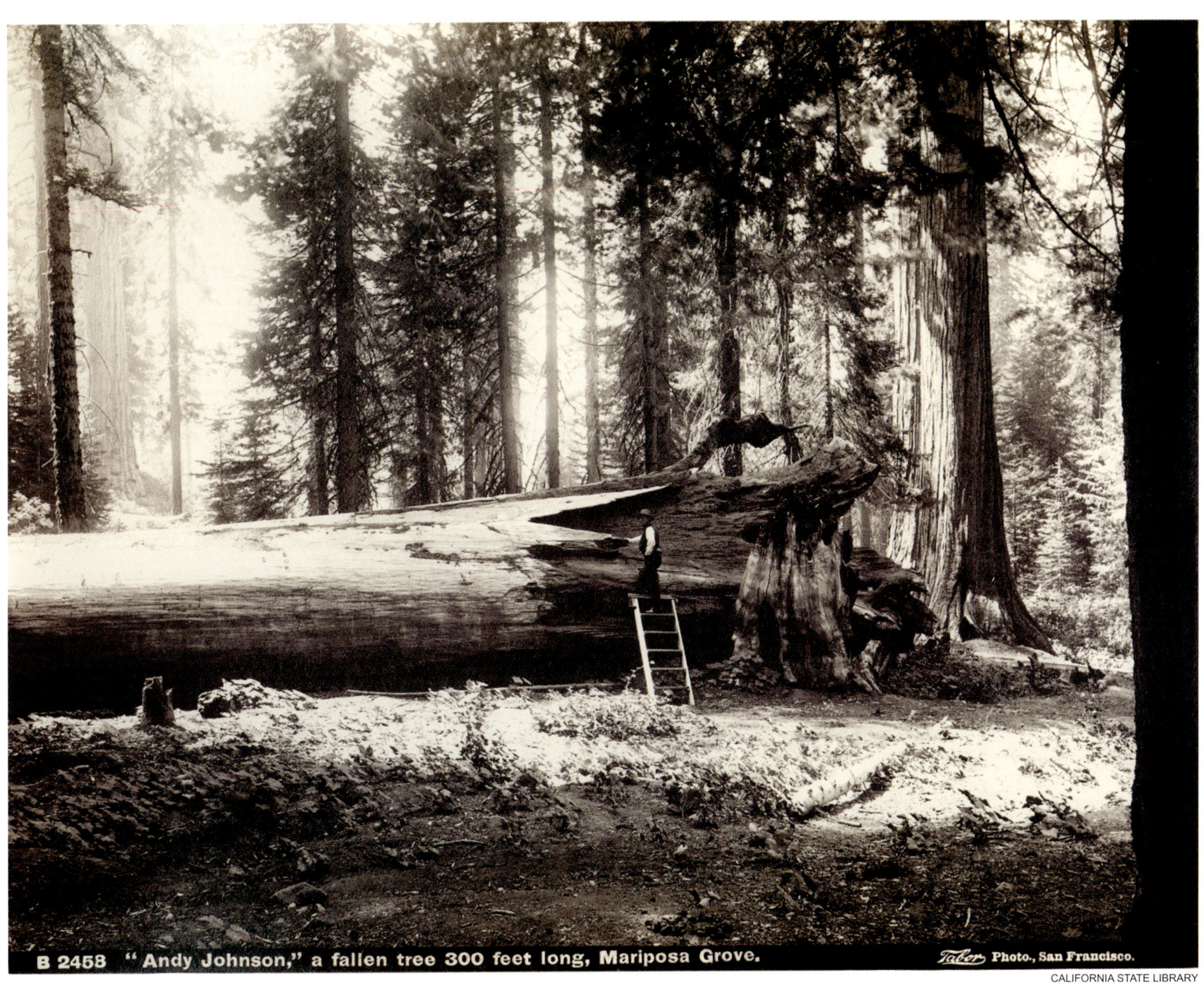

B 2453 "Andy Johnson," a fallen tree 300 feet long, Mariposa Grove. Tabor Photo., San Francisco.

CALIFORNIA STATE LIBRARY

CALIFORNIA STATE LIBRARY

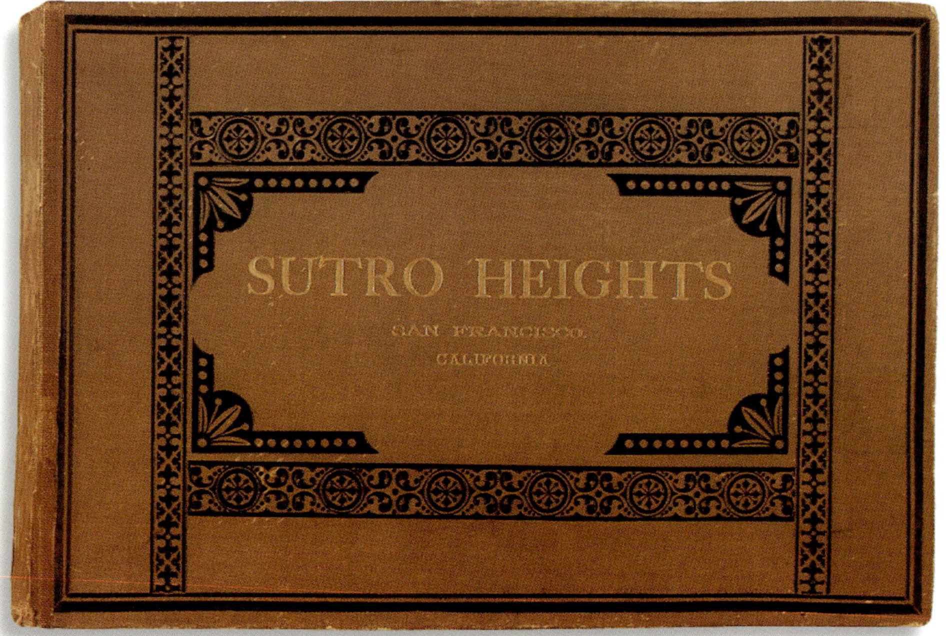

SUTRO HEIGHTS & BATHS

Before his death in 1898, Adolph Sutro was well known for having made millions in the Comstock Lode, founding a great library of rare books and manuscripts, building the most elaborate of all the Cliff Houses, and creating a museum and immense natatorium known as Sutro Baths. He was also elected mayor of San Francisco in 1894 on the Populist Party ticket. Photographing his estate overlooking the Pacific Ocean with its sublime vistas, formal gardens, faux classical statuary, and imposing entrance gates, was a particularly fascinating assignment for Isaiah Taber. Sutro, himself, was a photogenic figure known for his sartorial splendor. Taber and his assistants trooped out to Sutro Heights and took dozens of views.

Clearly the photographs were made for Mr. Sutro but evidence indicates that a wider audience would also enjoy the photographs made of this fascinating place. Several of these views Taber mounted in albums probably for presentation to Sutro. The Sutro Library in San Francisco, formed by the great bibliogent, contains two oblong albums of Taber's views with gold-stamped cover entitled Sutro Heights. One contains 51 images and the other, 30. All measure 8 ½ x 5 inches. As he did with virtually all his jobs, Taber sold individual images at his downtown gallery.

Taber also photographed Sutro's other project, Sutro Baths. Taber's views of the baths featured a number of interior shots that fully demonstrated the immensity of the structure. Sutro, a public-spirited man, wanted to share the bounty of his earnings with the general public. As shown by Taber's images, these included many amenities such as an elegant promenade adorned with tropical plants and a museum loaded with all kinds of curiosities, some of which came from Woodward's Gardens, the former San Francisco amusement park. The Cliff House, completed in 1894 and the third to be built on that ocean promenade, with its spectacular chateauesque-style façade, likewise received the photographer's attention.

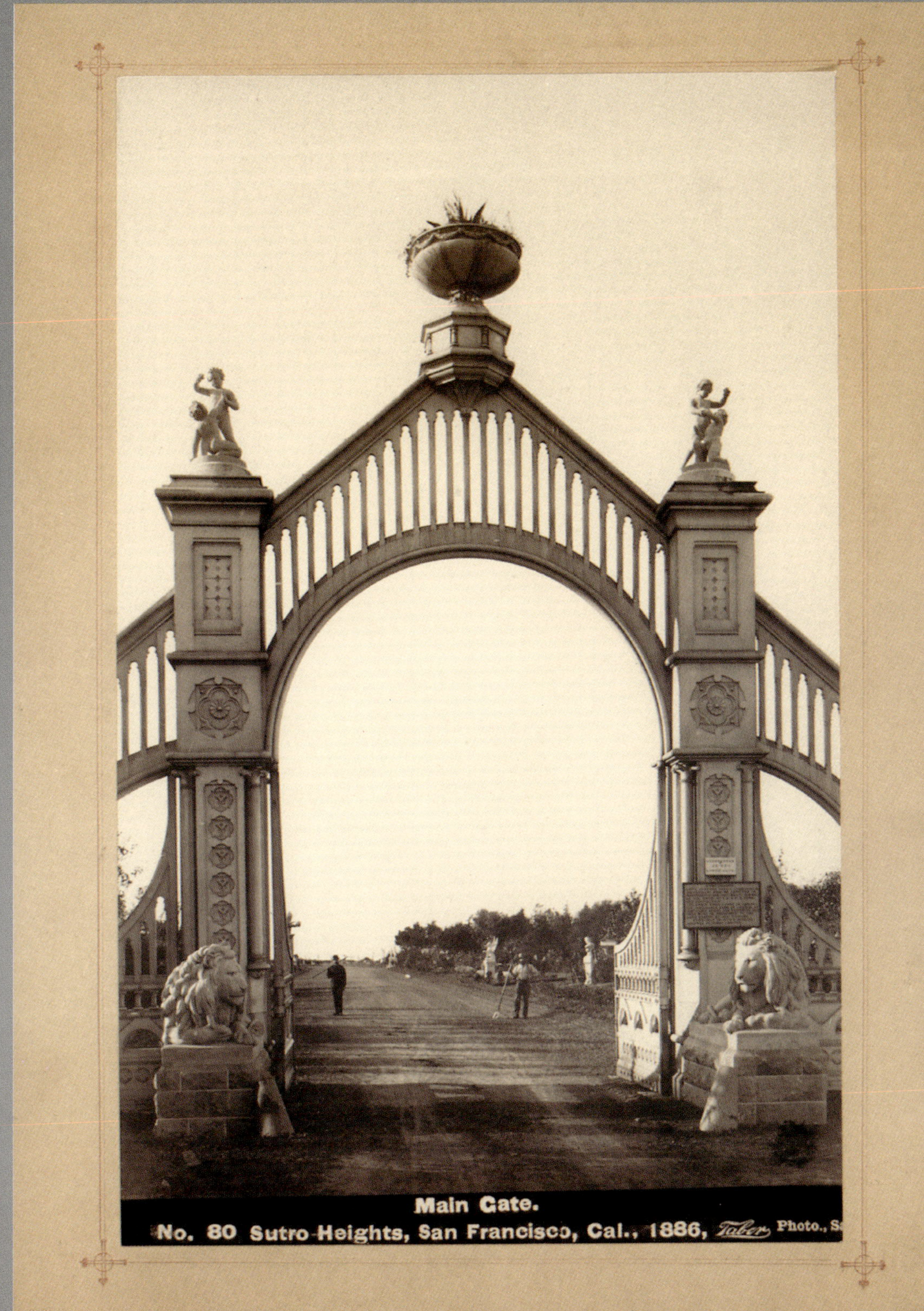

Main Gate.
No. 80 Sutro Heights, San Francisco, Cal., 1886, Taber Photo., S

CALIFORNIA STATE LIBRARY

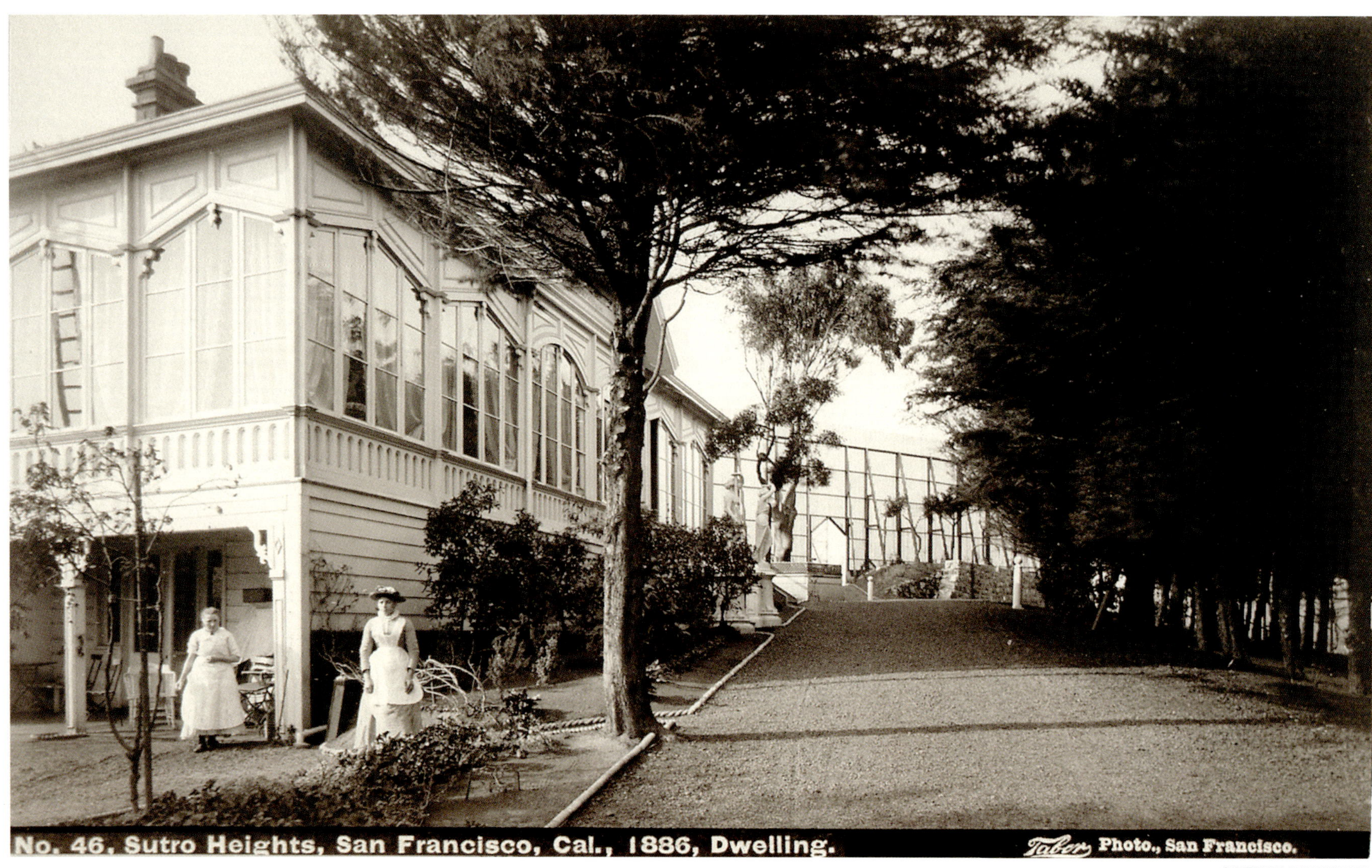

CALIFORNIA STATE LIBRARY

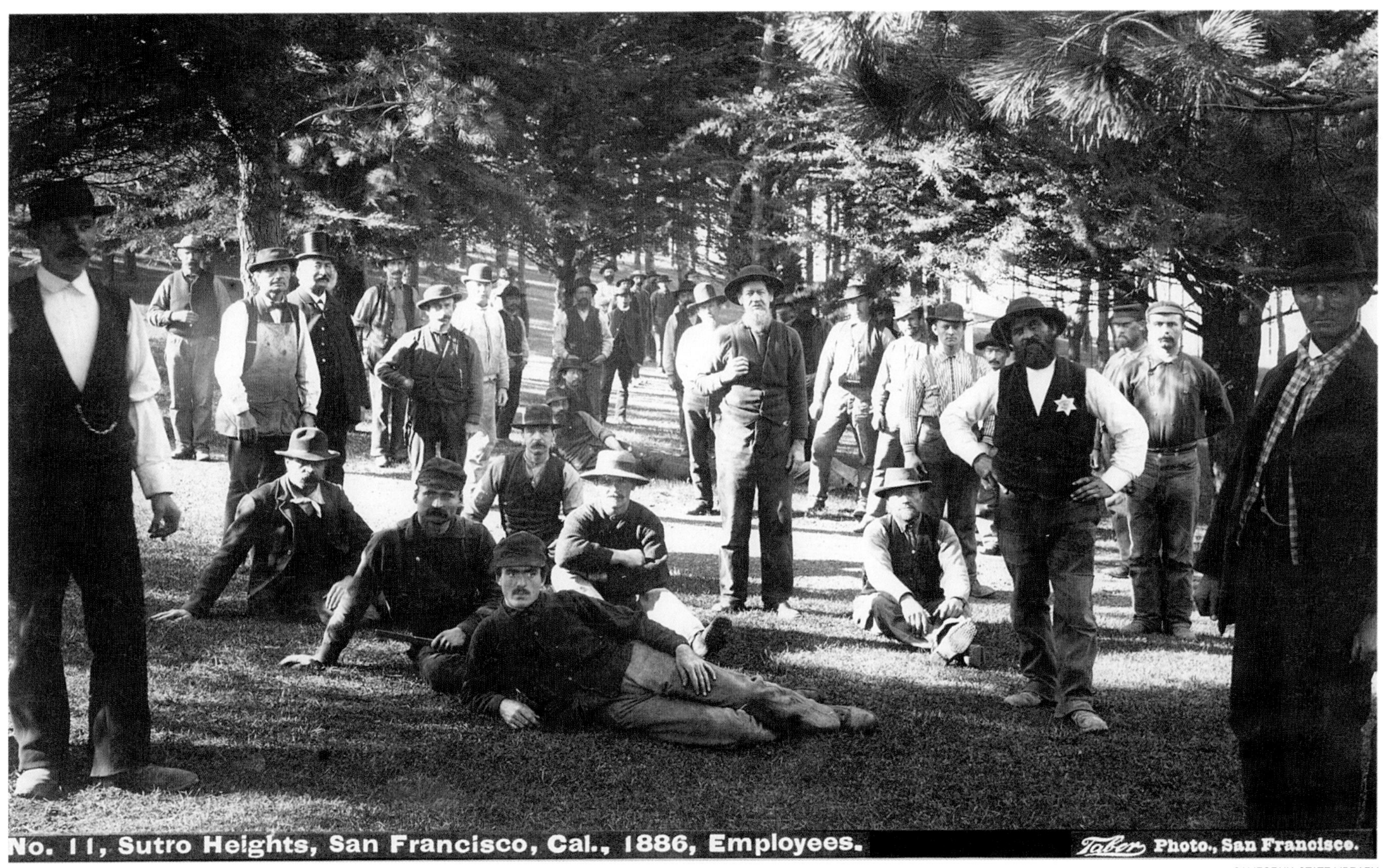

CALIFORNIA STATE LIBRARY

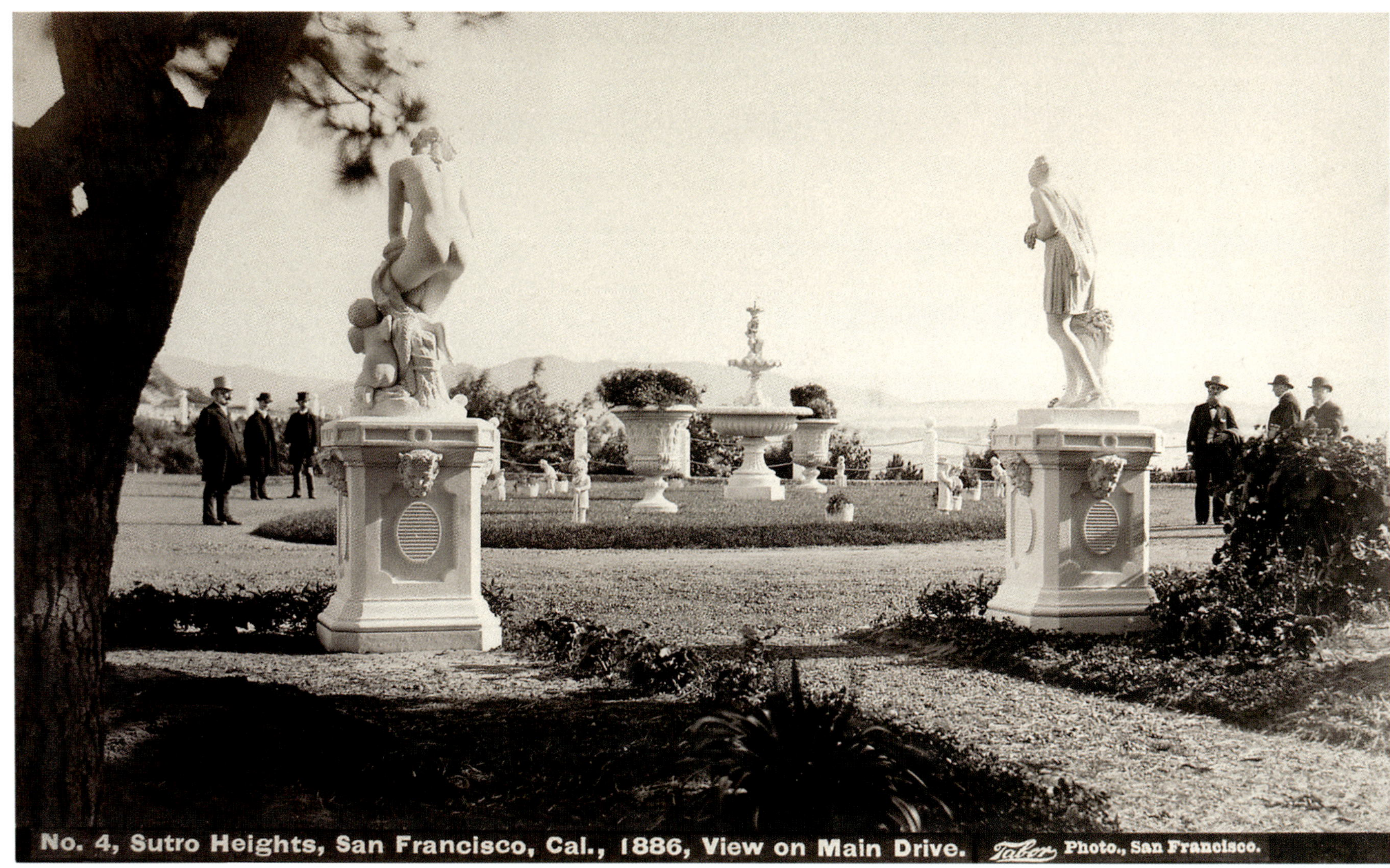

CALIFORNIA STATE LIBRARY

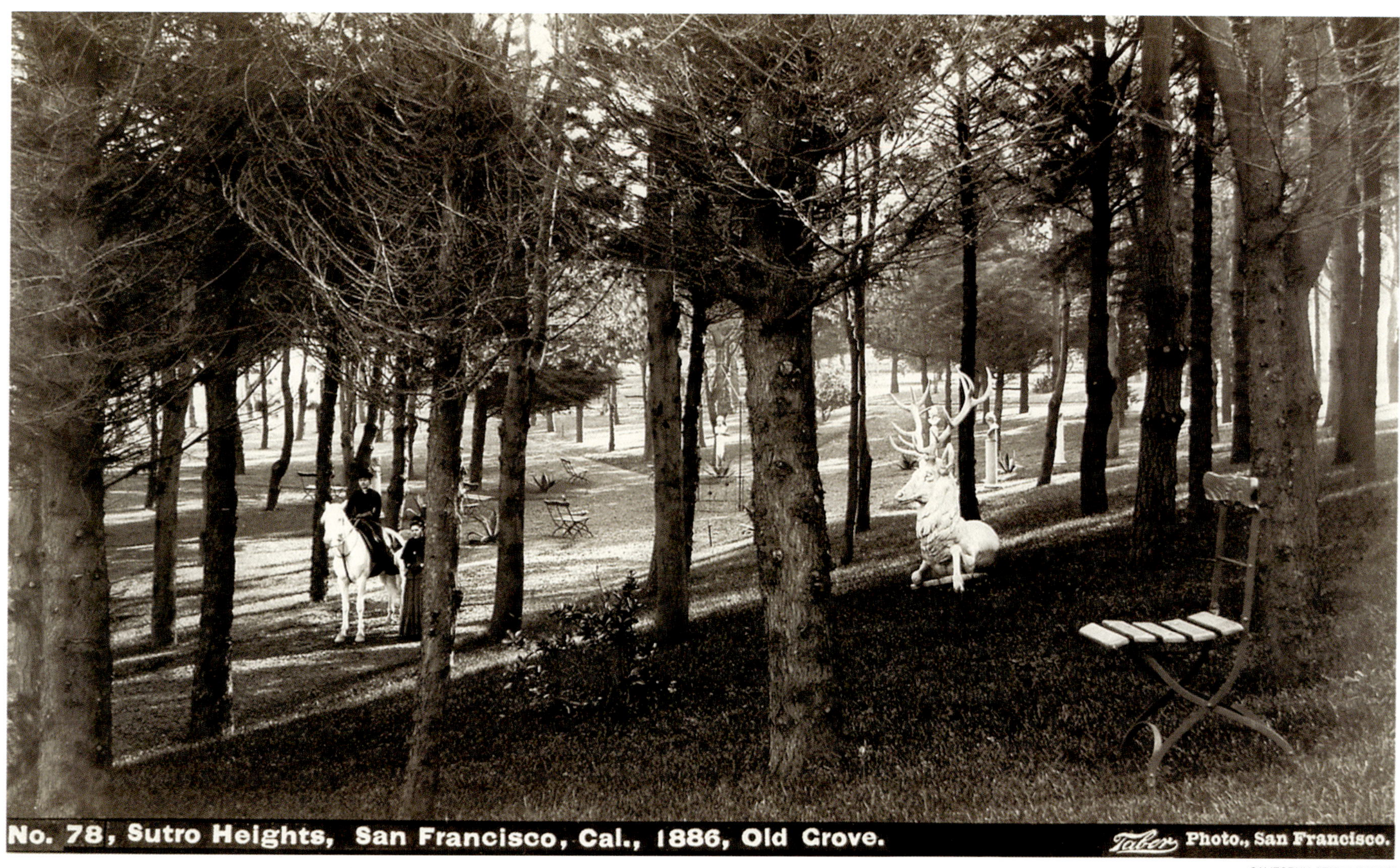

CALIFORNIA STATE LIBRARY

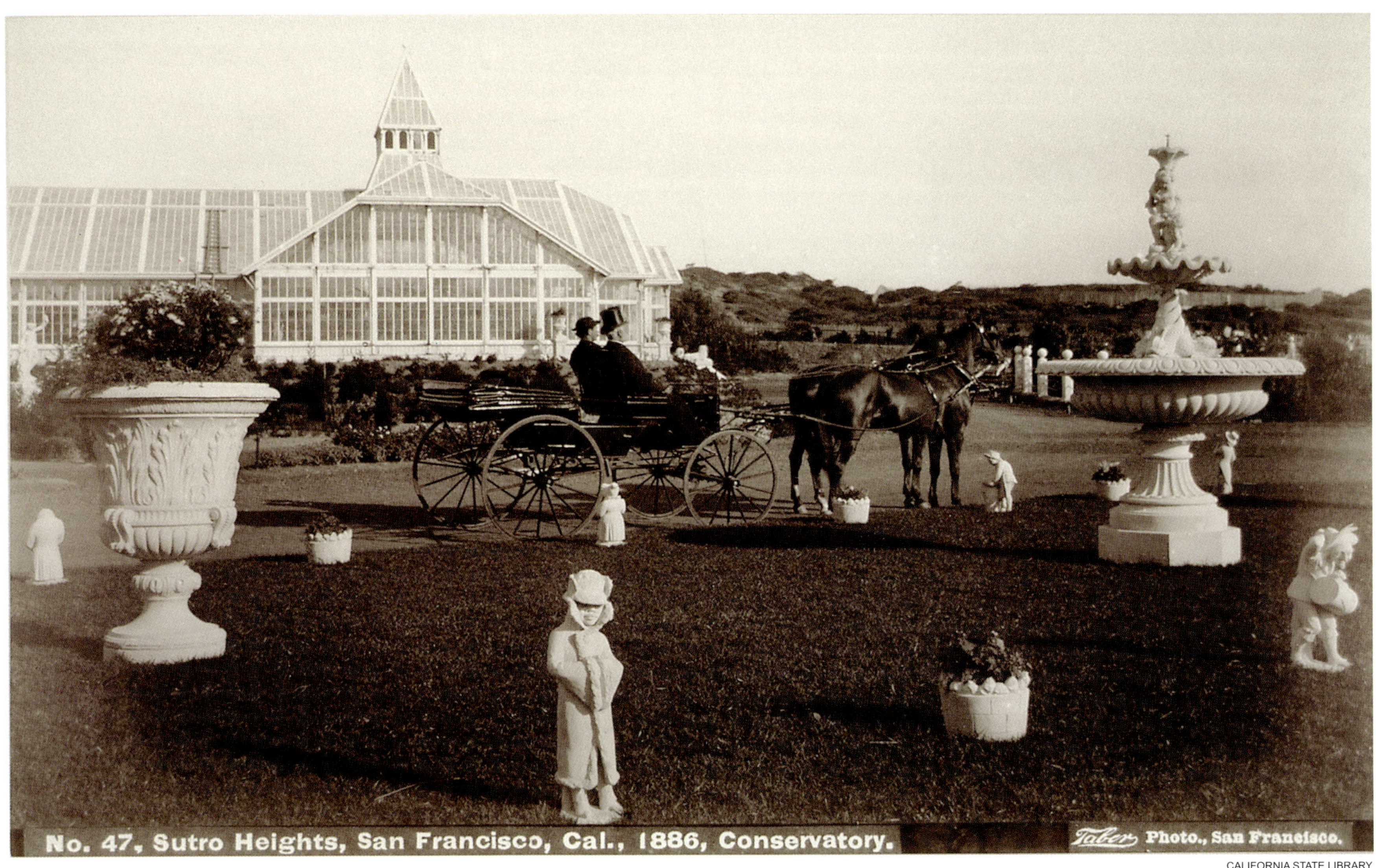

CALIFORNIA STATE LIBRARY

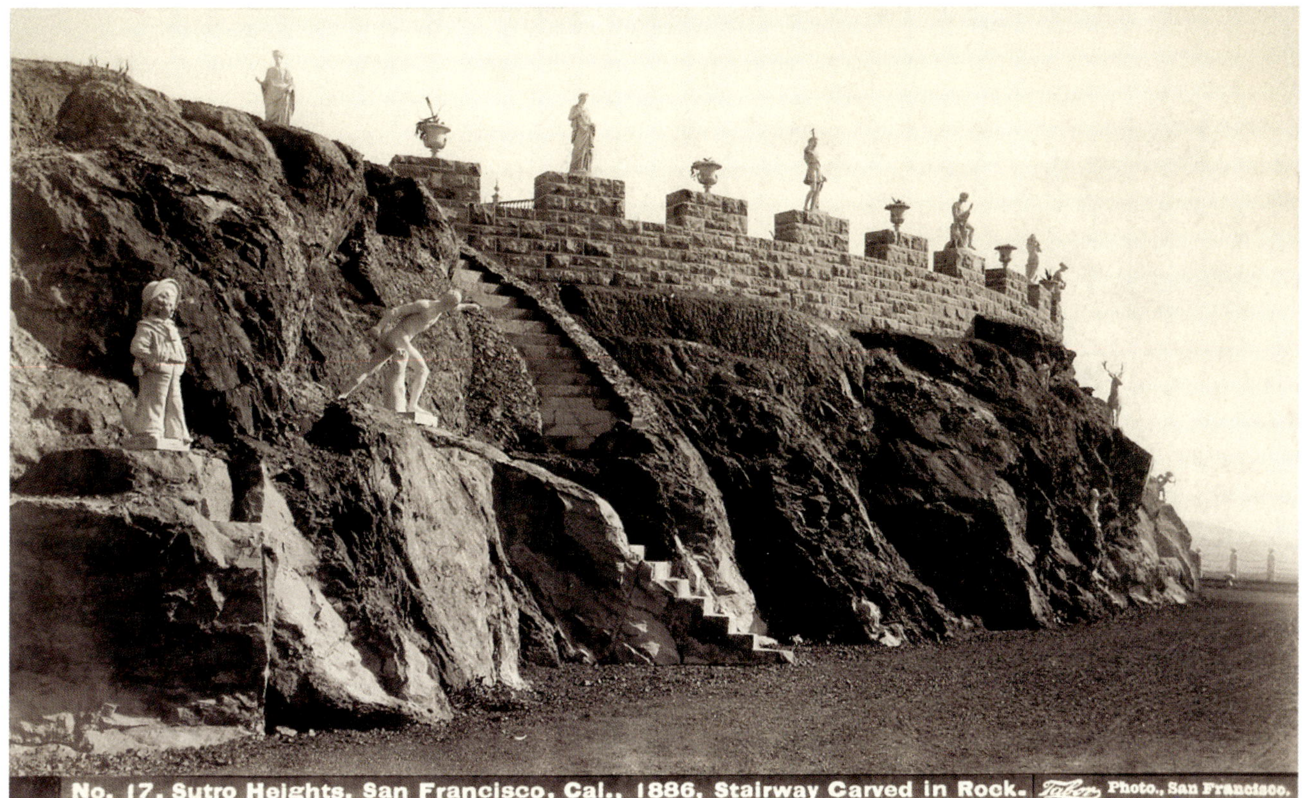

No. 17, Sutro Heights, San Francisco, Cal., 1886, Stairway Carved in Rock. Taber Photo., San Francisco.

CALIFORNIA STATE LIBRARY

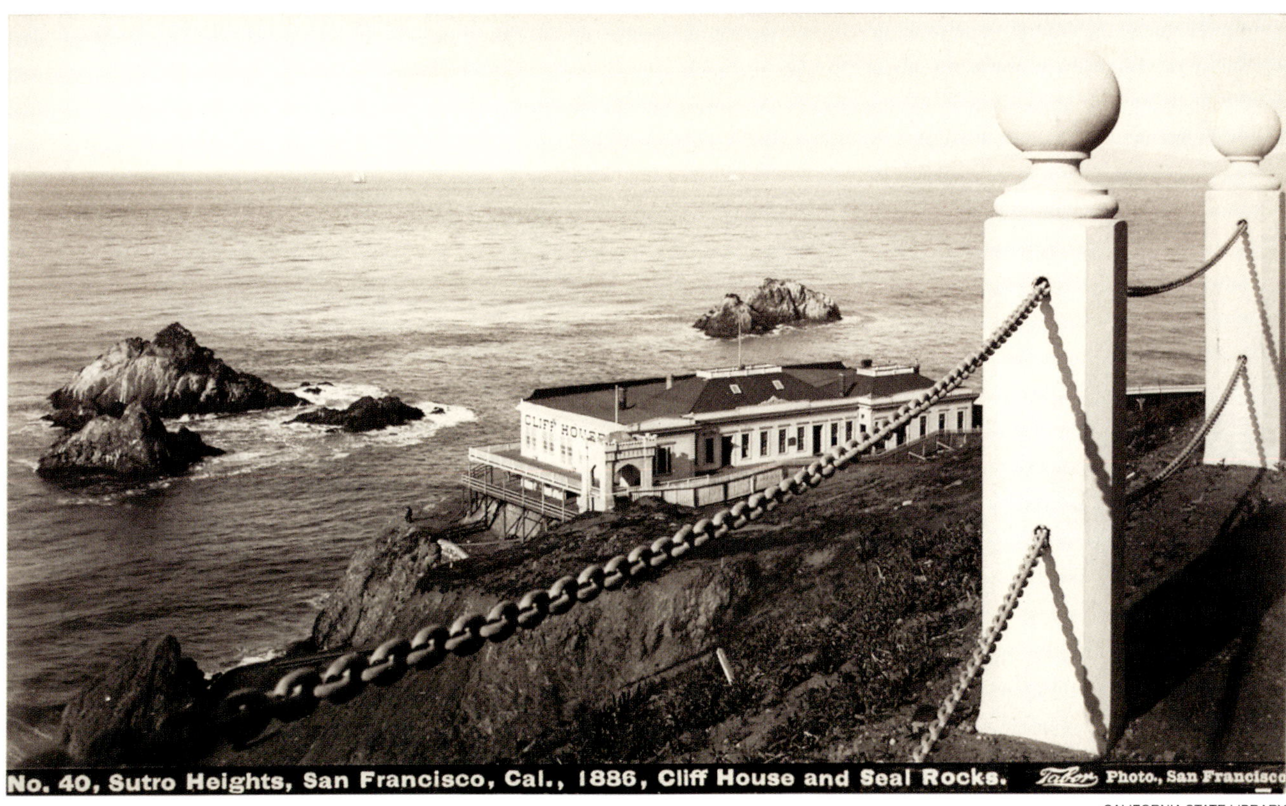

No. 40, Sutro Heights, San Francisco, Cal., 1886, Cliff House and Seal Rocks. Taber Photo., San Francisco

CALIFORNIA STATE LIBRARY

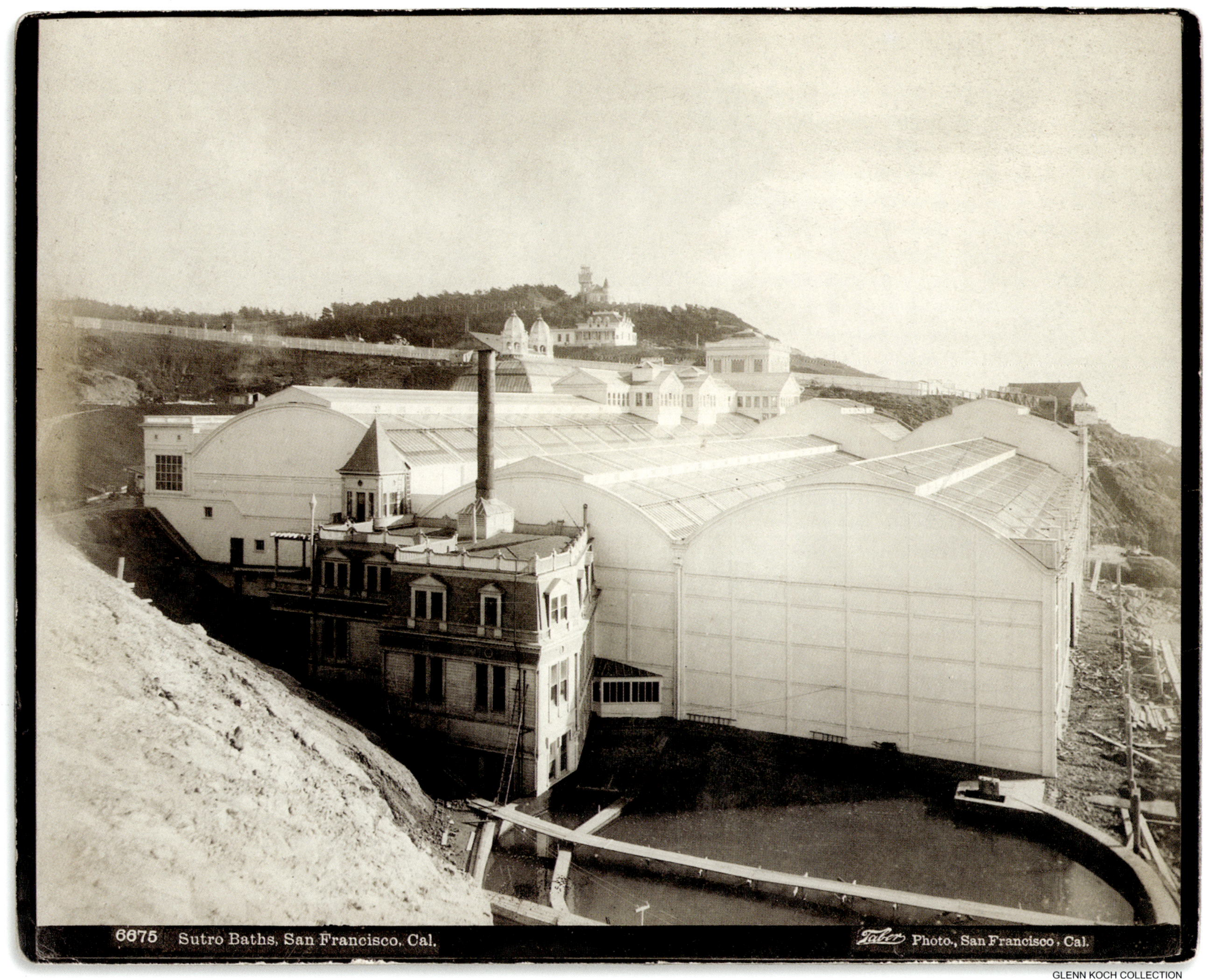

GLENN KOCH COLLECTION

Taber and his assistants went to Adolph Sutro's two pleasure domes, the Sutro Baths and Cliff House around 1895. The baths would not formally open to the public until 1896 but Sutro enjoyed showing select groups around what he called the "Sutro Coney Island." Above, Sutro Heights is visible in the background.

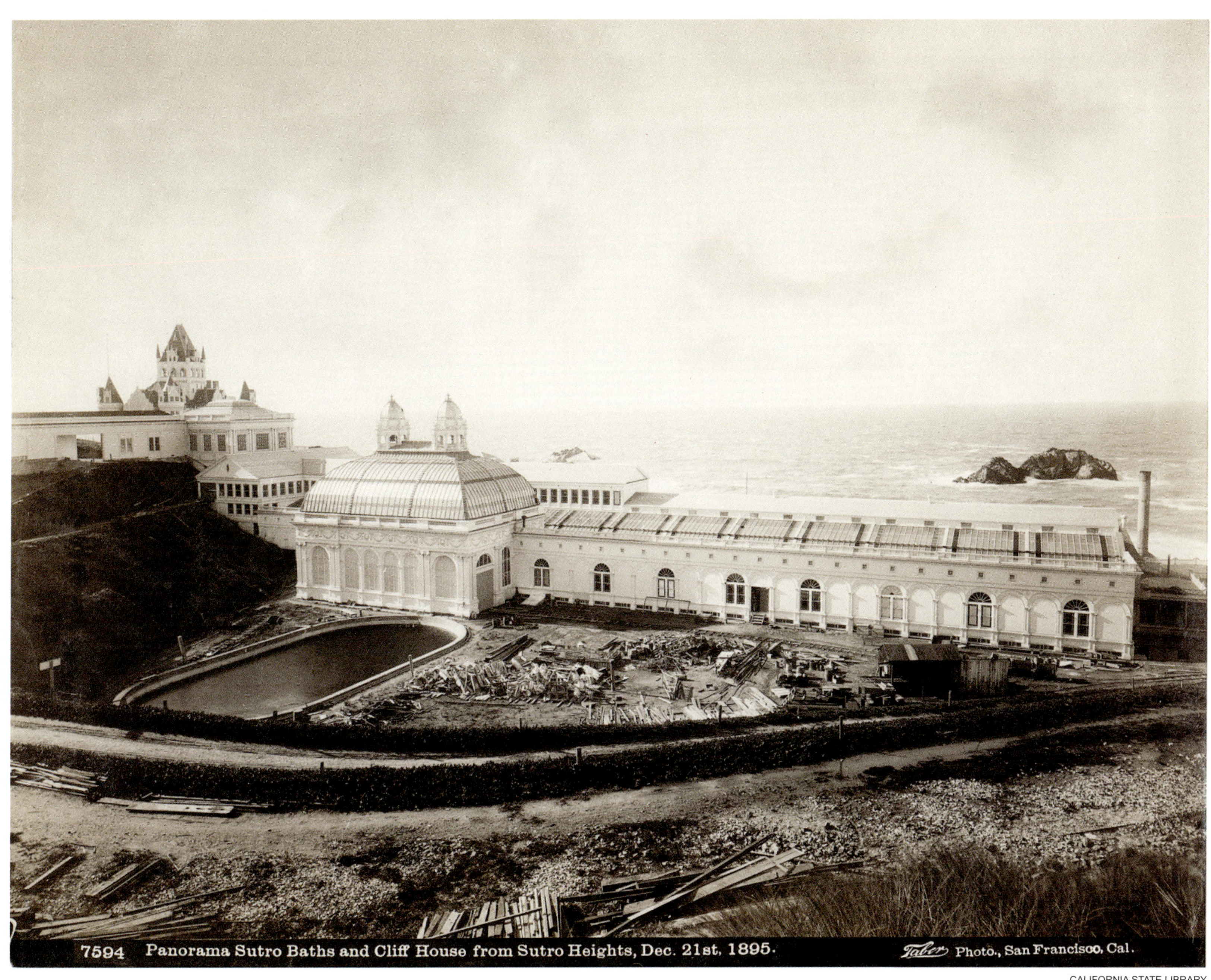

CALIFORNIA STATE LIBRARY

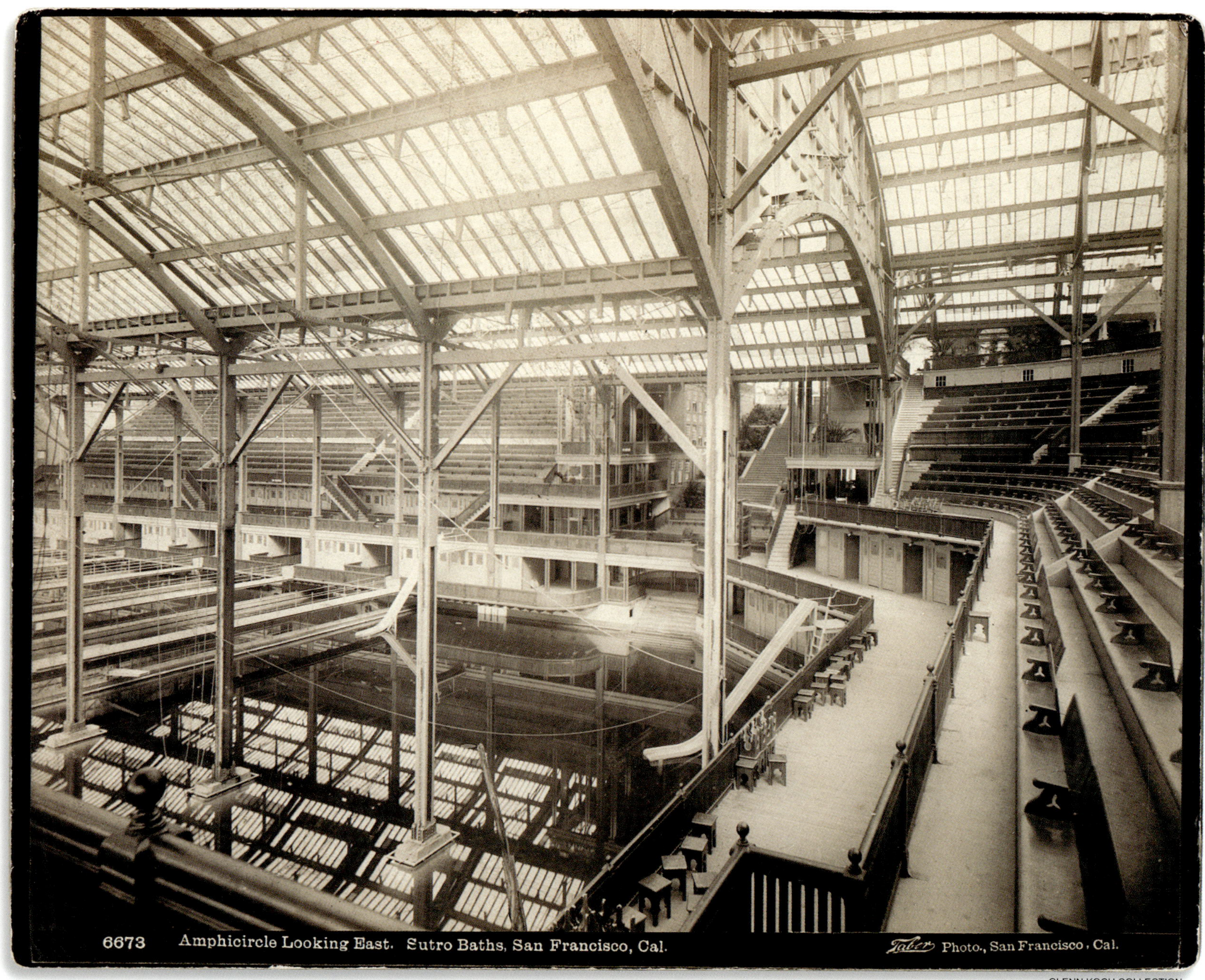

GLENN KOCH COLLECTION

c. 1896

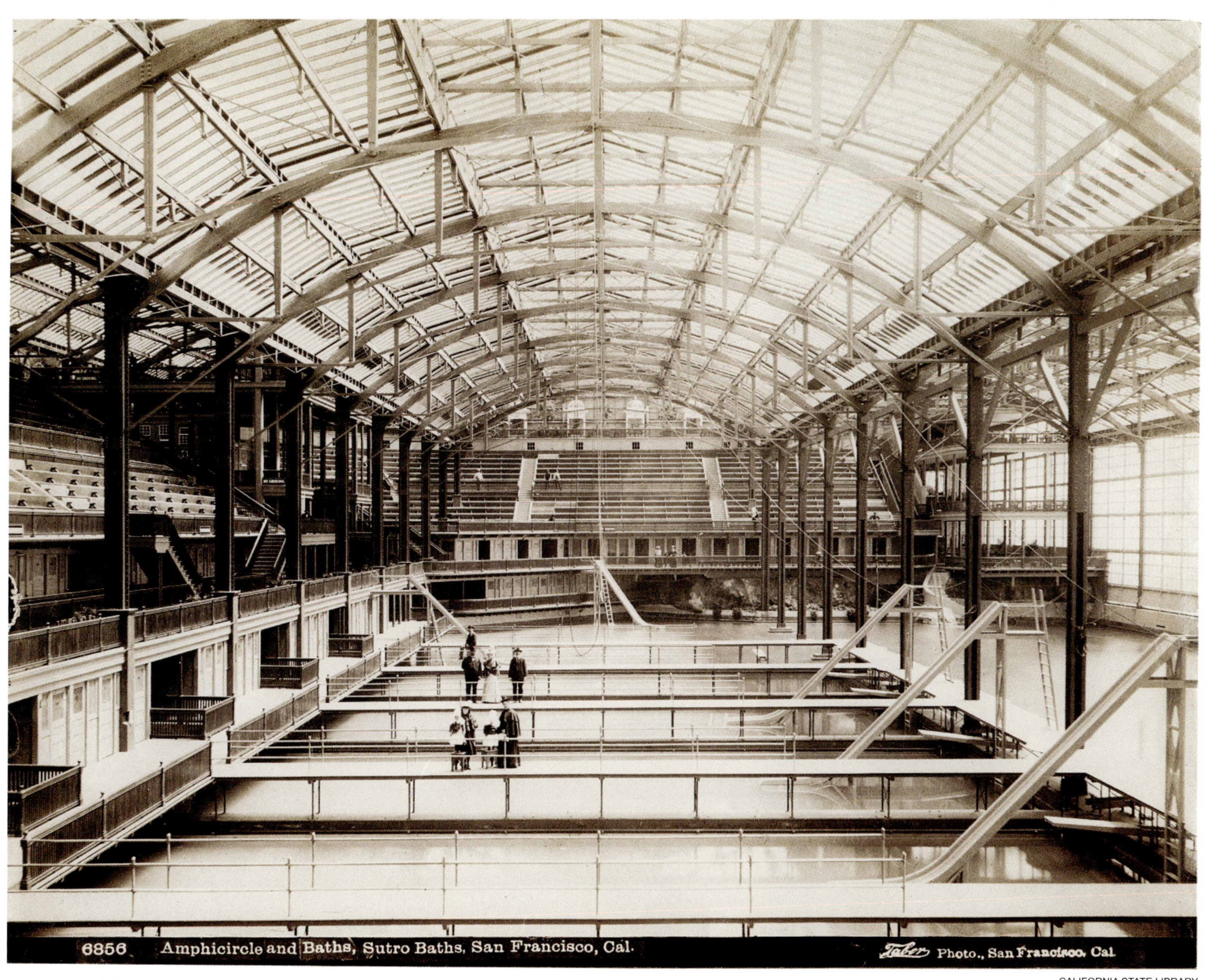

c. 1896

CALIFORNIA STATE LIBRARY

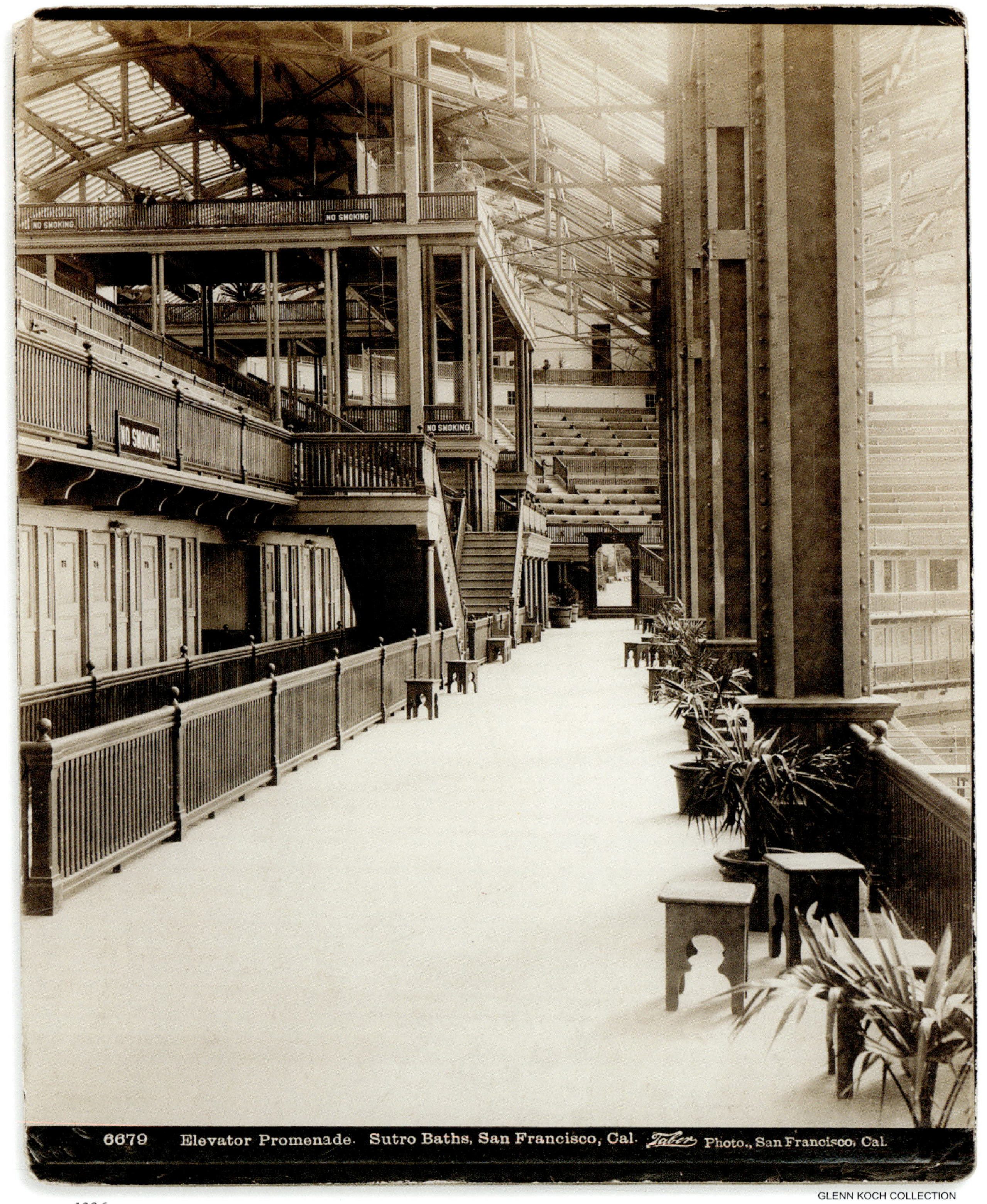

GLENN KOCH COLLECTION

c. 1896

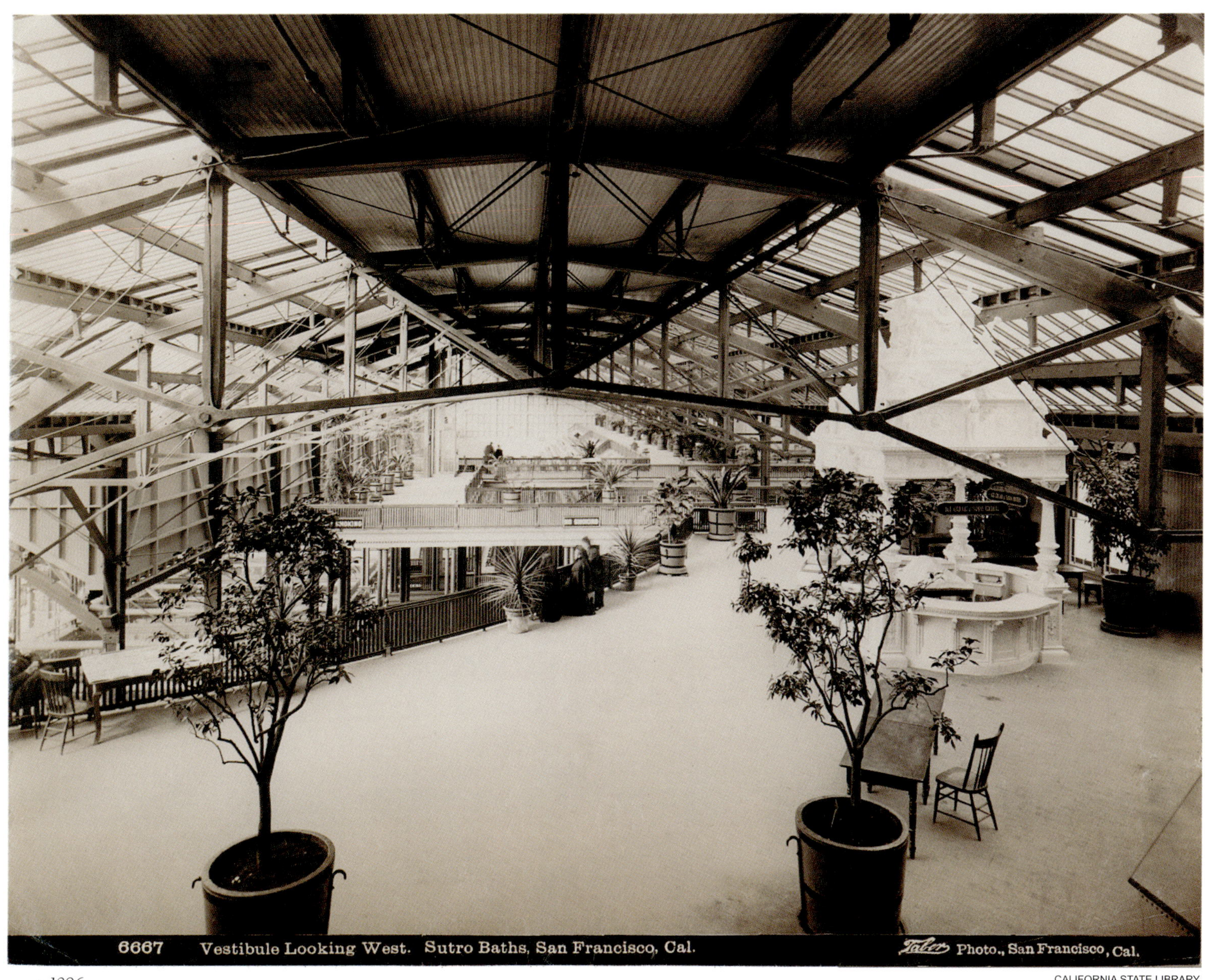

c. 1896

CALIFORNIA STATE LIBRARY

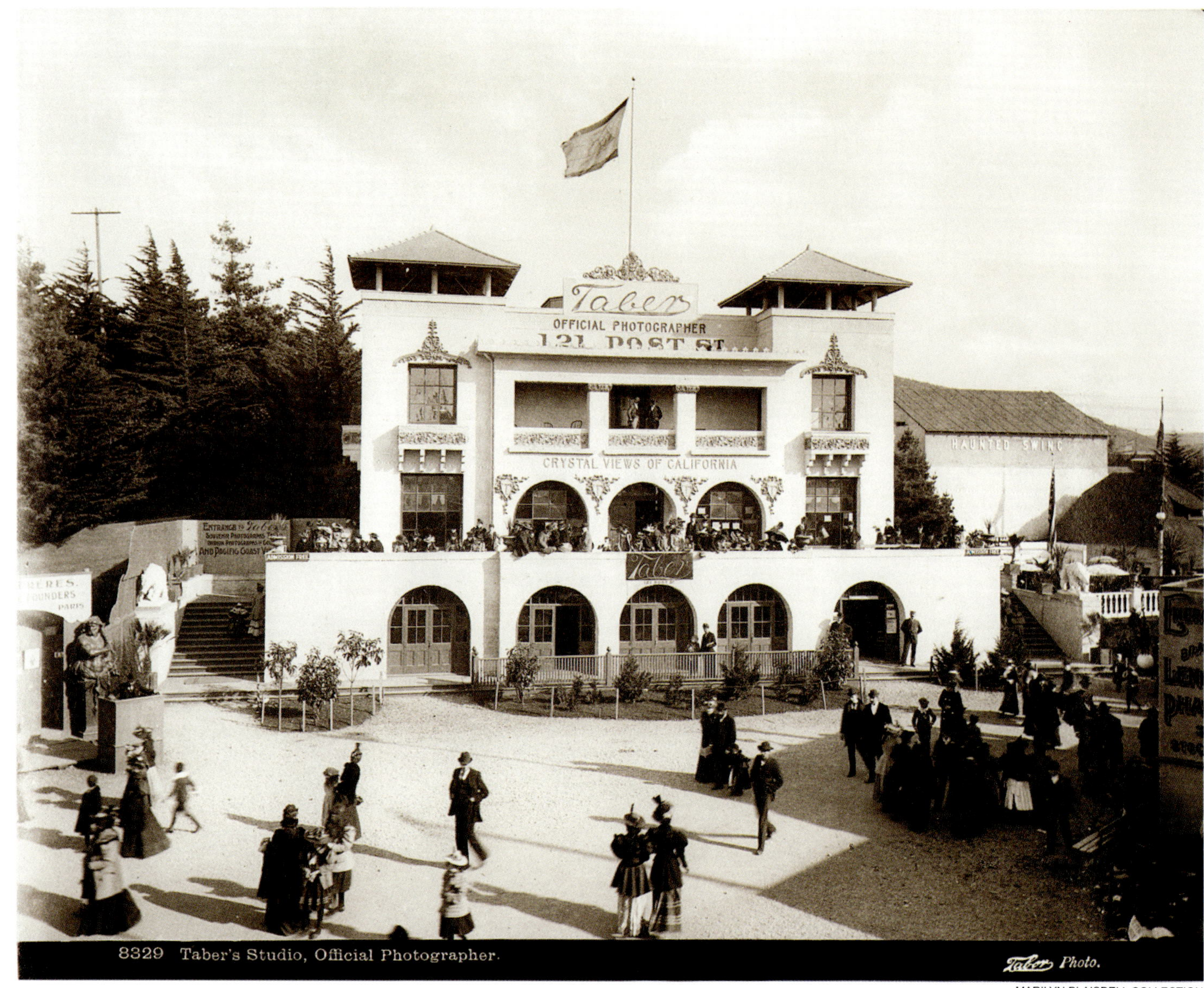

MARILYN BLAISDELL COLLECTION

1894 MIDWINTER FAIR

Isaiah Taber's commission as official photographer of the 1894 California Midwinter International Exposition in Golden Gate Park marked a high point of his career. Conceived by newspaper publisher Michael de Young and other businessmen to promote their city, the Midwinter Fair put an international spotlight on San Francisco and put Taber in a unique position to meet and photograph any and all important visitors to the event. His pavilion within the fairgrounds provided an excellent opportunity for self-promotion as well as sales of his scenic views and portrait services. Taber invited other photographers from around the state to assist him in the monumental project of recording construction and operation of the fair.

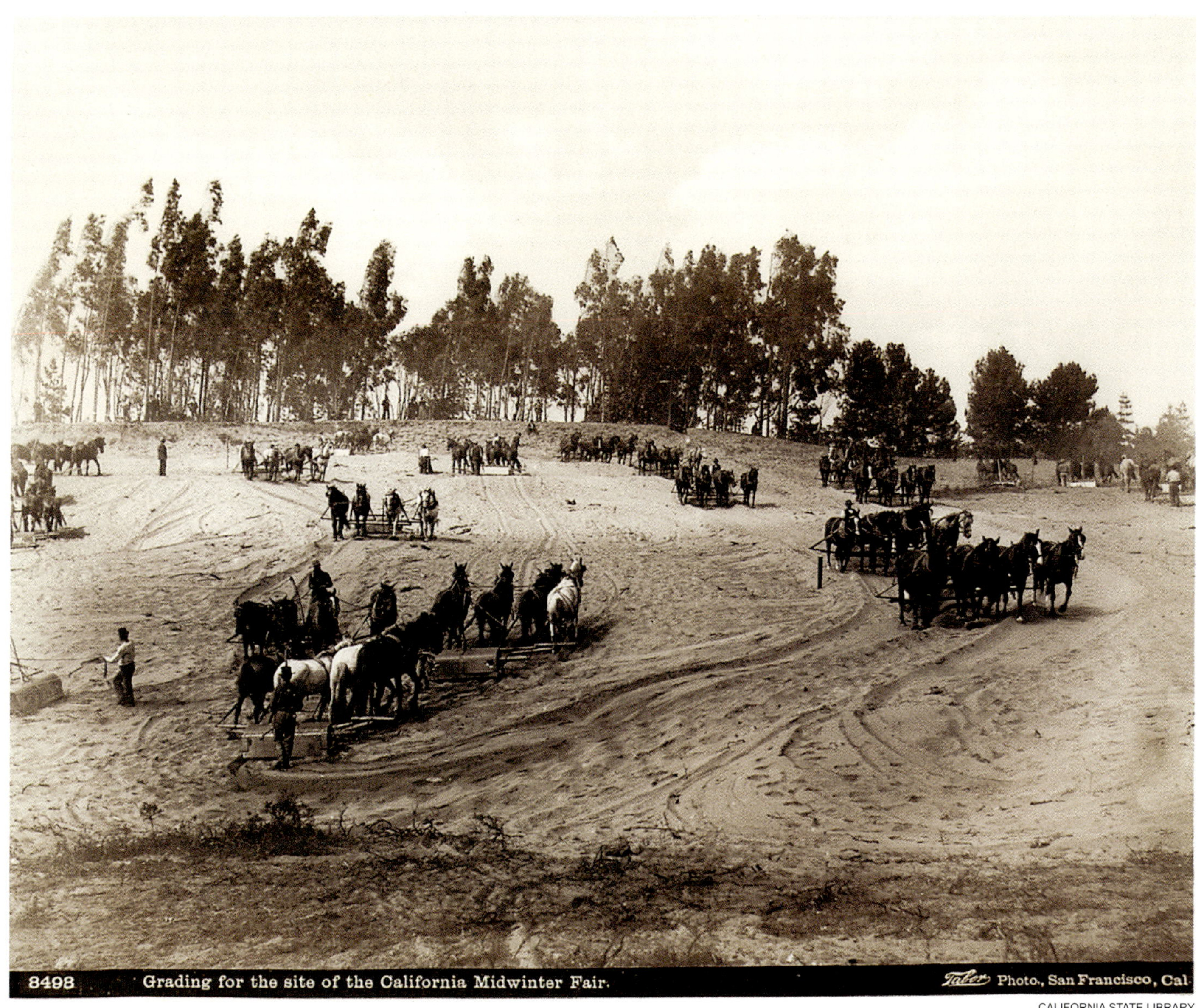

CALIFORNIA STATE LIBRARY

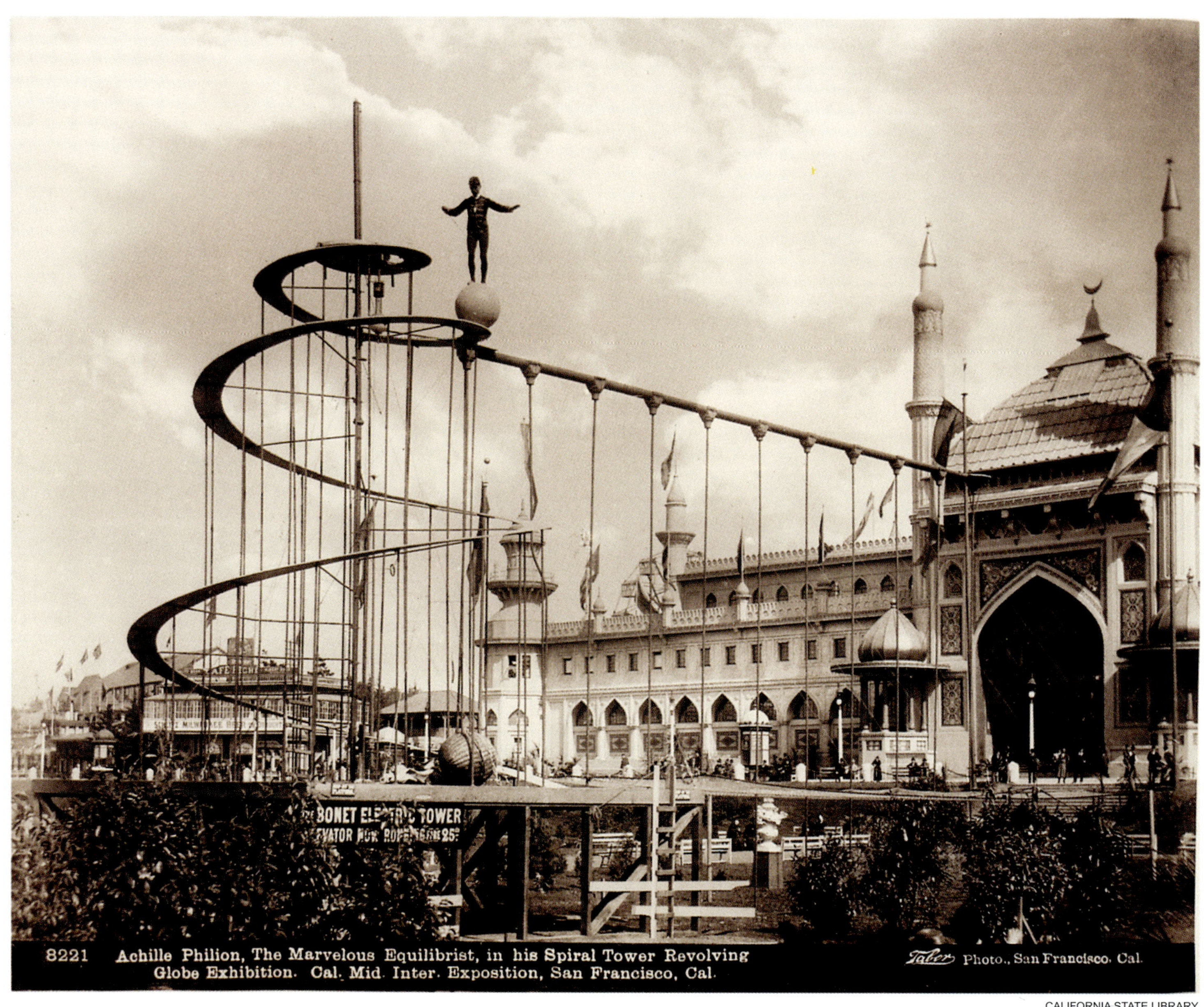

8221 Achille Philion, The Marvelous Equilibrist, in his Spiral Tower Revolving Globe Exhibition. Cal. Mid. Inter. Exposition, San Francisco, Cal. Taber Photo., San Francisco, Cal.

CALIFORNIA STATE LIBRARY

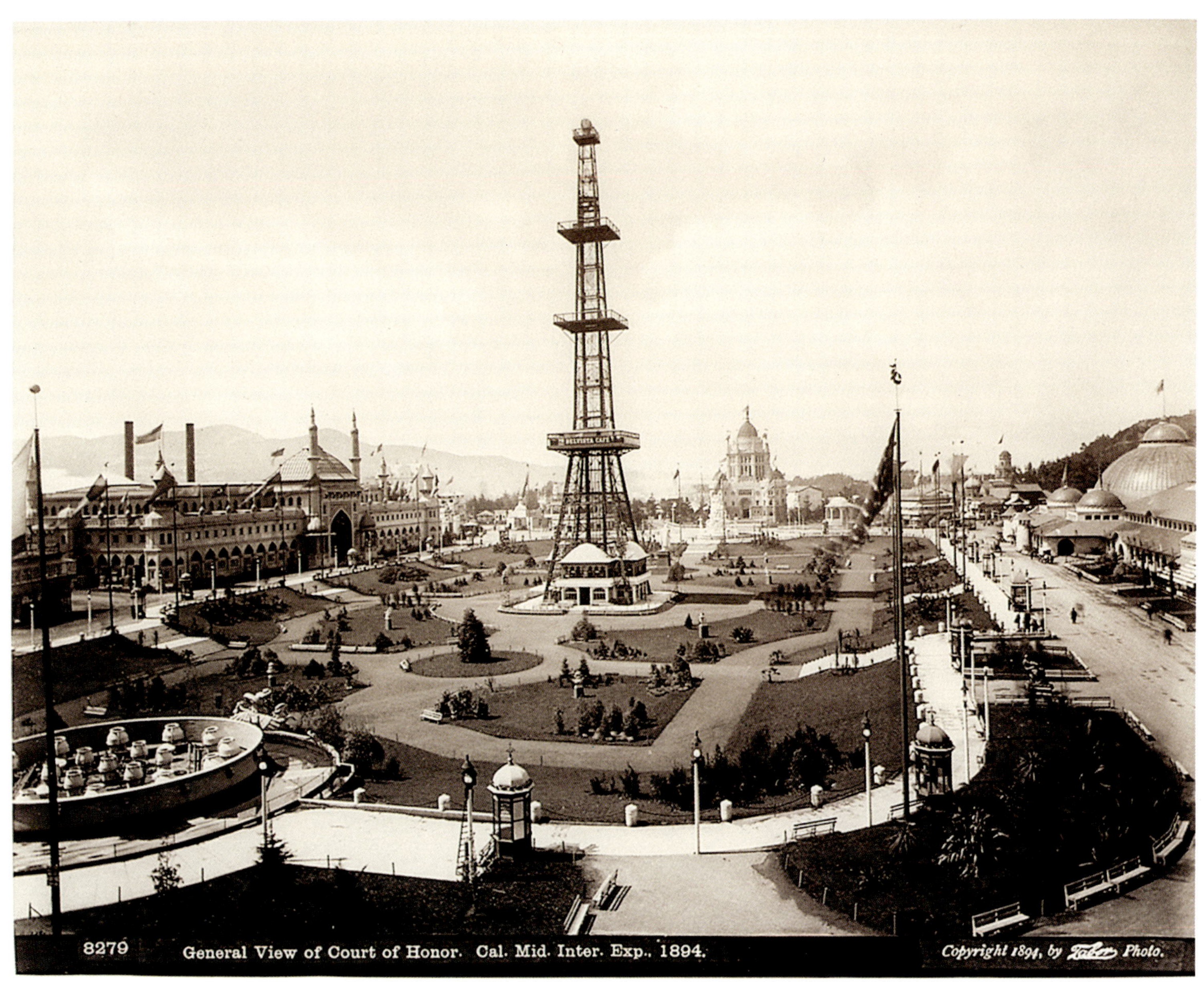

CALIFORNIA STATE LIBRARY

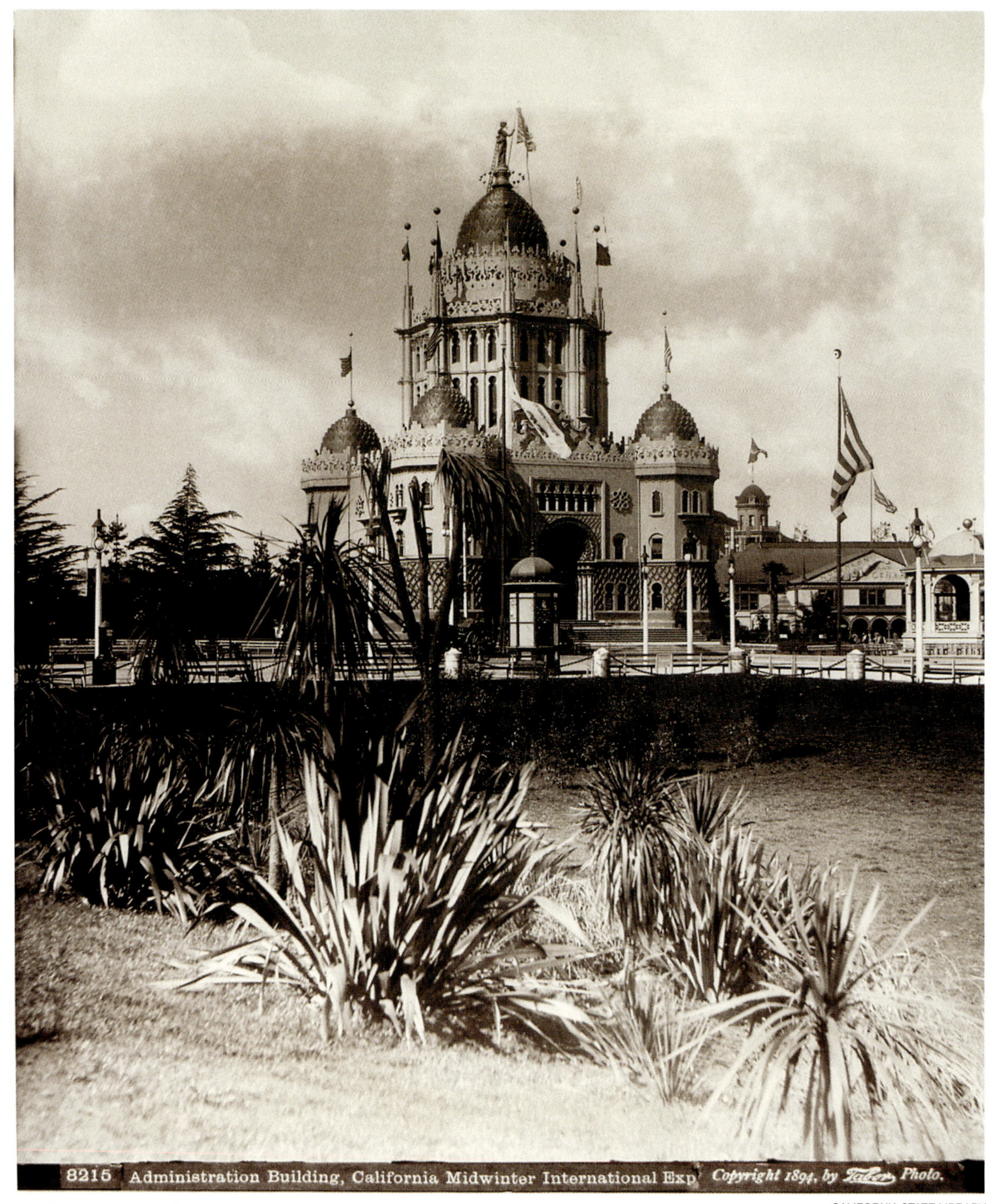

CALIFORNIA STATE LIBRARY

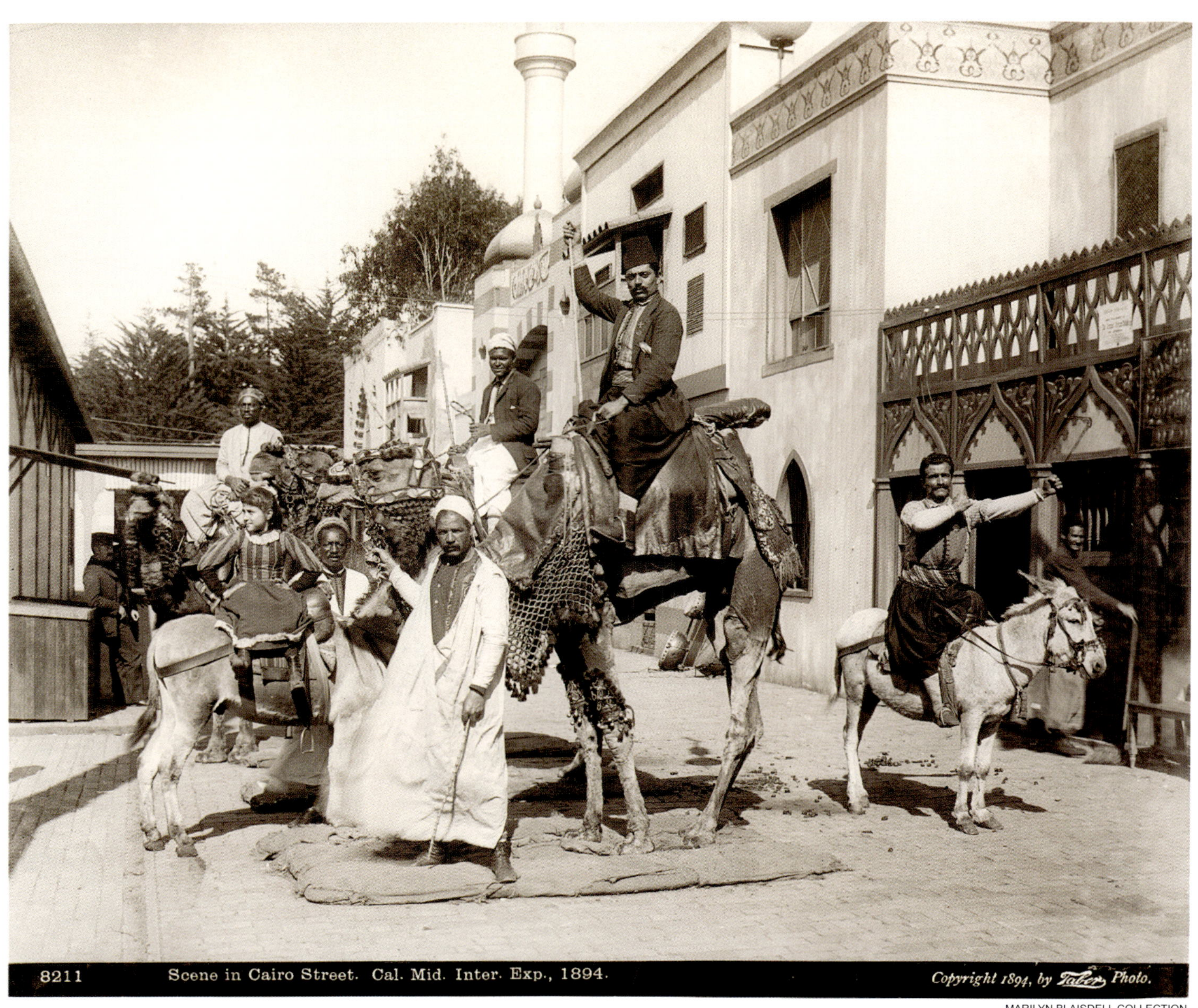

8211 Scene in Cairo Street. Cal. Mid. Inter. Exp., 1894. Copyright 1894, by Taber Photo.

MARILYN BLAISDELL COLLECTION

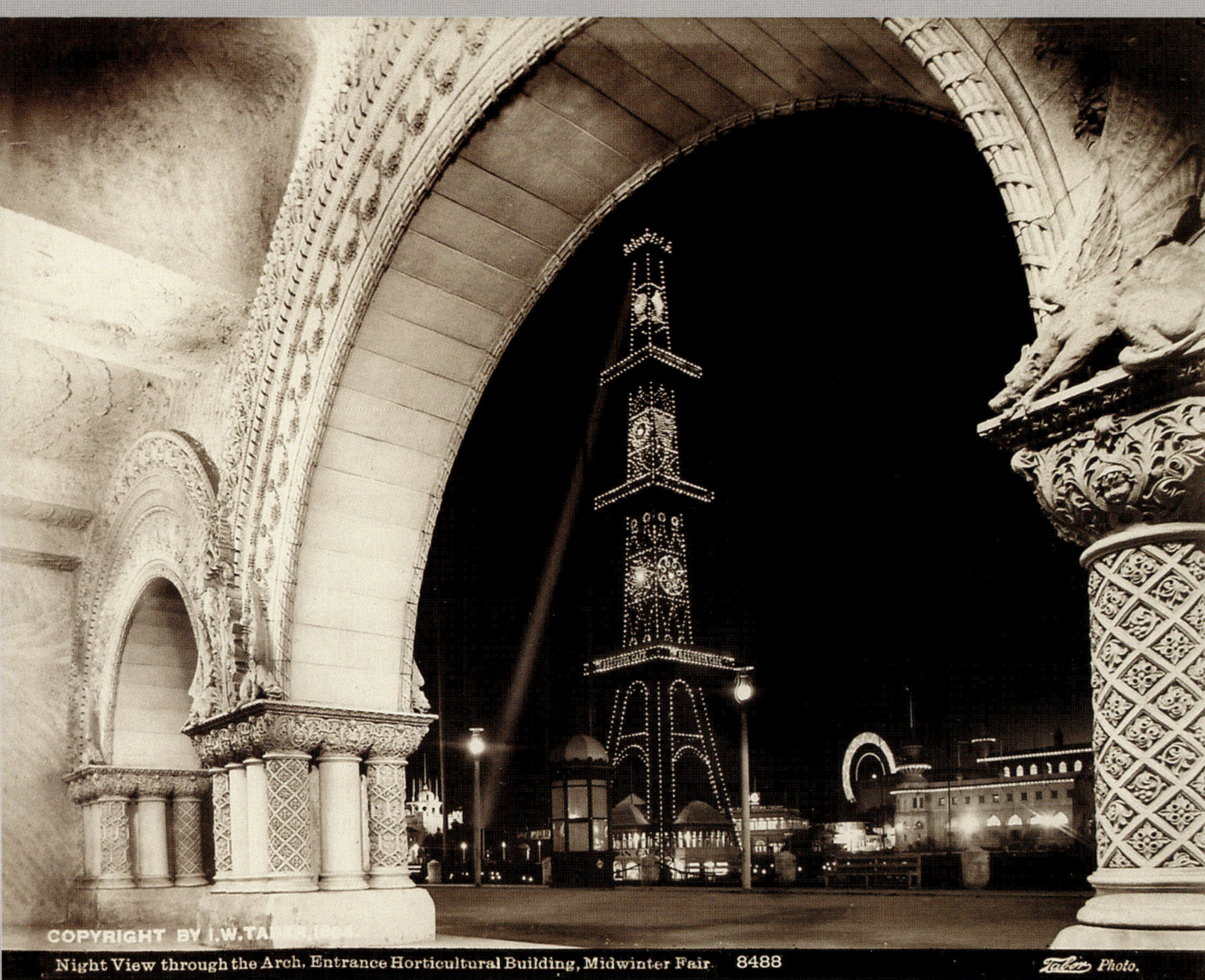

Night View through the Arch, Entrance Horticultural Building, Midwinter Fair. 8488 Taber Photo.

CALIFORNIA STATE LIBRARY

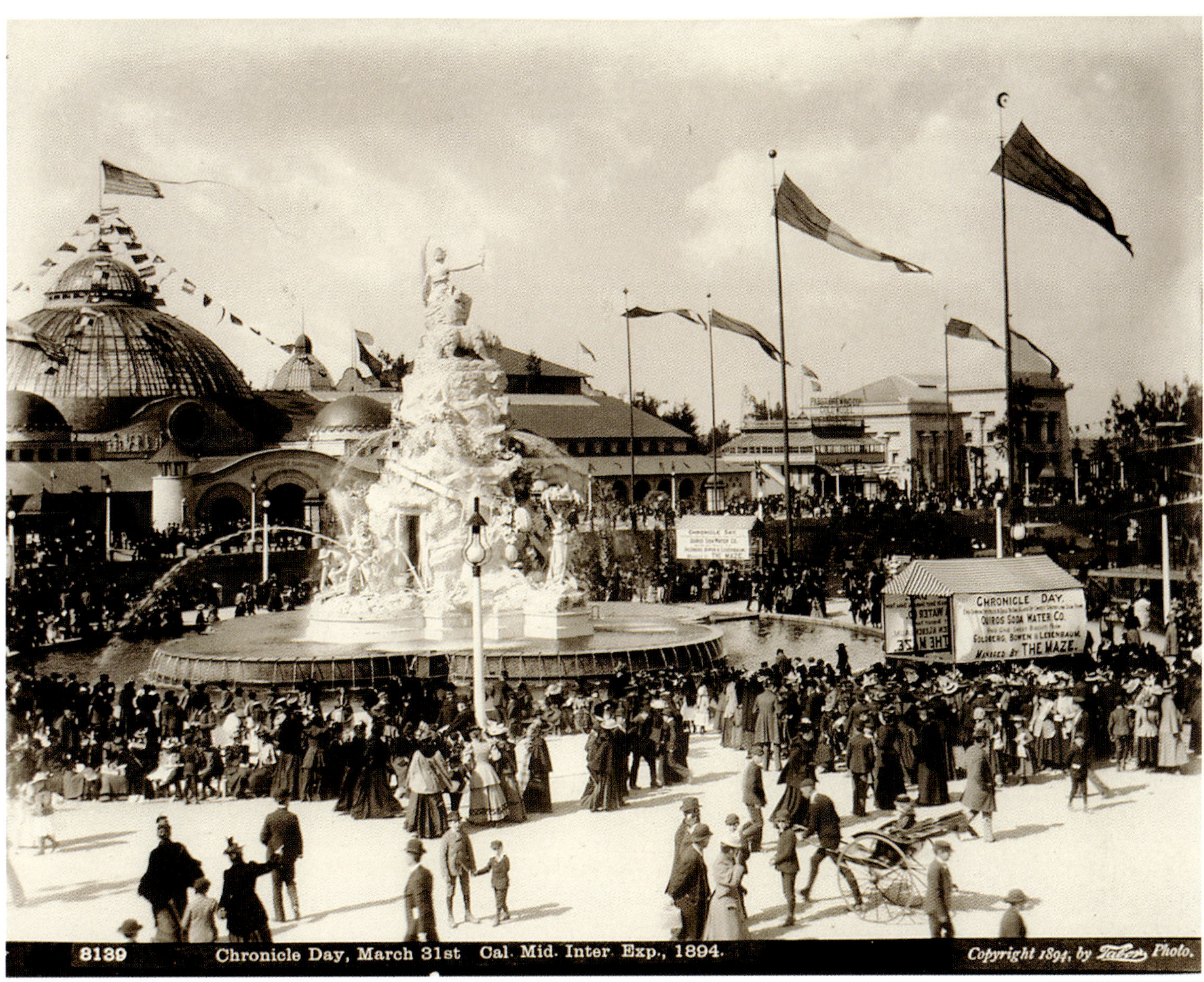

8139 Chronicle Day, March 31st Cal. Mid. Inter. Exp., 1894. Copyright 1894, by Taber Photo.

CALIFORNIA STATE LIBRARY

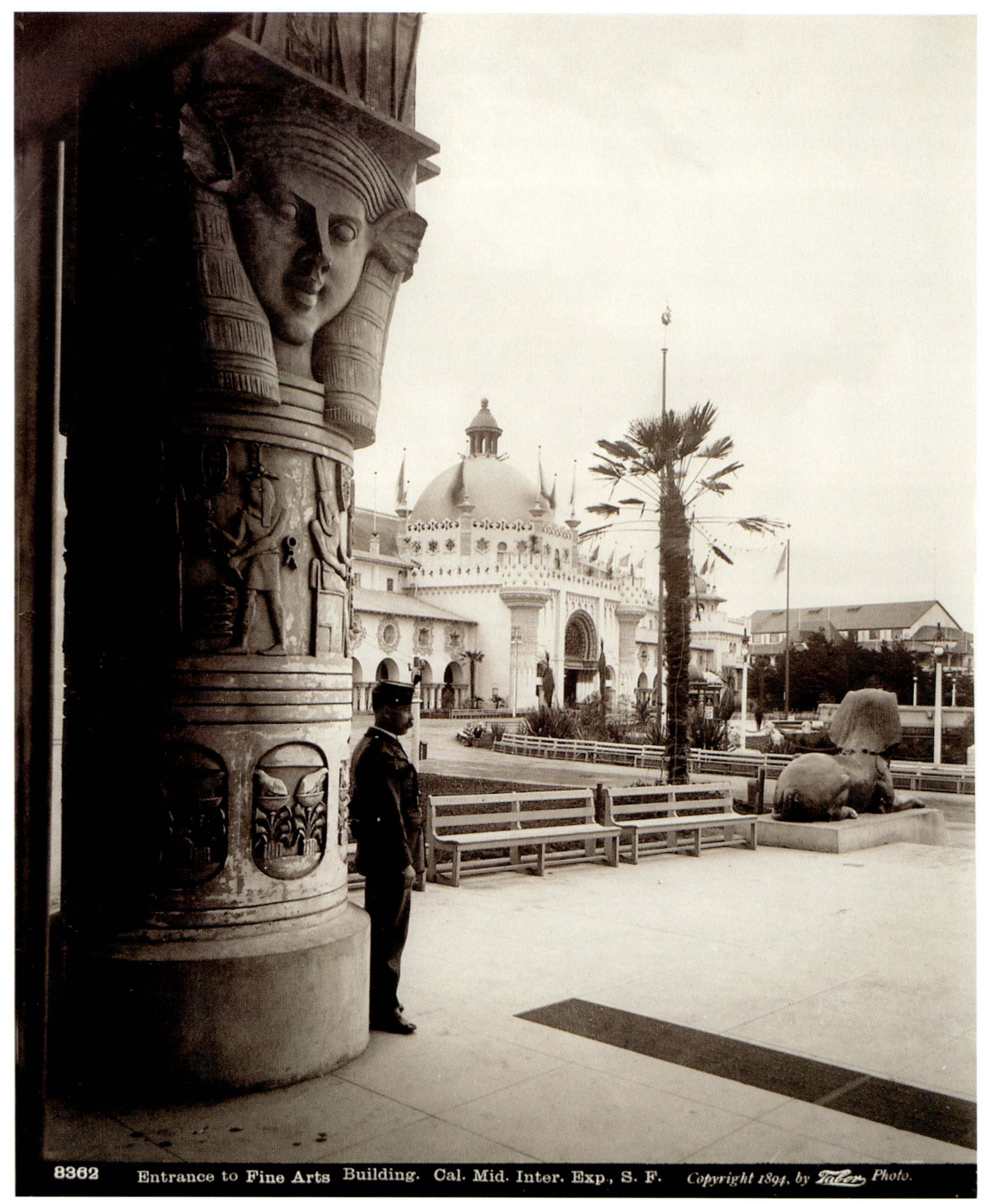

CALIFORNIA STATE LIBRARY

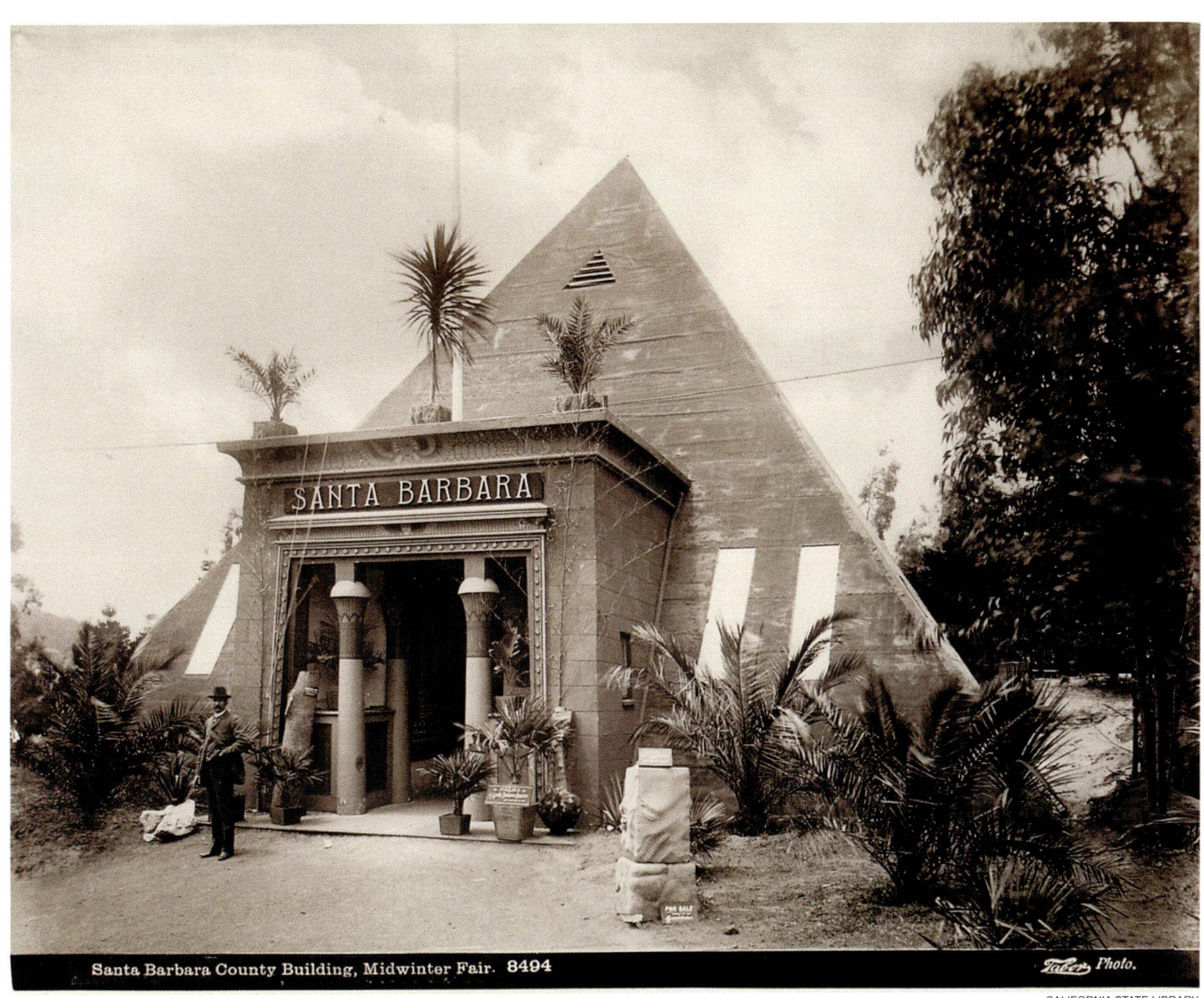

CALIFORNIA STATE LIBRARY

LONDON AND PARIS

By the late 1880s Isaiah Taber's interests had expanded beyond San Francisco. Already well-known in the United States, he wanted recognition in Europe as well. He had met and photographed almost all the foreign dignitaries, princes and princesses, diplomats and adventurers that had visited San Francisco over the previous decade. By carrying examples of his work back to their home countries, they had laid the groundwork for his European expansion. Taber felt the right time was 1887, the event, Queen Victoria's golden jubilee celebration recognizing her fiftieth year on the throne. Taber made inquiries, probing for an invitation to go to London. He sent a gift of several photographs to Queen Victoria but was politely rebuffed by Buckingham Palace. The queen, it seems, liked the photos and wanted to keep them, but as she could not accept gifts, she instructed her agent to pay Mr. Taber for them.

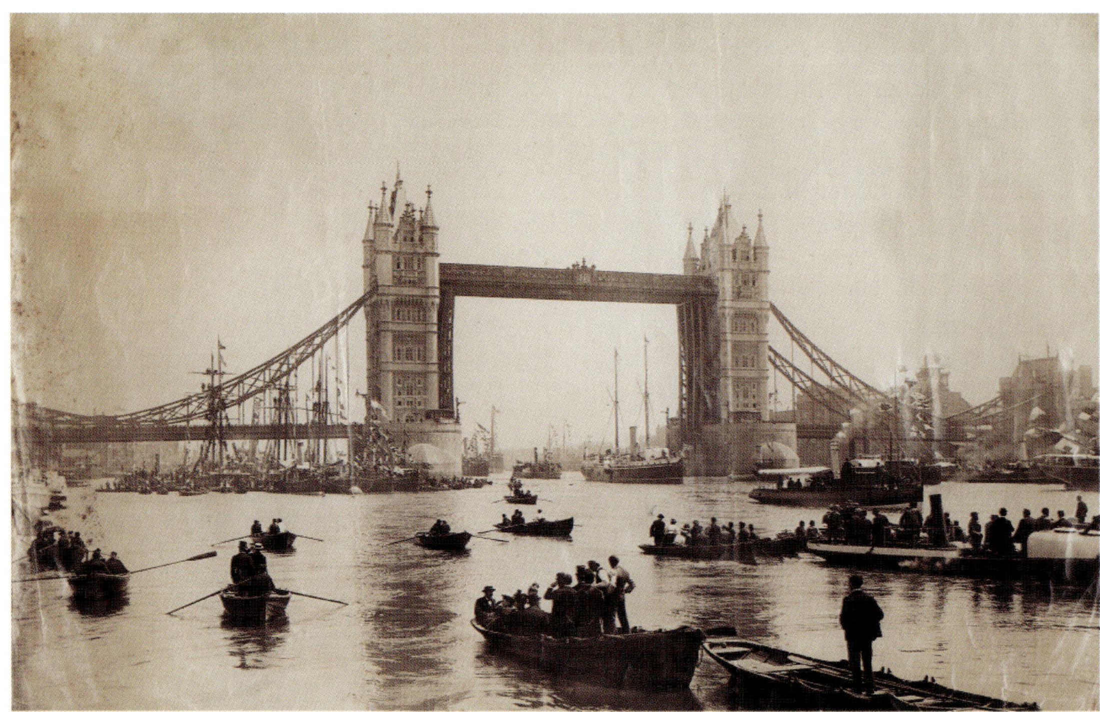

CUNEO COLLECTION

Taber lost his opportunity but, in his usual manner, did not surrender. He turned his attention instead to securing the position of official photographer for the upcoming 1894 Midwinter Exposition planned by his friend and patron Michael deYoung of the *San Francisco Chronicle*. Taber was awarded the commission and, during the course of the fair, met any and all foreign visitors of note, especially English nobility. He took a portrait of Henry Morton Stanley, of Stanley and Livingston fame, and renewed their acquaintance. Taber had first met Stanley in Monterey in 1891 when Stanley was touring the country promoting his new book *In Darkest Africa*. Stanley, an American expatriate living in London, was a rising star in British affairs and had been recognized by Queen Victoria. Apparently Taber enlisted him in his quest to photograph Queen Victoria's next jubilee, the sixtieth year of her reign to be celebrated in 1897. This time, perhaps with help from Stanley, Taber was successful, receiving an invitation from Buckingham Palace.

His moment had come in his sixty-sixth year. Taber, still vigorous and industrious, made plans that would have wilted a younger man. He would introduce his bas-relief portrait process to England well before the Queen's jubilee so that after the event, he could establish permanent studios and galleries, first in London, then Paris and Berlin. Taber began writing to former clients, friends and acquaintances in England and France, informing them of his plans. There was Nelly Bly, famous woman journalist who had surpassed the fictional Phineas Fogg in his dash around the world in eighty days by completing the journey in sixty days. He had met and photographed her in San Francisco at the end of her celebrated journey when her employer and publisher Joseph Pulitzer sent a special train to greet her. She was living in Paris, married to millionaire Robert Seaman and she agreed to make introductions there for Taber. Henry Stanley would assist from

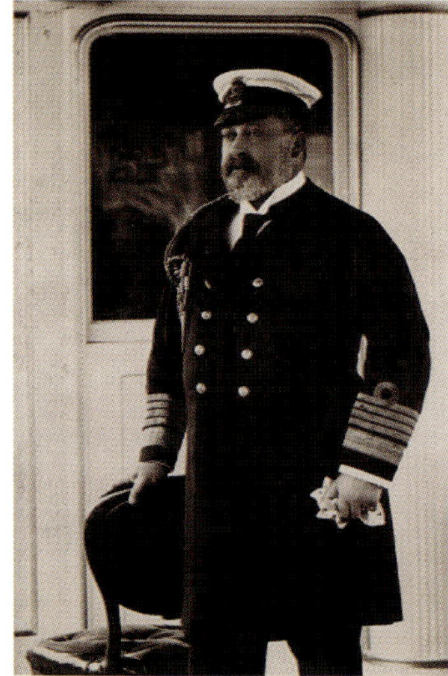

CUNEO COLLECTION

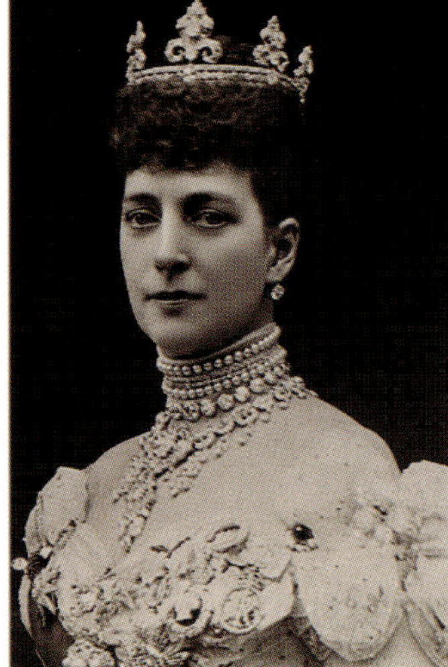

CUNEO COLLECTION

Top: The Tower Bridge, London, during Queen Victoria's jubilee.

Above: King Edward VII and Queen Alexandra, c.1901.

London. Loie Fuller, world-famous dance sensation (Taber had photographed her as well) would let Isaiah Taber use her Follies Bergere stage address as a Paris mail drop. Probably through Fuller, Taber met and charmed Sarah Bernhardt, and was invited to photograph her Paris home.

Taber traveled to New York and sailed for England, arriving there in June, 1896, almost a year in advance of the Queen's jubilee celebration. For the next six months, working out of the Hotel Cecil in London, a fashionable spot for visiting Americans, he broadened his contacts, renewed old acquaintances and promoted his bas-relief process.

He toured England and Scotland and met Sir George Bullogh, who owned the Isle of Rum, one the Inner Hebrides off the coast of Scotland. Stopping for lunch with Sir George at a small inn, Taber was surprised and pleased to see the walls adorned with Taber scenic photos. The proprietor had once visited San Francisco and purchased the photos at Taber's gallery. The proprietor presented Taber with a plate frequently used by Queen Victoria's uncle, King George IV, when the king visited on hunting trips.

In the summer of 1897, in time for Queen Victoria's jubilee celebration, Taber opened a London portrait studio on Dover Street, Piccadilly. Taber's photos must have been well received at Buckingham Palace because he was invited to Marlborough House to make portraits of the Prince and Princess of Wales, who, after the death of Queen Victoria in 1901, became King Edward VII and Queen Alexandra.

Taber's Paris quarters on the Rue de la Rochefoucauld may or may not have been a portrait studio. It was, however, the Paris office of his European publishing venture, the Taber Bas-Relief Photographic Syndicate, Ltd. An impressive sounding name, but little is known of its fate.

Taber returned to San Francisco in the early spring of 1898 and resumed operation of his Post Street studio. He had left his San Francisco business in charge of James Jay Cook, his old financial backer and Yosemite entrepreneur, and Cook, with Taber's many capable employees and assistants, had kept the studio running smoothly in Taber's absence. Taber soon learned, however, that he could not be in two places at the same time. Without his driving energy and talent, his European enterprise evaporated.

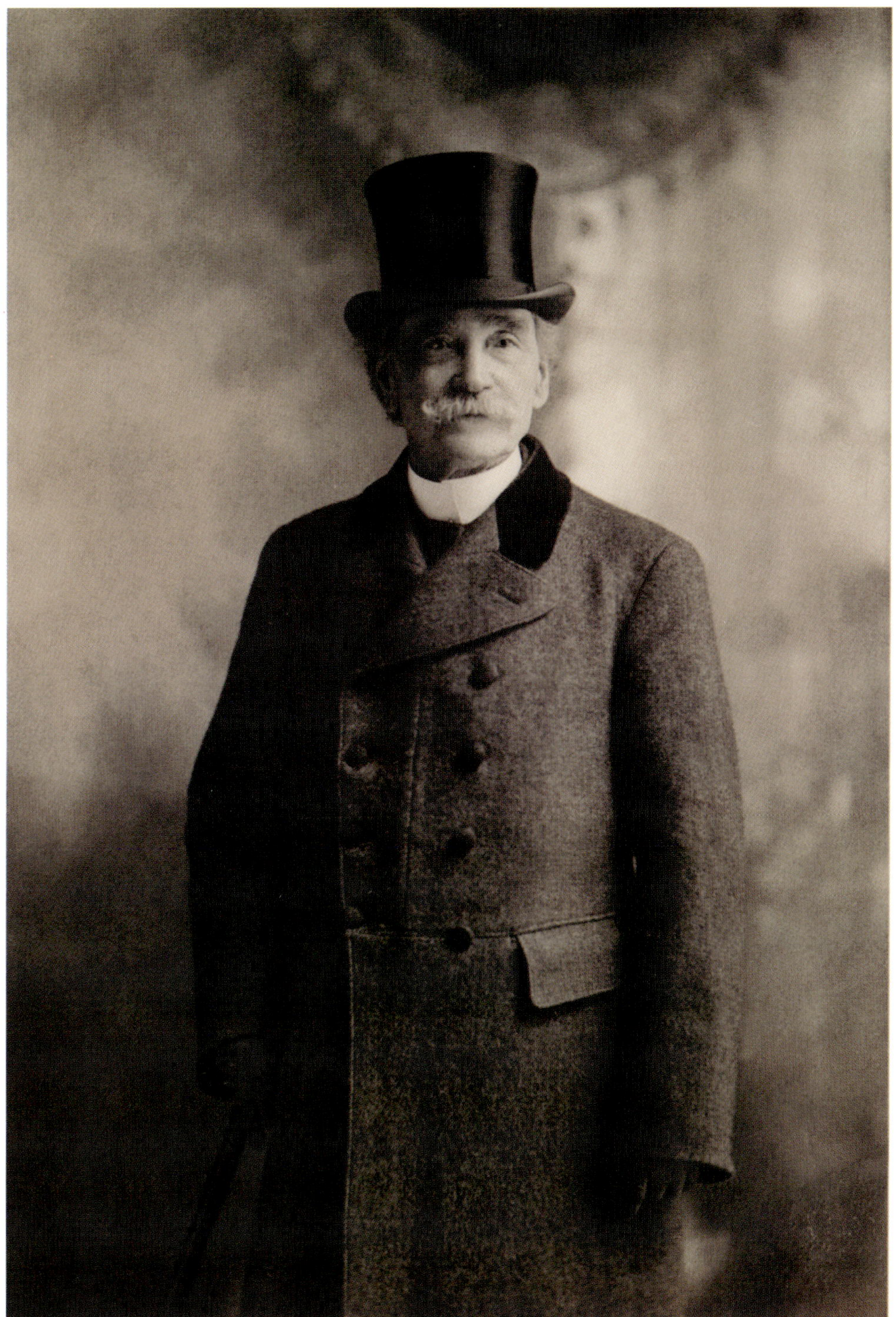

CUNEO COLLECTION

Isaiah West Taber, c. 1897.

Taber
Bas Relief Studios.
Telegraphic Address "Tabernilla, London."
Telephone No 1745, Gerrard.

38, Dover Street,
Piccadilly. W.

CUNEO COLLECTION

4 TABLE TALK. [Oct. 14, 1896.

CELEBRITIES FROM HOME.

MR. J. W. TABER AND THE NEW PHOTOGRAPHY.

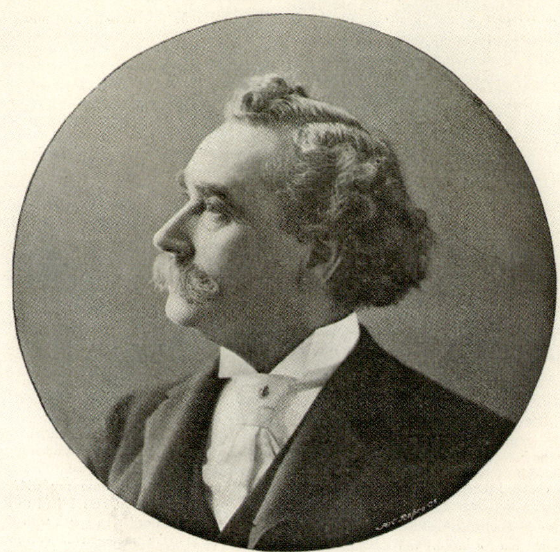

IN the Book of Panegyrics that will one day be written on the improvements and inventions of our nineteenth century, it may be taken for granted that the art of photography will occupy no obscure or unimportant position. For to assert that photography has contributed in no small degree to our material prosperity, as well as to our æsthetic development, is but to enunciate an obvious platitude.

If we were asked off-hand to determine under which of the two categories "art" or

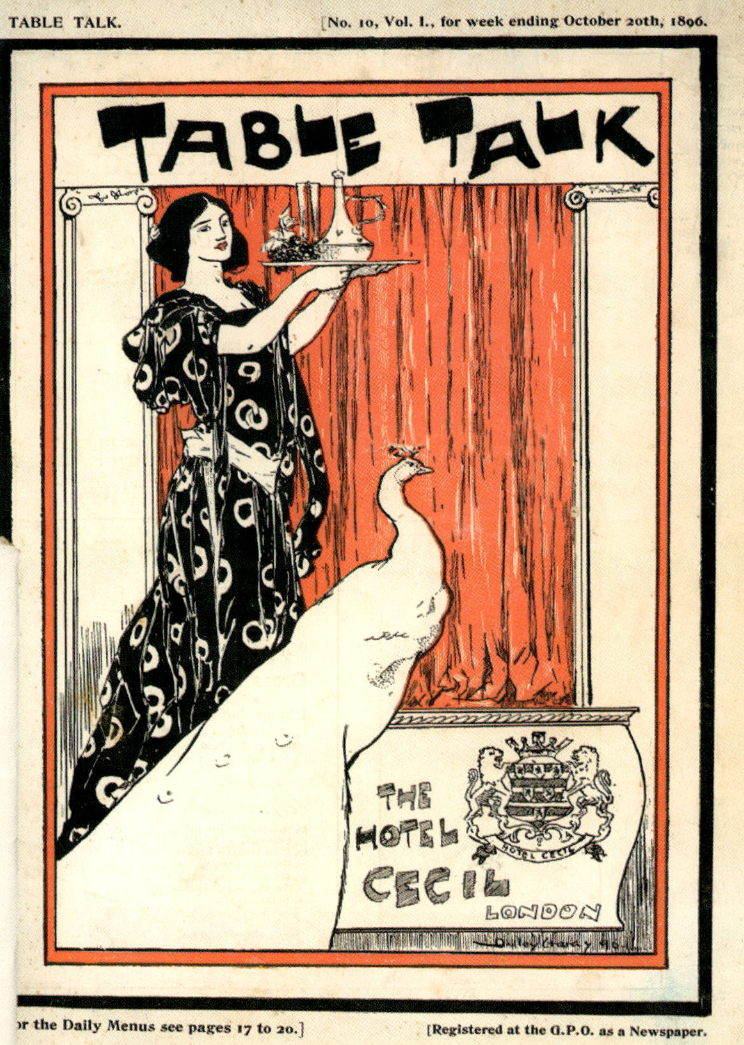

TABLE TALK. [No. 10, Vol. I., for week ending October 20th, 1896.

TABLE TALK

THE HOTEL CECIL LONDON

[For the Daily Menus see pages 17 to 20.] [Registered at the G.P.O. as a Newspaper.

CUNEO COLLECTION

Far left: Taber's London letterhead with a cable address allowing his San Francisco and London studios to communicate directly.

Above and left: The weekly events and menu booklet published by the Hotel Cecil where Taber first set up his London Studio in 1896. The bas-relief self-portrait of Taber, left, was made several years before he went to London. The interior of his Piccadilly studio is shown on page 6.

From "Table Talk," October 20, 1896:

"If anyone deserves the title of "artist" in the true sense of the word, in the field of photography, it is surely Mr. Taber of San Francisco, for he has done more than any other to perfect the art. We may regard painting and photography as sister arts, whereas painting gives us color and the general effect, photography approximates more closely to nature, and reproduces line for line, and detail fro detail. Two things there were, it was thought, that photography could not adequately reproduce, depth and color. Although the platinotype of today is immeasurably in advance of the early photographs on tin, the progress in England has only been in one direction, that of finish and permanency.

"But San Francisco in the person of Mr. Taber has come to our assistance, and by his new bas-relief process one of the problems has been solved, and photography can now give us depth. Mr. Taber has quite a miniature gallery in the room at the "Cecil," consisting of both portraits and landscape reproduced by the new process, which gives the effect like that of a cameo. I noticed portraits of the two rival candidates for the presidency, Mr. Bryan and Mr. McKinley, of Mr. H. M. Stanley, and a host of others too numerous to mention, for the list of celebrities who have sat for Mr. Taber is almost interminable.

"The inventor of the process has been in London some five months now, and hopes to develop his ideas here and in Paris, and perhaps Berlin as well. He is an enthusiast on the subject of photography, to which he has devoted forty years of his life. He first began in New York, but soon moved to the more congenial climate of San Francisco. In 1866 he introduced the Rembrandt process, which marked so great an advance in the art. I took the opportunity of asking Mr. Taber his opinion on the other great question, that of color photography. There have been so many promises and so few performances in this matter that he naturally acknowledges to being somewhat skeptical about the possibility of a solution to the problem, at any rate, at present."

Letter to Isaiah Taber in Paris from Nelly Bly, Hotel Metropole, London, 1897

Mr. Taber
c/o Miss Loie Fuller
Follies Bergere
Paris, France

Sunday Evening

Dear Mr. Taber:

I have written to Mlle Guilbert, 79 Avenue de Villiers, Paris: and if you will take some examples of your bas-relief, I am sure she will be glad to look at them, and for both your sakes, I hope she will consent to give you a sitting. I have explained fully to her who you are and if you send your card and Paris address with this letter, she will make a reply.

I would suggest your sending her samples of your work as she may not have seen it and so can have an idea of its beauty.

Trusting you will be given the privilege of photographing the charming and gifted Mlle Guilbert, I am

Very truly yours

Nellie Bly Seaman

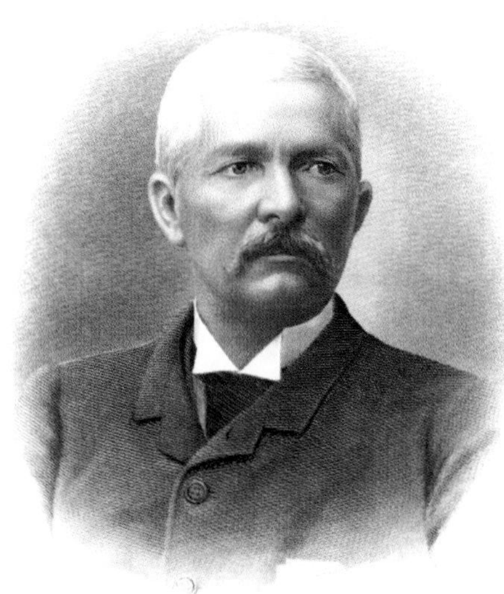

Henry Morton Stanley, from the frontispiece of his book *In Darkest Africa*, 1890. In 1895 Stanley was elected to Parliament and, in 1899, knighted by Queen Victoria.

Letter to Isaiah Taber from Henry Stanley, 2, Richmond Terrace, Whitehall, S.W.

April 30th 1898

Dear Sir

I did not reach my house in time to acknowledge the receipt of your kindly gift before your departure to America – nor did I wish to lay the Hotel Cecil under the obligation of forwarding my letter to you. I therefore send my acknowledgment direct to San Francisco.

The photos have been inspected by my family and they are all unanimous in saying they are veritable works of art. Personally, I have seen nothing like them in this country, except your own productions. It strikes me that the sculptors will have much to thank you for it will now be possible for them to reproduce one in marble with the utmost fidelity years after he has withdrawn from this earthly sphere.

I beg you to accept my best thanks for your munificent present. I had no idea that my visit to a photographer at San Francisco would have yielded such rich returns. I cast my bread upon the waters and it has returned to me a hundred fold after many days.

Believe me Dear Sir
Your much obliged
Henry M. Stanley

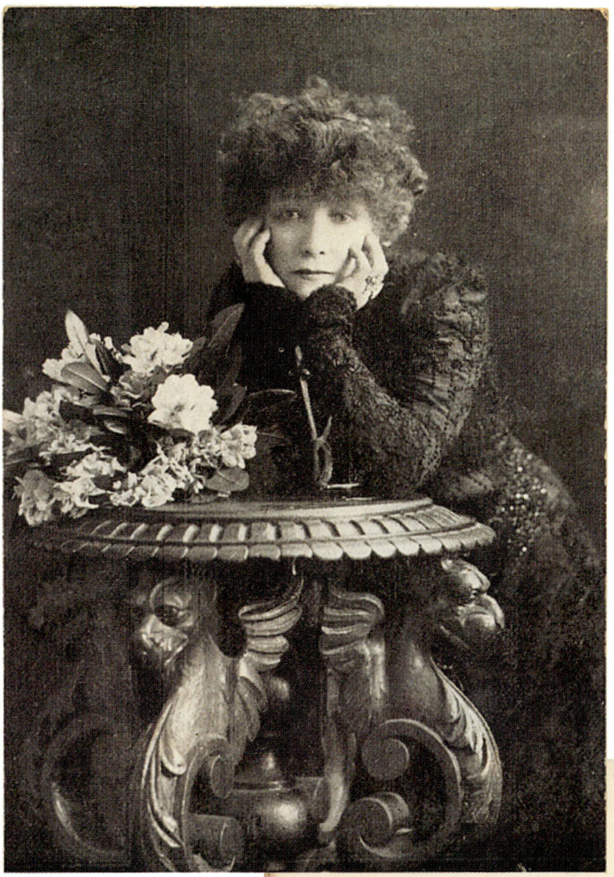

CUNEO COLLECTION

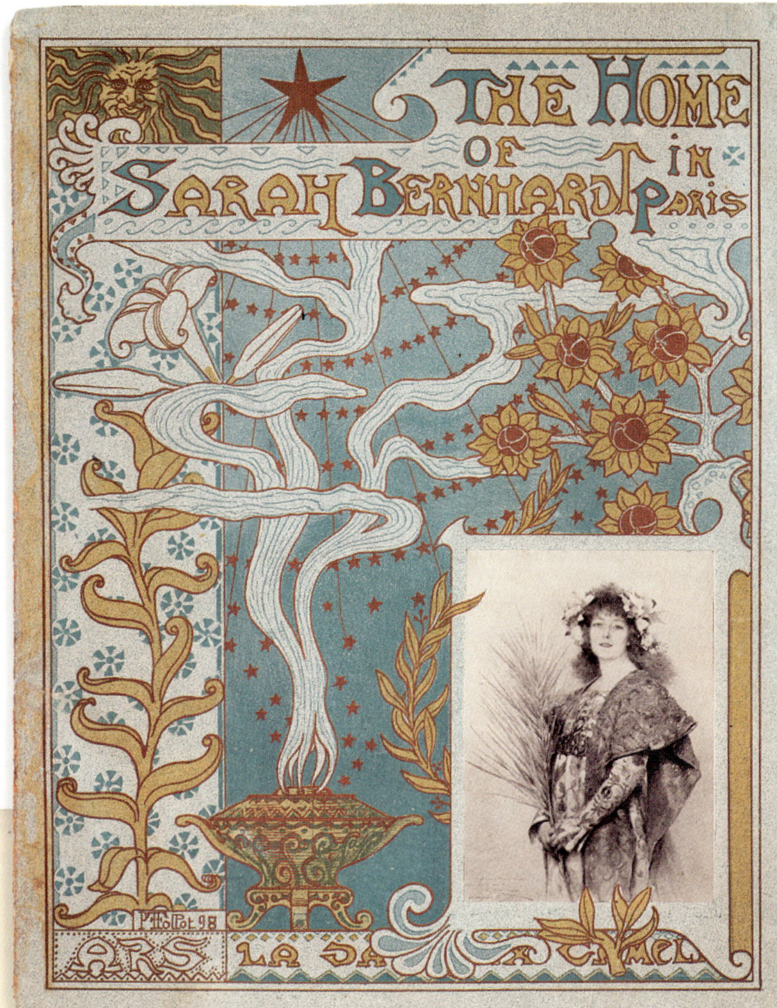

CUNEO COLLECTION

Above: Sarah Bernhardt in Paris, c. 1897.

Right: the booklet published by Taber in 1898 after photographing Bernhardt's Paris home and beach cottage.

The inscription on the fly leaf reads:

Dear Mr. Taber,
I authorize you with pleasure to publish your little volume of photographs just as you have presented them to me.
Sarah Bernhardt

PUBLISHED BY

The Taber Bas-Relief

PHOTOGRAPHIC SYNDICATE, LTD

PARIS :

16, Rue de La Rochefoucauld

LONDON :

38, Dover Street, Piccadilly, W.

CUNEO COLLECTION

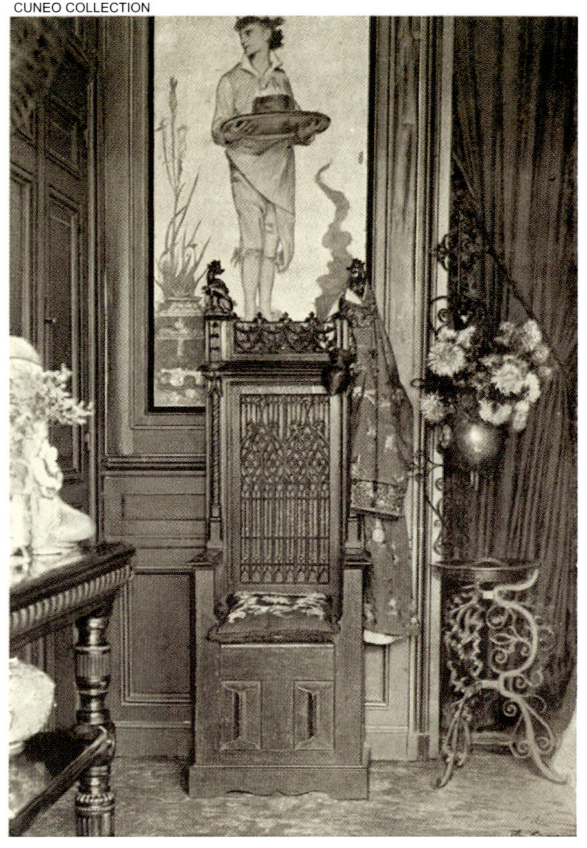

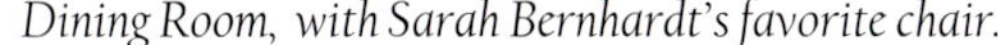

Dining Room, with Sarah Bernhardt's favorite chair.

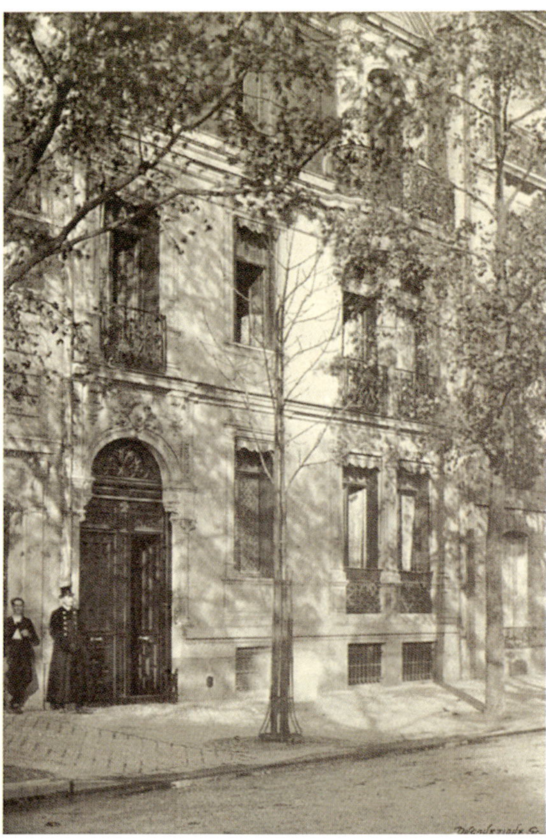

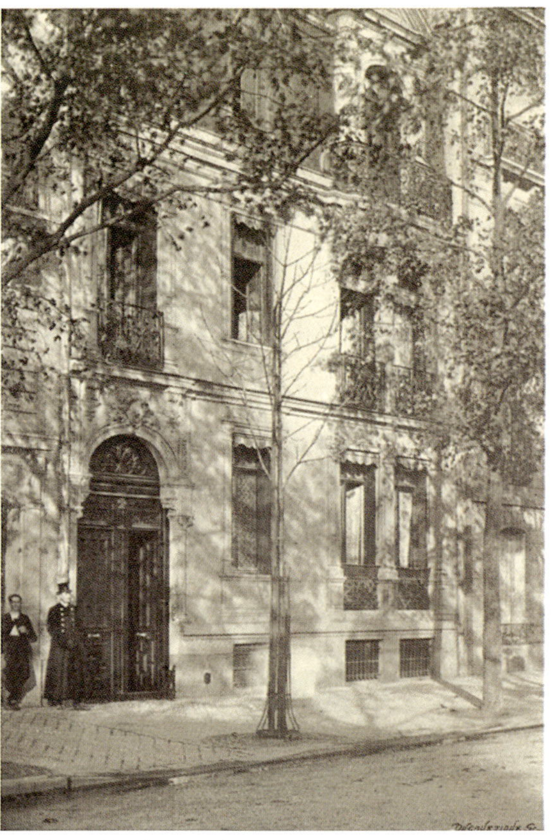

Sarah Bernhardt's Residence in Paris.

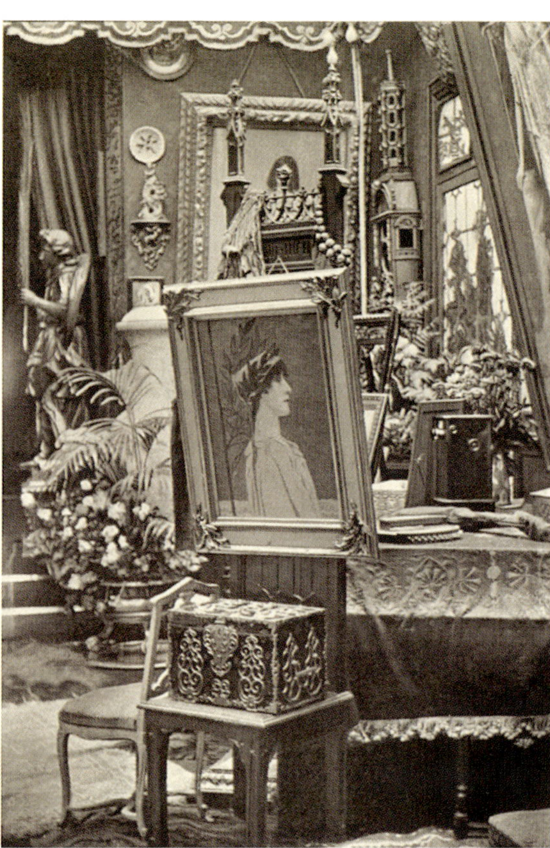

Corner of Sarah Bernhardt's Studio

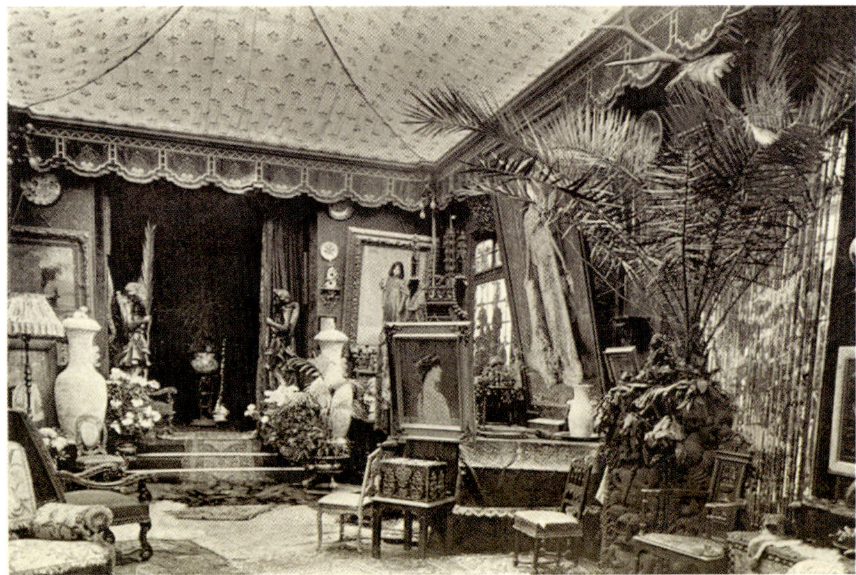

Studio.

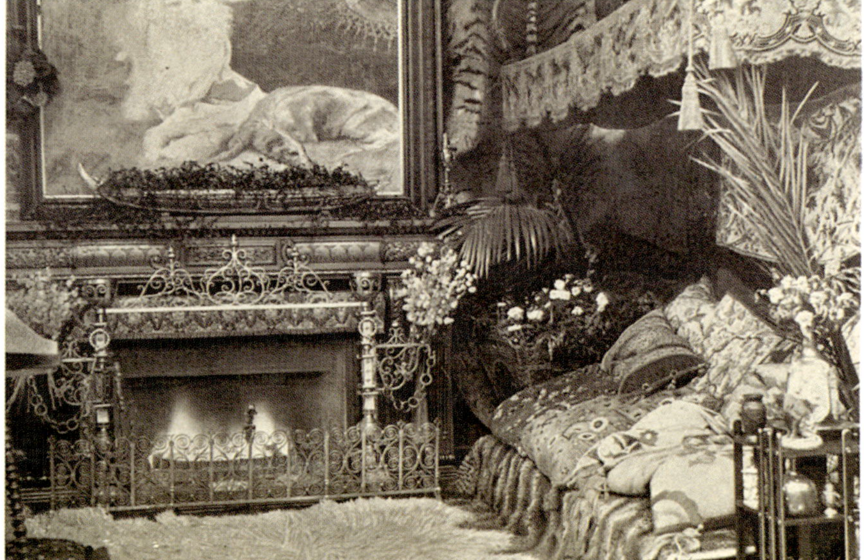

Bed Room.

1906 EARTHQUAKE AND FIRE

In the early morning of April 18, 1906, in little more than a minute, one epoch of San Francisco history ended and another began. The earthquake and subsequent fire left no one unchanged. As with any disaster of that magnitude, the stunned survivors experienced an unimaginable range of emotions and personal tragedy. One survivor was Isaiah West Taber. Luckier than many, he and his family were uninjured, and his home near Golden Gate Park, out of the fire's reach, was undamaged. Isaiah Taber watched the distant growing fires, consuming everything in their paths, he knew he had lost his life's work.

Among San Francisco's photographers, Isaiah Taber was not alone in suffering catastrophic loss. Much of the photographic history of early San Francisco from then on would consist of surviving prints and those few negatives that were stored elsewhere in April, 1906. Of course, uncountable prints burned along with the negatives, many of them single copies. Lost also were the photographers' workbooks, journals, and records.

A month before the earthquake, Taber's wrote to his life-long friend in New Bedford, retired admiral George Winslow, explaining his upcoming move. His lease had expired at 121 Post Street and the ground floor firm was taking over the entire building. Taber, therefore, was moving to the building next door at 131 Post Street. He planned the move meticulously, deciding to take only his negatives and photographic equipment. He wrote, "You can imagine I have got my hands full, so much has accumulated in the past thirty years that I have got to dispose of." Taber had just completed the move when disaster struck. Shortly after the earthquake, Taber wrote again:

Dear George:

As the excitement is passed and we are getting more used to our condition and having more leisure time than I care for, I will devote some of it to giving you an account of our experience. I know I cannot tell you much about earthquakes for I remember that your ship was thrown from the sea onto dry land some years ago in South America. But we have had another element to contend with.

After the earthquake had shattered the City, the fire started and swept everything before it. It was the most appalling disaster since the destruction of Sodom and Gomorrah in Bible history. The beautiful modern structures of iron, stone and brick were not spared. They stood the shock, but the intense heat of the fire brought ruin to most of the imposing buildings in the City. The whole business portion, including all the resident districts east of Van Ness Avenue to the waterfront and, in the Mission district, all are in ashes.

Russian Hill and Telegraph Hill are blackened by the dying embers of the dwellings. Chinatown and its underground dens have been purified, never again to taint the atmosphere of that district or the magnificent City that will rise up from the ashes.

In 1850 I saw the town swept by fire. I saved my blankets and camped on the side of Russian Hill amongst the poison oak. The howl of the coyote was a familiar sound at night in those days. The town was built of light material and was soon swept away. In May 1851 San Francisco was again destroyed by the devouring flames, fanned by a high wind and could not be controlled. The burnt district was three-quarters of a mile long. The June fire soon followed and the people thought the City was doomed. Many New Bedford men were among the builders of the City in those early days, but few are left to view the ruins of today.

Thousands of people are camped in the Golden Gate Park. It was an appalling sight to see three or four hundred thousand men, women and children fleeing for their lives from the fire. Everyone was loaded with the articles they had snatched from their homes in their flight. Some were dragging bed ticks filled with various articles, others with bundles. Every kind of vehicle you can imagine, filled with their treasures, was being pulled and pushed by men and women with children tagging to their skirts.

Our residence you may remember is on McAllister Street, one of the main avenues to the Park. The rush passed our house was the most novel and exciting scene I have ever witnessed. The earthquake was a rattler, and caused dismay. I have since looked over a part of the City that is left standing and viewed the havoc, but it is nothing in comparison to the fire. The earthquake was forgotten in the terror of the flames.

Golden Gate Park is a city of tents. Made of sheets, blankets and all kinds of material and color, also army tents. But it does not resemble and army camp as the occupants are men, women and children. It reminds me more of the Millerite Camp Meeting to the east of Fairhaven in 1843, the year that Miller predicted the world would come to an end. Of course the camp was small in comparison. I was a boy of thirteen and with other playmates we hovered around the camp to see the ascension and hear the prayers of his deluded followers for the savior to appear. San Franciscans are praying for the continuation of life and planning for a new City with structures of iron which will stand the trembling of the earth's crust while adjusting itself for a more solid foundation.

I have been photographing in the fire district. Nothing is left in the neighborhood of 500 blocks but tottering walls, melted glass, twisted iron, bricks and stone. It is the most desolate sight I have ever seen. I have stood on the brink of a volcano and have seen the fiery waves of red-hot lava throbbing and dashing in the crater below, but to me it was not so appalling as the flames that swept with such terrible fury our fair City.

My photograph gallery on Post Street was entirely destroyed. I had just completed a new studio in the next building to my old quarters. I had furnished it entirely new and up to date. It took nine men four weeks to move my portrait negatives, eighty tons, containing portraits of celebrated people from all parts of the world. Many were of historic value as the people have passed away. The negatives are not only a great loss to me, but to my patrons. Three and four generations were represented in this collection. Besides the pioneers of the state and the early businessmen of San Francisco whom I have taken in the past forty years, my view negatives, about twelve tons, contained views of San Francisco as far back as 1849 and up to the present time, showing the growth and progress of the City. After the shake up and the flames were subdued, I took account of stock and found that I had just $8 in my pocket to start life anew, after passing the three-scoreyear and ten mark. Bit I am not discouraged nor disheartened. My health is good and the problem has got to be solved.

All of my photographic apparatus is gone, but I managed to borrow a camera and am in the field among the ruins. What income will be from it I don't know, but I have got to do something and have commenced in the ashes and will try to rise again. We are living now almost like campers, our water and gas have been cut off and we are doing the cooking in the gutter by putting a few bricks together in front of the house. No fires are allowed inside as all the chimneys have been wrecked. The water we are bringing from two blocks away, and have to stand in the bread line to get something to eat. Provisions are plentiful at present and no one goes hungry. We have not been allowed to light a candle in the house until a few nights ago. The City is under martial law and soldiers are patrolling all the streets. Everything is orderly and quiet excepting the dynamite used in blowing down the dangerous walls. My determination now is to stay in San Francisco and in some way try and get established again.

Mrs. Taber and Louise are well and join in love to you and Mrs. Winslow. I received the sad news of my daughter Daisy's death in the midst of our trouble. She died in Buffalo, New York.

Hoping you are all well I am yours very truly,

I.W. Taber

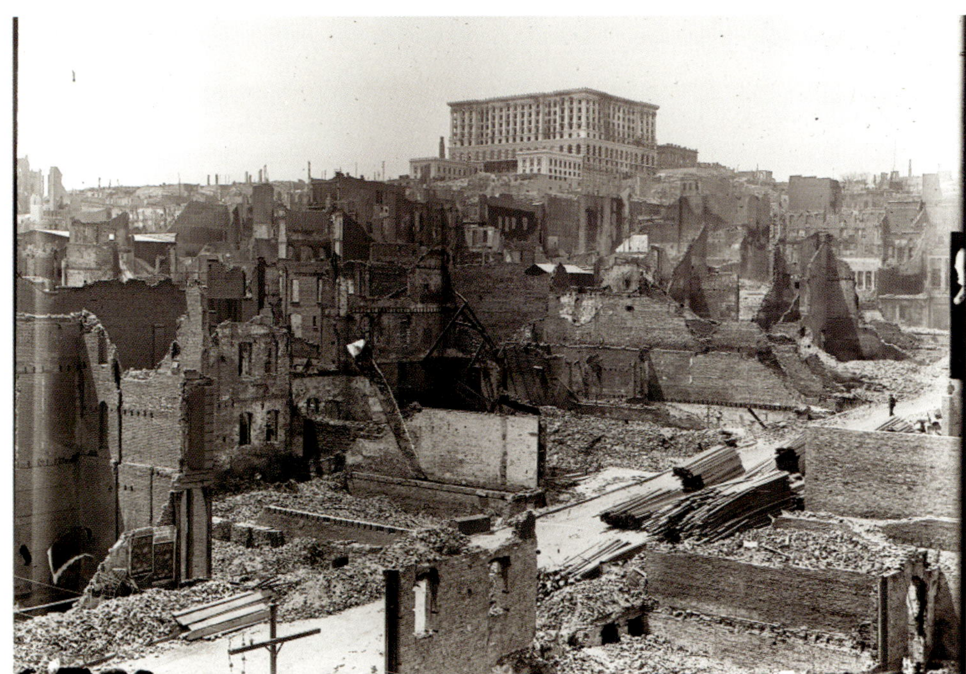

CUNEO COLLECTION

Top right: the downtown district near Taber's studio after the fire, with the Fairmont Hotel on the skyline. Photo by Taber with a borrowed camera.

Right: Even in the face of disaster, Isaiah Taber kept his sense of humor. Here, Taber, his wife Annie and daughter Louise, prepare a meal at their outdoor kitchen with its sign board proclaiming "The Poodle Dog," named after San Francisco's famous old eatery lost in the fire. The sign reads: "Meals served while you wait (a long time). Ham and Eggs, Porterhouse Steak— all gone. Roast Beef, Lamb Chops—across the Bay. Pork and Beans—in Boston." Photographer unknown.

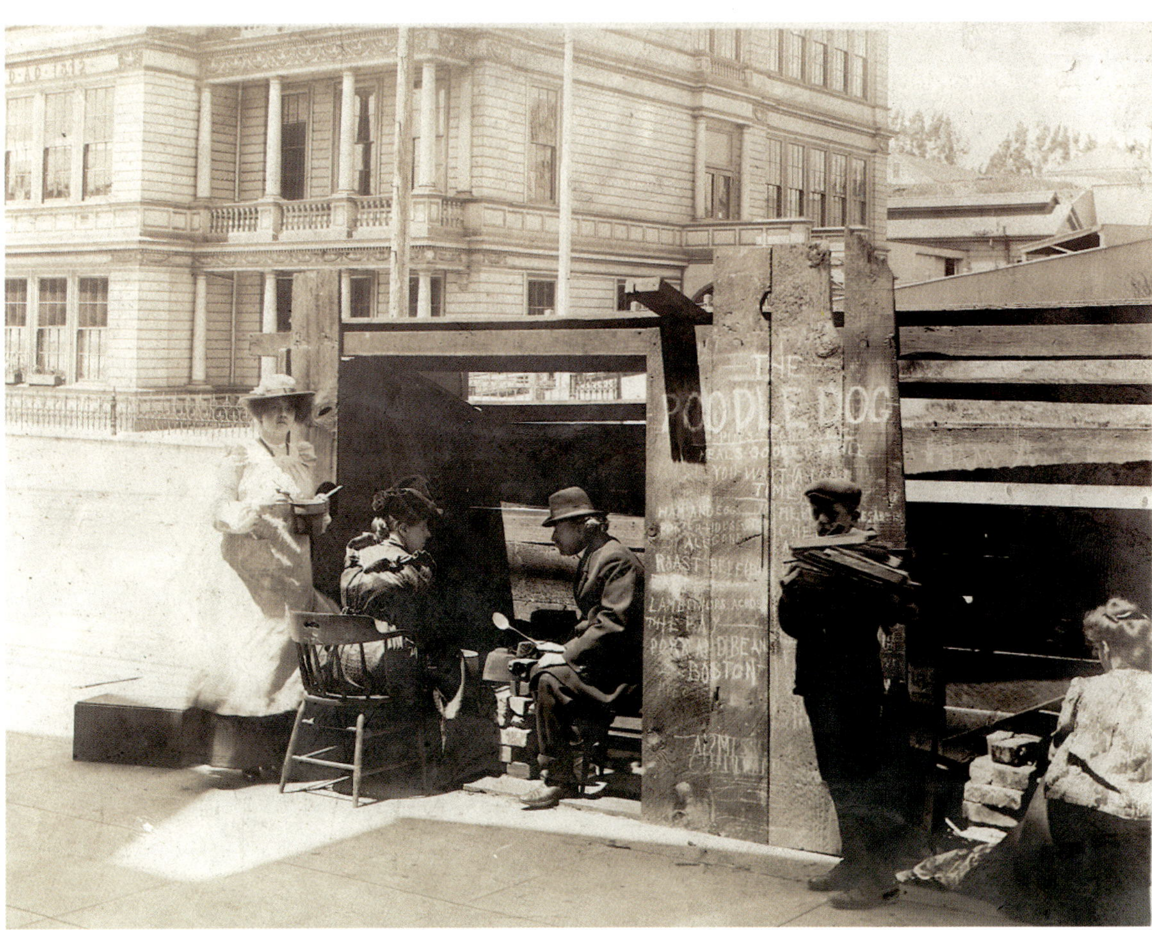

CUNEO COLLECTION

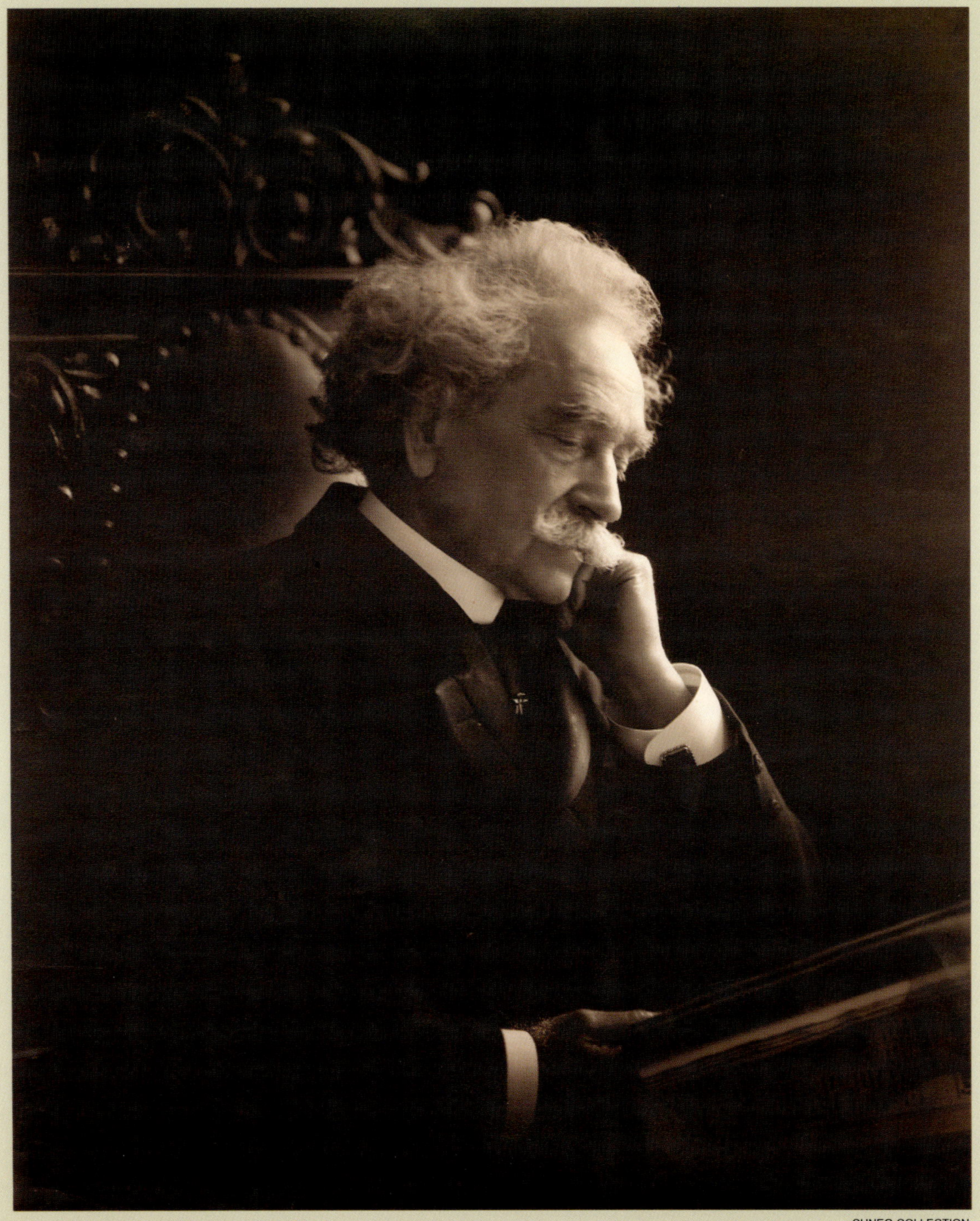

CUNEO COLLECTION

Isaiah West Taber, c.1909

Following the earthquake and fire, Isaiah Taber never fully recovered from his shattering loss. In 1908 he opened a portrait studio at 118 Geary Street, next door to the Stanford Studio run by G. H. Wichman and G. N. Thomas, who had run the Yolo Photographic Art Gallery in Woodland, California in the early 1880s. Taber joined them in 1908, forming the Taber-Stanford Studio, but apparently their personalities clashed. Taber wrote, "I soon found I had made a mistake for they had no enterprise and were drawing one deeper into the mire. Their books did not show any profit for me. They would not advertise or try to push the business or listen to any advice that would cost a dollar to stimulate trade. On this account I withdrew my name and they have since been obliged to go out of business." Taber's name continued to be linked with the studio until 1912.

By 1911 his stamina and health began to fail. He wrote to George Winslow in September of that year: "I passed my 81st birthday last month and am still in good condition, considering that my first arrival in San Francisco was over 61 years ago. My only trouble is a weak heart and I have to go slow. I have stood the wear and tear of the strenuous life of a sailor, miner, rancher, photographer and now an idle life which is the hardest struggle of all my experiences. The destruction of my business and the city that I had grown up with came when the fire of my energy was nearly exhausted, and too late to recuperate.

"My age and lack of capital has prevented me from re-establishing myself under the old and well-known name which I made famous in the photographic world. My only course now is to try and weather the breakers on a lee shore towards which I am now drifting. I am sailing close to the wind and hope to make my final port in safety."

On February 22, 1912, Isaiah Taber died peacefully at home from heart failure, his wife and daughter at his side. Word of his death spread quickly throughout the photographic world and he was eulogized in magazines and newspapers.

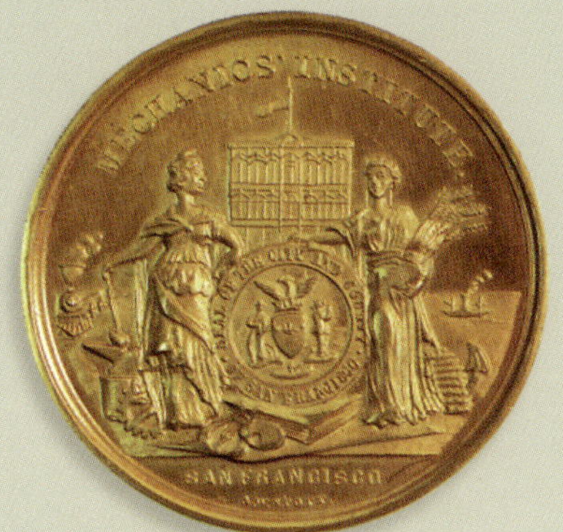

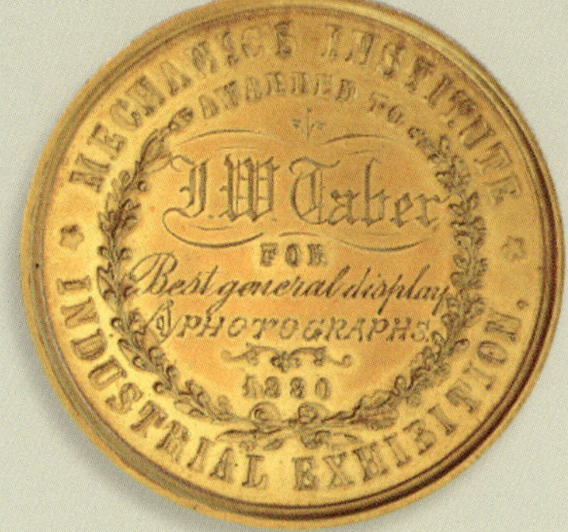

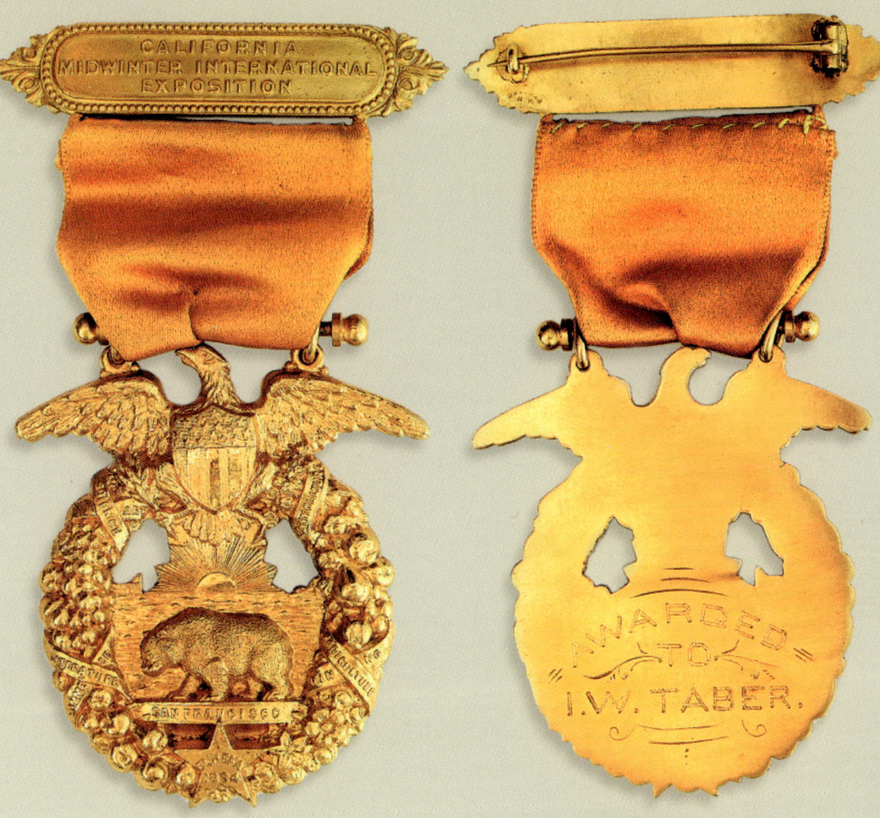

Obverse Reverse

Mechanics Institute Gold Medal, San Francisco, 1880

Obverse Reverse

California Midwinter International Exposition Gold Medal, 1894

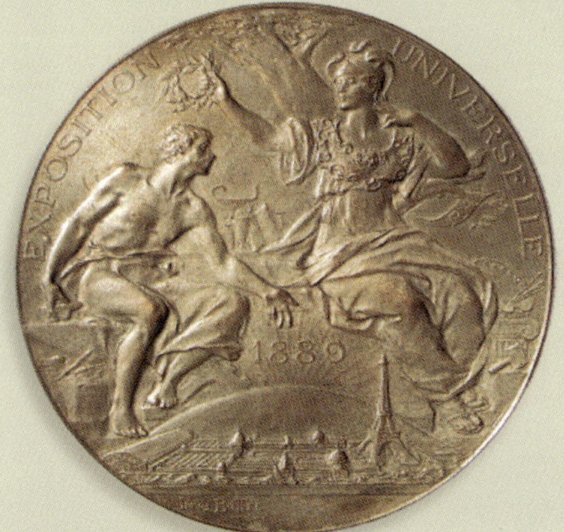

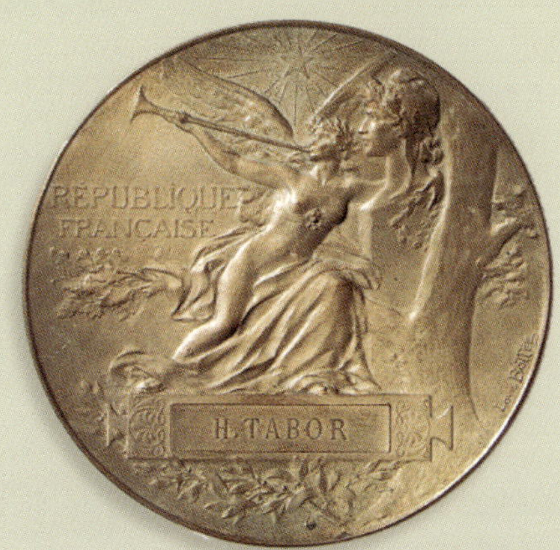

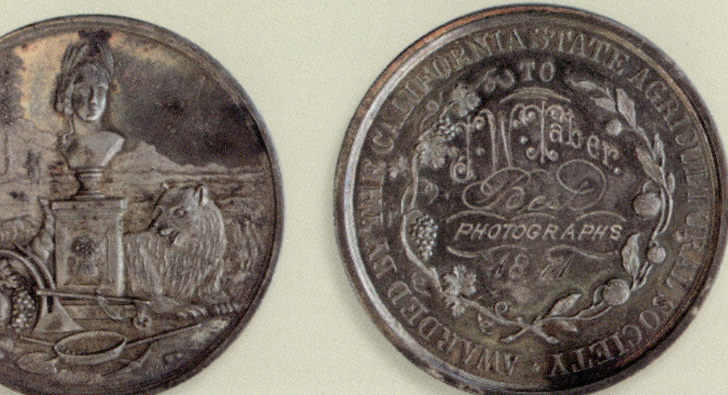

Obverse Reverse

Exposition Universelle Bronze Medal, Paris, 1889

Obverse Reverse

California Agricultural Society Silver Medal, 1871

ALL MEDALS, CUNEO COLLECTION

Appendix A:
PORTRAITS BY TABER

Although known as both a portrait artist and scenic view photographer, Isaiah Taber's first love was portraiture. Framing his clients through the lens over a span of sixty-four years, he never tired of the personal interaction between photographer and subject. Surviving examples of his work can usually be identified by his trademark signature printed or embossed on the mount. Over the years, Taber's studio offered dozens of styles and finishes in the most popular sizes. The most frequently seen are cabinet cards, 6 ½ by 4 ½ inches, and imperial mounts, 7 by 10 inches. Vignettes, seen at right, were common, but Taber also produced many full length and three-quarter length portraits, as shown below.

WINDGATE PRESS

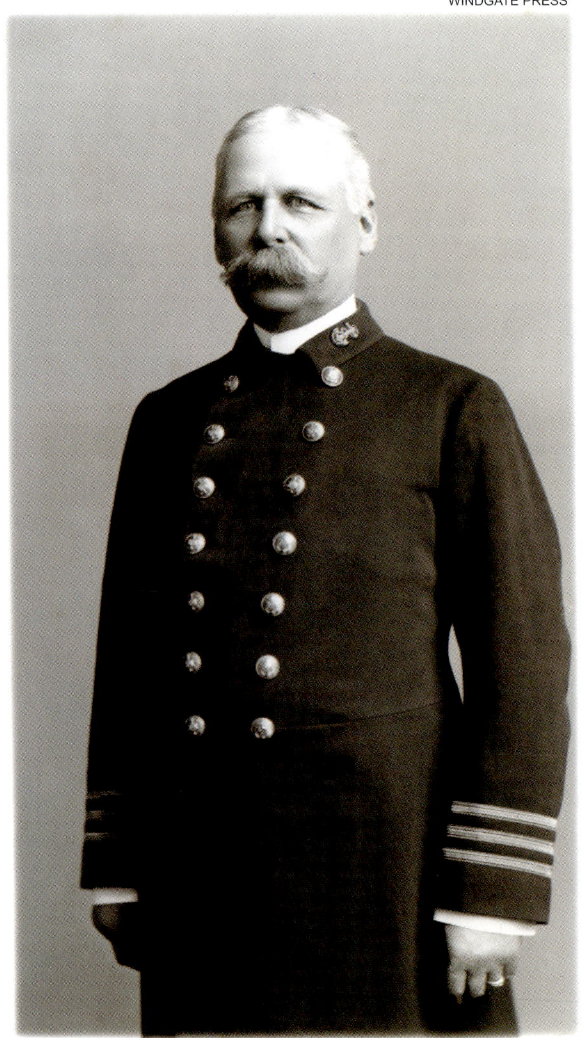

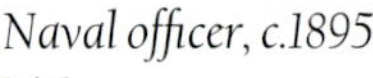

Naval officer, c.1895

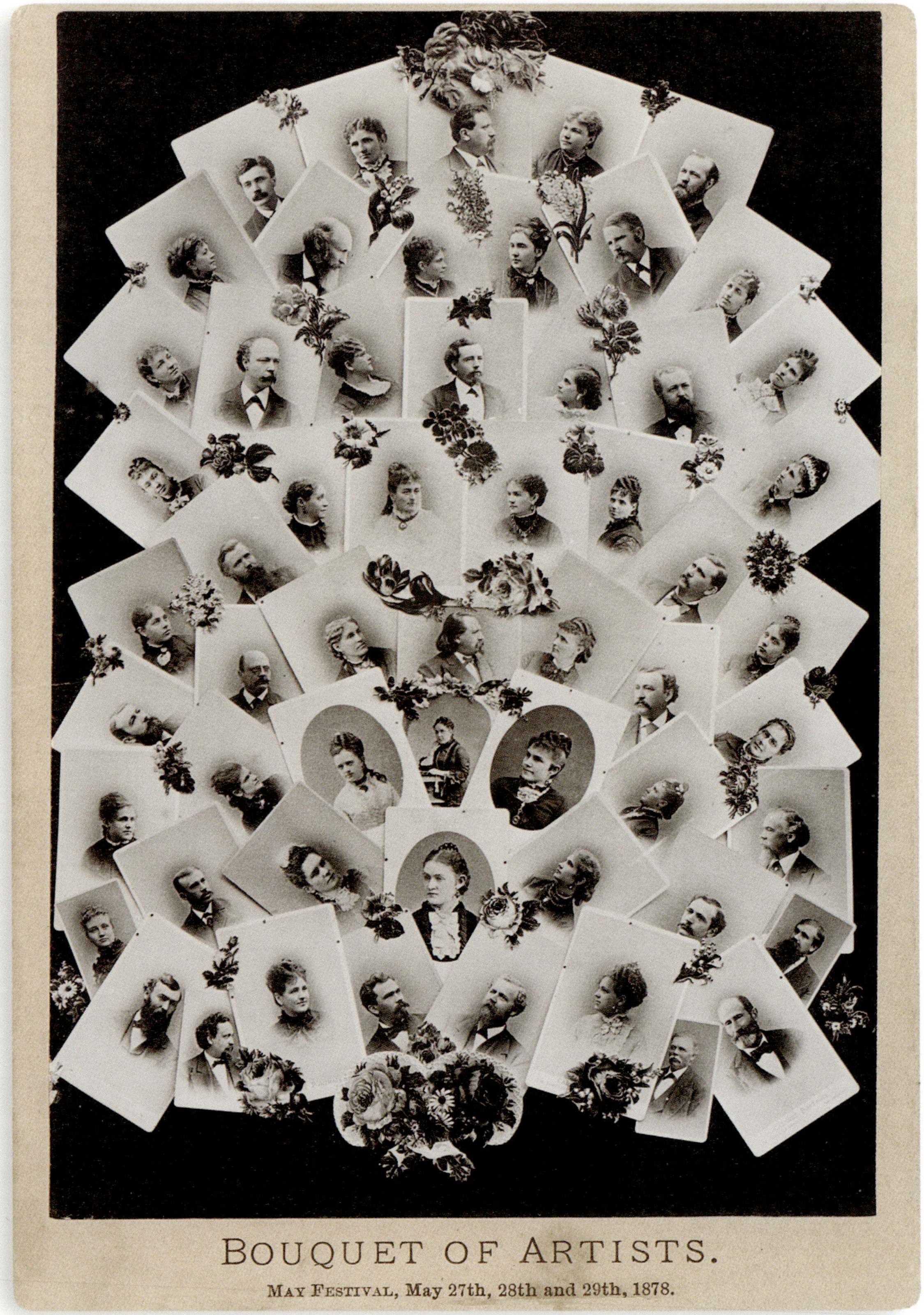

BOUQUET OF ARTISTS.

MAY FESTIVAL, May 27th, 28th and 29th, 1878.

MARILYN BLAISDELL COLLECTION

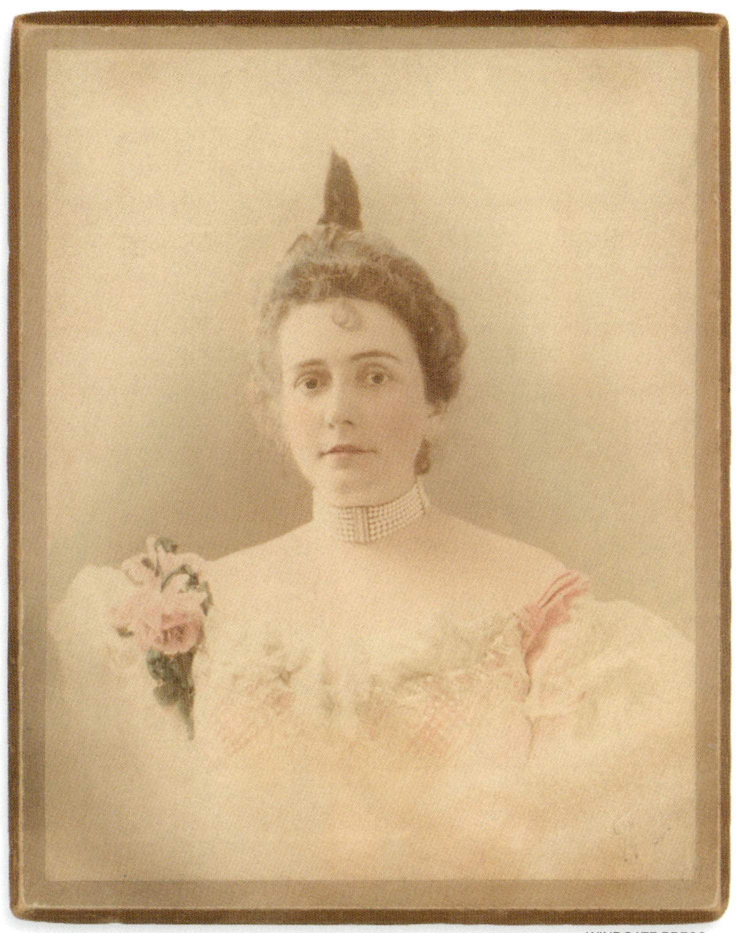

WINDGATE PRESS

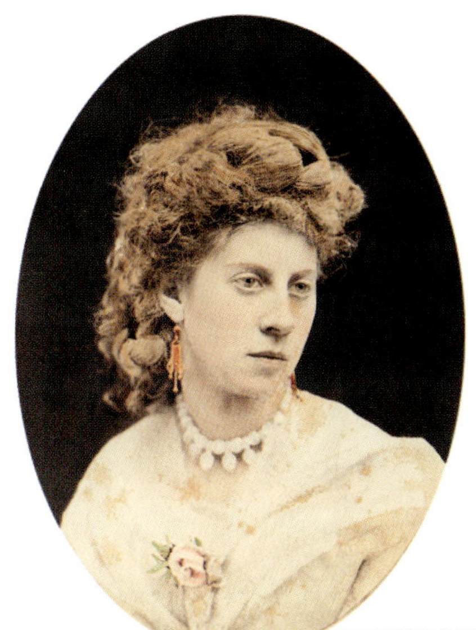

CUNEO COLLECTION

Far left, a hand tinted portrait by Taber, 1898, 5 ½ by 7 inches.

Left, hand tinted portrait by Taber of his wife Annie, c.1871.

COLOR PORTRAITS

Like many photographers of the time, Isaiah Taber was intrigued by the possibilities of color. Hand painted and tinted photos were nothing new, they had been around since the earliest daguerreotypes. Taber saw the commercial appeal of color and, over the years, tried ways to perfect hand coloring. As early as 1856 he offered colored ambrotypes. By 1880 he advertised the "Rembrandt Process," in which Hugo Nahl and other artists hand painted Taber's work.

The culmination of his color experimentation was the "bas-relief" process shown at right. It involved both hand coloring and three-dimensional sculpting. After the portrait was taken, a sculptor would carve a bas-relief likeness in plaster, guided by the portrait. A high-contrast print was made on special paper, the print then was softened by soaking in water. The artist then pressed the damp print onto the carved model, carefully embossing the details. After drying, the print was removed from the model and tinted with watercolors. The prints, usually about 8 by 10 inches, were mounted with special deeply embossed mats and framed behind glass.

Derided by critics as impure photography, Taber's patented bas-relief portraits nonetheless found an appreciative audience in the 1890s among his wealthy patrons in San Francisco and in Europe. The process was costly and time consuming. That plus the difficulty Taber had engaging suitably skilled artists capable of handling the complex process led, no doubt, to its demise.

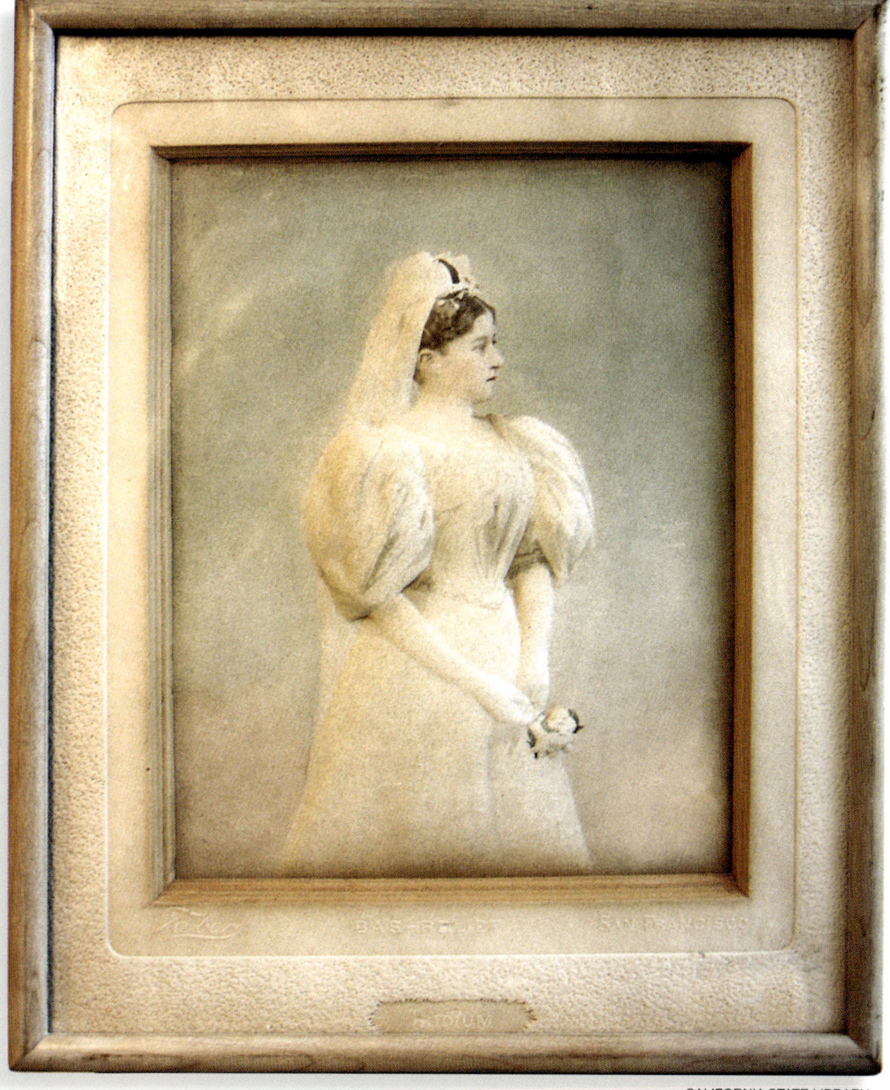

CALIFORNIA STATE LIBRARY

The majority of Taber cabinet portraits printed from 1880 to 1900 bear on the front the Taber script logotype. Script signatures were common to many photographers of the era. Taber, however, used the device more consistently than most. He seemed to possess an instinctual knowledge of self promotion and, as a publisher as well as artist, used his "brand name" to identify his entire range of products.

Since many surviving Taber portraits are not dated, assigning a specific year of origin can be difficult. Even when a hand-written date appears on the back, it can be deceptive. For example, a hand-written or stamped date might refer to the year the original photograph was taken, or to the date the print was made. Taber, like most portrait photographers, encouraged patrons to order additional prints. This was done sometimes months or years after the original portrait session.

The typical mounts of unidentified portraits shown below indicate the slow transition of the Taber imprint. The script logotype made its first appearance around 1878, before Taber moved to 8 Montgomery. The earliest mounts using that address, 1880 to about 1883 read: "Opposite the Palace and Grand Hotels." The word "Elevator" was added around 1884 and the line "Over Hibernia Bank" a short time later. A new look, lower right, appeared around 1886 when the address line was embellished with fancy hand-lettering. The portrait of Adolph Sutro, opposite page, lower left, identifies Taber's new location at 121 Post Street, around 1893, using the same flourish style for the address. Some early versions, 1893-4, of the 121 Post Street address include the line " has removed to 121 Post Street." The letterhead at top right dates from after 1894. The portrait of Julie Duraind, opposite right, bears a simplified Taber address line. Taber used many variations on these forms on a variety of mounts as fashions changed, including gold and silver stamping, colored and metallic inks, and embossed logotypes.

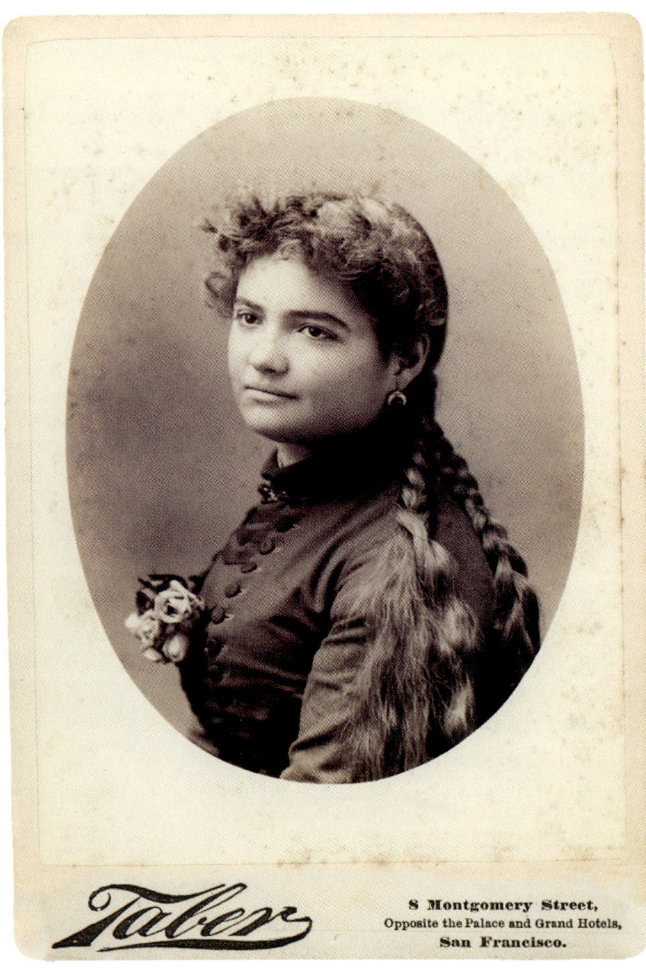

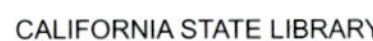
CALIFORNIA STATE LIBRARY

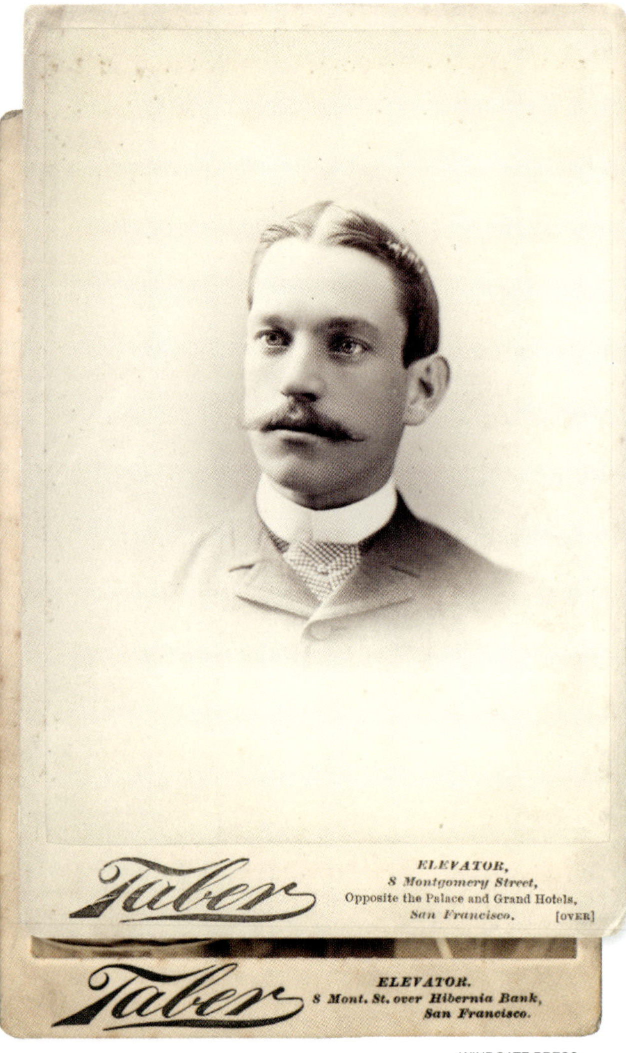

WINDGATE PRESS

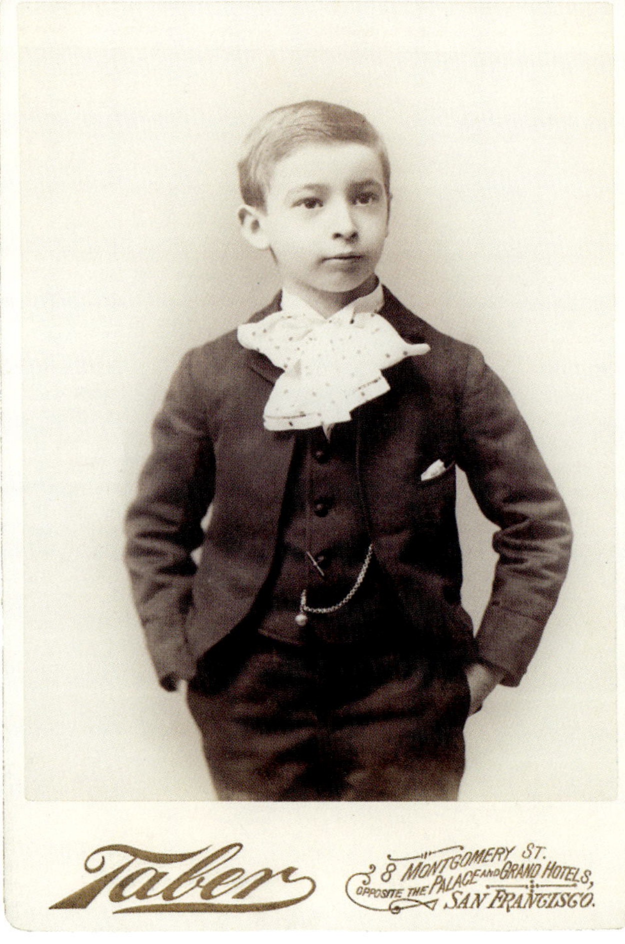

CALIFORNIA STATE LIBRARY

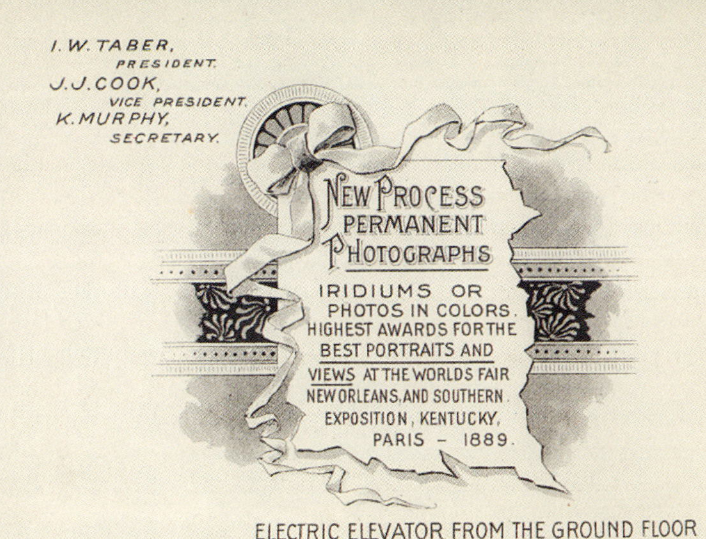

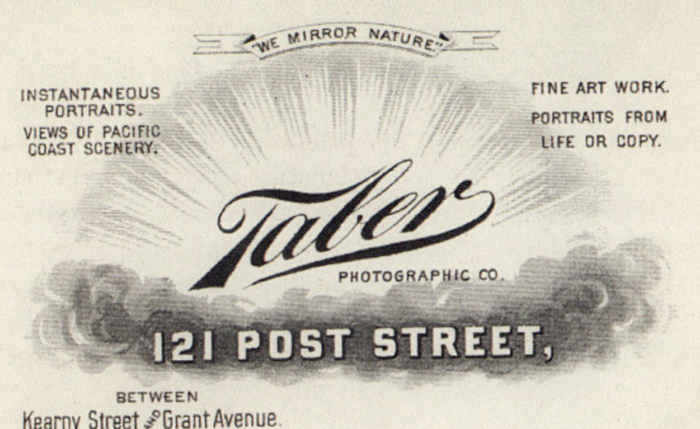

HIGHEST AWARD CALIFORNIA MIDWINTER INTERNATIONAL EXPOSITION. 1894.

San Francisco,

CALIFORNIA STATE LIBRARY

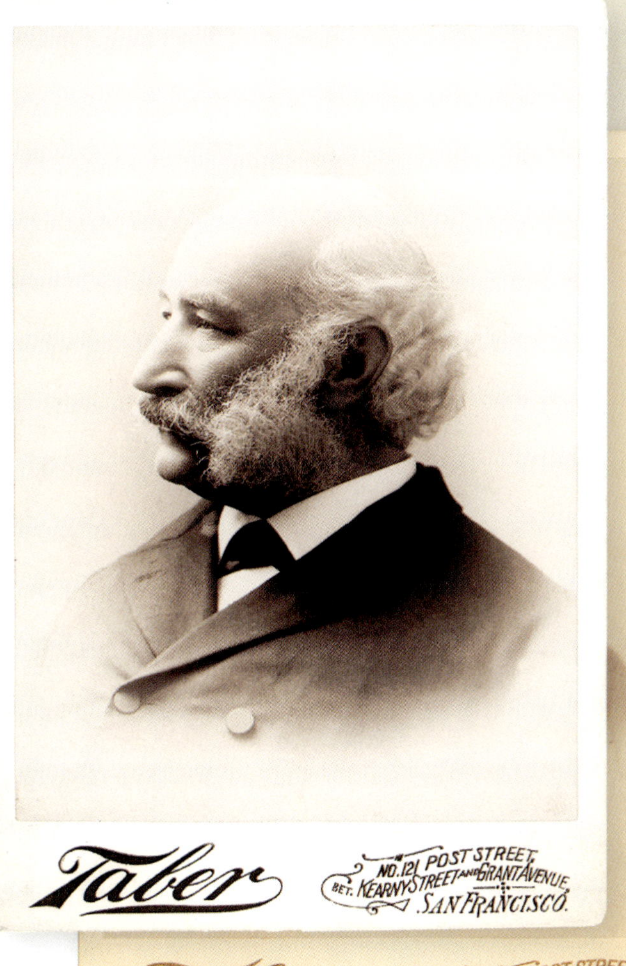

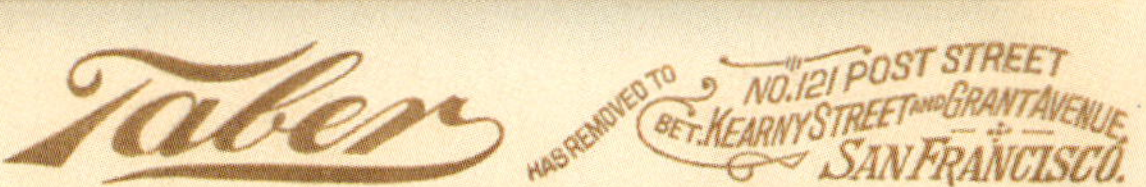

CUNEO COLLECTION

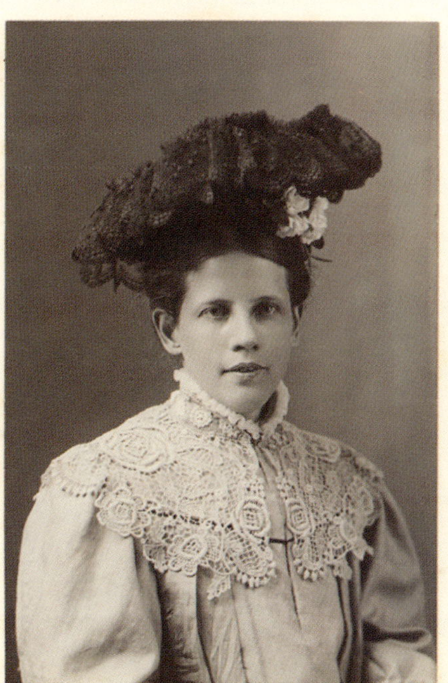

Affectionately
Julie A. Durand

Taber

121 Post St. S. F.

CUNEO COLLECTION

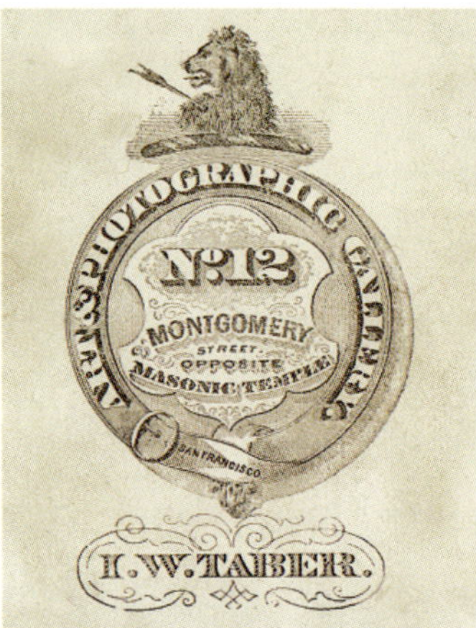

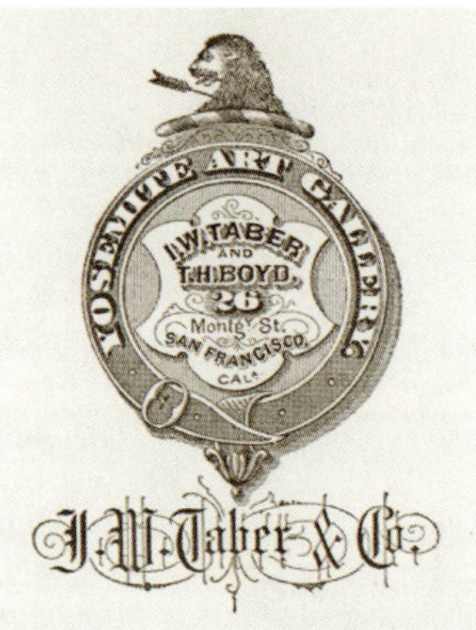

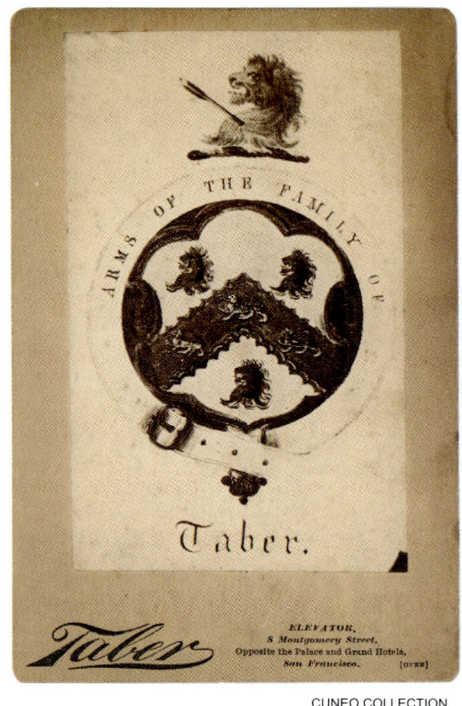

CUNEO COLLECTION

The reverse or back of Taber photo mounts carried advertising as well as identification. Early examples, far left, bear a design based on the Taber family coat-of-arms, dating back to fifteenth-century England. The design, top left, is from Taber's first gallery at 12 Montgomery Street (ca 1871-74). Below it a similar logo bearing the address 26 Montgomery Street (ca.1876-79) when Taber merged his portrait business with the Yosemite Art Gallery using Carleton Watkin's scenic negatives.

Below left, the reverse of Taber's photo mounts after his move to 8 Montgomery Street around 1879. This design, with variations, remained in use until around 1889 when he reorganized the Taber Photographic Company. The new design in shown below, center. Below right, when Taber moved to 121 Post Street around 1893, he used a simplified version of the design.

Opposite page: After Taber returned from Europe in 1897, he revised the Taber logo again, reverting to a design based on the Taber coat-of-arms, but stillretaining the little "Taber" script logo he had employed consistently since 1878. The 1905 portrait below left, bears the tiny Taber crest in the upper left of the mount. Above it is the crest enlarged and the original design painted by Isaiah Taber himself as a guide to the artist.

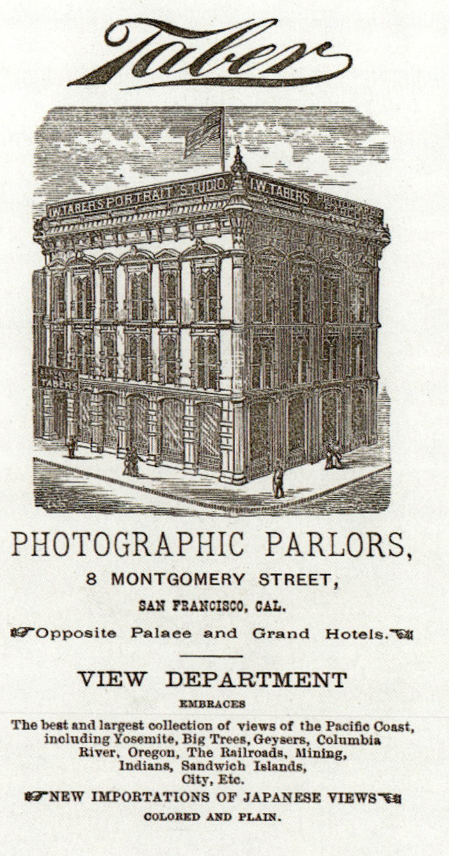

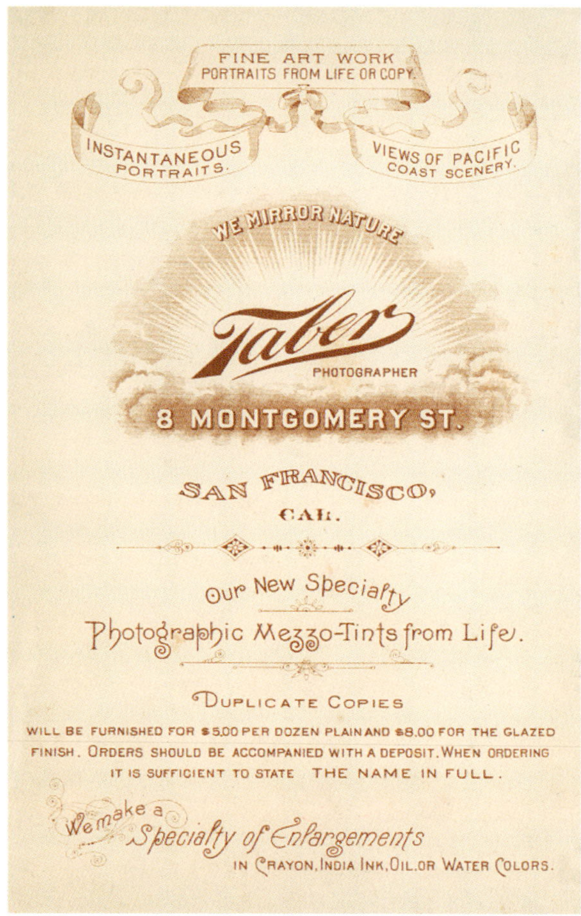

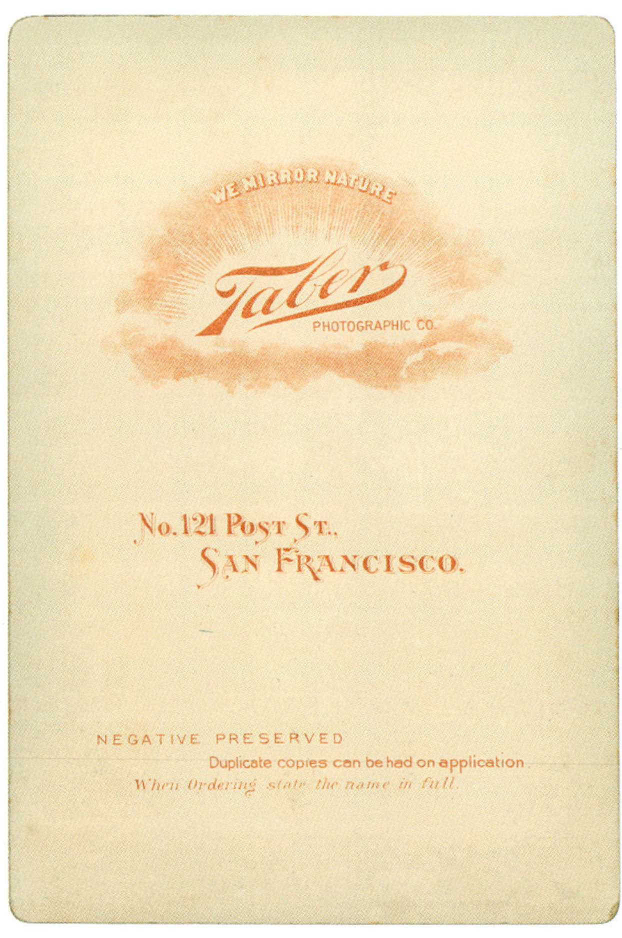

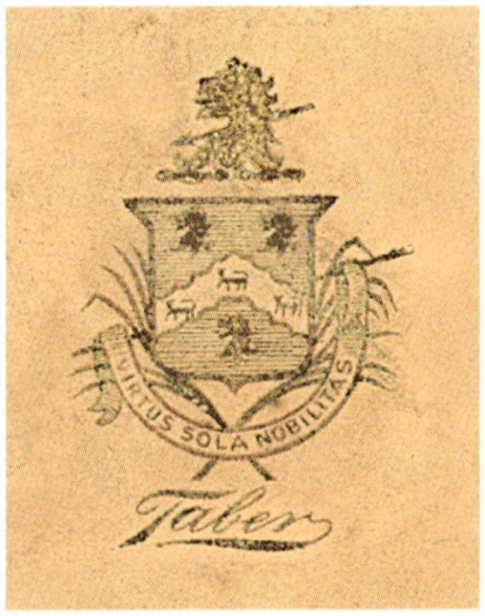

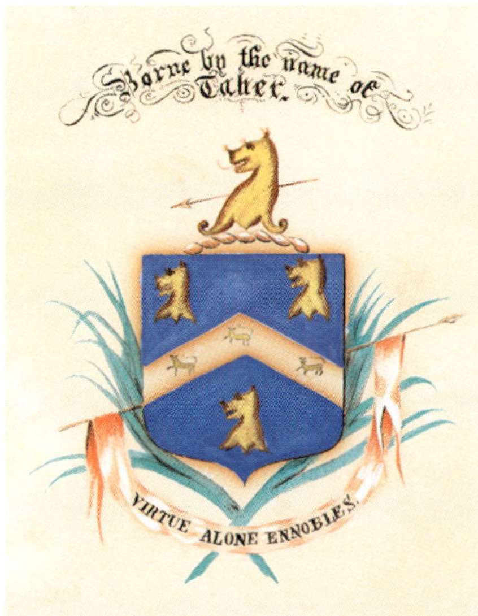

CUNEO COLLECTION

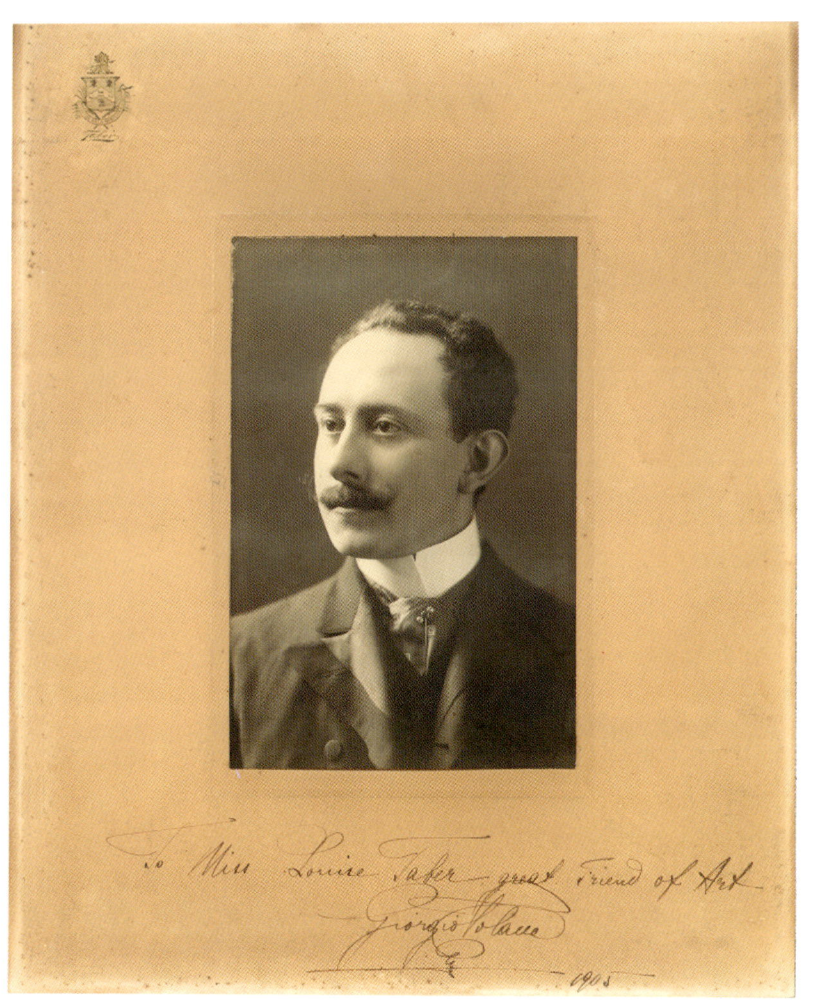

CUNEO COLLECTION

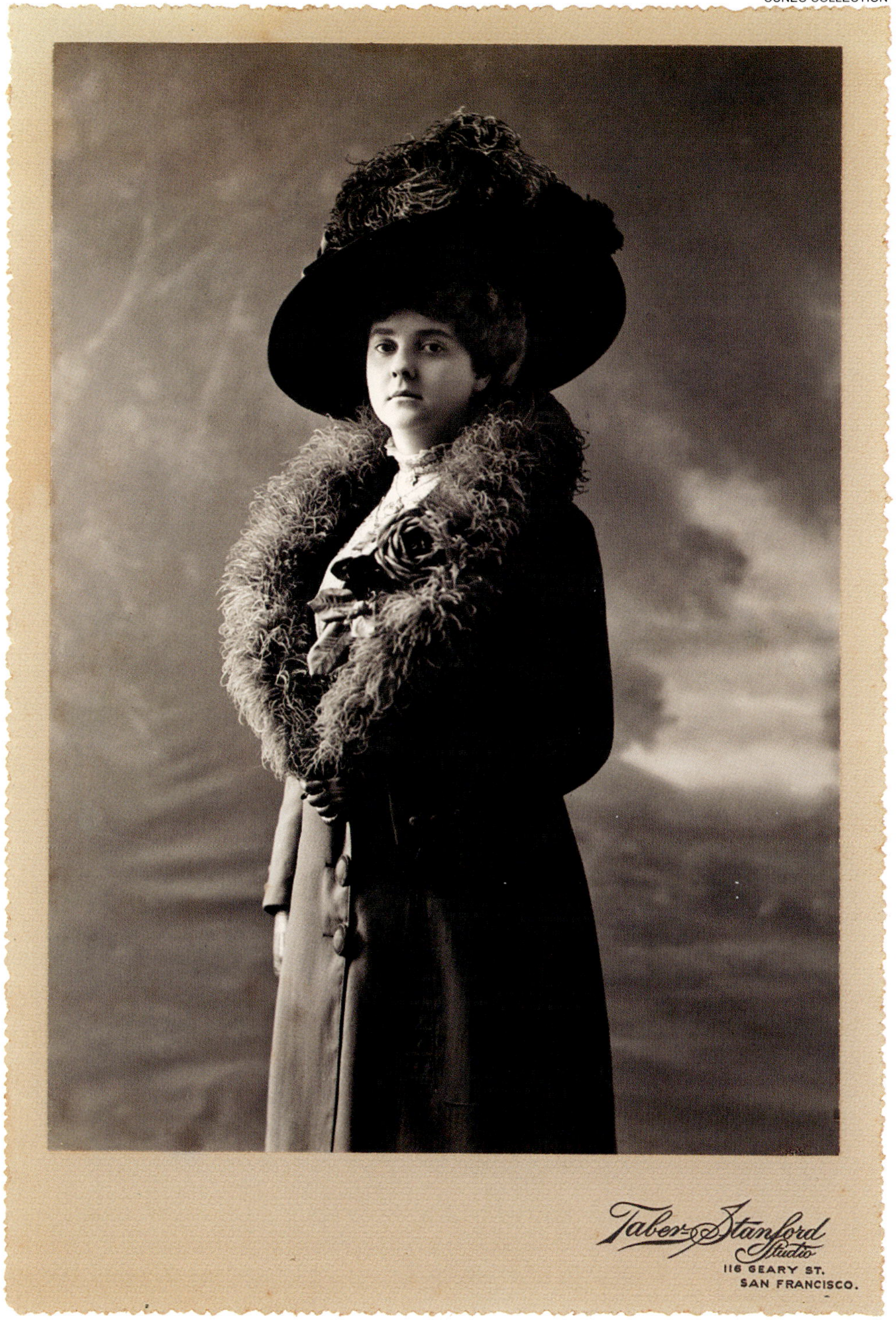

CUNEO COLLECTION

Taber-Stanford Studio
116 GEARY ST.
SAN FRANCISCO.

Above is a rare example of Isaiah Taber's last studio venture, after the 1906 earthquake and fire. He teamed with G.N. Thomas and G. H. Wichman of the Stanford Studio to form the Taber-Stanford Studio. This unsuccessful collaboration lasted from 1908 until early 1911, when Taber left. This portrait of Louise Taber, around 1911, is one of the last photographs taken by Isaiah Taber. At eighty-one years of age, the master had not lost his touch.

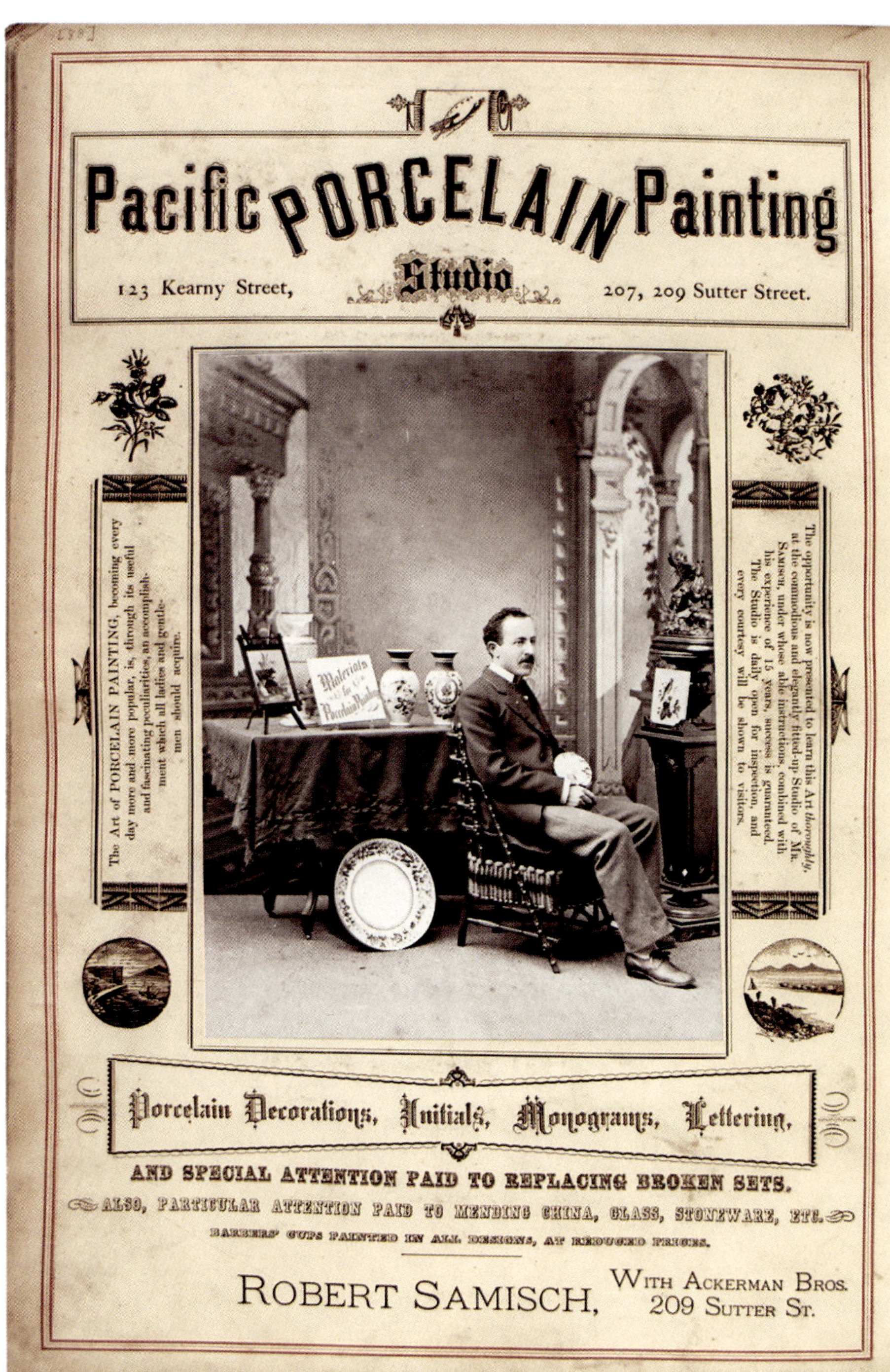

CALIFORNIA STATE LIBRARY

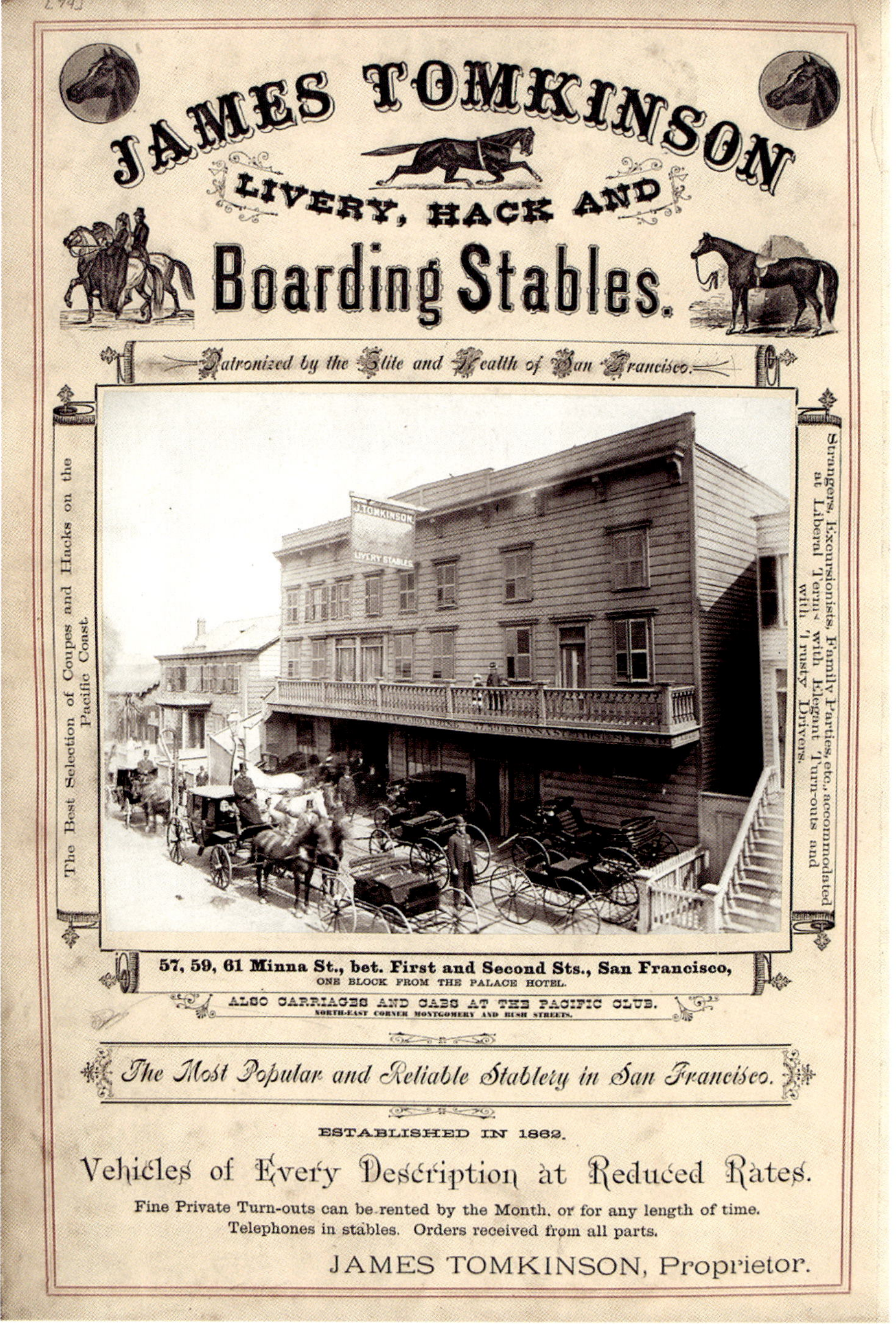

CALIFORNIA STATE LIBRARY

Taber's two commercial photographic albums contain fine examples of how he applied his portraiture and landscape skills to specific commissions. The album pages, above, from the Taber Photographic Album, 1880, *also contain lively examples of the typographer's range of ornate wood and lead type.*

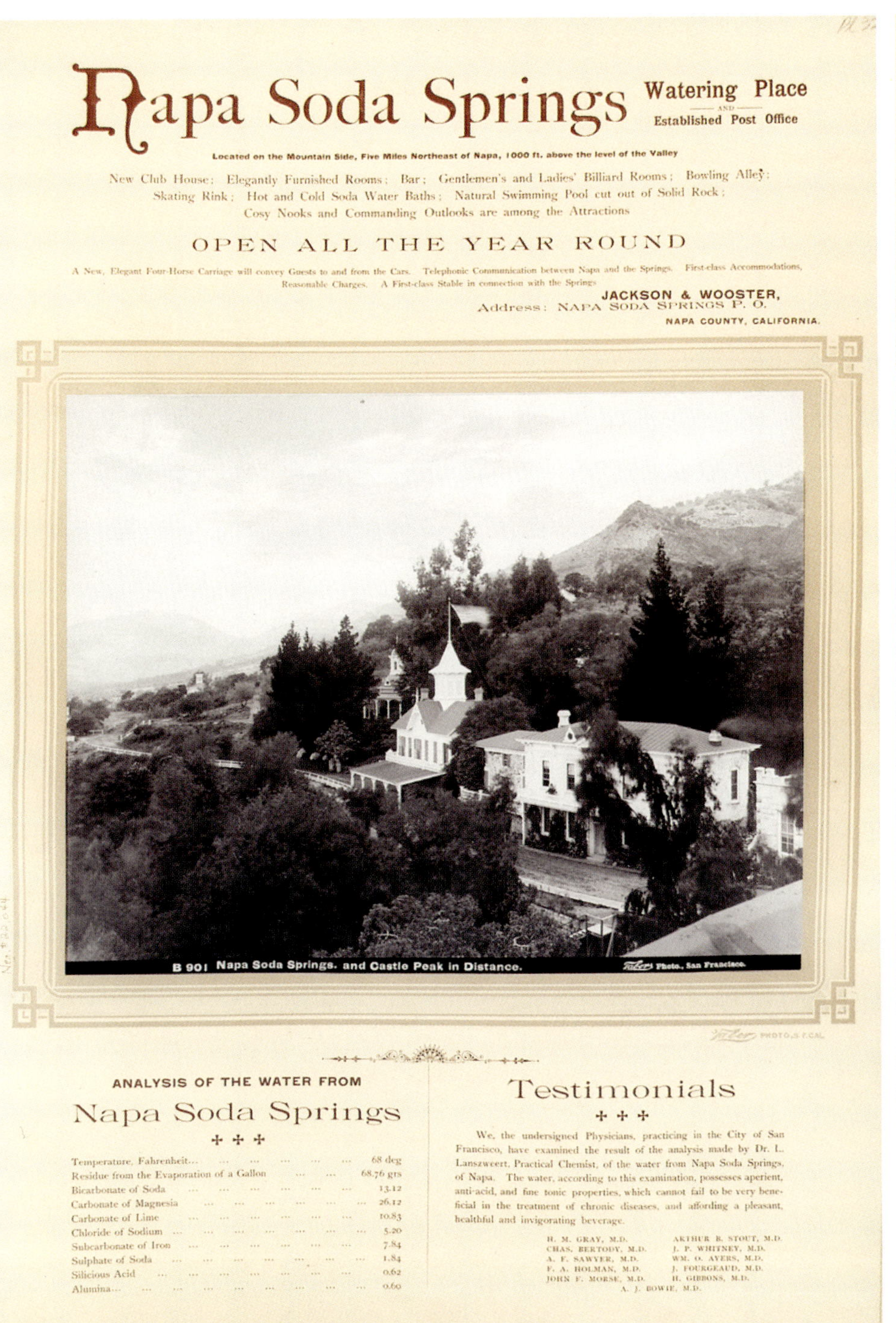

Napa Soda Springs

Watering Place
AND
Established Post Office

Located on the Mountain Side, Five Miles Northeast of Napa, 1000 ft. above the level of the Valley

New Club House; Elegantly Furnished Rooms; Bar; Gentlemen's and Ladies' Billiard Rooms; Bowling Alley; Skating Rink; Hot and Cold Soda Water Baths; Natural Swimming Pool cut out of Solid Rock; Cosy Nooks and Commanding Outlooks are among the Attractions

OPEN ALL THE YEAR ROUND

A New, Elegant Four-Horse Carriage will convey Guests to and from the Cars. Telephonic Communication between Napa and the Springs. First-class Accommodations, Reasonable Charges. A First-class Stable in connection with the Springs

JACKSON & WOOSTER,
Address: NAPA SODA SPRINGS P. O.
NAPA COUNTY, CALIFORNIA.

B 901 Napa Soda Springs, and Castle Peak in Distance. Taber Photo., San Francisco.

ANALYSIS OF THE WATER FROM

Napa Soda Springs

✢ ✢ ✢

Temperature, Fahrenheit...	68 deg
Residue from the Evaporation of a Gallon	68.76 grs
Bicarbonate of Soda	13.12
Carbonate of Magnesia	26.12
Carbonate of Lime	10.83
Chloride of Sodium	5.20
Subcarbonate of Iron	7.84
Sulphate of Soda	1.84
Silicious Acid	0.62
Alumina...	0.60

Testimonials

✢ ✢ ✢

We, the undersigned Physicians, practicing in the City of San Francisco, have examined the result of the analysis made by Dr. L. Lanszweert, Practical Chemist, of the water from Napa Soda Springs, of Napa. The water, according to this examination, possesses aperient, anti-acid, and fine tonic properties, which cannot fail to be very beneficial in the treatment of chronic diseases, and affording a pleasant, healthful and invigorating beverage.

H. M. GRAY, M.D. — ARTHUR B. STOUT, M.D.
CHAS. BERTODY, M.D. — J. P. WHITNEY, M.D.
A. F. SAWYER, M.D. — WM. O. AYERS, M.D.
F. A. HOLMAN, M.D. — J. FOURGEAUD, M.D.
JOHN F. MORSE, M.D. — H. GIBBONS, M.D.
A. J. BOWIE, M.D.

CALIFORNIA STATE LIBRARY

Pacific Mail Steamship Co.

COMPANY'S FLEET:

City of Tokio,	5000 Tons	City of Sydney,	3000 Tons	Colon,	2700 Tons	Clyde,	2000 Tons
City of Peking,	5000 "	Zealandia,	3000 "	Granada,	2700 "	Crescent City,	2000 "
City of Para,	3500 "	Australia,	3000 "	San Blas,	2000 "	South Carolina,	2000 "
City of Rio de Janeiro,	3500 "	Colima,	3000 "	San Jose,	2000 "	City of Panama,	2000 "
City of New York,	3000 "	Acapulco,	2700 "	San Juan,	2000 "	Honduras,	1500 "

New York, Panama, Mexican and Central American Line.

Steamers leave Pier 42, foot of Canal Street, New York, for San Francisco via Isthmus of Panama on the 1st and 20th of each month.

Steamers leave P. M. S. S. Co's Wharf, First and Brannan Streets, San Francisco, for New York on the 1st and 15th of each month. These Steamers call at Aspinwall, Panama, Punta Arenas, La Libertad, Acajutla, San Jose de Guatemala, Champerico, Acapulco, San Blas, Manzanillo, and Mazatlan.

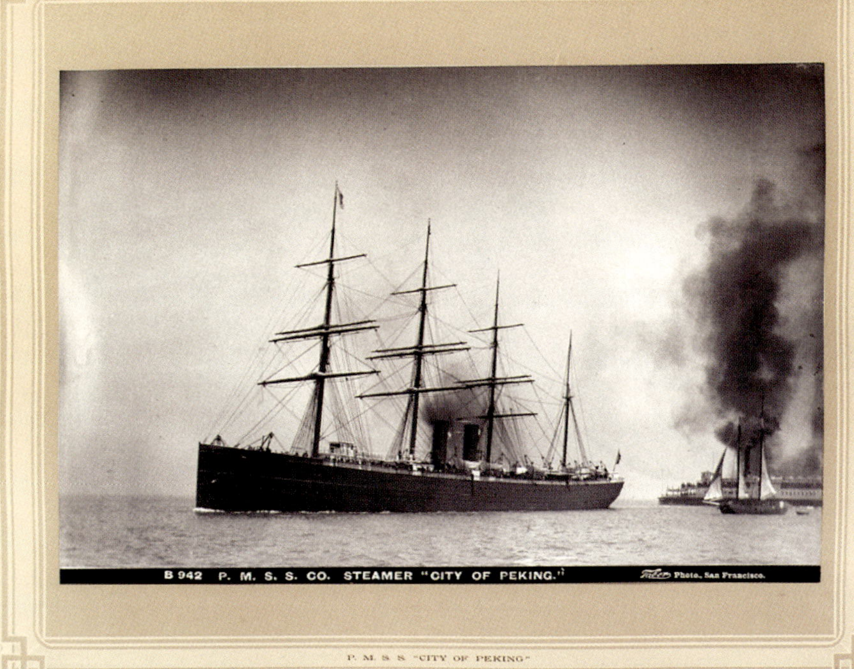

P. M. S. S. "CITY OF PEKING"

Taber PHOTO. S. F. CAL.

China and Japan Line

Steamers leave the Pacific Mail S. S. Co's wharf, First and Brannan Streets, San Francisco, as advertised, for

YOKOHAMA AND HONGKONG

Connecting at Yokohama with the Mitsu Bishi Mail S. S. Co. for Shanghai and Japanese Ports and at Hongkong with Steamers for all East Indian Ports

Australian Line

Steamers leave the Pacific Mail S. S. Co's wharf, First and Brannan Streets, San Francisco, for

AUCKLAND AND SYDNEY, CALLING AT HONOLULU

Every four weeks, as advertised.

Connecting at Auckland with local lines for New Zealand Ports, and at Sydney for Melbourne, Brisbane and all Australian Ports

WILLIAMS, DIMOND & CO., General Agents, San Francisco
B. MOZLEY, General Superintendent, New York

H. J. BULLAY, Superintendent, New York
J. B. HOUSTON, President, New York

CALIFORNIA STATE LIBRARY

Above, examples from Taber's album California Scenery and Industries, *1884.*

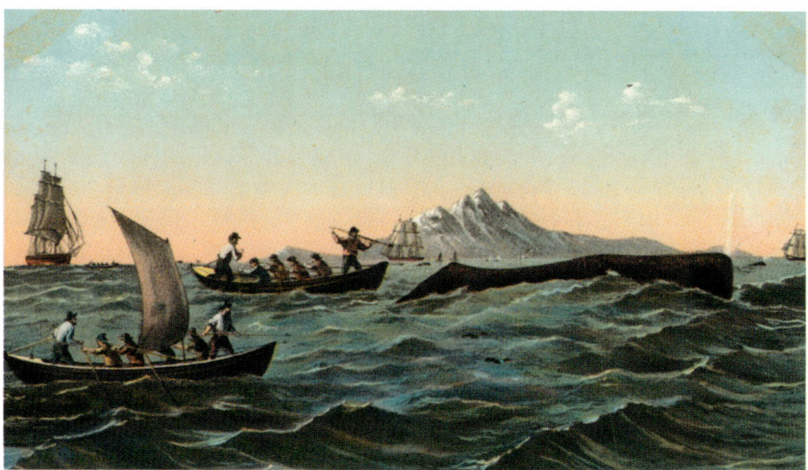

New Bedford whalers in the Arctic ice, from a print Taber kept in his possession.

ISAIAH WEST TABER: A BIOGRAPHICAL SKETCH

Isaiah Taber carefully cultivated his public persona throughout his long career. Known simultaneously as businesslike and artistic, energetic, thoroughly professional and cordial, he worked diligently and enthusiastically at his chosen field. But he also recognized the importance of a public image as the consummate photographer and publisher. Early on he prepared a stock biographical résumé of his early days in New Bedford, his gold-rush experiences, and his early pursuit of photography in New York and San Francisco. These stories changed little over the course of his life. In interviews he preferred to emphasize the present and future rather than the past. Even in old age he declined to write his memoirs or elaborate on his early life. What is known about his early experiences can be gleaned from biographical vignettes, a few surviving personal letters, and business directories and public records. Add to that a little interpolation of probability and we get a fuller picture of Isaiah Taber the man.

When Isaiah Taber was born in New Bedford, August 17, 1830, the Tabers had been in Massachusetts for two hundred years. His English ancestors, among the original group of Quakers who had settled along the Acushnet River in 1630, married into families who had come to the new world aboard the Mayflower. The first settlers in the region, including the Tabers, had been farmers, working in the Acushnet River valley, or fishermen working along the coast.

By the late 1700s, whale oil and by products had become a big cash business in New England. New Bedford with its wide, deep harbor, sent an ever increasing number of whaling vessels around the world in search of whales. New Bedford men became seafarers. New Bedford and Freehaven, its sister town across the harbor, became America's most active whaling ports. Many of the original families intermarried and, as the population grew, most new families included one or more of the old names. Young Isaiah learned he had many cousins, some close and some distant, linked by marriage through the old original settlers. His siblings were Charles Austin Mendall (1824-1911), Joanna Mendall (1826-1893), William Dean (1828-1871), Harriet Snow (1835-19?), and Freeman Augustus (1841-1910).

After a typical brief and simple New Bedford childhood attending the local grammar school, Isaiah was ready at fifteen to follow his family's tradition. He went to sea after the whale. Almost all the young males in New Bedford did the same. Isaiah's grandfather, Antipas Taber, and his father, Freeman Taber, a shipwright by trade, had gone to sea as youths. Two of his father's brothers had been lost at sea off whalers. The Taber family tree had wide branches and deep roots, including sea captains, boat builders, and provisioners to the whaling trade. Isaiah West Taber's namesake uncle, Isaiah West, was a whaling captain. Among his many relatives were the Howlands, and several of them were sea captains and ship owners. A Howland became the first mayor of New Bedford. Benjamin Taber was one of New Bedford's earliest boat builders.

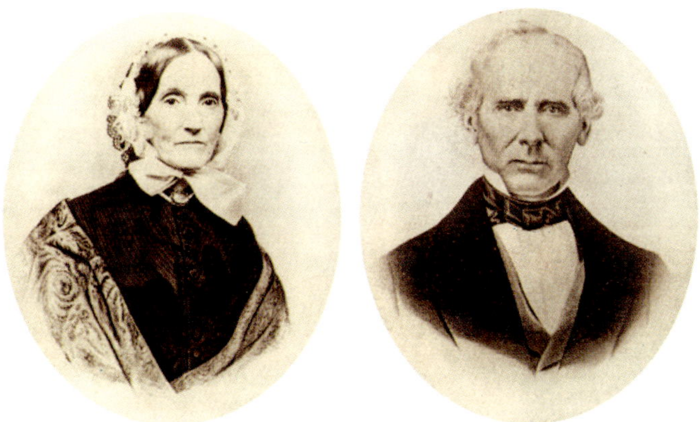

Isaiah Taber's parents, Louisa Mendall Dean Taber, left, and Freeman Taber, c.1860, from ambrotypes by Taber.

Isaiah's older brother Charles had gone to sea at fifteen, a "greenhand" aboard a relative's ship. A typical whaling voyage lasted from one to three years until the ship had filled its hold with barrels of whale oil. The vessel might track the whales in the Atlantic from Greenland to the Azores, or in the Pacific ranging as far as Australia or north to the Arctic Circle. New Bedford, the world's busiest whaling port by the 1840s, might see a ship arrival or departure every day of the year. In addition to deaths at sea, whaling crews were reduced by desertion, illness and injury, and crewmen switching vessels at distant ports. So, there was always room for anyone who wanted to sign on in New Bedford. Every member of the crew, from captain to lowest, most inexperienced hand, shared in the profits, usually as a percentage of the "lay," the take in whale oil. A boy might go to sea, but he returned, if at all, a man. And if he was lucky, a man with gold in his pocket, as much as thirty to fifty dollars worth for each of his years at sea.

After one voyage, many took up land occupations and professions. Some returned to the sea. Charles Taber chose the sea, becoming at age twenty-six, one of New Bedford's youngest sea captains. Isaiah Taber might have followed the sea if other events hadn't intervened. As ship's "boy," he knew life aboard the *Adeline Gibbs* would be hard, even though the captain, Isaiah West, was his uncle. Their course was Cape Horn to the Pacific. The first stop for provisions was Valparaiso on the coast of Chile, then west to the Marquesas Islands. From there they headed north to the Bering Sea. When the ship returned to Fairhaven on July 1, 1848, two changes in America had come about that would forever change the life of Isaiah West Taber.

The first was the daguerreotype camera. Capturing elusive images on glass had been a dream of artists for a long time. Experiments in the 1830s has shown that such a thing was possible if not practical. Jean Jacques Daguerre had developed in France his practical application of capturing images in 1839. By the time Isaiah Taber returned to New Bedford, "daguerreian" photo galleries had sprung up in cities and towns across America, over 100 in New York City alone. A least 10,000 people in America people called themselves daguerreotypists. No record exists of when Taber saw his first photographs or how he reacted to them. The process was exhibited in Boston as early as 1840, and was being practiced in San Francisco during the gold rush.

The second, more immediate event that changed Taber's life was the discovery of gold in California. News of the January 1848, find along the American River, reached New England within months. When Isaiah Taber stepped ashore, among the first things he must have heard was "gold in California." Some men had left for the gold fields, many others were planning their journeys. His older brother Charles, lucky devil, was already in California, running a schooner along the Sacramento River and a store in Sacramento City. His brother William would soon be on his way too.

Isaiah Taber learned that a group of New Bedford men had charted a whaling vessel, the *Friendship* to take them around Cape Horn to the gold fields. Isaiah Taber signed on. The *Friendship* sailed from Fairhaven on August 20, 1849 and headed south to Cape Horn. They put in at Valparaiso, the old whaling port in Chile before heading north to San Francisco Bay. After 186 days, on February 22, 1850, they entered the Golden Gate and landed at the foot of Clay Street. Upon learning that the gold fields were overrun with miners, and seeing the phenomenal prices for food and supplies, Taber and some New Bedford men, all experienced sailors, cooked up a plan. They pooled their money and chartered a vessel from the many available in the Bay and sailed south to Valparaiso, a voyage of several weeks. In that port they purchased a quantity of muskets, powder and ball, and set a course northwesterly. Following the Pacific currents and trade winds, they came to the Marquesas, another whaling port familiar to the New Bedford men. There they traded the firearms for a ship load of the islands' abundant wild pigs, rounded up for them by the natives. After sailing back to San Francisco, they sold the pigs for a handsome profit.

Taber passed the winter of 1850-51 looking for gold, probably in the company of New Bedford men. He did this with some degree of success until 1852. That summer he tried growing hay in the Sierra foothills on land purchased from his gold profits. In the spring of 1854, Taber returned to New Bedford. He never explained why, or, if he did, it is unrecorded. His brother Charles had returned to New Bedford due to ill health and temporarily had taken up farming before returning to the sea. His brother William was still in California. Perhaps Isaiah Taber, age twenty-four, decided it was time to settle down.

New Bedford in the mid-1850s had changed. The California gold rush had temporarily drained the supply of crewmen for whalers, giving rise to and expanding other trades ands industries. Among them was Charles Taber & Company, booksellers specializing in engravings, charts and imported goods, Henry Taber & Company, merchants, and Isaac C. Taber of Taber & Company, hardware and stoves . Both Charles and Isaac Taber were Isaiah's fourth cousins. To Isaiah Taber, it must have seemed that a Taber was involved in every business enterprise in New Bedford. Over sixty Tabers were listed in the city directory. Besides mariners and shipwrights, there were bakers, masons, coopers and clerks, and at least two "daguerreotype artists," Lemuel Taber and James H. Taber, and one "ambrotype artist," Daniel G. Taber. Barton R. Taber, possibly related, was a dentist. No doubt relatives and friends had advice for twenty-four-year-old Isaiah Taber.

His interest in things technical and mechanical led him to study dentistry, a trade at that time just emerging from the pliers, hammer and chisel stage to a profession that included the design and manufacture of dental prostheses and oral surgery. A field not entirely unrelated was the new photographic art, which entailed working with chemicals, tools and fine instruments (One of the earliest daguerreotypists in New York, Alexander S. Wolcott, was a manufacturer of dental supplies). Taber took up photography as well, learning to make ambrotypes. In 1856 Isaiah Taber listed himself in the directory as a dentist. That same year he became a photographer.

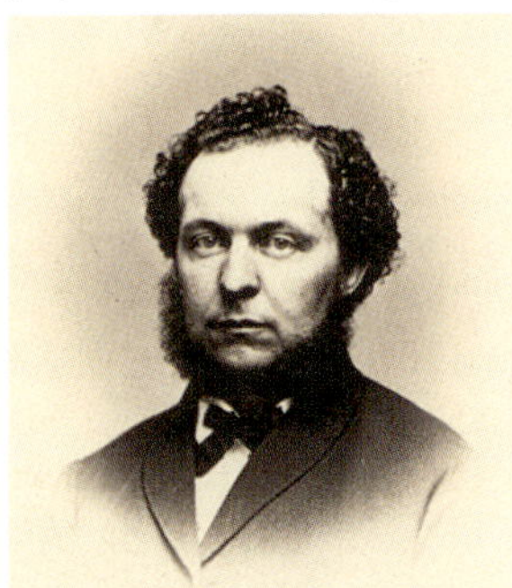

Benjamin Franklin Howland, c.1859, Syracuse, New York.

ONANDAGA HISTORICAL ASSOCIATION

Taber formed a partnership with Benjamin Franklin Howland, a distant cousin by marriage, a man six years his senior but with a similar background. Howland had gone whaling in his teens, spent several years at sea, gone to California in the gold rush, and returned to New Bedford around the same time as Isaiah Taber. Quite likely the two men had shared some experiences in California since the New Bedford men tended to stick together. He may have taken up photography around the same time as Taber.

The newly formed Taber & Howland moved to Syracuse, New York, in the summer of 1856, and listed themselves as "Ambrotypists." They may have felt the competition in New Bedford limited their chances, or, because

Syracuse was a larger city, opportunities were greater. There were Tabers living in Syracuse at the time, and Howlands as well. Syracuse, close to the western end of the Erie Canal, saw many people passing through on their way west, all in need of a good photographic likeness. The fact that Taber's name appears before Howland's may indicate a larger financial stake on his part or his more aggressive personality. Taber and Howland's new venture, at No. 4 Franklin Building, East Genesee Street, was duly announced in the *Syracuse Journal*, June 9, 1856: "Messrs. B. F. Howland and I. W. Taber, of New Bedford, Mass., have, as many New England business men have done during the last few years, selected our city as the place for their future home. They have taken the large, commodious and appropriate rooms in the Franklin Buildings, lately occupied by [the Daguerrean Gallery of] Barnard & Nichols [same entrance as Dr. Skinner's Dental rooms], and have fitted them up in elegant style, with a view of pursuing the new and popular business of ambrotyping, or taking likenesses on glass. They opened their rooms today, and are now fully prepared to accommodate customers, We bespeak for them a full share of public patronage. We know them to be polished gentlemen, honorable and enterprising men, and superior artists."

From the start, Taber got on well with the press, a relationship he maintained throughout his career. He wrote his own advertising copy and began promoting the new ambrotypes over daguerreotypes. "These pictures," he wrote, "are destined to take the lead of all others, as they have done in all our eastern cities." He went on to describe ambrotypes as "a new style of picture on glass, being hermetically sealed between two plates of fine, polished glass (by a cement which not only secures, but gilds and beautifies the pictures) and renders it as permanent as the glass itself. They may be seen in any light, are not reversed, will not corrode at sea, or change in any climate. Wherever taken, they are universally admired, and take the place of every other style of picture. They are clear and bold, vastly more perfect in detail than the Daguerreotype, and taken in one fourth of the time."

Taber and Howland, youthful inexperienced upstarts, hit Syracuse with a bang. To the consternation of established Syracuse competition, Taber announced, "The proprietors flatter themselves as Artists of long practice, from the East, to give entire satisfaction, and so confident are they of producing the best picture, that they are willing to forfeit $100, if any picture made in this city shall surpass them, and will leave the public to judge. This is no game of brag to deceive a generous public with, but a determination to convince the citizens of Syracuse and the surrounding community that there are such Artists in their community."

When the competition stiffened, Taber became bolder: "Rouse Ye, Rouse Ye. Awake from your slumbers and behold the [Taber & Howland] Banner which floats upon the breeze, from the Franklin Buildings, Central City Ambrotype Gallery, may it remind each of you the duty you owe your friends to have your picture taken at once, while in the bloom of health." It must have worked. In the month of October 1858, Taber reported selling 687 ambrotypes and only five daguerreotypes.

The following year, 1857, Taber designed a unique advertising device, perhaps the earliest motorized revolving store sign. It consisted of a conical frame, about four or five feet high, resting on its base and revolving upon a shaft, turned by a clock spring mechanism. On the surface of the cone were vertical grooves in which he slipped examples of his ambrotypes. "The cone," he said, "is enclosed in a glass frame, and presents a revolving panorama, quite pleasing to the eye. Crowds of admiring spectators are constantly surrounding this sign, and expressing their pleasure in enthusiastic terms."

The city of Syracuse held a celebration in August 1859 marking completion of the first trans-Atlantic telegraph cable. The party got out of hand and the *Syracuse Standard* reported the results: "A Mean Act—The revolving cone and stand in front of Taber & Howland's Daguerreotype establishment was stolen on Friday night, and it is supposed the frame was burned in the street bonfire that night. The cone, with its revolving machinery and elegant pictures, was valued at $100." Undeterred, Taber built a bigger and more elegant revolving cone.

Isaiah Taber's energy and creativity found other outlets during this period. In 1858 he designed and patented his "Helion Light," an improved whale oil burner that produced superior illumination. He solicited investors at $200 apiece to start manufacturing the lamp. Taber and a man named Baker set up a factory in town to produce kerosene oil. Traveling between Syracuse, New Bedford, and New York kept both Taber and Howland abreast of the latest photographic equipment and styles. During one stay in New Bedford, Taber married Benjamin Howland's sister, Mary. He was twenty-seven and she, twenty-three. She accompanied him back to Syracuse. Things went well for Taber in 1858. He and Howland announced that they had "secured the services of Mr. Parlow, of Washington City, a gentleman noted for his skill in photographing."

The next year, however, Taber & Howland and their competition must have faced hard times. Taber cut prices and offered special deals including life-size portrait heads printed on canvass and colored by John Winter, a local artist. They pushed the new ambrotypes mounted with metal backs rather than glass. Taber wrote, "Since the introduction of the beautiful Metallic Back Ambrotype into this city, by Messrs Taber & Howland, the old Daguerreotype has been fast fading away. It is but seldom they are ever heard of, except occasionally the name is faintly murmured by some old fogy artist, who cannot make a good durable ambrotype. All those having old Daguerreotypes that are fading out, can preserve them by having them copied at Taber & Howland's Gallery, from the size of a small locket to that of life size. Remember the place, Taber & Howland's, No. 4 Franklin Buildings, sign of the Revolving Cone."

His persistent barbs at the competition sparked not only a price war but a battle of words in the local press. Photographer H. Lazier complained of Taber's price cuts. "Every sensible person must know that good photographs, either plain or colored, can only be produced at a fair remuneration. We have thus far endeavored to hold our prices at a figure which would allow us to compete with the best galleries in New York and other leading cities. But since another firm in our city [Taber & Howland] has been disposed to run the business down by offering work at a less price than can be afforded; and as said firm has thrown down the gauntlet, *we pick it up*, and would say to all who feel disposed to procure either plain or colored photographs, that we have the very best facilities, and if the business must go down we will do our best to save it, in offering each individual *better work* for less money than any other establishment in the Central City. So get your lowest figures and come on. We can live as long as any one by doing our work a little lower."

Taber responded: "Doubtless the readers of our daily papers have noticed that the *modest* artist who was throwing stones at the Revolving Cone, a few months since, has again appeared on the stage, and *boldly* acknowledges that his business is going down. Poor fellow, if he had taken a *nobler* course than the one he advertises, perhaps he might have been saved. By the article he had written he seems to think our Syracuseans will stoop so low as to accept of his invitation to run around to other galleries and get their lowest figures and then call upon him and witness his *small* way of doing business. Say no more, Mr. Photographer. Our noble-hearted Syracuseans will not endorse such sentiments as you advertise. They are willing to pay a fair price for good work. Our friend has yet to learn that to do business successfully is to deal fairly with his customers. Such has ever been our motto, and we think it the secret of our success. We fix our prices, as usual, regardless of any other establishment in this city, and will convince our neighbor that the course we pursue will not drive away one of the many customers that daily visit our gallery."

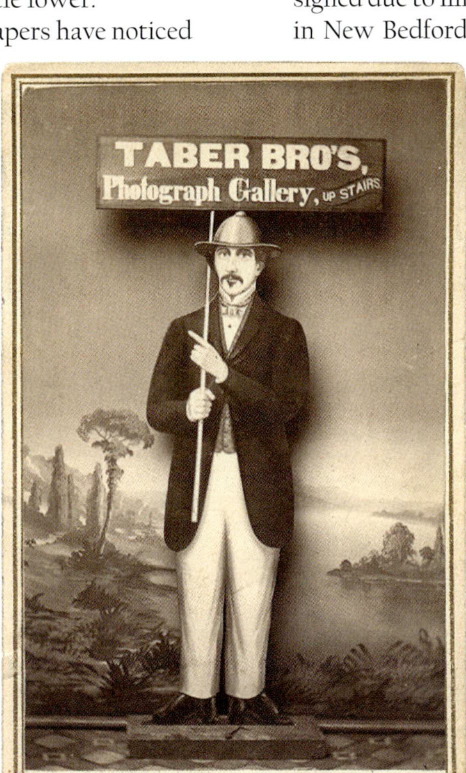

Carte de Viste *by Taber of his wooden cutout sign, a self-portrait, Syracuse, New York, c.1863.*
ONANDAGA HISTORICAL ASSOCIATION

Two months later, on April 19, 1859, Taber and Howland announced dissolution of their partnership by mutual consent. Perhaps Howland had become uncomfortable with Taber's brash approach, or possibly sales slumped to an unsustainable point. In any case, Howland kept the premises, calling the firm "Taber & Howland's Old Gallery—Sign of the Revolving Cone." Within a short time he renamed it B.F. Howland & Company. Taber dropped his name from the directory and may have returned to New Bedford in 1860 for a short time. He pursued his patented whale oil lamps, exhibiting them in Boston and New York. The *Syracuse Journal* called him, "Our friend I.W. Taber," and said of his lamp, "We don't know of a more flattering prospect for a fortune, than friend Taber has; may his usual success ever attend him, is our sincere wish."

Massachusetts on the eve of the Civil War was a center of abolitionist sentiment. Citizens, particularly the Quakers, including the Taber family, had long supported the underground railway and the human rights of escaped slaves (William C. Taber in 1837 had aided the runaway Frederick Douglass in finding sanctuary in New Bedford). When war broke out in 1860, Massachusetts strongly supported the Union cause, but to Quaker families opposed to war, difficult decisions had to be made. Isaiah Taber and his older brothers did not participate in the Civil War. Freeman Taber, Isaiah's younger brother, enlisted at age twenty as a lieutenant in the Second Army of the Potomac. He fought at Gaines Mill and Malvern Hill, then resigned due to illness in July 1862. Isaiah and Mary Taber had a daughter born in New Bedford, July 24, 1861, whom they named Louise (or Louisa) after Isaiah's mother Louisa.

Isaiah Taber returned to Syracuse with his recovered brother Freeman in the fall of 1862. They took over the photographic studio of J.F. Coonley, next to Benjamin Howland's studio and gallery. The *Syracuse Journal* wrote on Dec. 31, 1862: "Taber Brothers have opened a new photograph establishment, at No. 6 Franklin Buildings. They have provided everything necessary for carrying on the business in the highest style of the art. Mr. Taber was formerly engaged in the photograph business in this city, and secured, by his uniform courtesy and earnest efforts to satisfy his customers, troops of friends, who will welcome his return to our city. We are glad of the opportunity to recommend the new firm to the favorable notice of the public."

Benjamin Howland, meanwhile, had a new partner, C. F. Perry. Wether the relationship between the Taber brothers and Benjamin Howland was cordial or not is unrecorded. Complicating matters was Mary Howland Taber's relationship with her brother. What happened between Isaiah and Mary is a mystery. Perhaps they separated, even divorced at that time. Mary had ambitions to be a photographer (she became one in San Francisco in 1876), perhaps their ambitions clashed. No record is found of their daughter beyond her birth. Perhaps tragedy intervened similar to what befell Benjamin and Alice Howland. On February 28, 1862, the newspaper announced the death of their infant son.

In Syracuse, Isaiah Taber resumed where he had left off three years earlier, promoting and advertising heavily. He had a sign made, a wooden cutout of himself pointing upwards and placed it on the street next to the entrance staircase leading to his studio. A large glass enclosed cabinet filled with samples of his work stood at the entrance as well. In an ad, he pledged, "No work of inferior quality shall be imposed on the public— *none but the best shall go from our hands.* On this principle we intend to establish a business. Our gallery is now open to the public, and we invite them to call and be convinced of the above fact. Our instruments for taking pictures are new, and attached to them are the Latest Improvements!"

In 1863 Taber sensed a demand for pictures of wartime leaders and heros who's names appeared in the press. He obtained a good portrait of General Rosecrans, the "Hero of Murfreesboro," and found that *Carte de Viste* copies of it sold well. Soon he advertised, "Persons wishing card pictures for their Albums of any General in the Federal Army, can obtain them at Taber Brothers new Photographic Gallery." By this time Taber had dropped ambrotypes in favor of the more popular *Carte de Viste* mounted on thin board.

WINDGATE PRESS

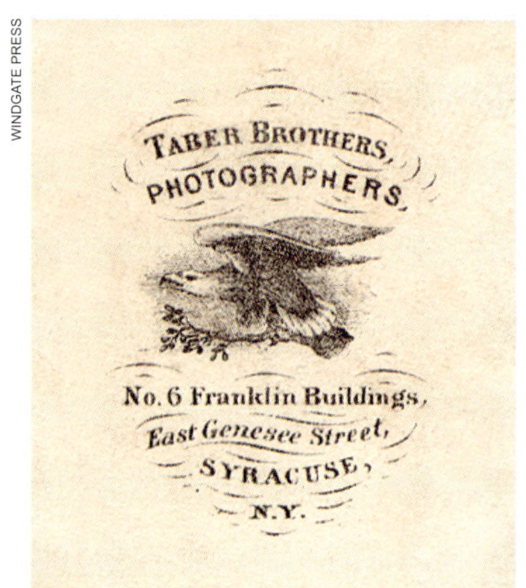

In the fall of 1864, Isaiah Taber left Syracuse for San Francisco. He said in later years that the San Francisco firm of Bradley and Rulofson, having heard of his fame, offered him a position. In June 1864, Taber Brothers were still advertising in the Syracuse papers. In January 1865 the ads read "Taber Brothers, successor Geo. K, Knapp & Co." It seems unlikely that he would make a snap decision of that magnitude. Most probably Taber had been considering a move for some time. In December 1862, on one of his trips to New York, he may have seen Carleton Watkins' mammoth-plate views of Yosemite on display at Goupil's Gallery. Taber no doubt heard about the "discovery" in the late 1850s of Yosemite Valley and recognized the sales potential of California's scenic wonders. Perhaps he regretted having left California, particularly since photographic technology had advanced, making large scenic prints possible. In the East, money was tight during the Civil War, but California was booming. Taber, always one step ahead of the pack, probably saw the future and it wasn't in Syracuse. Given his ambitious and assertive nature, he most likely solicited Bradley and Rulofson, sending them examples of his work and telling them of his California experience and his acquaintance with important people there.

Benjamin Howland may have left for California about the same time, perhaps accompanying Isaiah Taber. By December 1865 Howland, either divorced or a widower, was in California and married Mary Slauson in Marysville. Freeman Taber, by then a skilled photographer, appears to have stayed behind in Syracuse.

Taber rented rooms near Bradley & Rulofson's Montgomery Street Studio and went to work. Having been absent from San Francisco for a decade, he probably was astonished at the changes that had taken place. There were many more people, and new business blocks of brick buildings and fine homes and mansions on Rincon Hill. Taber's contemporaries Carleton Watkins and Eadweard Muybridge were the leading photographers. They and others appeared to have the scenic view market sewed up. Isaiah Taber, although a highly skilled photographic artist and technician, had a lot to learn. Over the next eight years he was with Bradley & Rulofson he learned about running a large photo studio with multiple technicians and employees. He learned the competitive nature of photography in San Francisco, and how to survive in it. He made friends and business relationships. His brashness mellowed as he matured into a professional artist and business man. During this period he began making scenic views of Yosemite Valley and the Sierra.

In 1871 Taber felt ready for his big move. He left the security of Bradley & Rulofson and went on his own. That same year he married Annie Slocum, a twenty-nine-year-old transplanted New Englander, and began a new family life. It is unknown whether or not he had any contact with his former wife Mary, who was probably living with her brother Benjamin Howland in San Francisco. Benjamin Howland had opened a gallery in 1865 near Third and Market Streets, and by 1872 had a well-established business. In 1875 his sister Mary, Taber's ex-wife, went to work for him as a bookkeeper. The next year she was listed as a photographer and, in 1878, she went with her brother to Marysville where she died, age forty-four, September 27, 1878.

Isaiah Taber's relationship with his new wife Annie got off to a good start. Annie was twelve years younger than Isaiah and had no aspirations toward photography. Her portraits show a proper and fashionable but somewhat dour young lady. In reality she was lively and playful. Like Isaiah, she had a sense of humor, an artistic nature, and loved music. In accordance with the times, Isaiah Taber never mentioned his wife in his public statements. She remained in the background, a silent partner in his success.

CUNEO COLLECTION

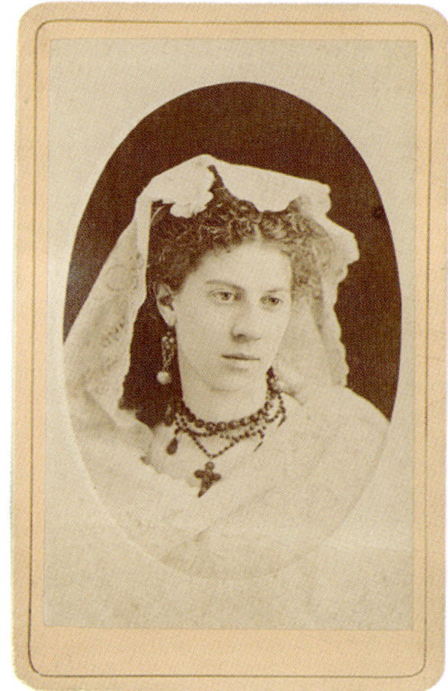

Annie Slocum Taber, by Isaiah Taber while at Bradley & Rulofson, 1871.

The Tabers moved from San Francisco to the shores of Lake Merritt in Oakland, where, in 1873 they settled into a lovely, quiet suburban neighborhood of large Victorian homes with broad lawns. Their house on Madison street was a block from their friend Dr. Samuel Merritt, self-described capitalist and developer who had created Lake Merritt as the centerpiece of a fashionable residential development.

The Taber's first born was Daisy, in 1876, followed by Louise in 1883. The Taber children played in a special fenced playground next to where

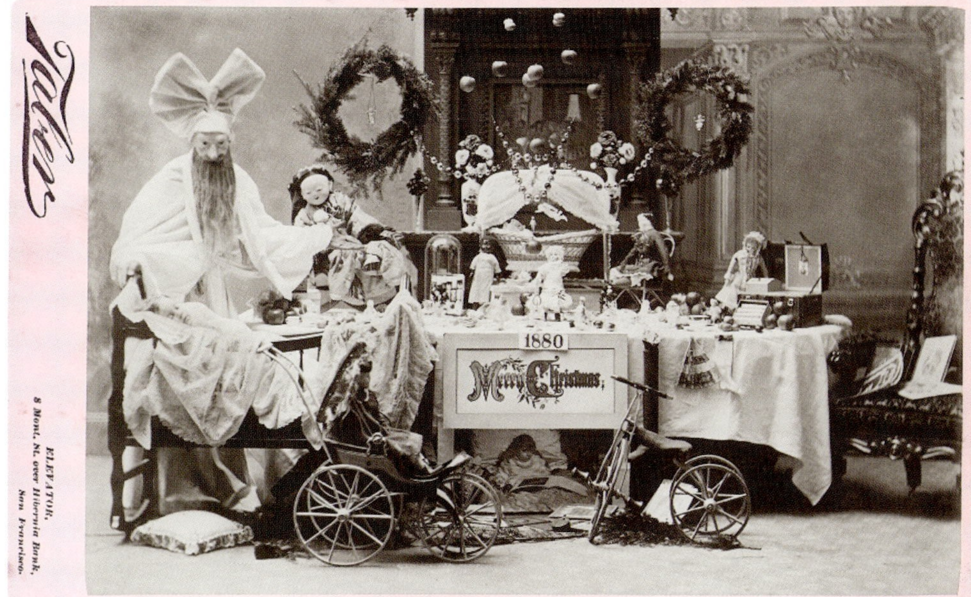

MARILYN BLAISDELL COLLECTION

Each year the Tabers produced a photographic Christmas card. This rare example from 1880, taken in their Oakland home, shows an elaborate tableau with four-year-old Daisypretending to be asleep, dreaming of toys and delights to come. The rather odd looking elf with rubber nose and stringy beard is Isaiah Taber himself. the photo was taken, no doubt, by Annie Taber.

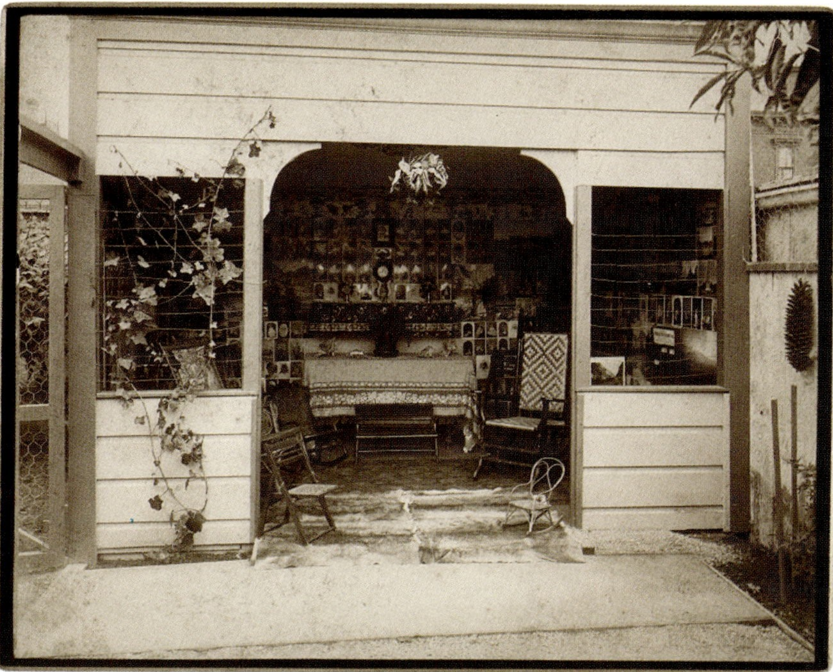

THE BANCROFT LIBRARY

This miniature backyard photo gallery features a series of ballet dancers in motion on the back wall, an indication that the gallery was for the benefit of the children. The two little chairs in front are further confirmation.

Annie raised roses in the big back yard. Annie Taber ordered the latest style furnishings from Boston for their home. With her sense of fashion and good taste in decor, she probably selected furniture and props for Isaiah's San Francisco salons and galleries too.

Isaiah Taber commuted daily to his San Francisco studio by ferry from Oakland. He could not, however, entirely separate his work from his home life. He set up a photo gallery in his basement, possibly for friends or East Bay customers. In the back yard Taber built a miniature photo gallery for his children, and the house was filled with family and celebrity portraits, all photos by Taber. He and his wife delighted in dressing and posing their daughters as fashionable ladies. Annie made copies of the latest Paris and New York fashions in miniature for the little girls. The children had several large dolls and, these too, carefully costumed and posed, appear in family photographs.

The Tabers enjoyed the opera and apparently attended regularly. No doubt, Isaiah Taber saw it too as an opportunity to meet visiting celebrities and potential patrons. Their daughter Louise developed an early love of music, opera in particular. Just as Isaiah Taber kept an autograph book in his photo gallery, young Louise began gathering autographs of musicians, condusctors and composers. The children received special tutoring in music and attended the finest grammar schools.

For the most part, Isaiah Taber enjoyed a fine reputation and was not distracted from pursuing his goals. He had his detractors, however, as well as competitors. Critics at times took exception to his unabashed self promotion or his clever marketing approaches. Yet he was well liked and admired by his many patrons who favored him with repeat business. One detects a tinge of envy in some of the critical barbs aimed at Isaiah Taber. No one disputed the consistent superior quality of Taber's prints and mounts. Isaiah Taber was criticized for his practice of publishing the work of other photographers without acknowledging them. At the time, however, other photographers did the same. Taber never attempted to hide the fact that he published the work of others, indeed he advertised it. Taber stated in his advertising that he employed the finest artists available and selected works from photographers in Japan, Mexico and Alaska. While some photographers may have resented the lack of attribution, others apparently were delighted to have in the Taber Photographic Company a sales outlet for their scenic views. In portrait studios then as today, the finished product went out imprinted with the proprietors name. Just as Isaiah Taber no doubt begrudged working for Bradley and Rulofson for years without individual recognition, some of Taber's assistant photographers felt resentment and left his employ to strike out on their own. That too was common practice in the competitive hotbed of San Francisco.

As his business grew, Isaiah Taber found himself spending more time in San Francisco and less in Oakland with his family. Around 1890 Taber, then sixty years old, made some major changes. His brother Freeman, age forty-nine, arrived in San Francisco. Freeman, after parting company with his brother in 1864 back in Syracuse, had joined the William Page Company, a Boston brass fabricator, as a designer. He had risen to manager and stayed for eighteen years. Isaiah made Freeman, with his extensive knowledge of photography, manager of the Taber Photographic Company. At the same time, Isaiah Taber and his family moved to San Francisco and settled on McAllister Street near Golden Gate Park. One reason for the move may have been that Daisy Taber, now fourteen and Louise, seven, were enrolled in San Francisco schools and no longer needed the big play yard in Oakland. Certainly the daily commute for Isaiah improved. The cable car rolled right by his house and carried him down Market Street to the doorstep of his Montgomery Street studio. The Tabers remained at the McAllister Street address for the rest of their lives. Although the residence survived the 1906 fire, no interior photographs of it exist among the Taber family records.

Isaiah Taber in his prime earned a comfortable income and lived well. And he was able to sustain for thirty years a highly competitive business employing, at one time, up to sixty people. A remarkable achievement given San Francisco's rapid changes during those years. As head of the largest photographic business in San Francisco, Isaiah Taber looked the part. Straight backed and trim, he stood five-feet, six inches. As his dark hair turned grey, it only added to his dignified appearance. Always carefully groomed and immaculately dressed in the latest fashion, Isaiah Taber cut a dashing figure.

CUNEO COLLECTION

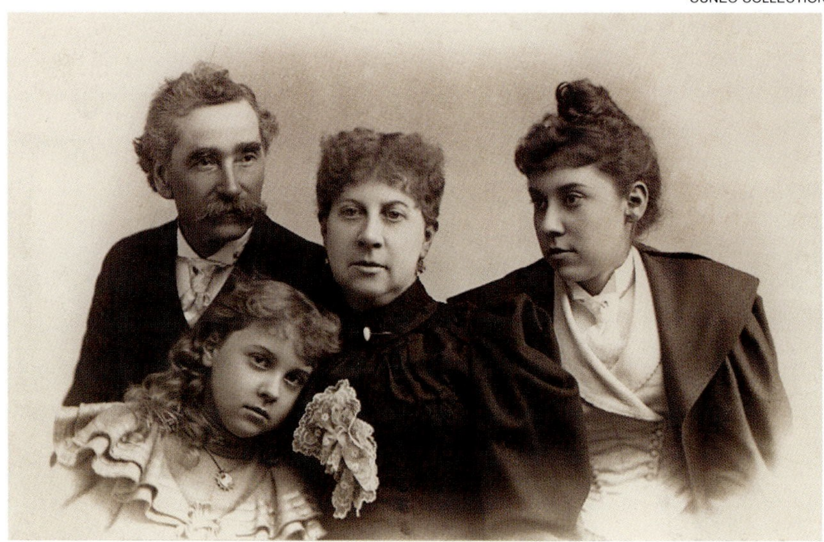

The Tabers around 1891, when the family moved to San Francisco from Oakland. Isaiah, Annie, and Daisy, rear, and Louise at lower left.

THE BANCROFT LIBRARY

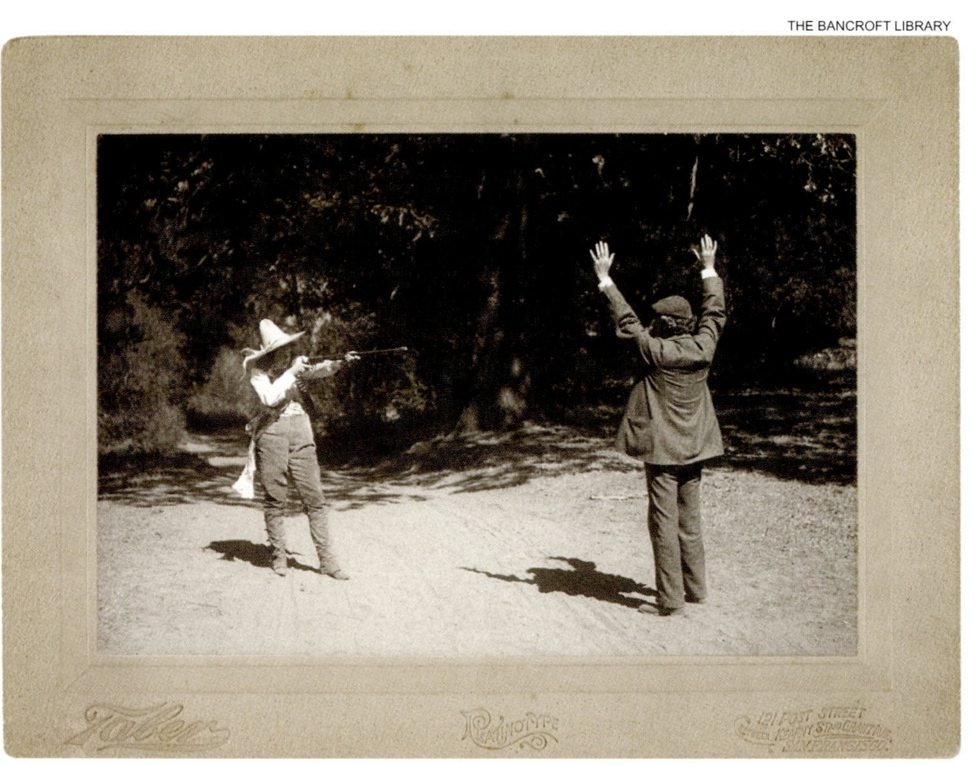

Out for a walk in the Oakland countryside, Isaiah Taber encounters a highwayman, his daughter Daisy, c.1887.

Isaiah Taber had a gift too, the ability to making his clients and their wriggling children at ease before his camera. Many of his customers had never sat for a portrait and viewed the big dark camera box draped in black as we might today view some ominous piece of equipment in a medical clinic. Taber charmed them with his friendly, yet professional manner. He liked people and knew his business. No doubt he engaged his subjects in polite conversation as he posed them and arranged his reflectors and light baffles. "Mr. Taber," his promotional literature reads, captures the "individuality of his subjects [with] a gracefulness of pose given to every figure, so there is no trace of awkwardness in any photograph that leaves his hands."

With an unflagging dedication and interest in his subjects—people or places—Taber produced a body of work that is a significant contribution to the history of the West. More than any other photographer, he captured the entrepreneurial spirit of nineteenth-century San Francisco. The photographic legacy of Isaiah Taber has withstood the test of time.

Much of what is known of Isaiah Taber is due to his daughter Louise Eddy Taber. She kept family photos, letters, her father's awards and medals, most everything that survived the 1906 fire, and passed them on for posterity. Gregarious like her father, she also developed a keen interest in early California history. Isaiah Taber's determination to record photographically the California pioneers impressed young Louise. She remembered the stories told by pioneers, friends of her father, who had come west in the gold rush.

In her teens, Louise became a devotee of opera and opera performers. She discovered too, she possessed al talent for writing. She composed poetry and wrote short stories and plays, mostly in a romantic vein appropriate for Victorian young ladies. As she matured, Louise improved her writing skills and became a serious writer. She published several short stories and in 1911, at age 28, she published her first novel, *The Flame*, a "romance of California." the novel's modest success encouraged Louise to write a second, entitled *Amata*.

Louise wrote articles for local newspapers and magazines about the history of San Francisco's opera companies. She later broadened her scope and penned colorful pieces about early days in San Francisco. By that time, around 1915, many of the gold rush pioneers were dying off, and a new generation of San Franciscans seemed eager to hear the stories that Louise Taber had heard at her father's side since childhood. In the late 1920s, Louise began reading her stories on the radio, her warm, confident voice attracting a large local audience. Her radio scripts were published in two popular booklets called *California Gold Rush Days* and *The Mother Lode Country*. In 1938 Louise became a member of the Promotion Board for the Golden Gate International Exposition held to be held on Treasure Island, and became a radio regular on KFRC, every Thursday evening at seven on the "1939 Exposition Program."

In the early 1940s, her radio programs branched out to include famous personalities of early San Francisco. At that time she also managed the San Francisco Community Opera Company, an organization of local performers who presented over several seasons popular arias at the Native Sons Hall on Mason Street.

Despite her local notoriety as "historian of the air waves," Louise Taber led a quiet life. After her mother died in 1922, she sold the family home on McAllister Street and moved to a small Telegraph Hill apartment. A good cook and conversationalist, she continued to entertain artist and musician friends until her death in 1946.

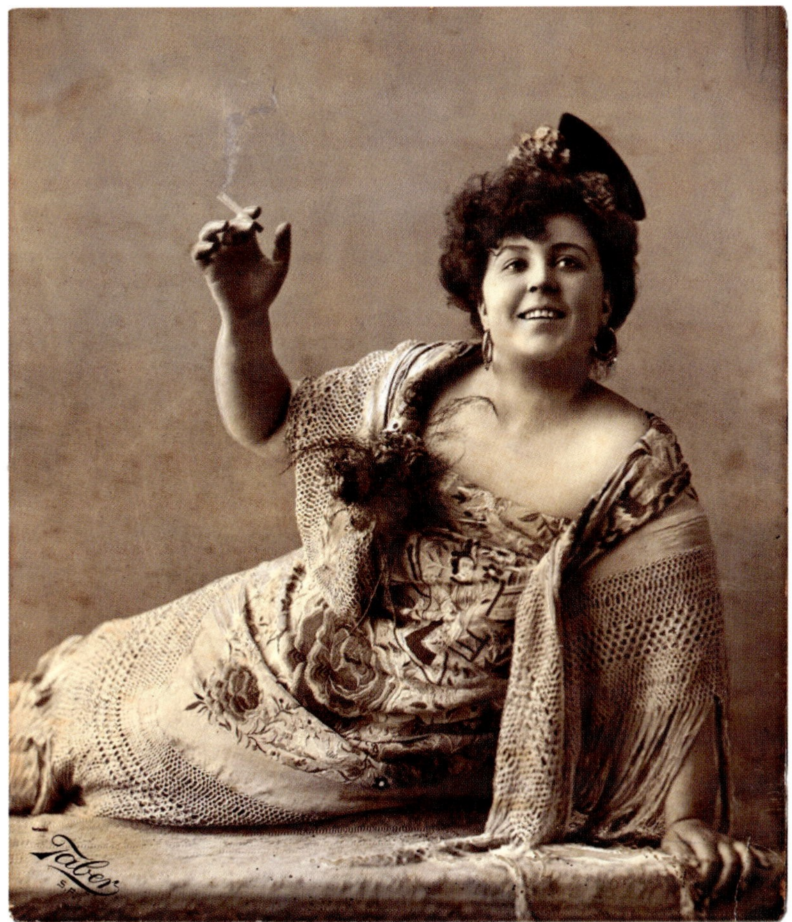

CUNEO COLLECTION

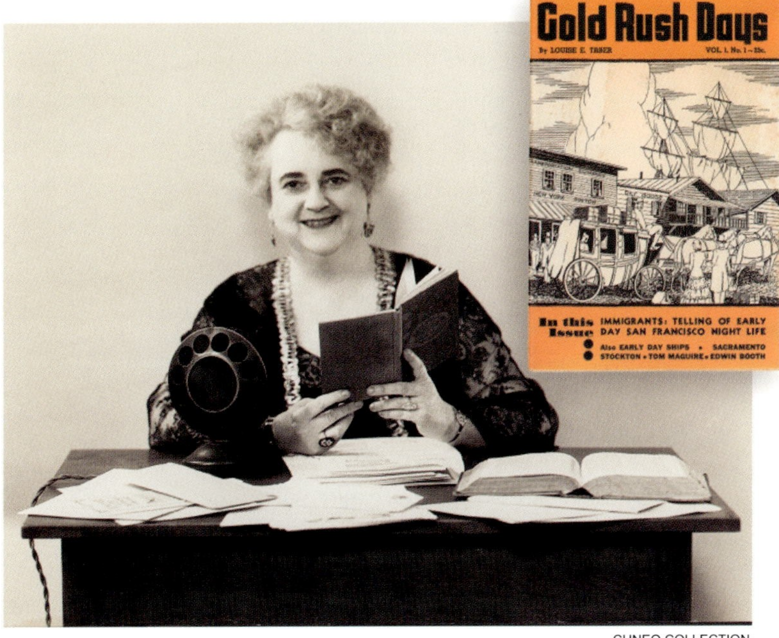

CUNEO COLLECTION

Above right: Louise Taber, around seventeen, in a parody of the Alphonse Mucha posters popular around 1900. This 16 by 18 inch-portrait by her father reveals some hand work including the painted cigarette smoke and the inked Taber logotype, done, no doubt, by Isaiah Taber.

Right: Louise Taber, c.1936, in a publicity shot for her radio broadcasts.

Inset: One of Louise Taber's collections of pioneer stories.

CALIFORNIA STATE LIBRARY

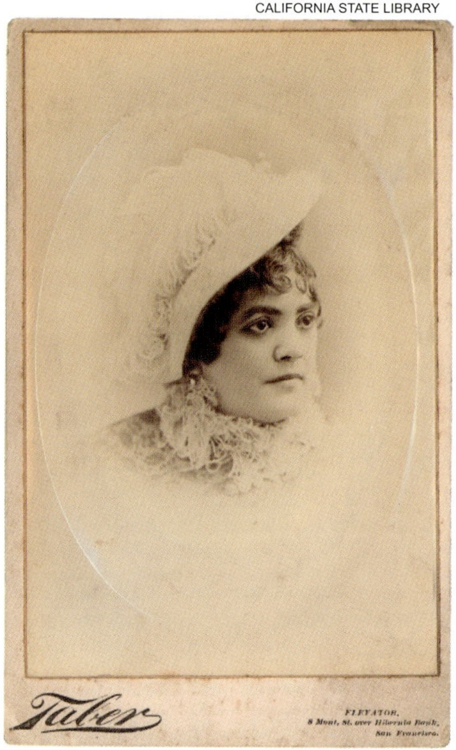

CALIFORNIA STATE LIBRARY

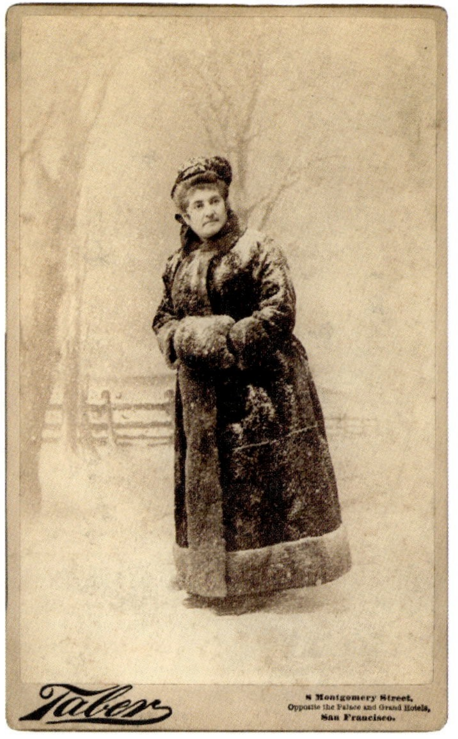

CALIFORNIA STATE LIBRARY

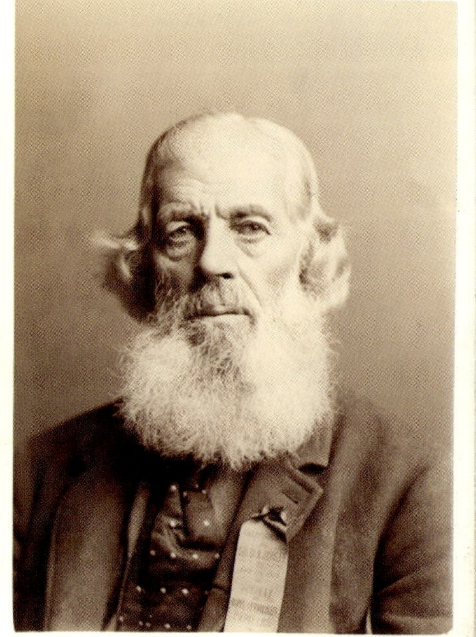

Left: Maria Vallejo Cutter and Adela Vallejo, daughters of General Mariano Vallejo, and near left, William Cooper Graves, a survivor of the ill-fated Donner Party of 1846.

Below: Isaiah Taber's older brother Charles, who then lived in Wakefield, Massachusetts, returned his completed form for the pioneer project in October 1906, six months after the San Francisco fire. Seen today, with its precise dates and spellings in the subject's own hand, one can only imagine the magnitude of the loss of Taber's pioneer project.

ISAIAH TABER'S PIONEER PROJECT

By the nature of his business, Taber had an interest in the state's young history and its colorful individuals. After all, he participated in the Gold Rush and could readily identify with the pioneers who built the state. To this end, Taber embarked on a project to create a collection of portraits and biographical data on "representative Californians."

He planned to present his collection to the California State Library in Sacramento. The portraits were cabinet card in size and the verso of each carried the following notice: "Taber's State Collection of Portraits of Representative Californians. In Memoriam, To Be Presented To The State Library, by I. W. Taber. That the State may preserve the names and faces, and keep alive the memory of those who made it what it is."

Tragically, Taber's pioneer portrait albums, almost complete, were lost in the earthquake and fire of April 1906. In a letter dated July 25, 1906, to Eudora Garoutte, head of the State Library's California Historical Department, Taber wrote: "In answer to a letter from Mr. Gillis, State Librarian, for information about my collection of representative Californians, on which I had been working and collecting data for the past 20 years, I regret to say that it was destroyed by the fire with my Gallery at 121 Post Street. I had six large Albums, holding 300 portraits each, with Autographs, Date of Arrival in California, Occupation, Address, birthplace, Date of birth, and first occupation in California, with other biographical history. They contained nearly a thousand of the pioneer business men of the State, many have now passed away, and many professional men and others who have not figured prominently in public life, but who were among the builders of our state."

Only a smattering of these portraits survives today. The State Library, however, does have an album of California Supreme Court justices and, perhaps not coincidentally, all the photographs were by Taber.

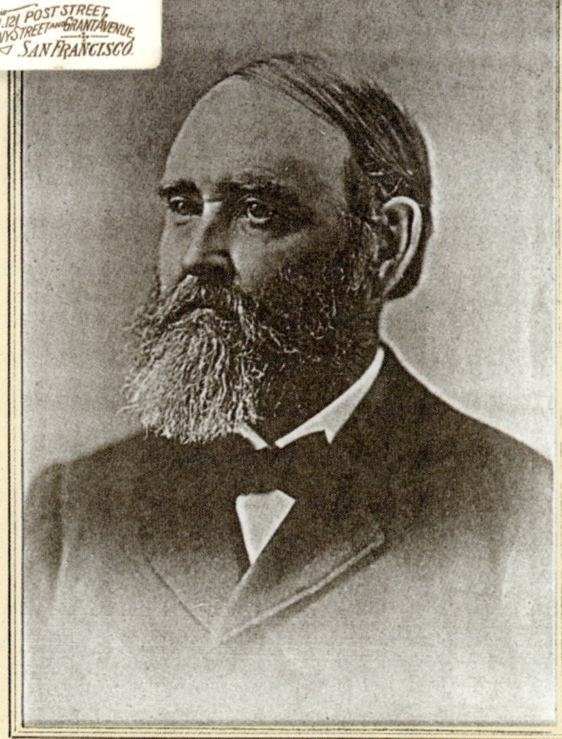

Autograph Charles Austin Mendell Taber

Date Oct. 10 1906. Occupation Author. last work 'The cause of Geological Climates'.

Address Wakefield Mass.

Birthplace Rochester Plymouth County. Massachusetts.

Date of Birth April 3 1824. Date of Arrival in California August 1848.

First Occupation in California Transporting government troops and supplies

For Biography see

CUNEO COLLECTION

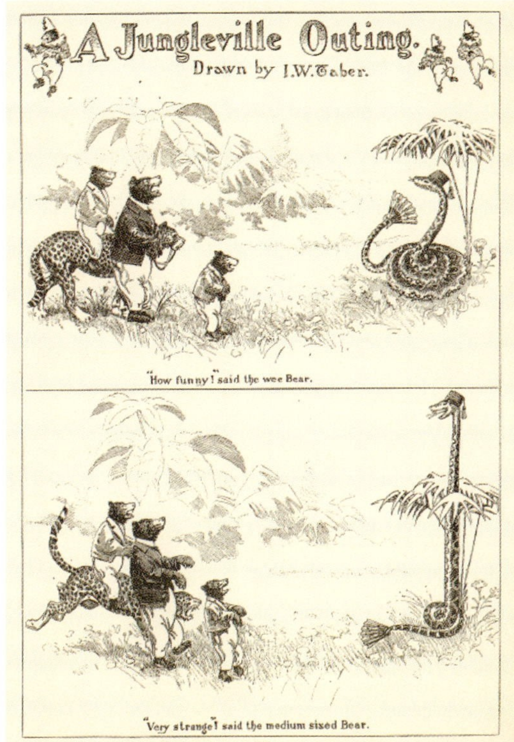

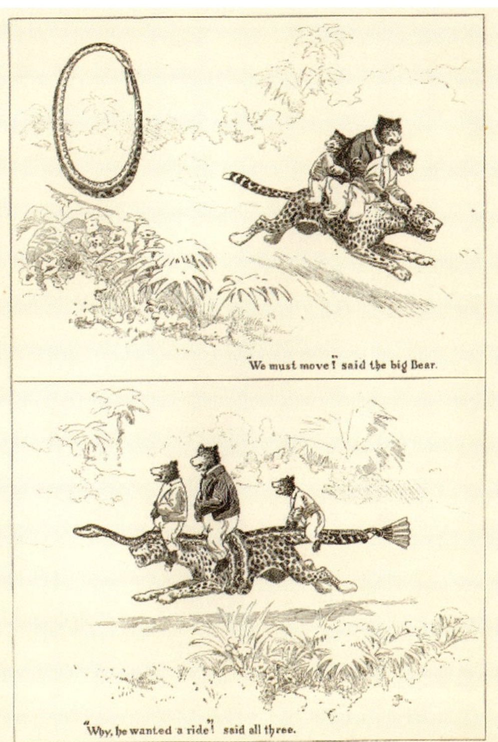

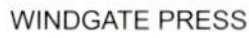
WINDGATE PRESS

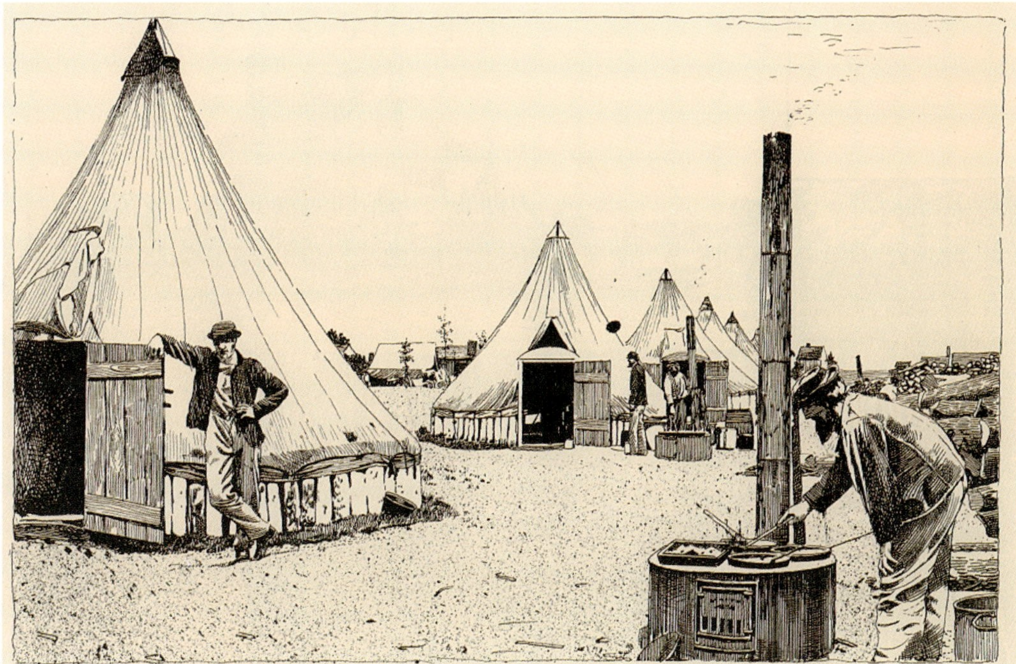
WINDGATE PRESS

THE OTHER I.W. TABER

Photographer Isaiah West Taber is sometimes confused with his artist cousin Isaac Walton Taber because both men were known as "I.W. Taber." The two Tabers, both from New Bedford, shared the same great-great-great grandfather Joseph Taber (1678-c.1752). Isaac Taber's father was Isaac Congdon Taber, Civil War mayor of New Bedford for whom Fort Taber in that city is called. Not much is recorded about Isaac Walton Taber, born around 1849, other than he became a well-known illustrator in the 1880s and 1890s for *Century Magazine* and *St. Nicholas Magazine* for children. He was a principal illustrator for the popular history series *Battles and Leaders of the Civil War* published in the 1880s. In addition he made sketches and oil paintings of maritime subjects including whaling scenes. Most of his earlier work was signed simply "Taber" or "Walton Taber," but by the 1890s, he began signing "I.W. Taber." Today, because of that signature, galleries occasionally exhibit drawings or paintings by Isaac Walton Taber incorrectly attributed to Isaiah West Taber.

Clearly Isaac Taber knew his cousin Isaiah Taber, but there is no record of any contact between them. Perhaps they both were amused by the minor confusion their signatures created. Isaiah's older brother Charles Taber, captain of whaling vessels, writer, and an accomplished sketch artist, commissioned Isaac Taber to illustrate a book he wrote entitled *The Voyage of Columbus*.

Above left is a cartoon panel by Isaac Taber drawn for *St. Nicholas Magazine*, March 1892. Below it is a pen and ink drawn by Isaac Taber, based on a photograph, for the series *Battles and Leaders of the Civil War*, c. 1884.

Below are signatures by Isaiah West Taber (top), and two typical examples (bottom) by Isaac Walton Taber.

Yours very truly,
I. W. Taber

Taber/84

I.W.Taber

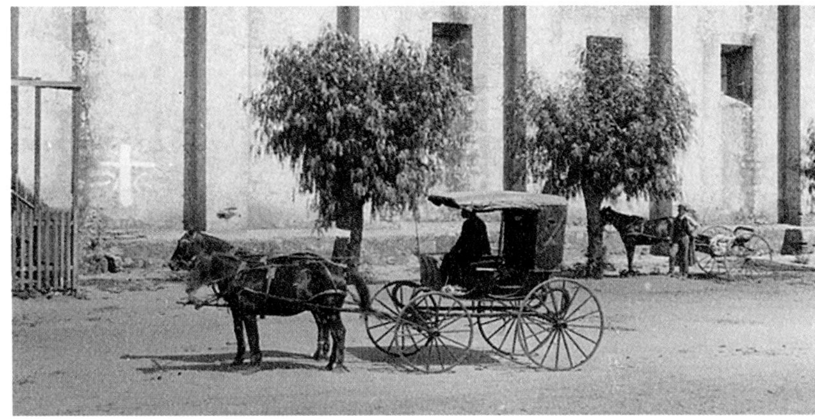

CUNEO COLLECTION

ISAIAH WEST TABER CHRONOLOGY

1830 Isaiah West Taber is born second of six children to Freeman Taber and Louisa Dean Taber, New Bedford, Massachusetts.

1840 Isaiah Taber attends grammar school in New Bedford.

1845 Fifteen-year-old Isaiah signs on as ship's boy on whaler *Adeline Gibbs* out of New Bedford. The captain is his namesake and uncle, Isaiah West.

1848 After a three-year voyage to the Pacific and Bering Sea, Isaiah Taber returns to New Bedford, July 1, 1848, learns that gold had been discovered in California.

1849 Isaiah Taber joins company of New Bedford men in chartering whaler *Friendship* to take them to California, departs New Bedford August 1849.

1850 After 186 days around Cape Horn, Isaiah Taber arrives at San Francisco, joins other New Bedford men in successful speculative voyage to Valparaiso, Chile and the Marquesas Islands to bring live hogs to San Francisco.

1851 Isaiah Taber tries gold prospecting and farming until 1853.

1854 Isaiah Taber returns to New Bedford, practices dentistry and learns to make Daguerreotypes and Ambrotypes.

1856 Taber moves to Syracuse, New York, with Benjamin Franklin Howland and opens a photography studio.

1857 In New Bedford, Isaiah Taber marries Mary F. R. Howland, sister his partner of B. F. Howland.

1859 Taber and Howland dissolve their partnership by mutual consent. Howland continues to operate the studio.

1861 Isaiah and Mary Taber have a daughter, born in New Bedford.

1862 In December, Taber and his younger brother Freeman Augustus Taber open a studio in Syracuse called Taber Brothers.

1864 Isaiah Taber leaves for San Francisco where he joins the firm of Bradley and Rulofson as a portrait photographer. He remains in their employ until 1871.

1870 Isaiah Taber (apparently divorced) meets Annie Slocum when he makes her portrait at Bradley and Rulofson.

1871 September 29th, Isaiah Taber marries Annie Slocum in San Francisco. He wins medal for best photographs at the California State Agricultural Society.

1872 Taber opens his photo gallery at 12 Montgomery Street with Thomas Henry Boyd.

1875 Taber gallery closes. Isaiah Taber and Boyd join George Daniels Morse Photographic Art Gallery, 417 Montgomery Street.

1876 Carleton E. Watkins loses his San Francisco gallery and negatives to James J. Cook, who forecloses on loans to Watkins. Cook enters into agreement with Isaiah Taber to publish prints from Watkins' negatives. Taber and Boyd leave Morse and take over Yosemite Art Gallery, 22-26 Montgomery. Isaiah and Annie Taber's first daughter Daisy born; the family moves their residence to Oakland.

1877 Taber wins gold medal for photography at Mechanic Institute Exposition in San Francisco.

1878 Taber opens I.W. Taber Photographic Art Gallery in new Hibernia Bank building at 8 Montgomery Street, corner of Market Street. Boyd leaves the firm. Cook, meanwhile, stays at the Yosemite Art Gallery at 26 Montgomery Street, and forms a new company is formed called Rieman & Tuttle. Taber's ex-wife Mary Howland dies in Marysville, California.

1879 Taber photographs visiting former president Ulysses Grant.

1880 Isaiah Taber produces *The Taber Photographic Album of Principal Business Houses, Residences and Persons*, the first of his large photo-illustrated commercial albums for subscribers. Taber photographs president Rutherford B. Hayes on his visit to San Francisco. Taber joins with his friend Dr. Samuel Merritt on eight-week voyage to the Sandwich Islands and the South Pacific aboard Merritt's schooner yacht *Casco*. In Hawaii Taber photographs King Kalakaua. Taber wins gold medal for photography at the Mechanics Institute Industrial Exhibition , San Francisco.

1883 The Tabers move their residence temporarily into the Palace Hotel after the birth, in Oakland, of their second daughter, Louise Eddy Taber. The same year the Tabers move back to Oakland. Taber and his wife voyage to Hawaii at the invitation of King Kalakaua attend his belated coronation

1884 Taber produces the second of his large photo-illustrated commercial albums, *California Scenery and Industries.* He wins gold medal for best photographs in the Southern Exposition, Louisville, Kentucky.

1886 Taber begins his monumental project to record photos and biographical sketches of California pioneers.

1887 Isaiah Taber tries and fails for a commission to photograph Queen Victoria's Golden Jubilee in London.

1888 Isaiah Taber is named a Yosemite commissioner, serves four years.

1889 Isaiah Taber voyages to Alaska to photograph native villages and scenic views. He wins medal for photography at the Paris Exposition Universelle.

1890 Freeman Taber arrives in San Francisco and joins Isaiah Taber as a photographer.

1891 Isaiah Taber reorganizes his operation, changes name from I.W. Taber Photographic Art Gallery to the Taber Photographic Company, with himself as president, his younger brother Freeman Taber as manager. Isaiah and his family move their residence to 1715 McAllister Street, San Francisco. He photographs president Benjamin Harrison during his visit to San Francisco.

1893 Taber moves his studio to 121 Post Street. He is chosen official photographer for the 1894 Mid-winter Exposition to be held in Golden Gate Park.

1894 Taber sets up a studio and photo gallery at the Mid-winter Fair and makes portraits of many visiting dignitaries, including dancing sensation Loie Fuller. He meets Henry Stanley (of Stanley and Livingston fame) and enlists his help in securing an invitation to photograph Queen Victoria's Diamond Jubilee to be held in England in 1897.

1896 Taber is awarded a commission to photograph the Queen's Jubilee. He appoints James Jay Cook as vice president of Taber Photographic Co., San Francisco. He travels to London and sets up his "Bas-Relief Gallery" at the Hotel Cecil and later opens a gallery in Piccadilly.

1897 In London, Isaiah Taber invited to photograph the Prince and Princess of Wales, who later become King Edward VII and Queen Alexandra. Taber establishes a gallery in Paris and forms the "Taber Photographic Syndicate." He photographs the home of Sara Bernhardt and parlays his connections with celebrities and royalty into expanded portrait business. He returns to San Francisco. Without his presence in Europe, his overseas operations fail.

1901 Isaiah Taber gains increased notoriety for photographing celebrities who visit San Francisco as well as important state officials. Photos by Taber appear regularly in *Sunset Magazine* and other publications. Taber photographs president William McKinley on a visit to San Francisco.

1905 Taber nears completion of his portrait albums of pioneer Californians, containing over 1,800 portraits gathered from all over California. Taber intends to present the albums to the California State Library as a visual record of early California. James Jay Cook dies.

1906 April 18th earthquake catches Isaiah Taber at home on McAllister Street. The subsequent fire destroys Taber's gallery and negatives at 121 Post Street, including his pioneer portrait albums. Taber borrows a camera and shoots aftermath of fire. That same year, Taber's eldest daughter Daisy, age thirty, dies in Buffalo, New York.

1908 Isaiah Taber, now seventy-eight years old, rents space at 118 Geary Street as a portrait studio.

1909 Taber joins with G. N. Thomas and G. H. Wichman, who operate the Stanford Studio next door, to form Taber-Stanford Studio, 116-118 Geary.

1911 Taber leaves Taber-Stanford Studio, dissatisfied with his partners' lack of advertising and promotion of his work. He retires from photography.

1912 Attended by his wife and daughter Louise, Isaiah Taber dies at home, February 22, exactly sixty-two years after he first set foot in San Francisco.

1922 Isaiah Taber's widow, Annie Taber, dies in San Francisco.

1946 Taber's remaining daughter, Louise Eddy Taber, dies in San Francisco.

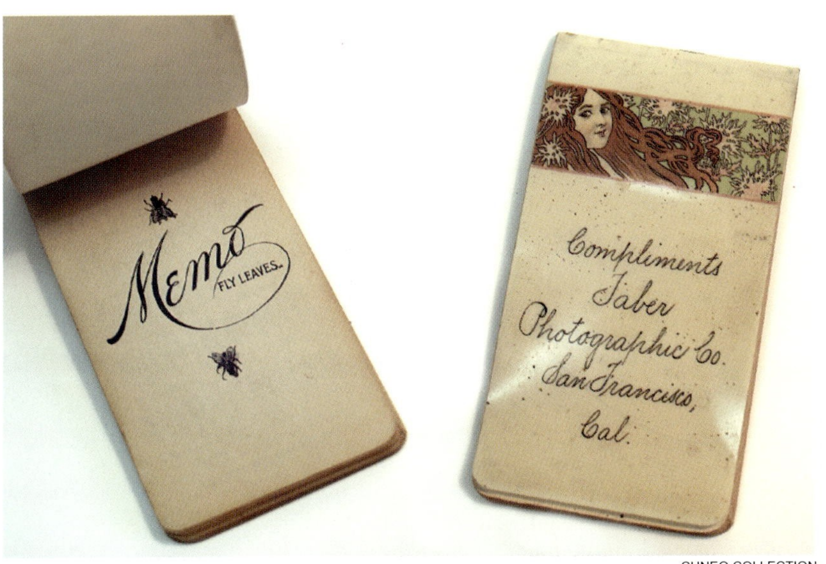

CUNEO COLLECTION

INDEX

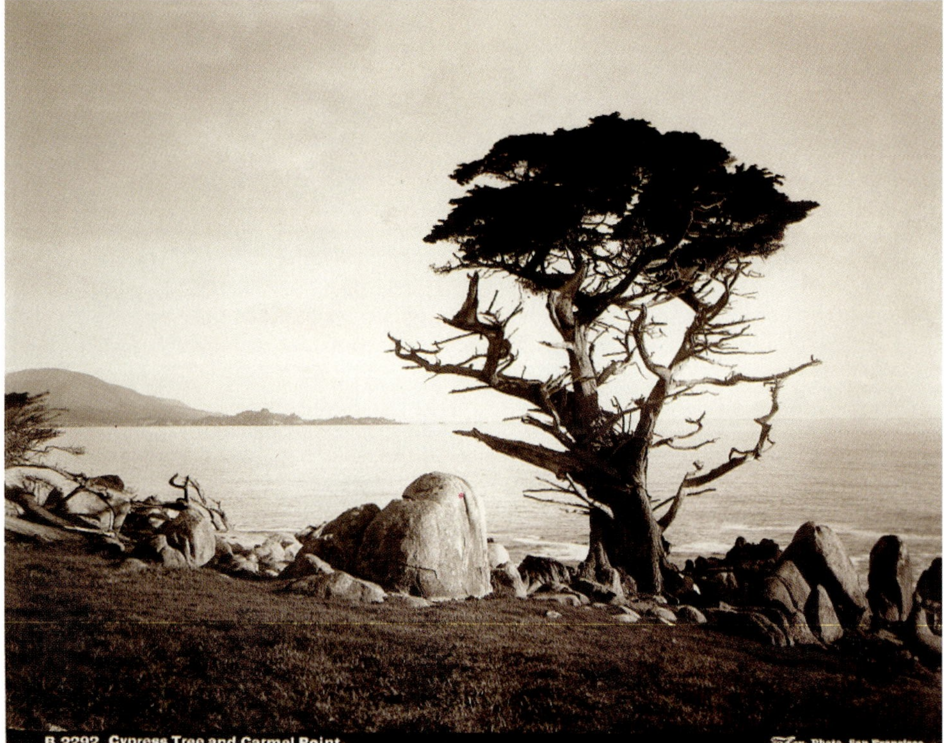

CALIFORNIA STATE LIBRARY